RENASCENCE PORTRAITS

Photo. E. Walker.

THOMAS CROMWELL.

AFTER THE PAINTING IN THE NATIONAL PORTRAIT GALLERY.

RENASCENCE PORTRAITS

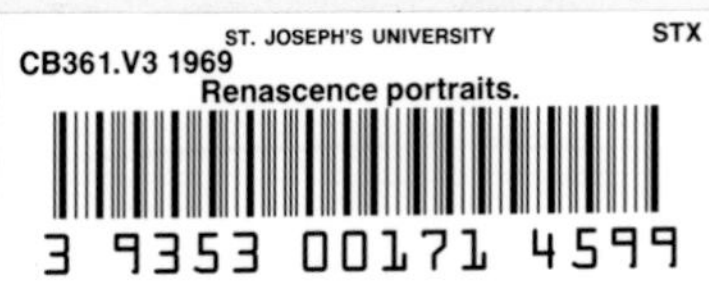

BY

PAUL VAN DYKE, D.D.

PROFESSOR IN HISTORY, PRINCETON UNIVERSITY

Essay Index Reprint Series

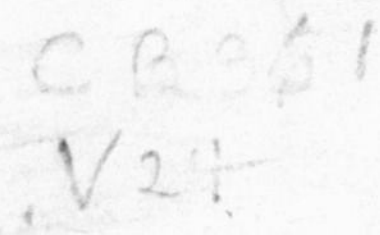

BOOKS FOR LIBRARIES PRESS
FREEPORT, NEW YORK

First Published 1905
Reprinted 1969

LIBRARY OF CONGRESS CATALOG CARD NUMBER:
69-17593

PRINTED IN THE UNITED STATES OF AMERICA

NEC · FAMAE · NEQVE · AVRO ·
SED · GAVDIO · STVDIORVM ·
SPE · QVOQVE · OTII · AMICORVM · OBLECTANDI ·

LIST OF ILLUSTRATIONS

This anonymous portrait was painted in the school of Holbein. It repeats, with slight variations, the head in the damaged and repainted Holbein portrait at Tittenhanger, representing Cromwell seated in his cabinet. A fine drawing by Holbein at Wilton bears Cromwell's name in an old writing, but is not now accepted as his portrait.

This portrait, one of the finest masterpieces of Marcantonio and of Italian engraving, was, according to Vasari, drawn from the life as well as engraved by the artist. Nearly all Marcantonio's work was done after the designs of others, notably Raphael; but there is no reason to suppose that he was not capable of drawing this portrait. At any rate, no painter's name can be put forward with any certainty as that of the original designer. Marcantonio was a friend and associate of Aretino's, and it has been suggested that this portrait was made in recognition of the latter's service in procuring his release from prison, about 1525 A.D.

Maximilian died in 1519, and this portrait is dated 1520. It has, however, all the characteristics of a portrait done from life. Presumably Lucas made the drawing on one of the emperor's visits to the Low Countries, and engraved it after his death. The print is rare, and executed with that combined delicacy and vigour which made Lucas van Leyden as supreme among engravers of the Netherlands, as Dürer in Germany or Marcantonio in Italy.

PREFACE

This book tries to illustrate the Renascence by describing three men who were affected by it and who were all living at the same time in Italy, England and Germany. For such an attempt to illustrate the Renascence a variety of reasons suggested the choice of Pietro Aretino, Thomas Cromwell and Maximilian I. One important reason is that they are all more or less unknown to the ordinary reader of history in English. On Aretino there is almost nothing in English except four pages of Buckhardt written many years ago. In German there is little more. The older French and Italian writers, and some of the newer ones, show him out of focus and without due regard to the perspective of history. Cromwell is known by a caricature rather than by a portrait. In the essay of the Appendix: Reginald Pole and Thomas Cromwell, the writer believes that he has shown the origin of the exaggerations of this current caricature in the distorted account of Cromwell's bitterest enemy. Of Maximilian there are accounts in English; a short one has recently been printed as the Stanhope Historical Essay by Seton Watson of New College, Oxford. But none attempts to use the best means for the interpretation of his character —Maximilian's own writings. Indeed, until recently it was not possible to do so for they were ascribed to his secretaries. Whatever light these three men may throw upon the Renascence will, therefore, seem to the ordinary reader more illuminating because it is new to him.

For this book is addressed to the ordinary reader and the writer frankly confesses a desire to be interesting. And though he is willing to plead guilty at once to a charge of dismal failure he insists upon a claim to credit for good intentions. Such a claim, however humble it may seem, is in reality a little bold. For a desire to be interesting in writing history is regarded by a number of historians as distinctly out of date. A school, which until recently threatened to become dominant, assures us that a writer on history has no more reason for trying to be interesting to the average reader of books than a writer on mathematics. One of them is credibly reported to have thanked God he had no style to tempt him out of the straight and narrow path of scientific exactness.

But the right of literature to try to keep the result of historical research in touch with life is happily being re-vindicated against this temporary fashion by men whose ability in the use of scientific methods cannot be disputed. Such words as these of Mr. Vinogradoff are gladly echoed in many minds:

"What I call literary history, has by no means done its work. There is too much in the action of men that demands artistic perception and even divination on the part of the historian to allow this mode of treatment to fall into decay."

To his desire to be interesting the writer has, however, set one limit. An Oxford Professor of history was once asked why he did not make his lectures more interesting. He replied,—he would be glad to do so if he saw any way except by making them less true. History cannot walk in the path of romance, and the writer has honestly tried to follow always the way of sober truth. He has never consciously exaggerated vices or heightened virtues to give scope for strong adjectives. He has tried to avoid the tone of the advocate, though it is easier to listen to than the tone of the judge. He has never tried to make up for the lack of exact knowledge about how things did happen by exuberance of imagination about how they might have happened, and there is no item in his description of any scene which is not suggested by contemporary evidence.

Beside the fact that he did not *mean* to be dull, the writer makes one other claim upon the indulgence of the reader. He has tried to be short. Of recent years a flood of historical monographs has been poured forth in French, English, German and Italian. Most of them describe with more or less minuteness various points in the original contemporary records of historical events. But as a whole they make the events they treat no clearer to the average reader than they were before. This is especially true of the American reader. These works are often difficult to read; they are written in foreign tongues —they are scattered in different libraries, many of them cannot be found in America at all. The monographs must be interpreted to the educated public even as they interpret the records to the specialist.

In Germany, the home of the monograph, this need has recently been clearly recognized. The words of Professor Baumgarten are an example of the recognition: " The most painstaking specialist cannot deny that collections of sources are not issued for their own sakes, that the highest purpose of the investigations of monographs does not consist in clearing up some detail. * * * When the most extensive publications, the most acute investigations remain for years as good as unused, when at last their enormous extent renders the review of them impossible even for the historian, unless he is willing to confine his interest within the narrow limits of a few decades, such a result does little to advance true historical knowledge. To increase them without limit, making no attempt to draw the sum of historic results out of these costly materials, is an undertaking which is in direct contradiction to the true understanding of scientific investigation."

Therefore the writer, having the materials for two books in his notes and the ideas for a third in his head, decided to condense them all within a single pair of covers.

It seems as if there were now some prospect that American writers on history might be emancipated from the tyrannous fad of footnotes. The value of pages is no longer estimated *everywhere* by the amount of space upon them occupied in small print by miscellaneous observations on more or less irrelevant topics and citations from obvious authorities to support commonplaces. The remark made by Mr. Armstrong in the Bibliographical Introduction to his recent most interesting Biography of Charles V. strikes a responsive chord. "I had a few scruples as to abandoning the explanatory or supplementary footnote which is often the fruit of laziness or literary incompetence, for it is far easier to bury a stubborn fact or episode at the bottom of the page than to make it a living portion of the text."

But in works so condensed as these short biographies there are occasional remarks in the nature of asides, which may make the subject clearer and could be worked into the text only by misplaced ingenuity. And it seemed wise to indicate the places where citations from contemporary sources are to be found. The writer was confirmed in this practice by the experience of searching all obvious collections for an interesting document partially cited by Mr. Armstrong, without being able to find and enjoy the rest of it.

The author of Don Quixote tells in his preface how being one day in his study very uneasy about his book because he had for it no quotations for the margin or annotations for the end, and no bibliography to place at the beginning "as all do under the letters A. B. C., beginning with Aristotle and ending with Xenophon or Zoïlus or Zeuxis," a friend came in and showed the way out of all his troubles. The bibliography was easily settled,—"Now," said the friend,—"let us come to those references to authors which other books have and you want for yours. The remedy for this is very simple. You have only to look out for some book that quotes them all, from A to Z, as you say yourself, and then insert the very same alphabet in your book. * * * For, at any rate, if it answers no other purpose the long catalogue of authors will serve to give a surprising look of authority to your book. Besides, no one will trouble himself to verify whether you have followed them or whether you have not, being in no way concerned in it."

The writer has not taken this very practical advice in the preparation of his bibliography. In regard to Cromwell and Aretino he has read everything which promised to throw any light on the men. He has not been able to do this in regard to Maximilian. The secondary literature on the period of Maximilian's lifetime in Germany is so enormous that Ulmann, publishing, after years of preparation, the first volume of a sixteen hundred page life of him, confesses that he "had not been able to reach an exhaustive review of all the writings related to his subject."

The brief list in the Appendix gives only a small part of the titles of the books that have been read in preparing these essays, and consists of full titles of the works cited in the footnotes. The writer's main reliance has been the Calendar of State Papers, the writings and letters of Aretino, the writings and letters of Maximilian.

He is indebted for control and suggestion to many secondary sources, probably to some not named in the bibliography. He owes very much for Maximilian to the great work of Professor Ulmann, for Pietro Aretino to the labors among the archives, the acute criticism, the able reconstruction of Signor Luzio and Prof. Rossi. But he is afraid that for the book as a whole no one ought to be blamed except himself.

Parts of the material, sometimes in the form under which it is here presented, sometimes in different form, have appeared in The Atlantic Monthly, The Outlook Magazine, Harper's Magazine, The Presbyterian Review (two articles), The American Historical Review (two articles).

CONTENTS

RENASCENCE PORTRAITS

I

THE RENASCENCE

THE historian is no more able to tell all the facts he finds in his authorities than the chroniclers and makers of documents were able to record everything that happened during their lives. He must select. And if he wishes to produce anything but a collection of anecdotes or a summary of miscellaneous happenings his selection must consciously or unconsciously follow some principle or purpose. For a history is not simply a record of facts. It is an account of the impression left upon the mind of the writer by his study of the records of facts.

One of the commonest impressions made upon the examiner of the records of facts in the lives of past generations is that history is not a mere mass of events. The events seem to compose currents or movements. Some men of the past appear to have idly drifted with these currents; some appear like those who try to dam and turn back a river, while others seem to so divert or guide it that the superficial observer thinks they created the movement or controlled its direction. This is simply putting into a metaphor the impression that there was a certain similarity between the thoughts and feelings of many men living at the same time which suggests a common influence or set of influences operating on all of them. A few familiar examples will show that this is an impression made by facts:

After the decline of the Roman Empire in the West and the unsuccessful attempts of the rulers of various German immigrant tribes to restore the order and prosperity it maintained, Europe, west of the Adriatic, suffered a series of catastrophes. The Northman plundered and burnt along the Atlantic coast from the delta of the Rhine to the Pillars of Hercules. The Saracen swept the shores of the Mediterranean with fire and sword and savage hordes of Slavs and Magyars pushed into the domain of ancient civilizations until the broad strip of desert they left behind them almost met the bloody trail of the Northman on the West. The Empire of Charlemagne broke down under the weight of these disasters. The suffering inhabitants found a shift for their desperate condition in a plan of defense and local rule, based on methods of land tenure and personal relations with which their ancestors, whether Germans or Romans, had been familiar. The shift devised was much the same in all localities. It spread and maintained itself, a certain concatenation between the parts of society thus organized arose, men formed a theory to explain the origin and internal relations of what had grown up illogically under the pressure of immediate need, and, from the ninth to the fourteenth century, what is sometimes spoken of as the feudal system exercised a great influence not only upon the acts but on the thoughts and feelings of the inhabitants of Europe of all classes.

So also the student of the sixteenth century finds it

hard to avoid the impression of something spreading like a contagion. For seven hundred years the Roman Church organized with the Papacy at its head had been the most powerful institution in Europe. There had been sporadic dissent with its doctrines or its management, protests like those of the Lollards, rejections of all for which it stood by inhabitants of certain localities like that of the Catharists—it had fallen into terrible disorder, as during the Great Schism—but in the minds of the enormous majority of western Europeans for more than twenty generations reverence for it had never been destroyed. Speaking broadly, Europe had during these centuries acknowledged its authority as the one visible common institution which actually survived the decay of the Roman Empire.

Within one generation of the sixteenth century, great masses of the people of Europe renounced its rule. And religion, which, for seven hundred years had been on the whole a unifying force in the history of Europe, became an influence making for disorder. It plunged Europe into a hundred years of intermittent wars whose chief underlying cause was the unwillingness of large numbers of men to accept the jurisdiction of the church generations of their fathers had obeyed.

So also during the last two generations of the nineteenth century privilege and disability before the law were abolished, and the idea of increasing the number of those who have a voice in the affairs of government found expression in legislation with a rapidity and to an extent seen at no time before in the history of the modern world.

These paragraphs state facts which are naturally summarized in metaphorical expressions. But the feudal system was never a definite thing like the Papacy or the English Monarchy of which you can say at any point in time and space, here it is. Nor can its spread be traced as we follow the spread of a flood or a tide. There was no bacillus of the Reformation nor was that movement a contagion either of good or evil. Democracy is neither a fruitful harvest nor a noxious weed flourishing more and more freely in European soil during the last half of the nineteenth century. And yet it would not be hard to find historians whose work has suffered from this fallacy, and still more readers of historians whose understanding of history has been impaired by it.

For this reason one of the most acute and scholarly of living French historical writers announces in a preface that he has avoided—"abstract nouns—such as royalty, the church, elements, tendencies, which so easily come to seem mystic forces. When I have had to describe the acts or ideas of groups of men, I have always designated the group either by its national or party or class name, or by a collective noun, such as government, ministry, clergy—so that the reader may be able to discover, behind this name, the men who have acted or thought." [1] The warning of this practical protest is a necessary and valuable one, but general terms when written and read with intelligence and care are useful because they do record and express a natural and true impression made on the mind of the student of the records of the past. It is necessary for history to be as accurate,

[1] Histoire Politique de l'Europe Contemporaine. Charles Seignobos.

and therefore as clear and explicit as possible, but it is hard to imagine how history can ever become an exact science and practically impossible to transfer to it the methods of the physical sciences. An over anxiety about exactitude has its dangers too. If historians confine their writings to descriptions of the programmes of political parties, to events which can be described by testimony acceptable in a court and things of that sort, it is to be feared lest the great mass of people from whom, of course, the future historians must come, may say—"well, in that case there seems no valid reason why the race should devote much time and energy to history. If the historians refuse to discuss the features of the lives of past generations we want to know about, what especial reason is there for any very large supply of historians?"

Such general terms as the "Spread of Feudalism,"—the "Growth of Democracy,"—the "Movement of the Reformation," conveniently connote facts and a natural impression they make upon the mind of every student. The defense of their use does not make it necessary to enter into discussions about the relation of mental categories to existence. Nor is it wise to attempt to trace causes of phenomena too complex to be explained. When the attempt is made to bring philosophy and history too close together, in the so-called Philosophy of History, the lamb of history generally lies down inside the raging lion of philosophical discussion. It is enough to say that history is a branch of literature and the historian should not suffer from any embargo on language. He may try to transfer to the mind of his reader the impressions made upon his own mind by the facts of the records, through any terms wisely fitted for the purpose.

About thirty years ago[1] English writers on history, literature and art began to use freely the word Renaissance, borrowed from French writers. It expressed and still expresses an impression made on the minds of students of the records of men from 1350 to 1560, that a rapid, progressive and similar change took place in the thoughts and feelings of many men of those generations which wrought out noticeable effects upon their life and institutions. The comparative rapidity of these changes in thought and feeling, the fact that many felt them at the same time,—that inhabitants of one country felt them at a period succeeding their first prevalence in another,—the new forms in literature and the plastic arts in which these changes found expression, their apparent influence in hastening the break up of the social institutions of past generations—these impressions made by facts are naturally and simply expressed by the phrases, the movement of the Awakening—the New Birth,—the Renascence.[2]

The more one learns of the life of the generations between the death of Petrarch and the days of Elizabeth, the more useful do the phrases, "Movement of the Renascence,"—"Influence of the Renascence," seem to be, and the more difficult to define. It is plain that there was a Renascence, but very hard to say what the Renascence was. The changes that it brought about or helped are plain.

[1] Encyclopædia Britannica, Article Renaissance.

[2] Usage is rapidly substituting the English word for the French word. The borrowing was a totally unnecessary confession of poverty in a language which had an exact equivalent then in use.

At the end of the thirteenth century Thomas Aquinas, the Universal Doctor, was the supreme master of European learning. In the beginning of the sixteenth century Erasmus was the king of letters. Both devoted their great industry and singular ability to the discussion of religion and the institutions and customs in which religious ideas were expressed. The Summa Theologiæ and the annotated Greek Testament were both issued with the highest sanction of the Church. The difference between them suggests the difference between the worlds in which Thomas Aquinas and Erasmus of Rotterdam lived.

In the middle of the thirteenth century there was built in Paris to receive the relics Louis IX, King of France, brought back from the crusade, the Holy Chapel; and the architect expressed his sense of beauty in an art whose mode was complicated, suggestive, mystic. Five generations later Brunelleschi built, on commission of a great Florentine merchant, the Pazzi Chapel by an art expressing itself precisely, with an almost logical order and relation of parts, more akin to mathematics than to metaphysics. In the end of the thirteenth century Cimabue painted for a Florentine church a picture of the Madonna; in the beginning of the sixteenth century Michael Angelo painted on the rear wall of the Sistine Chapel a picture of the Last Judgment. And five minutes' comparison of the two pictures will make certain differences between them plainer than twenty-five pages of description.

Now the difference between the work of these three pairs of men is much greater than the difference between the men. If Erasmus had been professor at Paris or

Bologna at the end of the thirteenth century he would have written books different from the Summa Theologiæ. But they would not, like his Praise of Folly and Enchiridion, be translated into the languages of modern Europe. They would remain in their original Latin, unread save by a few theologians. Had Brunelleschi been called north of the Alps to work for Saint Louis in the thirteenth century, he would not have built the Holy Chapel, but he would have built something as much like it as the façade of the cathedrals of Siena and Orvieto. Had Michael Angelo passed Cimabue on the streets of Florence every week, any skilled critic might still have been able to tell their pictures apart. But as it is, not even a child could confuse the work of one with that of the other.

And this general and average difference in modes of literary and artistic expression between the thirteenth century and the sixteenth century is matched by a difference in human institutions during the two ages.

A series of rough maps of Europe indicating by different colours political divisions uses thirty-six colours for the year 1420. The map in the same series for the year 1563 has twenty-six colours, and if we take out the leading states of the German Empire, which in the two maps are unchanged in number, the count would be thirty to twenty. One-third of the political units of a great part of Europe had been absorbed into others during four generations.

And the change in political conditions was greater than can be thus summarized to the eye. In the Iberian peninsula, within the Italian Peninsula, to some extent in England, what were in effect loose aggregations of semi-independent dominions nominally united into what must be figured on a chart as a political unit, had become unified and subjected to the more efficient control of a central authority. This political change, rapidly consolidating feudal aggregations not effectively controlled by the authorities they acknowledged into larger or more centralized states, shows itself plainly in a change in the character of the wars of Europe. Up to the end of the fifteenth century, leaving out of account the religious movements of the crusades, the greater part of the killing for generation after generation was done in private war, or at least in factional war. Even the Hundred Years War, though we think of it now as a struggle between nations, was, to a large extent, a factional, feudal and class contest. When the English kings invaded France in the fourteenth century, they were aided by large numbers of Frenchmen, vassals of the English king or rebellious vassals of the French king. But with the French invasion of Italy at the end of the fifteenth century begins a long series of battles, really between dynasties but apparently between nations—struggles in which the leaders appealed to their supporters to defend against the glory and interest of foreigners, the glory and interest of those who spoke or at least read the same tongue.

A great economic change had also taken place. The unique importance of land as the source of wealth and power had decreased. Men could gain comfort or riches by making things to sell or trading the products of one country for those of another. The use of money had replaced barter in all but primitive transactions and a system of credit had begun to make up for the scarcity of money.

This economic change had helped to alter the balance of society. From the tenth to the thirteenth century the land holder, because he was either vassal or overlord, and often he was both, must be a fighter. A woman did not freely inherit fiefs, and the knight, holder of enough land to support a horse, became the power in the world. But before the beginning of the sixteenth century the spears and clubs of burghers had more than once broken the charge of the chivalry—the professional warriors of the thirteenth century. And successful armies were made up not of vassals, unapt for discipline, anxious to get home, but of men paid to stay with the standard. Knighthood became an ornamental title rather than the symbol of a necessary activity. The burgher who lived within the walls of a town and tilled no land, but who could fight himself and whose money could hire other fighters, took his place beside the knight as a figure in society. Some attention must be paid to his feelings and interests. In the valley of the Po and the slopes of the northern Apennines, men who traded themselves and whose ancestors had been traders became rulers of states and rivalled in power and magnificence the proudest feudal families of the North.

The education of the world had changed. At the beginning of the fourteenth century, though there were students at the University who did not expect to enter the service of the Church, the instruction was in the hands of clergymen and to a great extent in the hands of members of monastic orders. At the beginning of the sixteenth century the most celebrated men in the world of learning were neither clegymen nor members of monastic orders. A new figure, the humanist, had taken his place alongside the monk and was waging with him a fierce and manifestly successful battle to substitute for the "Old Learning of the Schoolmen," the "New Learning."

Those who had the chance to do what they liked in the world, the nobles and wealthy burghers—had during the fifteenth century changed their minds about education. In the middle of the twelfth century the Earl of Arundel spoke to the Pope of himself and his friends as illiterate laymen. Men of the sword and horse took no shame for not knowing what belonged only to men of book and pen. That changed somewhat in the next hundred years. Young nobles began to enter the Universities. But noble society did not become intellectual. In the end of the fourteenth century John Froissart, poet, priest, traveller, courtier, wrote a book for "all noble and valiant persons." He and those to whom he read what he wrote thought, and, as the event showed, wisely thought, "it would in times to come be more sought after than any other." He could safely assume in it that the men and women of the English or French courts and the castles of minor princes would care for nothing but war, love and hunting. But during the fifteenth century the society of courts changed. The old learning taught by the monks had never appealed very strongly to the nobles. The new learning of the humanists captivated them. In the beginning of the sixteenth century Count Baldassare Castiglione repeated the attempt made by the Hainault priest a hundred and fifty years before to write a book for noble persons. He was equally successful. His "Courier" was read everywhere and soon translated into the chief languages of Europe. It pictures a society informed and cultured, women of wit and education, men who have joined the clerk to the knight and hold the pleasures of the mind as dear as the hunt and the tournament.

All these changes in the motives of learning and the forms of literature and art; in political institutions, in social conditions, and personal ideals, seem to be related to a change in methods of thought and habits of feeling promoted by a new ideal of education and life. That new ideal began to find numbers of adherents in Italy at the beginning of the fifteenth century. At the close of the century it spread across the Alps and during the next hundred years deeply affected the social, political, scholarly and artistic life of all nations. In the works of the Italian man of letters, Petrarch, who died in 1374, this ideal of education and life can be seen clearly expressed and sharply defined from the scholastic ideal of education and life, all but absolutely dominant thirty years before his birth.

And it would appear that if you are to give any definite meaning to the vague term Renascence, if you are to equate your *x*, you must make the Renascence equivalent to the new ideal of education and life suggested by Petrarch and the humanists and expressed in the plastic arts in Italy during the fifteenth century. The movement of the Renascence is the spread of that ideal, with the consequent, or at least contemporaneous, weakening of the power of the ideas of society and government and religion which had prevailed during the middle ages under the influence of feudalism and scholasticism. Feudalism, scholasticism and the mediæval church were indeed decaying before the end of the fifteenth century. Economic causes, intellectual criticism, their own corruption were weakening their power, but the Renascence spreading from Italy gave them a death blow—the new ideal of education and view of life separate modern Europe from mediæval Europe.

To define this ideal by positive and abstract terms is difficult. Petrarch, in whose works we first find it clearly though not always explicitly set forth, presented it in opposition to the prevailing scholastic ideal. He denied that teachers ought to have most in view the usefulness of knowledge and training their scholars to earn a living in the world. He said the first object of education was to lead men to love and seek truth for its own sake. Culture was higher than knowledge, skilled workmen could not repay the world for the lack of wise men.

He wanted a culture, broad, liberal, humane, to replace the narrow technical training of the schools. Therefore, he quarrelled with the methods of the scholastic learning as well as with its purpose. He asserted that literature was a fuller reflex and a better measure of life than logic; that poetry and rhetoric would set free the mind quicker than metaphysics and theology; that the languages containing the records of the civilizations of Greece and Rome were better instruments of training than disputations about entities which had never existed except in the minds of the disputants.

And when the reason of the scholar was thus set free from prejudice and ignorance, he wanted it relieved of the weight of authority. He said boys should be taught the thoughts of other men in order that they might learn to think for themselves. In a treatise "Concerning his own Ignorance and That of Many Others," he dared to assert that Aristotle did not know everything. He declined to admit that the works of Peter Lombard, of Aristotle, of Thomas Aquinas and other men, however great, had circumscribed the field of knowledge, said the best possible word, given the final judgment, on every topic worthy of serious attention. Therefore, he proposed to cease studying commentators, to break through them in every direction and study subjects. He reasserted the right of personal judgment and made his disciples conscious that they were personalities and not members of a class,—whether in the University or the larger school of life.

Such an ideal of education and the view of life it assumed, was a disintegrating influence in mediæval society. If a noble family was influenced by it for any time it came to pass that the son, or at least the grandson, of the man who read Froissart, preferred Castiglione. And this change in literary taste was an index of a change of thought, feeling, desire and habit. Social customs, political arrangements, civil and ecclesiastical institutions, common opinions, showed the influence of such changes.

To set forth this ideal of education and this view of life so pregnant with revolutionary influence, demanded the power of marked originality in Petrarch. And yet, of course, it was not new, nor did the movement we may date from him begin with him. History cannot be cut off into lengths as a stick of wood is cut with an axe and the pieces labeled "Dark Ages," "Middle Ages," "Age of the

Renascence," "Age of the Reformation." Neither do men launch "movements" as a ship is built in the yards and launched from the ways. Other men before Petrarch had uttered similar protests. A hundred years before he was born Abelard had used the methods of the schools to question the accepted conclusions of the schoolmen. And before Abelard the school of Chartres was leading its pupils to spend more time on Cicero and Virgil than on disputes over substance and accidents. There was a Renascence before the Renascence more or less plainly recorded in the works of some French artists and the writings of some French teachers. But these men were less certain of their aims—their influence was less widespread and effective than that of Petrarch and his disciples.

It may be that Petrarch only transmitted and increased their impulse as they may have transmitted and increased the lesser impulse of predecessors. It may be that if we could see history entirely we should find all processes continuous and that the source of spiritual energy was constant under all changes of form. If any man chooses to think that, he is going into a domain where profitable argument is impossible for lack of data. But, however history might appear if seen by omniscience, to men it seems that certain individuals have been independent sources of power and influence. During the life of some generations it does look as if hidden streams had suddenly broken out to the light of day or currents begun to flow with much greater rapidity. And in this sense it is possible for a wise man to speak of Petrarch as the father of the Renascence and to say that it began in Italy in the latter part of the fourteenth century.

The Renascence was not equivalent to the revival of the influence of classic antiquity. Nowhere has the undue liking of writers on history for memorable, sharp and picturesque statements made more plain its evil effects upon popular conceptions than in this matter. Large numbers of educated people believe that the Renascence began with the fall of Constantinople, which drove a crowd of Greek teachers into Italy and so revived the knowledge of the classic world—mother of arts, literature and learning. But Petrarch, Boccaccio, Salutato, Marsigli, Niccolo de' Niccoli, Leonardo Bruni, Traversari, Vittorino da Feltre and many other furtherers of the Renascence were dead before Constantinople fell. The typical humanists Bracciolini and Filelfo were old men when the Turkish army moved to the fatal assault in 1453; and six years before, the Renascence incarnate in the person of Nicholas V. had mounted the throne of the Papacy.

The truth is that the influence of classic antiquity in the art, the language and the literature of Rome and Greece was only the means of accomplishing the Renascence ideal. It became the symbol of its advocates against the "Old Learning" and the sign of their victories, but the Renascence did not mean simply better Latin and the reading of Greek, the influence of the Pantheon and the study of the Roman antiques in the gardens and cabinets of Lorenzo de' Medici. When Stephen Vaughan was travelling in the Netherlands on business for Thomas Cromwell, a leading London lawyer much given to hospitality, it was natural that he should advise his employer to buy a large dining table he saw in Antwerp; for it was decorated with carved inscriptions in Latin, Greek and Hebrew.[1] Thomas Cromwell had spent several years in Italy and imbibed the spirit of the Renascence. His attitude was prophetic of the part he was to play as Vicar of the King for ecclesiastical affairs and Chancellor of the University of Cambridge in replacing men of the "Old Learning" by men of the "New Learning." There came to his house a number of young students and writers who had either visited Italian Universities or studied under men educated in Italy, and when Vaughan saw a table thus symbolically decorated he said to himself—"There is the very thing for the dining-room of Cromwell's house." But this thought did not arise because Cromwell had any special interest in linguistic studies. The London lawyer knew only one of the three languages and was not particularly skilful in using that. Such a table seemed appropriate for Cromwell's house because he and his friends felt in the words of Reginald Pole, another Englishman, who, during many years' study at Padua had been affected by the New Learning, though he disliked it—"in these three tongues, Greek, Latin, Hebrew, *all liberal culture is contained.*"

When some students returned from Italy to Germany, moved all younger Germany to Homeric laughter by the parody of "The Letters of Obscure Men," they did not do it simply to make fun of scholastic Latin. They used the weapon of satire in defense of John Reuchlin, the leader of the progressive scholarship of Germany, threatened with the stake by the scholastics of Cologne

[1] Letters and papers Henry VIII, Vol. IV, Part 2, 5860.

because he advised the Emperor Maximilian not to permit the destruction of all Hebrew literature outside of the Bible. They were interested in something far more vital than good grammar and classic diction. They were defending against obscurantism clad in the garb of zeal for religion, the right of free inquiry, which is the breath of true learning and one of the conditions of a high civilization.

To suppose that the Renascence was nothing more than the stronger revival of the influence of classic antiquity, is to confuse the means of the men who shared and spread its ideal with their end. Aretino, a typical product of the Italian Renascence at its height,—who, judged by social and financial standards, was the most successful of all the professional humanists of his day—could not read Latin at all.

The end of the men of the Italian Renascence was a broader and more human culture of the mind, their favourite means the study of classic antiquity, but neither their means nor their end was the source of the impulse which moved them. Boccaccio saw his forerunner in Dante, a man trained in the "Old Learning," and looking at the universe under its rubrics. The promise and the potency of the development of art at Florence is in Giotto, who did not understand perspective and could not model his figures. When there arose in Italy generations of handlers of brush and chisel who had a new view of the beauty of this world we live in, they found a new technique. Having something to say they worked out a new language. They did it with the help of the marbles and bronzes of Greece and Rome in the society of men who were re-studying their literatures. But the new technique did not give them their ideas. Generations of Italians had seen the ruins and broken statues of the Romans before the time came when all artists were expected to have learned what they taught. It was the seeing eye and the hearing ear and the understanding mind among the men of the fifteenth century which made these dead things produce new life. A native impulse, a revival of the love of truth and beauty, making men more sensitive to the world around them and quicker to respond to its glories of form and colour with vivid emotions of pleasure, sought new and better means of expression. It seized upon classic forms and moulded them to its purpose, and they became the carriers of the generous contagion of the new enthusiasm for the beautiful. But that impulse would have found some means of expression if all the classic remains in Italy had dissolved into dust. Even as during the fifteenth century the van Eycks of Flanders and their followers learned to make more beautiful pictures by developing the mediæval technique.

In other words, men like Petrarch and Masaccio preferred a new ideal of education and form of expression because they had a new and more vivid view of the world and of life in it. Their ideal spread because it found men of similar feelings, thoughts, desires, or at least, men in whom such feelings, thoughts and desires were dormant and ready to be wakened. The reason why the world changed as much as it did between the death of Petrarch and the reign of Elizabeth was because generations grew up who were different from their forefathers. If we are to use the word Renascence intelligently, we must always see behind it the men of the Renascence.

Here we must tread carefully for we are again on the very border of the debatable ground of the Philosophy of History. Let us by all means steer clear of it. We may escape wasting time in repeating the disputes of generations of metaphysical speculators, in this way. Whether it be true that man helps to make the history of his own age or whether it is true that he is made by it, we act as if it were true that he helps to make it. If we did not assume this, all political discussion, scholarly argument or religious activity,—everything but commerce and the arts, would cease. There would be no use in an intelligent man doing anything but adjust himself to machinery which could not be changed. If we thought all problems were working themselves out by formulæ where human choice was not a chief factor, it would be useless to try to take a hand in the solution.

We live as if we were not mere straws in the rushing tides of history,—as if men made society rather than as if society made men. And it seems reasonable to look at past generations from the point of view we take to look at our own—to think of dead men as influenced by inheritance and circumstance, as limited by opportunity, but as making by their actions the inheritance and circumstance of coming generations. Practically we assume that personality is a chief factor in the life of our own day—we should have assumed it had we lived in the sixteenth century; why is it not wise to assume it when we try to find out what the life of the sixteenth century was like?

For there was no time when personality was a stronger factor in history than during the age of the Renascence. The mediæval man, the average man who lived during the thirteenth century, instinctively thought of himself as belonging to a class. He was serf or noble, burgher or ecclesiastic. It was taken for granted that a burgher would act differently from a knight, that a serf should be treated differently from an ecclesiastic. Every man's chances and duties were limited not only by circumstances and abilities but by obligations joining him to his fellows in every direction, by some inherited right or traditional authority of another man. The necessities of the barbarous condition of society which had forced feudalism to become a method of government, had made the social unit not a man or a family but the community. And the schoolmen had formed a theoretical description of the feudal system, which pictured society as a single great organization, ruled in ascending stages by a civil hierarchy of overlords, with every detail of life guided and directed by the spiritual hierarchy of the clergy. It is true that feudal life did not correspond with this theory. Feudalism left the way open for passionate assertions of a savage sense of individuality. Against general considerations of justice and the commonwealth, men were constantly asserting their rights by private, that is customary, local law, or avenging their pride by private war where no man thought it shameful to join robbery and arson to killing. But mediæval society, though it left a chance for savage assertions of individuality and fostered in the owners of castles a farouche unsocial pride, lacked the mobility and freedom needed to develop true individuality. If it had not been for the democratizing influence of the church, preaching universal ideals of justice and mercy and occasionally choosing for its head a man of humblest origin, European society might have hardened into a system of caste.

To give a man a humane training instead of the knowledge of the art of his class, to free the spirit from the habit of accepting traditional authority without question, was to broaden his horizon and to awaken in him the critical faculty, to make him more complex and independent. The consciousness of the ego increased, ambition was stronger and more diffused, activities became multiplied, men began to find keener pleasure in a greater variety of objects. The personalities of men counted for more. And because they had a clearer and wider view of the world they became more conscious of self. *Weltschmerz,* the fruit of chagrin, or a self-centred habit of mind, began to appear in literature. To the wonder of men north of the Alps, who had not felt the influence of the Renascence, able bastards gained or inherited political power, displacing feebler legitimate heirs. Many-sided personalities began to appear—artists who were poets, architects, sculptors, musicians, painters; rulers of states who were financiers, scholars, writers and connoisseurs of art. Feudal pride secure in its own sense of superiority, seeking only the applause of its peers, became personal pride fed by a mordant craving for praise that would give a sense of distinction in the eyes of all sorts and conditions of men.

The rapid creation of a new class of pictures marks the increased importance of the individual and the spread of the sense of personality. At the close of the fifteenth century artists everywhere began to paint great numbers of portraits, not put into corners of religious or historical works, not monumental effigies on tombs, but distinct records of personality made for their own sake. Portraits which up to the middle of the fifteenth century are rare outside of Italy suddenly become very numerous. We do not know what many of the great men of mediæval times looked like, but we have portraits of all the leaders of thought and action of the early sixteenth century. And the more noted were painted again and again.

There is therefore a reason for calling this book Renascence Portraits, and some grounds for believing that it might help a reader to a clearer understanding of the Renascence if I could succeed in showing him the character and life of three men who felt its influence, The German Emperor, Maximilian I; the English Chief Minister, Thomas Cromwell; and the Venetian Littérateur, Pietro Aretino.

The Renascence was firmly established in Italy before it had much influence in other lands. Men trained according to the new ideal of education were the leaders of polite society; all painters, sculptors and architects were following the methods of the new art, before the Renascence crossed the Alps. It spread first to Germany. For Germany was closer to Italy than any other part of Europe. In Germany great ecclesiastics were still what they had elsewhere ceased to be, political rulers. The Empire did not interrupt the connection of the episcopal sees with Rome as did the crowns of France, Spain or England. All central Europe from the Eider to the Tiber was nominally under one supreme ruler,—the Emperor of the Holy Roman Empire of the German Nation, who was elected on the banks of the Rhine but crowned by the Pope at Rome. The trade over the Brenner Pass linked together the Baltic and the Adriatic. Germany was in the fourteenth century waking to new intellectual life. And the commerce of thought followed the roads of trade. Students poured over the Alps into Italy. They brought back with them the New Learning and within a generation it produced most marked results. Luther and Zwingli, under whose lead the bulk of German-speaking peoples broke from the church of their fathers, would probably have perished at the stake but for the critical and independent spirit roused in the educated young men of the German Empire by the "New Learning."

Maximilian I died when these two great schisms, the first of a series which were to carry all Teutonic Europe out of the unity of Christendom, were scarcely begun. But it is easy to see that his attitude toward it would not have differed from that of his grandson and successor who regarded it as dangerous to church and state. Maximilian was sincerely religious. But he was not unwilling to question customary beliefs, and the plan he spoke of as his intention to become "both Pope and Kaiser," whatever it may have been, shows that he had no over-mastering reverence for the traditional form of the church. He thought a reformation conducted by himself would be safe, for it would leave the Hapsburg dynasty, where God had placed it, as the supreme arbiter of the highest destinies of the world. But a reform which originated from below—which found the bulk of its adherents in those classes whose interests God had committed to him—whose action gave the centre of the world's stage to someone else beside himself, left him cold. As soon as its leaders should begin to cross his plans they would stir a latent opposition in his mind into the rapid development of the conviction that they were enemies of truth and law.

For it was the same dominant desire of Maximilian which in his age made him cold and hostile to the first protests of the Lutheran Reformation, that made him eagerly accept in his youth the first influences of the Renascence. Maximilian saw in the Renascence a new ornament for the house of Hapsburg—in its art and literature loud trumpets to proclaim his glory to posterity.

In this Maximilian did not differ essentially from the votaries of the Renascence in Italy where it had reached its full power. It is not easy to find among Italian patrons, writers and artists of the sixteenth century any large number of men who loved art for art's sake. That society was then full of such men is a conclusion drawn by some advocates of a nineteenth century theory from a narrow study of the work of a few Renascence artists, and not from all the manifestations of their characters and the characters of their contemporaries. The rulers of the fifteenth and sixteenth centuries in Italy, all to some extent tyrants in the classic sense, had a full understanding of how much art was worth to them. Keen men of the world, they knew that, among a population lacking in moral simplicity, magnificence breeds respect. Pageantry helps to console a generation unworthy of liberty for the loss of it; even as new toys divert the grief of children. Some of them, it is true, gratified their own tastes, but in all they spent they found their account. And arrears were balanced by the asset of the tribute of fame which future generations would pay at their tombs.

Maximilian was like them in this. But he was unlike them in the fact that he never understood what he adopted. He never assimilated the Renascence and it never changed him from a mediæval into a modern man. The works he wrote and the monuments he planned are a standing proof that his taste was undiscriminating. He never could free his mind from the social and political ideas of the middle ages. And when he modified them, it was not by observing facts but by adopting the fantastic conceptions of servile humanists about the relation of his power to that of the Cæsars. It is very doubtful whether Maximilian was any more loyal in his diplomacy than his rivals; but it is certain that he was less successful. His schemes seldom failed to allow their victim to escape from the trap. A thing planned seemed to him done. He arranged men in day dreams, he did not think what living men would probably do. Hence, Machiavelli, who logically arranged, and by logically arranging exaggerated, the evils of the general political practice of his day, regarded Maximilian as a sort of living fossil inept at statecraft, entirely unable to take the world as it was around him.

Of the political ideal which relieves the sordid selfishness of Machiavelli's ideal of royal politics, Maximilian had no conception. For Machiavelli did more than display in logical arrangement the practical methods of statesmen of the Renascence. He sketched the ideal which they followed—the ideal of unified nations safe and prosperous under wise and skilful rulers. That ideal was in the air of Germany even more than in the air of Italy. But Maximilian never felt its power. Patriotism in its modern sense would have been a meaningless word to him, and he could never conceive the conditions of royal greatness from the modern point of view. A chance to promote the unity of Germany seemed to him of little importance compared to a raid into Picardy or the opportunity of taking a small town in Guelders. Maximilian simply put on the Renascence as he might exchange an armor worn by one of his house fighting the Swiss at Sempach, for a new suit from Brescia or Milan.

Thomas Cromwell on the other hand understood the spirit and ideals of the Renascence and assimilated them. No family traditions obscured his view of the world as it was. He readily accepted the idea that a man ought to look at it with his own eyes and not with the eyes of a dead philosopher. Any ideals he might follow never made him oblivious of facts. Henry VIII was destroying the ancient balance of the mediæval monarchy and trying to base a great throne on a united nation. He was calling to his service men who before had little career open to them in statecraft: the sons of country gentlemen and burghers. Cromwell followed the open road to service and fortune. He had his ambitions, but he also had his ideals. His ambitions were power won by intellectual ability, not by arms; fortune and distinction adorned by literature and art. He was not a scholar and too busy with practical affairs to write anything but letters and state papers. But he modelled his leisure hours after the society described in The Courtier.

And like his ambition, his political ideals were formed by the Renascence. The idea of nationality as opposed to loose confederacies of feudal communities—of the destinies of a nation as something whose guidance was a proper object of ambition for a man whose faculties were fully developed, was an idea whose hold on the human mind was strengthened by the Renascence. The strengthening of that idea was not merely a result of the revived study of Roman history and literature; for Imperialism was the dominant note there. It came rather from the broadening of the horizon of thought and feeling—from the beginnings of vernacular literature replacing partly the universal Latin—from the breakdown of feudalism and the abandonment of the scholastic methods of thought by which the universe had been feudalized in the imagination of men. Wherever the influence of the Renascence touched, this idea sprang into new life. In Germany, Celtes, Hutten and their friends caught fire at the image of Germania Rediviva and talked like the makers of the modern empire of the glories of Hermann, who had stood for Teutonic liberty and checked the flight of the Roman eagle. The idea of united Italy, mother of arts and letters, driving the hordes of plundering barbarians back over the Alps, shines like a star through the craft and cruelty of Machiavelli's Prince.

This idea of nationality was not new to England. Pride in one's nation as including all men who spoke the same tongue, can be seen among Englishmen long before the influence of the Renascence touched the island. But that influence deepened and strengthened the English pride of nationality.

During the sixteenth century this pride of nationality broke England from obedience to Rome and under the pressure of the Spanish crusade, blessed by the Pope for England's conquest, expressed itself in a deep reverence for Elizabeth as Britannia incarnate. It was because Cromwell had felt the influence of the Renascence that he saw this ideal of nationality and flung himself with all his energy into the struggle to unite England and to vindicate her independence of all foreign authority. The means by which he hoped to do this was one which most men who had been affected by the influence of the Renascence, from Machiavelli to Martin Luther, approved; the power of an absolute king wisely used.

A great wave of absolutism swept over Europe in the early sixteenth century. The need of breaking finally the disorders of feudalism and the renewed study of the Roman Empire inclined men of the "New Learning" to believe that the destinies of nations were safest in the hands of strong kings. And because he was a man of the Renascence, Cromwell served not only his ambitions but also his ideals in helping Henry VIII to destroy the political independence of the nobility and clergy and to control parliament as far as possible. He looked to the future, not to the past. And the way to the future seemed to him to be marked out by absolutism and nationality.

The influence of the Renascence when once it crossed the Alps spread with great rapidity. Men began to copy the Italian masters of painting and sculpture. They showed their liking for the new art in the forms of their houses and the decorations of their silver plate. English writers took both their material and their literary forms from Italian books. And these signs of the Renascence are so much more visible, the record of them is so much better preserved than any others, that we are apt to forget that the Renascence was not primarily an artistic and literary change. The Renascence began with an intellectual and moral ideal. Petrarch, in whose works we find the first clear record of that ideal, was deeply moved by the degradation and corruption of the institutions of Italy. A lover of freedom he saw the ancient seats of liberty fallen or trembling to their fall. Her city republics were so distracted by party hatreds, their citizens so averse to the discipline of arms, that her streets and fields were the hunting grounds of bands of foreign mercenaries, kept to the standard by the love of plunder and blood, or the ill-gotten gold of unscrupulous rulers anxious for more subjects to oppress. Rome, the symbol of the power of ancestors who ruled the world, was half in ruins. Her palaces were empty, her churches decayed. Wolves came into her squares at night; savage men, untouched by law, fought in them by day. The Papacy, which, a hundred years before Petrarch's birth, wielded power over all Europe, had crossed the Alps, established its seat at Avignon and sunk almost into an appanage of the French crown. This loss of liberty and ruin of the Church stirred Petrarch to indignation. The strong passion of his soul found vent in letters which made his name known from Sicily to the Baltic. He poured out upon the cardinals a flood of scorn, warning, entreaty, if by any means he could persuade them, to enable the Pope to seek power along the abandoned path of duty as the moral arbiter of the world; the Vicegerent of God on earth.

And the strong motive of his enthusiasm for a new ideal of education was the need of a new generation of men, to save church and state, to restore decadent Italy to her ancient glory.

The ideal of a new learning, humane rather than technical, producing the men the world needed, conquered Italian society in the letter but not in the spirit. When it was at its height Italy was profoundly corrupt. Refinement went hand in hand with licentiousness. Delicate taste was joined to forgetfulness of principle. The lives of the artists seldom matched the beauty of their pictures. Titian, in whose work Ruskin discovered such abounding moral quality, would have been entirely unable to understand the moral enthusiasm which made his modern disciple found the society of St. George. The Papacy was swept into the current. The highly developed ego of Alexander VI carried him without remorse into brutal crimes. Leo X admired pictures while the inveterate and notorious abuses of the church drove Germany into schisms and heresy. And at the very height of the Renascence Valois and Hapsburg fought over the spoils of helpless Italy. It is true indeed that in the end men trained according to the ideals of the Renascence reformed the church. The leaders of the Catholic Reformation were for the most part advocates and products of the "New Learning," and the Jesuits, the most active agents of the decrees of Trent, made the humanities the centre of the system of education by which they raised up a generation of princes faithful to the church. But for a time the men of the Renascence in Italy forgot moral ideals. Individuality ran riot in a carnival of egotism.

The humanist, a new type of man, as representative a figure of the Renascence as the knight was a representative figure in feudal times, gives the plainest proof of this declension of the Renascence from the ideals and purposes of its first great advocates.

By the middle of the fifteenth century the failure of the reform Petrarch had hoped from his new learning is prophesied by two distinguished humanists like Poggio and Filelfo, alternately flatterers and blackmailers, envious, malicious, obscene, of unlimited vanity and greed. There were, it is true, humanists, poets and artists of a type far higher than this notorious pair. But from 1475 on, few, even among the most respectable, escape some taint from the moral corruption which was like a disease in the bones of the men of the Italian Renascence. And the volunteer humanist, Aretino, the man who without the humanities became rich and famous by his pen, is an exponent of the declension of the Renascence on the soil where it started.

PETRVS ARRETINVS ACERRIMVS VIRTVTVM AC VITIORVM DEMOSTRATOR

PIETRO ARETINO.

AFTER THE ENGRAVING BY MARCANTONIO RAIMONDI

II

PIETRO ARETINO

In the middle of the eighteenth century, Count Mazzuchelli, one of the most distinguished littérateurs of his day, published a life of Pietro Aretino. The preface to the second edition begins thus: "The name of Pietro Aretino has always been so famous in the world that it never could be hid from the knowledge of even the least learned." And Addison in a Spectator written at the beginning of the century, declines to tell the career of Aretino as an illustration of his point because he is "too trite an instance. Everyone knows that all the Kings of Europe were his tributaries."

Neither of these sentences would be written now. The fame of Aretino, so vivid two centuries after his death, has declined until today many people of cultivation would know little more of him than his name. It is perhaps just as well not to know anything about Pietro Aretino, because up to the last few years it was difficult to know the truth about him. Pietro's life was written by enemies. And as his contemporary, Cranmer, said of his own foes,—"They dragged him out of the dunghill." The scandal mongers of later generations enlarged their invectives into the following story, and features of the disreputable career thus created appear in every mention of Pietro Aretino except those of a few Italian writers of the last dozen years.

He was the illegitimate son of a gentleman of Arezzo and a notoriously bad woman. After such an upbringing as might be expected from his parentage, he fled from Arezzo because of an impious poem (a variation of the legend makes him steal from his mother). He made a living in Perugia as a book-binder and picked up his education by reading the books he handled. There was a picture in the city representing the Madonna at the foot of the cross. Aretino painted a lute in her outstretched arms. After this sacrilege he fled to Rome, where he became a servant in the house of Chigi, the great banker. He stole a silver cup from his master and fled to Venice, where he led a life of extraordinary debauchery and won an evil reputation as an atheist and writer of pornographic literature. He was fatally hurt by falling over backward from his seat in a fit of laughter at an anecdote about a dishonorable adventure of one of his sisters, whose lives were worse than his mother's. And this scene was painted in 1854 by the German painter Feuerbach. Finally he died uttering one of the most profane sayings in the annals of blasphemy. In addition to this unsavory life history, entirely false, Aretino has been labeled with a larger number of strong epithets than any other man in the history of literature,—"The ignominy of his century," "The Cæsar Borgia of literature," "Perverter of morals and letters," "The synonym for all infamies." These are a few of the judgments that have been passed upon him.

To know Pietro Aretino in the four thousand letters from and to him, which have survived in print, is to recognize that he had great capacities and some amiable qualities which won him many ardent admirers and a number of warm friends. But it is also to perceive that he was essentially selfish and corrupt. In spite of the strain of religiosity in Pietro's character, it is hard to raise any very strong objections to the epitaph falsely supposed to have stood on his tomb,—"Here lies Pietro Aretino, who spoke evil of everyone except God. He never spoke evil of God simply because he never knew him."

If, then, the epitaph is just, why trouble to retell correctly the story of a bad life? Simply because to put Pietro Aretino aside labeled and classified by an absolute moral judgment,—to make him a scapegoat for the sins of his times—is to miss knowing a vivid and illuminating personality. To judge him sympathetically, to see his career as it appeared to himself and to many of his contemporaries, is to throw upon the society of the late Renascence in Italy gleams of light comparable in revealing power to those which shine from the pages of Benvenuto Cellini. If this cobbler's son, who in an age of pedantry gained fame and fortune by an untrained pen, whom Titian painted out of close friendship, whose head San Savino cast on the bronze doors of Saint Mark, of whom Ariosto wrote in Orlando Furioso,—"Behold the scourge of Princes, the divine Pietro Aretino"[1]—to whom his native city gave the title Salvator Patriae,[2] and the King of France sent a gold chain of eight pounds' weight, whom the Pope rose from his seat to receive with a kiss of welcome and who by command rode in a stately procession in the post of honour at the Emperor's right hand,—if this man be a degenerate type, his degeneration

[1] Canto XLVI, S. 14.

[2] Lettere al Aretino, page 83, Vol. I, Part I.

cannot be diagnosed by a fixed moral judgment—for his character and career are symptomatic of the disease of his times.

Pietro was born in Arezzo in 1492, of a poor shoemaker, and his wife.[1] He always had a very tender memory of his mother. Years afterward he got his friend and fellow-townsman, Vasari, to copy the Virgin in an annunciation over the door of a church in Arezzo, for which she had served as a model, and was delighted to trace a resemblance to the picture in the face of his little daughter.[2] He left his birth-place to seek his fortune and went to Perugia, where probably he studied painting without success.[3] When about twenty-five years old he went to Rome.[4] There he found a patron in Agostino Chigi. This descendant of an influential Siennese family inherited from his father the business of a banker. His skill and success gained enormous wealth. And this joined to his personal qualities made him the friend of the Pope. He became papal banker, and to a certain extent finance minister. His social position was even more imposing than his standing in the business world. He was permitted by Julius II to take the coat of arms of the della Rovere, which made him a sort of adopted relative to that Pope. He was a great friend and patron of the study of Greek literature, a most liberal and skillful connoisseur of art. The best creators of beautiful things in Rome, Sodoma, Peruzzi, Viti, Raphael, worked for him and gathered round his ta-

[1] Luzio, La famiglia di Pietro Aretino. Giorinale Stor, della Letteratura.

[2] Lettere V, 113-65.

[3] Luzio, Pietro Aretino nei primi suoi anni, etc., page 109. Torino, 1888, Bertani's answer, note page 12, is incomplete.

[4] Unless this age must be set back by examination of the poem alluded to in the note on page 37.

ble. The poets, scholars and wits flocked to his house, where his entertainments displayed the insolence of wealth amid the graces of literature and art. At a banquet he gave to celebrate the signing of his will the tables were laid in front of the frescoes where Raphael's hand has told the story of Psyche. The courses rivaled in their strangeness and profusion the days of Heliogabalus. And at the end of each service the gold and silver dishes were flung out of the window into the river; though in order to save his pocket book without lowering his pride the Pope's host had nets stretched beneath the waters to catch them. In such a household the wit and literary talent of young Pietro could find the stimulus of applause. His natural edacity and insolence would grow by what it fed upon.

From the house of Chigi, Pietro passed to the Court of Leo X, that Pope who "enjoyed the papacy God had given him," spent eight thousand ducats a year on his kitchen, a hundred thousand in gaming and presents to Court favorites, gave Michael Angelo six thousand for painting the Sistine Chapel and showed equal zest for a hunting trip, a fresco of Raphael, an indecent comedy, a discussion between Bembo and Bibbiena or the elaborate farce of a wild practical joke.[1] In the cultivated company gathered in Leo's palace, Pietro soon made a place for himself among the best—not by learning, for he had none, but by the vigour of his language.[2] A poet known for skill

[1] Lettere Aretino, I, 26. Also the Buffone di Leone X in Arturo Graf Attraverso il Cinquecento. Torino Ermanno Loescher.

[2] Apparently Pietro went to Rome and gained fame there earlier than any of his recent Italian biographers are aware of. At all events Le Glay Correspondence de Maximilien I et de Marguerite d'Autriche tome II, page 409, note 2, quotes the first lines of a poem written at the command of Leo X immediately after the battle of Guinegate (Aug., 1513), to celebrate that victory of Maximilian. It is printed in "Nouvelle Edition d'un poëme sur la Journée de

in reciting improvised verses to the lute mentions him among the famous men of Leo's Court, Bembo, Castiglione, Sadolet and others, as "a singer sweet and free, whose lithe tongue had the mastery both of praise and blame." [1] But, either because the men he knew were not laudable or because his spirit was acrid, blaming evidently came easier to him than praising. A pastoral dialogue of the time makes one speaker advise the other,—"Try your best to have Aretino for your friend because he is a bad enemy to make. God guard every one from his tongue." [2]

In 1521 Leo X died. It was centuries since Rome had seen so young a Pope, for Leo was consecrated at the age of thirty-eight, and his sudden death after a pontificate of eight years suggested the idea of poison. But such a charge is too common to be serious and historians are now disposed to see in the accusation a proof not of the crimes of ecclesiastics, but of the bitter hatreds bred by their strifes. We have every reason to believe that Leo X died of disease. Hate followed his bier. Every enemy of the Medici family and party took arms, the ready arms of voice and pen. Cardinal Soderini delivered an oration in which he thanked God for having delivered the church from Leo's tyranny.[3] A letter from Rome reported that no Pope since the church of God existed ever left a worse memory after his death, so much so that all Rome is say-

Guinegate 4° dedié by M. de Fortia to the Roxburgh Club and La Societé des Bibliophiles français. I have not been able to examine this pamphlet. The account given by Le Glay indicates that Aretino was well known in Rome three years before the tentative date assigned by Rossi and Bertani for his arrival there.

[1] Cited from MSS. by Vittorio Rossi, Pasquinate di Pietro Aretino, etc. Palermo-Torino, 1891.

[2] Pasquinate, etc. Appendix, page 161.

[3] Sanuto XXXII, C. 158, v. Quoted Rossi, X.

ing "He came in like a fox, he lived like a lion (Leo), he died like a dog." His wasteful extravagance and family ambitions had led him into all sorts of unseemly schemes for raising money. The Venetian orators sent to greet Leo's successor interpolate some descriptions of ancient monuments in their relation to the Senate. In describing the Pantheon they say,—"The great ancient portal is entirely of metal which contains so much gold that many say it is as good as the best gold florins, a saying not to be believed, for if it were so, Pope Leo would never have left the doorway in place."[1] A poet left the following epitaph: "That throne great and ornamented with riches he left as it were, extinct and ruined. See what a man has worn the crown. Murderous Tyrant is his true title. St. Peter have patience, for if you take another Medicina he will be to thy good flock a Catilina."

These were, of course, the utterances of Leo's enemies, and the friends of his family rallied at once to the defence. They did not pay much attention to the dead, they looked to the future Pope. For the eighteen months of one of the longest conclaves on record the family faction did all in their power to force the election of Cardinal Giulio de' Medici, Leo's cousin, with the bar sinister. In the long struggle behind the closed doors of the voting rooms where the Cardinals were shut up, Rome took the greatest interest. Pools were sold on the result and the prices of the favourites rose and fell according to the rumours more or less authentic which leaked out from the secret conclave. Medici started as a prime favourite. But his price soon fell as it became evi-

[1] Alberi, Relazioni degli Ambasciatori Veneti. Serie II, Vol. III, page 109.

dent that the majority, however discordant, were willing to unite against another Pope with the arms of the triple balls. One of his backers, however, was not discouraged. Pietro waged during the whole conclave, and even after the struggle was lost, a bitter fight for his patron, putting forth a succession of mordant satires on every Cardinal except the Cardinal de' Medici.

The form which he gave them foretells the vigorous originality of his talent. He never cared for the fashionable style and methods of the trained littérateurs of his day. His bent took him into unbeaten paths. Six times in his life he gave to a literary form, as yet but little used, power and vogue. In this way he made, while fighting for his patron, the beginning of fame which could be called Italian. Pietro Aretino was, so far as we know, the first man whose name became noted outside of Rome as a writer of pasquinades.

The Italians of the fifteenth century adopted the habit of their classic ancestors and were fond of writing verses to fix on walls of their friends' gardens or in places where the public might see them. So Shakespeare, read in Italian romances, makes the love-sick Orlando hang verses on the trees for Rosalind to find. But the verses which the early passers in the piazzas of Florence or Rome found from time to time, were not often love verses. The Italians, and especially the Romans, inherited from their forefathers that taste for satire which had avenged itself against the yoke of the Cæsars by epigrams sharper than swords. Their dialects lend themselves easily to rhyme, and the power of talking in meter has never been rare among them. One can still find among the Tuscan hills improvisatori, who given a subject and the proper number of rhymed words will compose a sonnet faster than it can be written down and, the first sonnet finished, will frequently succeed in making another on a different subject with the same rhymes reversed. This facility in rhyming and this satiric temper made the Romans delight in epigrams and poems playing upon the weakness and the vices of the great men of the day. And the most shining mark for these arrows of wit winged with rhyme were the members of the papal court from the Pope down to its secretaries.

This taste found at the beginning of the sixteenth century a means of expression and a symbol—Maestro Pasquino, a personage who for nearly four hundred years held up to laughter the crimes and follies of the first society of Rome. At last in 1870 when the law gave entire freedom to the press, unable to breathe the air of liberty, he died, and his voice, which was wont to take especial delight in the malevolent or scandalous rumours which flew around the closed doors of every papal conclave, has not been heard since. The long series of his poems is finished. Just how they began and where he got his name is not quite certain.

In the year 1501 the Cardinal of Naples had the caprice to place a fragment of an antique statue on a pedestal at an angle of his palace, and the statue received the name of Maestro Pasquino. Tradition says the name was inherited from a man; according to one report a witty cobbler with an evil tongue; according to another a tailor; according to another a schoolmaster, who had lived near, and whose festival was for many years celebrated by hanging Latin verses on his stone namesake. The festival celebrated by Latin verses on the statue certainly took place, for the verses were printed "with the biting ones left out." And whether the schoolmaster ever drew the breath of life or not, it seems certain that the tailor and the barber are creatures of myth. This annual fête of Master Pasquino so raised the fame of the statue that in the course of a few years it became a more and more favoured place to fix the biting verses the Romans loved. So a young German poet, Ulrich von Hutten, a warm adherent of the Emperor Maximilian, visiting Rome about 1514, wrote a satiric song and fixed it on the statue of Pasquino.

Popular leaflets in the vulgar tongue gradually displaced the Latin verses of the supposed pedagogue, who thus became, in the course of a generation, the terrible gossiping censor he remained until his death. It is not possible to trace exactly the victory of this satiric Pasquino who talked Italian, over the scholastic Pasquino who talked Latin. But the earliest manuscript collection of Pasquinades, as the world came to know them during the four hundred years of Pasquino's life, was made in the year of the death of Leo X and is filled mainly by verses of Pietro Aretino—the first man to win the dangerous but envied title of Secretary of Pasquino.

The deadlock of the conclave ended to the stupefaction of every one, in the election of the Cardinal of Tortosa (Adrian VI), an absent man who had not even been named as a possibility—one whom Italians spoke of as a Flemish barbarian—ignorant of literature, blind to art, a monk and a scholastic. Aretino gave full voice to that disgust which continued during all Adrian's life to cover with ridicule his honest efforts to live and rule like a Vicar of Christ and, at death, crowned his doctor's door with laurel and the motto Salvator Patriae.

When the Pope-elect slowly drew near to Rome Aretino thought it wise to leave. Adrian wanted to throw Pasquino into the Tiber and was only dissuaded by being told it was useless to try to drown him; "like a frog he would talk out of the water." If the Pope could have laid hands on Aretino, he certainly would have tried whether the Chancellor of Pasquino could talk out of a dungeon. He wrote to get him from Florence, where he had taken refuge with the Cardinal de' Medici. The Cardinal, of course, would not surrender his supporter but deemed it best for Aretino to go to the camp of his distant cousin, Giovanni de' Medici, called of the Black Bands. He was the first soldier that the Medici had yet produced, a formidable antagonist, a leader adored by the black mercenaries who followed him—perhaps the most famous Italian man of arms of his day. A close friendship at once united the dreaded captain and the dreaded satirist. Aretino became the comrade of Giovanni.

But this intimacy was interrupted by the death of Adrian VI, and Aretino went back to Rome to share the fortune of the man for whom, to cite his own phrase, "My virtù which fed on your praise, took arms against Rome when the throne of Leo became vacant." When Aretino came back to Rome he was not at first disposed "to make Pasquino talk." The man whose fortunes he had followed as a literary bravo had at length won. Leo X, son of Lorenzo de' Medici. had been succeeded as

Vicar of Christ after the brief pontificate of a northern barbarian, by Giulio de' Medici as Clement VII. The whole set of those who lived by their talents or their wits rejoiced that a Pope representing the reactionary ideas of the Middle Ages was replaced by a man of progress in touch with the times. Adrian had taken great interest in religion and none in art. They hoped that Clement would not spend too much energy in trying to foster the old fashioned virtues, and would give a great deal of attention to promoting men of virtù who could create with pen, pencil or chisel things to please the mind or the taste. The temper of the secretary of Pasquino was soothed by golden hopes, his dreaded and applauded tongue was still.

His contemporaries were ill content with that silence. After colour and form in the plastic arts, the Italians of the early sixteenth century seem to have found most pleasure in satire, and Aretino had shown himself able to give them a satire suited to their taste, suggesting no ideals, hoping no reforms,—so local and personal that it is hard for another generation to read and understand it; no bitter passion of the soul but just a delicate morsel for the intense "schadenfreude" of the day. They called on him not to stop his career. What stood for the public of our time demanded something from his pen. So a poet wrote in a dialogue between a Traveller and Marforio, a gossip of Pasquino:

Traveller:—"Marforio, since the day when this Pope was elected, your brother Pasquino is grown almost dumb and Aretino no longer reproves vice. What have you to say about it?"

Marforio:—"Why, don't you know that Armellino has cut short Pasquino by giving him to understand that if he makes a sound they'll slit his tongue for him, so the poor chap doesn't dare to breathe, much less talk."

Way:—"Pietro Aretino, who is in such high favor, was taken with a mouthful of bait like a frog, and now he sings but he doesn't want to touch the court. That would be a mistake, because it is giving him means to play the swell like a baron, etc."[1]

But it was difficult for Aretino to keep his pen still, and he used it in a kind of writing which, though it occupied but a small part of his works, has fixed the attention of posterity to the neglect of all the rest. Giulio Romano, one of the most distinguished painters of the day, painted a series of sixteen pictures and Marc Antonio Raimondi engraved them. The plates have fortunately perished but descriptions are enough to tell us that in English-speaking countries printer and seller of such plates would now be sent to the penitentiary. At the instance of the Datario, his most trusted counsellor, the Pope put Raimondi in prison. But Aretino appealed to the Pope to set him free and was successful. Then Aretino proceeded to write for the series, sixteen sonnets which matched the pictures. The Datario was indignant and Aretino found it best to retire from Rome to Arezzo. That the disgrace was not very serious is shown by two letters from Giovanni de' Medici, addressed just at this time to "The Stupendous Pietro Aretino, my true friend," and to "Pietro Aretino, Miracle of Nature." [2] And in a short time we find him back a Rome

[1] Printed from MSS. by Luzio, Nuova Antologia, Aug., 1890, Vol. 28, third series, page 693.

[2] Lettere al Aretino, Vol. I, pt. 1, Letters 1 and 2.

in high favor with Clement VII, who made him a Knight of Rhodes.

One of the most distinguished littérateurs of the day, whose presence was sought by every cultivated court of Italy,[1] was Bernado Accolti, the reasons for whose great esteem among his contemporaries do not appear in any of his verses which have survived. He was known everywhere by the title of L'Unico Aretino, because he had been born in Arezzo. This recognized model and authority in the poetic art on one occasion turned to Pietro, in the presence of the Pope and the whole court, assembled to hear him recite his verses, and said:—"Holy Shepherd, I rejoice in your presence because I leave behind me another self from my own city."[2]

Pietro's thanks for the renewed favour and increased reputation he received at the Court of Clement VII, appeared in verses praising the Datario and the Pope, than whom,—"Christ could not find today a better Vicar."[3] For that praise he also found another expression in a literary form to which he gave new force and vigour. In the first of his comedies, which showed less dependence upon the form and method of Roman comedy than any of the few which had previously been written in Italian, he interpolated into the dialogue, somewhat after the fashion of the modern "gag," complimentary references to the Pope and his Court.[4] But this sort of writing did not sat-

[1] Castiglione, Il Cortigiano.

[2] Aretino, Lettere, V, fol. 45.

[3] Laude di Clemente VII del divino Poeta M. P. Aretino, Roma, 1524. Quoted by Bertani, page 44, from an article by Luzio on a unique copy of this book.

[4] Luzio, Pietro Aretino nei primi suoi anni, etc., page 2, note 2. Report on a MS.

isfy either himself or his admirers. On the seventh of June, 1525, the Marquis of Mantua wrote to Pietro by the hand of his secretary,—"You promised several days ago to send some beautiful and pleasing compositions made for Pasquino, and we have been continually in eager expectation because we want always to have some new fruit of your active talent and we don't know why we suffer such a dearth of them unless it is to make us more hungry for them. But remember that your poems cannot be easily concealed and when they are known all over Rome and, as it were, all over Italy, we don't take as much pleasure in them, not because they are not the same after as before publication, but because novelty commends everything and adds value to valuable things, etc., etc."

To which the Duke added a postscript in his own hand, —"Please M. Pietro send me some of your compositions and kiss the feet of His Holiness for me. And I am entirely yours, entirely yours, the Marquis of Mantua."

Pasquino was talking again and the result was that Aretino, riding alone one day, was dragged from his horse and left for dead with dagger wounds. Certain letters suggest that it was not the first time his quill had been answered by steel. But this time his wounds were more serious. He barely escaped with his life.

Such an accident might easily happen to anyone in that day. Nor were artists and literary men exempt from the danger of the knife or free from a desire to use it. Bembo was stabbed in his youth. Benvenuto Cellini made deadly assaults on several men who had insulted him. Leone Leoni tried to murder three rivals, among them the son of his friend Titian.

Pietro was not always very severe against this way of "vindicating honour." Many years later when his own henchman, Ambrogio Eusebeii, cut Franco in the face with a dagger for attacking his master with sonnets, Aretino writes of it in a letter destined for publication with a pleasure lessened only by the reflection that the wound will win for the victim a charity he does not deserve. He solemnly denied that he had instigated the deed for, though Franco's "insolence deserves punishment, it was cruel to punish it with steel." [1] But his regret veils ill his satisfaction in the loyalty of his servant.

Circumstances, however, alter judgments. Pietro left no stone unturned to get Clement to punish his assailant.

Everybody knew who had tried to kill Aretino, a certain Achilles della Volta, of the household of the Datario Ghiberti, and years afterward Achilles, on trial for another deadly assault, confessed the deed. It was taken for granted by all Rome that the master had ordered the servant to avenge the insults of Aretino, an accusation which Ghiberti, years afterward, when Bishop of Verona, solemnly denied in a letter to the Marquis of Mantua.

All Pietro's efforts to get his enemy punished were vain. Achilles remained untouched of law in the service of the Papal Datario, and Pietro, vowing vengeance, left Rome for the camp of Giovanni de' Medici.

Of that famous captain he became the intimate friend and he wrote afterwards that the great soldier swore to make him lord and ruler of Arezzo when the war was over. The friendship and the hopes of the two were cut short by a bullet which fatally wounded Giovanni, Novem-

[1] Aretino, Lettere, III, page 203.

ber, 1526. Aretino has described the death of his friend and patron in one of the best of his letters.

"When the hour drew near, which the fates, with the consent of God, had fixed as the end of our Master, His Highness was attacking with his usual terrible force Governo around which the enemy had entrenched themselves, and while thus engaged a musket ball broke the leg which was already wounded by an arquebus. As soon as he felt the blow, fear and melancholy fell on the army and joy and ardor died in all hearts. Everybody forgot himself and in thinking of the occurrence wept, complaining of fate for having so senselessly brought to death the noblest and most excellent general in the memory of centuries, at the very beginning of more than human achievements and in the midst of Italy's greatest need. The captains who followed him with love and veneration, blaming fortune and his temerity for their loss, spoke of age ripened to bear fatigue sufficient for every undertaking and apt for every difficulty. They sighed over the greatness of his thoughts and the wildness of his valour, they could not control their voices in remembering the good fellowship which made them his companions and not forgetting his foresight and acuteness, they warmed with the fire of their complaints the snow which was falling heavily while they carried him to Mantua. * * * Then the Duke of Urbino came to see him and said, seeing the situation,—'It is not enough for you to be great and glorious in arms if you do not also distinguish your name by religion under whose sacraments we are born.' And he, understanding that these words meant the last confession, answered,—'As I have done my duty in all things, if need is, I will do it in this also.' Then when he went out he set himself to talk with me, calling for Sire Antonio with great affection. And when I said that we would send for him,—'Do you want,' he answered, 'a man like him to leave the field of war to see sick men?' Then he remembered the Count of San Secondo, saying,—'I wish he were here to take my place.' Sometimes he scratched his head with his finger, sometimes he laid it on his lips, saying,—'What will happen?' Often repeating,—'I have nothing to repent of.' Then, by the wishes of the doctors, I went to him and said,—'It would be an insult to your soul if I tried to persuade you that death is the cure of ills, made heavy only by our fears. But because it is the highest happiness to do everything with free will, let them cut off the leg broken by the artillery and in eight days you will be able to make of Italy, now a slave, a queen. And your lameness will serve instead of the royal order you have always refused to wear on your neck, because wounds and the loss of limbs are the medals of the friends of Mars.'

" 'Let them do it,' he answered at once. At this moment the doctors came in and praising the firmness of his resolution, ended their services for the night and, after giving him medicine, went to put their instruments in order. It was already the hour to eat when he was taken by violent nausea. Then he said to me, 'The signals of Cæsar! I must think of something else than life.' And with hands joined, he made a vow to go to the Apostle of Galatia. But when the time was come and the skillful men came in with their instruments, they asked for eight or ten assistants to hold him while the terrible sawing lasted. He smiled and said, 'Twenty couldn't hold me,' got ready with a perfectly calm face, took the candle in his hand to light the doctors himself. I ran out and closing my ears heard only two cries,—and then he called me. When I came to him he said, 'I am cured,' and turning himself all around, made a great rejoicing about it. If the Duke of Urbino had not stopped him, he would have made them bring in the foot with the pieces of his leg to look at, laughing at us because we could not bear to look at what he had suffered. And his sufferings were far greater than those of Alexander and Trajan who kept a smiling face when the tiny arrowhead was pulled out. He smiled when his nerves and sinews were cut.

But finally the pain which had left him returned two hours before day with all sorts of torments. I heard him knocking hastily on the wall of the room. The sound stabbed me to the heart and getting dressed, in an instant I ran to him. As soon as he saw me he commenced to say that the thought of cowards gave him more disgust than pain, trying by thus gossiping with me to set free by disregarding his misfortunes his spirit tangled in the snares of death. But as day dawned, things grew so much worse that he made his will, in which he divided many thousands of scudi in money and stuff among those who had served him and left only four julii for his burial. The Duke was executor. Then he turned in most Christian mood to his last confession and seeing the friar come, —'Father,' he said, 'being a professor of arms I have lived with the habits of soldiers as I should have lived like the monks if I had put on the dress you wear. Were it allowed I would confess before everyone for I have never done anything unworthy of myself.' At last he turned to me, ordering me to have his wife send Cosimo to him. At that, death which was calling him to the under world doubled his sadness. Already the entire household without any more thought of the respect due to rank, swarmed round the bed, mingled with his chief officers and shadowed by a cold melancholy, wept for the living hope and the service which they were losing with their master, each trying to catch his eye with a glance of theirs to show their sorrow and love. Thus surrounded, he took the hand of the Duke, saying, 'You are losing to-day the greatest friend and the best servant you have ever had.' His Excellency, masking his face and tongue with the appearance of false joy, tried to make him believe he would get well. And he who was not frightened by death even when he was certain of it, began to talk to the Duke about the result of the war, saying things which would have been remarkable if he had been in full health, instead of half dead. And so he remained working with his mind until almost the ninth hour of the night of the vigil of St. Andrew. And because his suffering was very great be begged me to put him to sleep by reading to him. I did it and he seemed to waste away from sleep to sleep. At last, waking after fifteen minutes' dozing, he said, 'I dreamed I was making my will and here I am cured. If I keep on getting better like this I'll teach the Germans how to make war and show them how I avenge myself.' Even as he said this the lamp of his spirit which cheated his eyes began to yield to the perpetual darkness. Wherefore of his own accord he asked for the Extreme Unction,

Having received the sacrament, he said, 'I don't want to die among all these poultices.' So we fixed a camp bed and put him on it and there while his mind slept, death took him."[1]

"He is dead—a force of nature. He is finished—the example of antique faith. He is gone—the right arm of battle."[2]

Aretino seems to have felt this loss more than anything which happened to him, and for the rest of his life never tired of praising the character of his dead friend and patron.

He was welcome to stay with his old admirer, the Marquis of Mantua. But Federico found himself much embarrassed by his guest's quarrel with the Pope whom Aretino ceaselessly attacked with bitter satires. And he had found for them a new and striking form. The belief in astrology was very common among all classes of the day,—educated and uneducated. For at least thirty years astrologers had issued their predictions based on the conjunctions of the planets; about the weather, the harvests, the war, the governments and other topics of interest. These publications, called giudizî, were taken seriously and had a large sale. Aretino conceived the striking idea of parodying these giudizî, making them a comment on what had happened spiced with satire and witty reflections. This gave him the chance of telling at once the scandals of the day and his opinions on them. Just when he began to write giudizî we cannot tell. Until very recently only a fragment of these admired productions was known. It was written at Mantua and en-

[1] Aretino, Lettere, I, 5-9.
[2] Aretino, Lettere, I, 10.

titled Giudizio or prognostic of Maestro Pasquino, the fifth evangelist for the year 1527. To the Marquis of Mantua Pieto Aretino. The stupidity of Guarico (a noted astrologer) and of that brute who is with Count Rangone and the other stupid ribalds, the disgraces of the prophets, have made me this year turn philosopher to the shame of the stupid flock of Abumasar and Ptolemy. I have composed the Giudizio for 1527 and I will not be a liar like the above mentioned rascals whose smallest and least important lie was the flood, etc., etc.

Section first. Of the nature of the atmosphere and the entries of the sun (into the zodiacal signs).

According to the opinion of modern interpreters of the planets, for instance Zulian Levi and Ceccotto of Genoa, the entry of the sun will be into the first tavern he shall find and he will come out drunk at the end of eight days at the meridian of your horologe of Mantua. The atmosphere will be very apt to become corrupt by the breath of Germans gulping Italian wine, etc., etc.[1]

The body of the Giudizio, which is lost, was evidently a most bitter attack on the Pope, the Cardinals and the Roman court. For, in April, 1527, the Mantuan Ambassador wrote from Rome to the Marquis that the confessor of the Pope reported his Holiness much offended by a little book of Pietro Aretino's dedicated to the Marquis and full of evil speaking, especially against the Pope and the Cardinals and other prelates of this court. The Ambassador suggests that he must drive Aretino from Mantua. The Marquis could not afford to quarrel with the

[1] Quoted from MSS. by Luzio, Pietro Aretino nei primi suoi anni, etc., page 8.

Pope. He answered that although he had taken pleasure in some of Aretino's writings, he had never been pleased to have him write against the Pope and the prelates of the church. As soon as he understood the blackguardly mind of Aretino he had told him to leave the court and had given him money and other gifts only to avoid appearing mean. If this was not enough His Holiness had but to give him the word quietly, or otherwise express a wish that it should be done, and he would settle Aretino for good and all. If he escaped from other hands he could not escape his and he would manage it in such a way that no one would know who did it.[1]

Whether the Marquis of Mantua was lying to the Pope in saying that he despised Aretino's writings and was ready to have him assassinated if His Holiness wished it, or whether he was lying to Aretino in his expressions of esteem, is difficult to say. At all events, twenty-four days after he sent the above dispatch to Rome, he sent a letter to Aretino at Venice in which, among other compliments, he wrote,—"Very willingly I have done you the favour to look over again your Giudizio, although I had re-read it before and I find that it is the most truthful Giudizio which has been uttered for many years and that you are the best astrologer there is. * * * I shall expect now in recognition of this favour that you will keep the promise you made to send me whatever comes from your fine mind as I beg you to do, because no greater pleasure could be given me, and your writings are the merriest things I come across."

[1] Luzio, P. A. nei primi suoi anni, Documento II. Quoted here in summary form.

Aretino arrived in Venice a fugitive with a hundred scudi in his pocket in March, 1527, and lived there for twenty-nine years a life of honour, splendour and fame,—a political force courted by all, a celebrity of Venice,—visited by distinguished strangers,—the flattered correspondent of the leading artists and littérateurs and their noble patrons. There was talk at one time of making him a cardinal.[1] If this had been done, no literary man of his day would have received larger material rewards or had a more triumphant success.

Of this successful life and of his own character we have a most vivid and truthful record in eight hundred and sixteen letters to Aretino and thirty-one hundred and seventy-five from him, all printed during his lifetime. In those five thousand pages one can see the reflection of the man and the times.

In Venice he found the home which suited his tastes. He was never tired of praising the charms of life in "The crown and beauty of the world." "Venice impress of the joyful soul of wonderful and foreseeing Nature." "Venice alias the Terrestrial Paradise."

Venice was the richest and largest of Italian cities, and the only one free from foreign control. The lines of trade were indeed changing. Adventurous ships had traced on the ocean the great highroads of travel, and the centre of commerce was no longer at the head of the Adriatic. It was moving up the Atlantic coast toward the delta of the Rhine. But the decline of Venice was very slow. It was as yet scarcely noticeable. The State

[1] Lettere al Aretino II, No. 248. Titian wrote from Augsburg that the Emperor talked of urging his name upon the Pope for a red hat.

revenues were larger than those of the English Crown. The citizens were prosperous, and out of a population of 190,000 in 1585 there were only 187 beggars. So easy was living that, by the middle of the century, citizens could no longer be found to man the galleys and they must be filled with aliens. The common people were comfortable to an extent unknown elsewhere in Italy. They had rugs for the floor, good beds to sleep on, pictures on the walls, and some silver pieces for the well-spread table.

The homes of the Venetian nobles had long been magnificent. In the early fifteenth century a traveller wrote that not even the Queen of France or the Duchess of Milan had apartments as gorgeously furnished as those of a Venetian lady. At that time the ships unloaded their cargoes at the steps of the palaces, and the lower rooms stored the merchandise that made the family wealth. Bales of wool and rolls of silk rested unashamed beneath the banners and arms won by noble ancestors in glorious fight with the Turk. But in the sixteenth century the eighteen hundred patricians, leaving trade to the citizens, gave themselves to the cares of government and to spending the wealth laid up by their hard-working forefathers.

They spent it in princely style. It was traditional in their class to be well educated, and when the rude English nobles could scarcely read and write, the Venetian patricians had maintained a course of public instruction in philosophy whose chairs must all be filled by aristocrats. They were rapidly building the hundred palaces which rose on the banks of the canals during that sixteenth century which brought into being most of the Venice we know; for about half of the buildings mentioned in a modern guide-book were erected or restored in the sixteenth century. Their patronage was fostering the bloom of artistic power that made Venice succeed Florence and Rome as the third centre of the art of the Renascence. At the public celebration of the victory of Lepanto in 1575, the gates of the Rialto were draped in gold, blue, and red, and decorated with trophies of Turkish arms, among which the city displayed as its most precious possessions pictures of Raphael, Bellini, Giorgione, Michael Angelo, Pordenone, and Titian.

The luxury of living grew steadily, in spite of laws passed to restrict it by men who sighed for the good old times when generations of Venetian seamen, working and fighting hard and living simply, wrested wealth from the sea and power from the infidel. Venice gained from Rome the reputation of being the centre of license as well as art, and became the pander of the visitors who flocked to see her beauty.

In Italy of that time public sentiment was deeply depraved. One of the many Italian scholars who, in these last few years, have been doing such valuable work on the Renascence, says: "It is now a banal truism . . . that in the Italian Renascence the concept of morality underwent a transformation and a general lowering so great that it requires a strong effort for us to form a just idea of it." [1]

The solid reasons on which this judgment rests may be indicated by two examples: Luzio has published letters of the Marquis of Mantua in which he frankly shows

[1] Cian, Bembo, page 180; Virgili, page 58, speaks of "Il fango ed il lezzo di quei tempi d'oro."

willingness to render the most infamous service to Aretino's vices. And Molmenti quotes a contemporary who says that Alfonso d'Este was called a virtuous man, because he let other men's wives alone and never failed to provide dowries and husbands for the young girls he ruined.[1]

A sense of shame is the last bulwark against vice and the standard of morality is always higher than the practice. Nowhere in the world during the early sixteenth century was this very high. But Italy had a deserved distinction in evil. Roger Ascham visited Venice five years before Pietro's death. His judgment may have been somewhat coloured by religious prejudice, but it will bear a large reduction without being much weakened. It is expressed in language a little too virile to be quoted entire in days when indignation is less frank, but the gist of it is in these two sentences: "I was once in Italy myself; but I thank God my abode there was but nine days. And yet I saw in that little time in one city more liberty to sin than ever I heard tell of in our noble city of London in nine years." [2]

It is not possible to find in modern literature pictures of a society moving on as low a level of moral judgment as that on which the heroes of the popular Italian novelists of the sixteenth century show their heroes and heroines. Social custom did not exact from vice even the tribute of concealment or hypocrisy.

Aretino had no quarrel with this depraved moral judgment. Indeed it did not seem to him depraved, but just

[1] Molmenti, page 287.
[2] Ascham, The Schoolmaster, about the middle of the treatise.

and natural. Like most men of this day he would have smiled with indulgent pity at a higher standard of conduct as the dream of an idealist ignorant of what happens. Boccaccio had expressed the base of a depraved literature and a depraved life in the conclusion,—the same conclusion assumed in that extraordinary series of erotomaniac romances to which so many masters of French prose have in our day given their pens—that man cannot resist his passions. Aretino writes in one of his letters,—"It is in the power of few or rather of none, to resist the assaults of lust or of anger. Wherefore, every unfortunate occurrence produced by one or the other of these passions ought to be forgiven."[1]

Let it be said then, once for all, that the life of Aretino, so picturesque, so joyous, so adorned with the pleasures of literature and art, was frankly disorderly, based on Turkish morals, or rather on morals worse than Turkish, for he lacked none of the vices of the East and his harem was irregular and temporary. This viciousness was not in the least concealed. We know of it chiefly from the allusions and accounts of the collection of letters he himself printed, and in two of them he has frankly and brutally defended and recommended such a life.[2]

This disorder was thrown in Aretino's teeth by his assailants. But neither their reproaches nor its notoriety diminished the tribute of respect paid to him in Venice and out of it by all classes of society, including popular preachers, prelates of the church and ladies of the most distinguished families. It did not prevent honourable

[1] Aretino, Lettere, I, fol. 192.
[2] Aretino, Lettere, I, 105-259.

women from sending him wine, preserved peaches, and beautiful embroideries, nor stop a blue stocking of unreproachable reputation like Veronica Gambara from writing the most flattering letters or celebrating his love in a sonnet.[1]

Within two years of his arrival in Venice, Pietro moved into a house on the Grand Canal close to the Rialto in the very centre of the life of the city. In a letter to its noble owner, Domenico Bolani, he describes it,—"I should seem, most honoured Sir, guilty of ingratitude if I did not pay with praise a part of what I owe to the divine site where your house is built. I live there with the greatest pleasure in life because it is placed in a position which could not be improved by being moved up or down or in any other direction. To undertake the theme of its merits is as difficult as it is to write about the Emperor. Certainly the man who built it chose the best side of the Grand Canal. And because it is the patriarch of all streets, and Venice the popess of all cities, I can truthfully say that I enjoy the prettiest street and pleasantest view in the world. I cannot go to the window during business hours without seeing a thousand persons and as many gondolas. On the right hand I have the piazzas of the beccaria and the fish market and the Campo del Mancino,

[1] Preachers—Vergerio, Cerolamo d'Este, Fra Tommaso, Bernardo of Brescia, Aretino Lettere. Prelates—It will be enough to cite the Cardinals of Ravenna, Mantua, Urbino, the Archbishop of Palermo, the Bishops of Casale, Lucera, Vercelli. Lettere a Pietro Aretino. Ladies—Contessa di Monte Labate, Duchessa d'Urbino, Camilla and Ludovica Pallavicina, Ludovica San Sevino, etc. Camilla Pallavicina had his illegitimate daughter for a visit and sent her home with a gold chain.

Aretino, Lettere, III, 143.

Veronica Gambara. Lettere al Aretino, I, page 318 ff.

"Serena will be with Beatrice and Laura eternal in the circle of Heaven."

the bridge and the House of German merchants. Opposite both there is the Rialto crowded with business men.

* * * * * * * *

"I do not care to see streams which water the meadows when at dawn I can look at the water covered at the season with everything that grows. It is very amusing when the farmers distribute their great loads of fruit and green stuff to those who carry them where they are to go. But that is nothing compared to the twenty or twenty-five sailing boats filled with melons gathered together in a little island, while the crowd runs around testing the perfection of the fruit by smelling and weighing it. I don't speak of the pretty wives shining with silk, gold and jewelry standing proudly in the boats. * * * And who would not have died laughing to see, as I and the famous Giulio Camillo did, a bark filled with Germans just come out of the tavern upset on a very cold day. * * * And that nothing may be lacking to complete my view, on one side I am charmed by the orange trees touching with gold the foundations of the palace of the Camerlinghi and on the other by the canal and bridge of San Giovanni. The winter sun never rises without first giving notice at my bedside, in my study, my kitchen, my rooms and dining-hall. * * * I must not forget the lights which after dark seem like scattered stars, where the things we use for our dinners and banquets are sold, or the music which at night comes to my ears with its concord of harmonious sounds. It would be easier to express the profound wisdom which you possess for letters and politics than to come to the end of the pleasures I find in my view. And if there is any breath or spirit of genius in the rubbish I write, it is inspired not by the air nor the shadows nor the flowers nor the Summer green, but by the airy felicity of this habitation of yours, in which I hope, God willing, to count with health and vigour the full tale of years which a good fellow ought to live." [1]

Aretino was so much pleased with his house that he refused almost all the pressing invitations which came to him to visit France and various courts of Italy. He seldom left it except for a couple of weeks in the summer when he went to Gambarara, a few miles off on the mainland. And when he had to move, near the end of his life, he simply crossed the canal to the other bank.

His house was always full of servants, parasites and visitors, and the table was seldom spread for less than a score of persons. The rooms were decorated with pictures, statues and frescoes of friends like Titian, Tintoretto, Sansovino, Vasari, and he had choice glass-ware of Murano, specimen Majolicas, wood carvings of Tasso, medals and silver-ware of Leone Leoni, oriental hangings and tapestries.[2] He was fond of magnificent dresses. One of his costumes was a robe of black velvet ornamented with gold cords with the lining of cloth of gold, and a long gown and jerkin of velvet. Another given by the Duke of Mantua was a gown of ermisine trimmed with embroidered black velvet and lined with pure white fox skins and a simare of black satin. He received as presents many gold chains. One from the King of France weighed eight pounds. His letters abound with thanks

[1] Aretino, Lettere, I, 169.

[2] Aretino, Lettere, passim.

for such things as "white satin stockings wrought in gold," "green silk caps," "a flesh coloured jerkin embroidered with silver cords and trimmed with ermine." A list of his presents would be a catalogue of splendid stuffs, embroideries and jewels, enough to furnish the wardrobe of a small theatre.

But in spite of this apparatus of luxury there was nothing really aristocratic about the life of Aretino. The house was filled with confusion, robbed secretly by the servants, plundered openly by its disorderly guests.[1] When a present of wine arrived friends and neighbours crowded in to drink it up. He could not hide the shirts or fine stockings sent him so that the women of the house would not steal them.[2] When he received a dozen rosaries he had ordered, he describes with great humour how the whole "troop of his band" gathered "like hungry hens picking at a piece of bread, admiring, discussing, choosing until midnight." And he begs his friend if he loves him and wants him to escape alive to send six more of garnet so that all may be satisfied.[3]

Aretino was lavishly kind to the poor and exceedingly hospitable. If he heard of any one sick he sent a doctor. He often paid the rent for those about to be turned out of their home. He visited prisoners and his purse was open to young men going out into the world to try their fortunes. Those who knew him said he would take the shirt off his back to give to a friend in need. He did not hide the light of his good deeds under a bushel. But

[1] Aretino, Lettere, I, 29, II, 131-134.
[2] Aretino, Lettere, I, 86.
[3] Aretino, Lettere, III, 68.

ceaseless braggart as he is, there is little reason to believe him a liar and the above picture of his charity is painted not with his own words but with those of his intimates.[1] His friend and publisher Francesco Marcolini tells two good stories of the way his kindness and hospitality were imposed upon. The first is of an "excellent scoundrel who came and told you that a certain respectable young girl who had formerly been a neighbour of yours was dead and got from your purse the money to bury her. And when a few days afterward the poor brother of the said young woman came to ask your help to find her a husband and a marriage portion, before he opened his mouth you ran to meet him with open arms tenderly sorrowing with him over his sister's death. But the young fellow, all taken aback, answered, 'Signore, if she hasn't died within the half hour, she is living and well.' And since you would not believe it, he was obliged to go and bring his sister to your house with scarcely clothes enough to cover her. She left it very well dressed and with the promise of a marriage portion to find her a husband."

The second story is a comment on "the continual hospitality of your house which is so open to everybody that the mistake of the party of strangers in Venice made on the first of May, 1532, is not to be wondered at. They took your house for, what in one sense it is, a tavern; especially when they saw so many people come out boasting of having drunk the best wine in Venice. And so they went up stairs and took their places at the table, saying,—'Bring us a salad.' Having been served with it and

[1] Lettere al Aretino, II, part 2, page 352, and elsewhere.

everything else they asked for and ready to go, they called your Mazzone, who because he is young, good looking, white faced, tall, fat, merry and of pleasant humour, they took to be the host. But when he was asked by one of the good fellows 'What was the bill for supper?' the good Mazzone, understanding that he was being treated as if he was an inn-keeper, got ready to give him a thrashing. At last, from the sound cursing that you gave them, accompanied by four or five blows, the merry gallants recognized that you must be the owner of the house and not the gentleman stopping at an inn for whom they had taken you. And when the good fellows understood that having supped like emperors it was not going to cost them anything but hearty thanks and good wishes, they were full of bows and compliments to you and went off roaring with laughter." [1]

This open house of a royal good fellow in luck exactly suited Aretino, for his taste in art, his love of rich clothes and his easy-going kindness were mingled at once with the habits of a dissolute Bohemian and the likings of a cockney. He writes that it is a fixed habit with him never to spend more than a week in the country, otherwise it becomes a terrible bore.[2] No pleasures of summer, he says, are "worth a single bite of bread dipped in oil eaten around the December fire when one sits drinking several cups of new wine, picking off bits from the roast turning on the spit and not caring if he does burn mouth and fingers in the theft." And there is a strain of sincere pleasure in the letter he writes to a

[1] Lettere al Aretino, II, part 2, page 355.
[2] Aretino, Lettere, I, 145.

friend praising him for being careless of all the splendours of the world and acting his own servant. "How pleasant it is when you come back at night to the little shelter fitted for the condition you have been wise enough to choose in order to escape the grumbling of a wife, who is as apt to be just as cross when one comes home too early as when one comes home too late. If the hot coals covered with ashes are not out, a sulphur taper lights the lamp. If they have burnt out just call to your neighbour and she will hand you out of the window a brand or a bit of live coal on the little fire shovel. While the faggot blazes up you stand humming a tune until you begin to feel hungry. Then you settle with your back to the fire and peg away with a fisherman's appetite at the salad you dress and the sausage you roast, drinking big draughts without any fear that the confounded household will make wry faces behind you. Then going back to the fire you watch your shadow which gets up when you do and sits down with you,—in short, is a most polite companion. Meantime, you swap stories with the cat. * * * When you get sleepy you say good-night to yourself and jump into bed, made perhaps twice a month by your own hands and saying the Ave Maria and the Pater Noster and crossing yourself (you don't need any other prayers because the man who has no family has no sins), you fasten your head so tight to the pillow that thunder would have to do more than its best to wake you. In the morning you get up and enjoy the pleasures of your pleasant art; you wait until a little omelette claims your attention, and shaking out the table cloth and putting it on the table, always at hand and always guarded by the jug of wine ever ready to make love to you, you eat to live instead of living to eat. Then you take a stroll for as long as you like. * * * You buy a little fish brought in fresh at the moment by the fishermen, or a little capon or chicken to keep Easter and the feasts, not forgetting a goose for All Saints' Day. * * * In Summer you are satisfied with plums, a dozen figs, a bunch of grapes. And you venture buying a melon, heavy, small and covered with bloom. When you get home with it, fresh water on the table, you put the wine bottle into the well bucket and at almost the same moment plunge your nose and your knife into the melon. Finding it sweet and delicious you have the pleasure of a pope * * *."[1]

In spite of this praise of a simple life, Aretino was very fond of the pleasures of an elaborate table. But not in a coarse way. The traveller who passes from the shores of the North Sea and the Baltic to the Mediterranean and the Adriatic, remarks at once the temperance of the Italian as compared with the Teuton. The heavy eating and drinking of England and Germany struck the Italian traveller of the Renascence with disgust. While the letters of Aretino suggest the epicure they do not show him as either drunkard or glutton. They are filled with thanks for presents of delicacies or allusions to little impromptu suppers, but there is nothing gross or selfish in this talk about food and drink. On the contrary, Aretino felt instinctively that subtle civilizing influence of the table which Balzac has pointed out. It was to him a symbol of the pleasures of taste and sense refined by common enjoyment—a pledge of friendship—a centre of cultivated

[1] Aretino, Lettere, II, 27.

companionship. His imagination or his wit is quick to play about what he eats. Writing of the pleasures of a visit to his native Arezzo, he says he "never has a large appetite except when he remembers the cheeses, the ham, the sausages, the olives, the mushrooms, the ragouts, the salads and the jokes doubling the savour of these good things of the Reverend Canons Capuiciùoli and Bonci." And he adds, "My benedictions would have doubled the praises of the peasant woman who made the cates sent me, if their delayed arrival had permitted me to taste them; nevertheless, the fact that they were spoiled does not make me any less obliged for them." [1]

"In spite of my fever," he writes, "I could not help tasting two of the peaches you sent. Certainly the peach is a fruit which appeals to the heart. When I see it beside a good melon, moved by their charm, I feel the same pleasure which my eyes would have in seeing a king and queen together." [2] When Marc Antonio Veniero sent him "two little calves, some big cheeses and good bologna sausages," he is delighted, "not because they will furnish his table, but because man naturally rejoices at seeing an abundance of food." [3] A present of fruit makes him think of the Villa of Coreggio whose garden bore them—so beautiful—"that if the world liked to carry flowers it would carry it always for a carnation." [4]

"Instead of one 'thank you', for a good fellow which I should have given you for sending the mushrooms I am still waiting for, I ought to give you ten for sending me

[1] Aretino, Lettere, II, 243.
[2] Aretino, Lettere, III, 62.
[3] Aretino, Lettere, I, 86.
[4] Aretino, Lettere, I, 124.

the quails and thrushes I did not expect. Because they are safer eating than those dangerous things, and one cooks them in a couple of turns of the spit, where they are sandwiched between leaves of laurel and country sausages. But you can't do that with mushrooms, for you must boil them with two chunks of the inside of a loaf of bread, and then fry them in oil. And then too one ought to be chary of eating them except in the morning, for fear of poison, which could so entrench itself during the night,—thanks to sleep,—as to be able to put to rout their excellencies, the physicians. The Chietini (pietists) understand this very well for they confess and take communion before they swallow a mouthful of them. It amuses me when a greedy and timid man wants to stuff himself with them. And I smile to see his nervous antics when at the same moment fear and the savour of the mushrooms attack his heart and his nose." [1]

He confesses a great weakness for salads. In a letter humorously defending himself against a mock charge of gluttony, he admits,—"If one sins in devouring a whole salad with an onion, I am undone because there is in that dish a delicate pleasure which the kitchen hawks that flocked around the table of Leo didn't have." [2] And it is about the dressing of salad that he writes one of the best of his lighter letters.

"As soon, my brother, as your tribute of salad greens began to decline, turning my imagination to astrology and divination, I tried to find out the reason why you held back the regular payment of food to my appetite. But if I

[1] Aretino, Lettere, I, 166.
[2] Aretino, Lettere, I, 146.

had squeezed my thoughts in the press which makes oil out of olives, I never could have found out that you have stopped giving me this supply because of the citronella which pleases your palate as much as it displeases mine. Who can say whence quarrels come—they come even from two stalks of that herb you cannot help sending me and I cannot stop throwing away. What the devil! I think I'll become one of those who don't drink wine or eat melons, since you stop sending the scraps from your table to a good comrade all on account of a herb, yellow as an old woman, which flaunts in all gardens.

"Have you used it for some enchantment that you take its part so strongly? Hereafter I want to accustom myself to eat it and I hope to do so. For I have got used to being without a penny in my pocket—a far harder thing than opening the mouth and swallowing, so go on sending me the tax your courtesy has laid on yourself. * * *

"I notice the way you lessen the sour of one herb with the sweetness of another. And it is no small art to temper the bitter and the sharp of some leaves with the neutral flavor of others—making the mixture so dulcet that satiety itself would taste. * * * The flowers scattered in the delicate green of such appetite-sharpeners tempt my nose to smell them and my hand to take them. In short, if my servants knew how to dress your salads *à la Genoese,* I would give up for them the breasts of capercailzie which very often at dinner or supper Titian, the unique, gives me for the glory of Cadore. * * * Certainly I am astonished that the poets don't strain every nerve to sing the virtues of mixed salad. And it is a great mistake of the monks and nuns not to praise it, because the monks steal time from their prayers to keep the soil of their lettuce-beds free from little stones. And the nuns tend it like a baby, wasting hour after hour in watering and caring for it. * * *

"I believe that the inventor of such a delicacy was a Florentine. He must have been, because the arranging of a table, decorating it with roses, washing the glasses, putting plums in the ragouts, dipping cup-up liver in batter, making black pudding, and serving fruit after a meal, all came from Florence. Their brains, active, always working, with the subtlety of their foresight have grasped all the points with which the cuisine can charm the sated palate.

"And to conclude I acknowledge that the good name of citronella is excepted from my dislike for it. And for that reason I hope that tomorrow will be the beginning of my restoration to the favour of your garden. And inform the dead man's rue that, although I am the head of the party of mixed salads, with plenty of oil and lots of vinegar sharp enough to split the rocks, I would revolt from them if you should compel me just to take a whiff of it." [1]

Aretino's most intimate table companions were Titian and Sansovino. A couple of the many allusions of the letters will show this sufficiently. He writes to the Cavaliere da' Porto: "Sansovino and Titian, the reputation of marble and the glory of colour, since the first with the chisel gives to marble both senses and spirit and the second with the brush gives to colour both senses and spirit—

[1] Aretino, Lettere, I, 173.

they, I say, enjoyed with me the two pairs of red partridges you sent." [1]

He wrote to Pigra: "You told me when you sent the big jar filled with Ferrarese finocchi, 'Eat them at once with your friends, because I am keeping some more for you.' That being so, I give notice that Titian, Sansovino, and I, after having enjoyed the first lot, are waiting to get into the middle of the second lot with little less anxiety than the cardinals watch around a pope's bed for the hour of his creeping death." [2]

Of the two, Titian was the more intimate. Aretino spoke of him as his other self. They called each other "compare" the old English "gossip." They were continually at table together in the house of one or the other.

Pietro tells Conte Manfredo di Collalto: "The day before yesterday we were eating some hares caught by the hounds which Captain Giovanni Tiepoli had sent me, and while their praises went up, *cœli cœlorum*, one of your lackeys arrived with the thrushes, which in tasting them made me chant the 'inter aves.' They were so good that our Titian, seeing and smelling them on the spit, glanced out at the snow, which, while they were setting the table, fell in showers, and abandoned a crowd of gentlemen who had arranged a dinner for him. And all unanimously gave great praise to the birds with the long beak, which we ate with a little smoked meat, a couple of leaves of laurel and pepper. And we ate them for love of you." [3]

Aretino writes that he took refuge at Titian's for

[1] Aretino, Lettere, III, 93.
[2] Aretino, Lettere, II, 244.
[3] Aretino, Lettere, I, 25.

luncheon whenever he was bored by too many visitors. And the grammarian Priscianese has left a letter describing a more formal banquet at the painter's house:

"I was invited the day of the Kalends of August to celebrate that sort of holiday which is called 'ferrare Agosto.' I don't know why it is so called, although it was much discussed here the evening I spent in a delightful garden of Messer Tiziano Vecellio, as everybody knows, the most excellent of painters and a person truly fitted to ornament by his agreeable manners the best circles of society. There were met together with the said Messer Tiziano, for like always draws like, some of the most exquisite men of talent to be found to-day in this city, and particularly M. Pietro Aretino, new miracle of nature. Next to him was her great imitator with the art of the chisel as the master of the feast is with the brush, Messer Jacopo Tatti, called Sansovino. And beside them were M. Jacopo Nardi and I; for I was the fourth of such an able company. Because the sun, in spite of the shade of the place, made its power felt, we passed the time before we sat down to table in looking at the pictures of the most excellent painter, of which the house was full, and in talking of the truly beautiful and charming garden, the pleasure and wonder of all who see it. It is situated on the outer edge of Venice, upon the sea, looking out toward the lovely little island of Murano and other most beautiful places. That part of the sea, as soon as the sun went down, was filled with a thousand gondolas, ornamented with the most beautiful women and ringing with changing harmonies and tones of voice and instrument, which up to midnight made music for our gay supper.

"But to come back to the garden; it was so well arranged and so beautiful, and therefore so much praised, that the comparison which occurred to me with the delightful gardens of Saint Agatha quickened so much my memories and desires for it and you, dear friends, that I could not tell most of the time during the evening whether I was in Rome or in Venice. Meantime the hour of supper arrived. It was as beautifully served as it was generous, and furnished, besides the most delicate food and most costly wines, with all those pleasures and enjoyments which fitted the house, the company, and the feast. Just as we got to the fruit, your letters arrived, brought by a young man from my house. * * * I read them to the company * * * and because in them you praised the Latin language and had little good to say for the Tuscan, Aretino grew particularly angry, and if he had not been stopped, I believe he would have turned his hand to one of the cruelest invectives in the world, for he excitedly demanded pen and paper. However, he did not fail to give us a good share of it in words. At last the supper ended hilariously." [1]

The friendship of Titian and Aretino was the most natural thing in the world. Their tastes and view of life were the same, and each was anxious to make out of his talents fame and the means of luxury. Aretino had great skill as a critic of art; and the chief artists of the day were glad to have his advice, feared his blame and sought his praise. When he wrote to Michael Angelo, saying that he was tempted to come to Rome just to see the "Last

[1] Quoted Cavalcaselle and Crowe Tiziano, Vol. I, page 458, from De'primi principii della Lingua Romana. Venezia, 1540.

Judgment" and give a pen-picture of the stupendous effects which he felt sure the painter had produced, the great solitary, so little given to compliments, replied:

"Magnificent Messer Pietro, my master and brother, your letter gave me both pain and pleasure. I congratulated myself because it came from you, who are unique in the world in virtù, and at the same time I was very sorry that, having completed the great part of my picture, I could not use your imagination, which is so successful that if the day of judgment had taken place and you had seen it, your words could not have reproduced it better. I shall not only be glad to have you answer my letter, but I beg you to do so, because kings and emperors consider it the greatest of favors to be named by your pen. Meantime, if I have anything which pleases you, I offer it to you with my heart.

Always yours,

Michelagnolo Buonaruoti." [1]

It had long been the part of every finished man of the world to have some taste in art and to be ready to express a judgment upon a statue or a picture, but Aretino has the best possible claim to be regarded as the father of that *genre* of literature which is known as art criticism. His skill in this was so clearly recognized that his contemporary Lodovico Dolce, writing a Dialogue on Painting, makes Aretino the chief speaker. Any artist seems to have been glad to work for him. Half a dozen different medalists modeled his head, some of them several times. Six of the leading art collections of the world, Munich,

[1] Lettere al Aretino, I, part 2, page 334.

Windsor, the Belvedere, Berlin, the Pitti, the Hermitage, possess his portrait,[1] so frequently reproduced by the engraver that the Bibliothèque Nationale has thirty-eight different prints of him. These favors seem to have cost Aretino no money. He was able fully to repay them by the constant advertisement he gave to his friends. He never misses a chance of mentioning and praising the work of artists he approves. When the factories of Murano turn out a new style of glass vases, decorated with the arabesques of Giovanni da Udine, he sends a case of them to the Marquis of Mantua, pointing out their beauty and mentioning at the same time that they are called Aretini.[2] When Jacopo del Giallo sends him a miniature, he writes a letter which was worth a good many pieces of gold to the artist:

"I am not blind in painting, and many times Raphael and Fra Sebastiano and Titian have taken my advice, * * * and I know that miniaturists take their designs from the masters of painted glass work; they do nothing but a charming combination of deep blue, of azure green, of cochineal lake, and of powdered gold; they spend their utmost skill on a shell or a strawberry and similar little novelties. But your work is full of drawing and relief. * * * Everybody is pleased with the way in which the little children, resting their feet on the head of the eagle, hold up the letter addressed in capitals with the name of the Emperor. * * * But how shall I repay you for such graceful work, since you do not want money?

[1] Art critics have raised the question whether some of these are correctly named in the catalogues.

[2] Aretino, Lettere, I, 24.

I will give you back ink for your colours and effort for your labour. By which your name will have as much pleasure in the fame I shall give it as I have had delight in the work you have made for me." [1]

This was no idle boast of Aretino. He did the greatest service to the artists he knew. The fame of the other two members of the trio of friends, Sansovino and Titian, has outlived his. The biographers of Titian can only wonder why he had anything to do with such a man. But it never occurred to Titian that Aretino's friendship was anything but a great gain and a matter of pride. Aretino got commissions for him from the Emperor, he wrote sonnets for most of his portraits. When Titian's imperial pension was not paid, Aretino used every effort to get it, writing to his friends to use their influence, offering to Ottaviano de' Medici four portraits of members of his family from the masters' brush if he would make the treasury pay the arrears. Vasari, who knew both, says that the friendship of Aretino was of the greatest advantage to Titian, both "as a matter of honor and of material gain, because he made him known far and wide where his pen reached, and especially to princes of importance." [2]

He was equally useful to Sansovino. It was no small service to an architect to be told, in a letter which would be read by many of the patrons of art throughout Italy, that "the works of his genius had put the finishing touches on the pomp of the city of Venice." That he would be very foolish to leave Venice for Rome "in spite of the fact

[1] Aretino, Lettere, I, 103.
[2] Vite de' Pittori, part III, Vol. II, page 810.

that popes and cardinals continually torment you to do so." At the same time he adds they are not to be blamed for this because "they never look at the church of the Florentines, which you founded on the banks of the Tiber to the wonder of Raphael, Antonio da San Gallo and Baldassare da Siena, they never turn toward San Marcello, your work, nor towards the tombs of Aragon, Santa Croce nor Aginense that they do not sigh over the absence of Sansovino."[1] And Aretino was not content with advancing the reputation of his artist friends. He did everything in his power to foster the taste for art among those who paid for it. He makes the characters of his comedies discuss noted pictures and buildings and the glory of those who built them. His letters speak continually of art, and in one he touches with master hand the strongest motive of most of its patrons in the Renascence:

"The prince, who reigns solely because he is made in the image of God, ought to imitate the maker of all things, whose power, according to the model of his will, built Paradise for the angels and the world for men, placing on the façade of the great edifice of heaven, as it were, his coat of arms painted by the brush of nature—a sun of gold with its infinite stars and a moon of silver in a broad field of bright blue. And just as every one of us who is born, as soon as he opens the eyes of consciousness is astonished looking now at the heaven and now at the earth, giving thanks to Him who made one and created the other, so the descendants of your Excellency, wondering at the magnitude of the edifices begun and finished by you, will bless the generous providence of their magnanimous pred-

[1] Aretino, Lettere, I, 191.

ecessor with the blessing given to the mind of the ancients embodied in stone in their theaters and amphitheaters by one who sees the pride of the ruins of Rome—whose wonders show what were the habitations of the conquerors of the universe." [1]

Aretino judged in the taste of the day and wrote in its style. He told Vasari in regard to some drapery, "Raphael has drawn things of the same sort. He has not surpassed you so much that you need regret it." [2] He wrote to Giulio Romano that if Apelles and Vitruvius could see the buildings and paintings he was doing in Mantua, "they would approve the judgment of the world which preferred him for originality and charm to any one who had ever touched compass or brush." But in regard to one of his friends Aretino's enthusiasm was guided by knowledge and skill. Those who knew Titian best are most ready to admit that they do not understand the secrets of his art better than Aretino. The comments he has left touch the finest points of his friend's pictures. The angel of the annunciation "filling everything with light and shining in the air with fresh radiance, bending gently with a reverence which makes us believe he is really in the presence of Maria;" the portrait of the little girl of Roberto Strozzi, so true that if "art should say it was not real, nature would swear it was not imitation;" the lamb in the arms of the little St. John, "so natural that a ewe would bleat at sight of it"—these are not vague praises. The words come not only from the lips but the eyes. And it would be hard to find a better phrase than that by which

[1] Aretino, Lettere, I, 151.
[2] Aretino, Lettere, II, 184.

he places Titian in a sonnet alongside of the two most celebrated artists Italy had produced.

"Divine in beauty was Raphael, and Michael Angelo was more divine than human in his stupendous design—but Titian has in his brush *the sense of things.*" [1]

Pietro has perhaps shown most plainly how well he understood his friend in the following letter to him:

"Having, contrary to my own habit, taken my meal alone, Signor Compare, or rather in company with this quartan fever which does not let me taste my food, I got up from table, having dined on the desperation with which I sat down to it. Placing my arms on the window ledge and resting my chest and almost my entire body against it, I gave myself up to gazing at the wonderful spectacle made by the infinite number of boats which, full of foreigners as well as natives, enlivened not only those who looked on but even the Grand Canal itself; joy of everybody who furrows its waters with the keel of his boat. And when two gondolas with celebrated gondoliers had finished a race, I found great enjoyment in the people who had stopped to see it at the bridge of the Rialto, the quay of the Camerlinghi, the Fish market, the ferry of S. Sofia, and the Casa da Mosto. And while these crowds went their different ways with gay applause, I, in the mood of a man who begins to bore himself because he does not know what to do with his mind and his thoughts, turn my eyes to the sky, which, since God made it, was never touched with beauty by such lovely painting of light and shadows. The atmosphere was one of those which they

[1] Aretino, Lettere, VI, 203.

try to express who envy you because they cannot be you. Try to see it as I describe it. In the first place, the houses, which seemed not of real stone, but of some stuff of dreams—and then bring before your eyes the atmosphere, which in some parts appeared pure and fresh, in others turbid and wan. Think also of the marvelous view I had of the clouds of condensed dampness, which in the center of the picture *(principale veduta)* stood partly near to the roofs and partly in the middle distance, since the right hand was filled with a smoky vapor tending toward a dark ash color. I was truly astonished at the changing tints the clouds showed. The nearest blazed with the flaming fires of the sun. The more distant were reddened with the glow of red lead, not too well heated. Oh, with what beautiful touches the brushes of nature thrust back the atmosphere yonder, clearing it away from the palaces in the style of Titian when he paints landscapes. In certain parts there showed a greenish blue, in others a blue-green mixed indeed by the caprice of nature, mistress of the masters. She darkened and threw into relief with shadows and high lights what she wished to darken or bring out until I, who know that your brush is the very soul of her ministering spirits, cried out three or four times, "Oh, Titian, where are you now!" [1]

Between the lines of this letter the discerning eye may read how pleasant must have been the many hours the two spent together at Aretino's windows on the Grand Canal or in Titian's little loggia looking off across his garden to Murano and the hills of Cadore.

[1] Aretino, Lettere, III, 48.

On the other hand, Titian does not fail to tell of the triumphs his friend has won by the pen. He writes from Rome that in the highest society of the court one hears nothing but, "This is what Aretino said." He writes from Ratisbon to say that the Duke of Alva talks of the divine Aretino every day and the Emperor showed every sign of pleasure when he was told that all Italy believes that the Pope is going to make Aretino a cardinal.

For during his life at Venice, Aretino vastly increased the literary reputation he brought there and made himself an acknowledged power in the world. His work may be summed up under six heads,—poetry, tragedy, comedy, letters, pornographic writings, religious writings.

His non-dramatic poetry may for the purposes of this essay be dismissed in a few lines. He wrote great quantities of it, but except where verse was the medium for his satiric verve, it is hard to understand why it was esteemed highly in a day when everybody composed poetry. Most of it was never printed and the loss to the world is not thought to be great by any of his commentators except Bertani, who seems to consider Aretino in all respects one of the great lights of Italian literature. His tragedy of Horace was the most carefully composed of all his works, and the only one which is approved by those who wrote of him up to the last ten or fifteen years. A French critic considers it superior to Corneille and an Italian historian of literature ranks it with Shakespeare. Such judgments came rather from the ardor of discoverers than from the sobriety of critics. But the most esteemed of all general historians of Italian literature, Professor Gaspary, considers it "absolutely the most important tragedy of the sixteenth century."[1] One merit it certainly had, the merit of a new method of treatment. The few tragedies in the vernacular which preceded it were imitations of the Greek writers. Aretino did not, like Shakespeare, cast off entirely the fetters of the classic unities, but he tried to write like an Italian of the sixteenth century and not like a Greek of the fifth or a Latin of the first. And therefore he is certainly not unworthy of honour among the predecessors of the great modern, who, ceasing to imitate the ancient giants, won a place among them.

Even more original are his comedies. The three or four comedies worthy of mention which were in existence when he wrote the first of his were, to a great extent, imitations of Plautus and Terence, introducing the stock characters of the Roman stage. Aretino, who could not read Latin, was more inclined to draw from life as he saw it. He knew life on the shady side and the comic force of his scenes is coarse. But he made the characters who tread his stage out of his own recollections of men he had known. And to read his scenes is to know them too. The street urchin of Mantua tying fireworks to the school teacher's coat tail; Messer Maco, of Siena, come up to Rome to fulfil the wish of his father that he should become a cardinal, and the hawks into whose claws he flutters; the hypocrite, a parasite cloaking his greed with piety instead of flattery—these and a score of others are real people. They move against a background vile with

[1] Adolf Gaspary. Storia della Letteratura Italiana tradotto del tedesco da Vittorio Rossi. Torino, 1900. Vol. II, part 2, page 221.

[2] Aretino, Lettere, III, 48.

the vileness Aretino had learned at the courts and in the streets of the cities where he had lived. But obscenity was then considered a necessary element of comedy, and the atmosphere which surrounds the characters of Aretino's comedies is less turpid than that of the Suppositi by Aristo, acted in the castle of San Angelo with scenery by Raphael and to the delight of Leo X.[1]

The distinctively pornographic works of Aretino, aside from the sonnets already alluded to, consist of the two first parts of a book entitled Ragionamenti. Competent judges who have read them hazard the opinion that they earn for Aretino the primacy of that long succession of writers through all the ages of the history of literature who have sold their pens to the service of the goddess of lubricity. There are times when the imagination of a generation seems to be poisoned by a mephitic miasma and impelled to dwell with insane persistence on the shames of life. The result of such a diseased bias in our own literature may be seen in the dialogue of the dramatists of the Restoration, and page after page written in Italy during the first half of the sixteenth century reeks with the same stuff.

It is true indeed that coarseness of language is not the measure of corruption. Habits of speech change in the course of centuries. Shakespeare puts jests in the mouths of gentlemen and ladies which seem strangely out of place in the modern theatre. In the Latin reading book Erasmus wrote for boys, there are jokes of the kind that circu-

[1] Letter to the Duke of Ferrara from Rome, March, 1519.

[1] Lettere d' Ariosto A. Cappelli, Milano, 1887. Documenti, page CLXXVII.

[1] The Calandra of Bibbiena, a piece admitted by all commentators to be obscene, was also given before Leo X.

late in low drinking places. Queen Anne of France asked an ex-ambassador to teach her a few phrases of Spanish to greet the Spanish ambassador. He taught her some indecent expressions, which she conscientiously repeated until she had learned them by heart. When he told the King what he had done Louis XII, it is true, warned the Queen, but roared with laughter over what he thought an excellent piece of wit.[1]

Soiled waters do not come from a pure spring and that with which the heart is full runs over on the lips, but still it will not do to confound manners with morals, nor forget certain modern writers who have pandered to depraved instincts with a perfumed diction and the subtlest refinements of style.

We should keep in mind also the satiric intent of much of the writing of Aretino's day. It was frequently asserted that the best way to save people from vice was to show it to them. Both these extenuations, of social custom and the prevalent methods of satire may be plead for Aretino. One of the coarsest of his letters (most of which are not at all coarse) was written to a noble lady and printed in the collection to do her honour. And Aretino claimed that his dialogues were a warning to virtue and an exposure of vice. It is not possible, however, that he could have been unaware that such an exposure is never a warning. He ranked his dialogues in honour among his other works and in telling a dream where the gods on Parnassus presented him with a basket of wreaths, alongside "one of thorns for his Christian writings" and "one of laurel for his

[1] De Maulde la Clavière, "La Diplomatic au temps de Machiavel." Paris, Leroux, 1892, page 368.

verses on love and war," was one "of rue for his lascivious writings."[1] All of his modern critics agree that they are a shame to literature.

The assertion is made nowadays that such an absolute moral judgment has no place in history—that to see life truly in the perspective of the ages we must forget our own measures of right and wrong. But knowledge does not require us to limit conscience to the domain of conduct. Conscience has rights also in the realm of reason. The surrender of fixed principle is not the necessary preparation for sympathetic observation of men living or dead. History puts her students in no such perilous position between the risk of surrendering their moral heritage to obsolete barbarisms or of enslaving their moral judgment to decadent opinion. There is a righteousness against which we have the right to measure the past as well as the present. But every man lives not only under the eternal heavens but also in the changing horizon. To see Aretino as his admirers saw him, we must see him in his horizon, and in that horizon public opinion did not force license to wear the cloak of secrecy nor compel vice to find a decorous appearance convenient. There are tales of Boccaccio which seem as bad as possible until one opens the novels of some of Aretino's contemporaries. Two clergymen he knew, popular romancers, put on many of their pages scenes which could now be recited only in the secret sittings of the police court. One of them received praise and reward for reciting some of his stories before Pope Clement VII. The other in his later years was the temporary incumbent of a bishopric in France.

[1] Aretino, Lettere, I, 135.

The age bore with pleasure the empire of corrupt imagination; Aretino defended the rights of that rule which he did more than any other to confirm; to make him the scapegoat of the vileness of his people is not to do any particular injustice to him but it is to fail to see mirrored in his life the age in which he lived. The pornographic writings of Aretino did not make him infamous in his own day—they did not even make him famous. They were published before his death less often than his other prose works, and contemporary imprints of them are so rare that, in 1693, Bayle had some trouble in finding out whether they had been printed during the life of their author. It was subsequent generations who found in them his chief claim to be read, and attributed to him a number of similar works by other writers. Among all his works they have had the most continuous life in print. They have been translated into four languages and recently, re-translated into French and English, they have been issued in sumptuous editions. The type which gives vogue to such dialogues in the nineteenth century is more immoral than the pen which wrote them in the sixteenth century. Conscience has its rights in the realm of judgment but history cannot be read in the spirit of the Pharisee, and zeal in blackening by denunciation the dark spots in the lives of the dead is apt to lighten too much by contrast the vile shadows that lurk around the most brilliant centres of our modern civilization.

Judged by the statistics of the press, the most popular of Aretino's writings were his religious books. Eight editions of his Penitential Psalms appeared during his lifetime, eight of his Life of Christ, five of his Genesis and

Vision of Noah, five of his Life of Saint Catherine, three of his Life of Saint Thomas Aquinas, two of his Life of the Virgin. Their character can best be judged by a specimen extract. He dilutes the first verse of the fifty-first psalm,—"Have mercy upon me, O God, according to Thy loving kindness; according unto the multitude of Thy tender mercies blot out my transgressions," into the following,—"Have mercy on me, O God, not according to the small merit of my fasting, my prayers, my wearing of hair shirts, my weeping, but according to Thy great mercy with which Thou dost surpass in greatness the vault of heaven, the breast of the mountains, the bosom of the sea, the lap of the earth, the bottom of the abyss and the measure of immensity, and beside which any fault whatever is less than a tiny point marked in the center of the largest circle. Although the poison which iniquity generates in sin sometimes makes it swell up so that, moving Thee to anger, it turns to rise on wings until it seems to desire to equal the very summit of the height of that pity of Thine before which, because I am certain that it conquers in Thyself the severity of Thy justice, I have not despaired of my faults," etc., etc.

The Humanity of Christ is a life of Christ written to suit the taste of the age. The fact that it was translated into French and the quick succession of reprints show that Pietro succeeded in what he tried to do. He was not able to base his work, as the authors of the large number of lives of Christ which have been written in our own day all profess to have done,—upon a careful criticism of the value of the records of that life. Nor if he had been able would he have thought of doing it. For to begin any historical criticism of the documents of the life of Christ would have raised a charge of heresy so radical and profound that no writer, orthodox or schismatic, would have had the moral courage to face it. Out of the mass of all those stories about Jesus Christ which anyone had ever believed to be true, whether they were found in the canon or apocryphal writings, he takes what suits him, arranges his material in a series of interesting pictures and ornaments them with imaginary details to make them appear real. He carries this so far that he does not scruple to put into the mouth of Christ long harangues which, like the speeches of the heroes of the classic histories, are entirely invented. By these means he made a life of Christ very popular, and about as much like the gospels as the sacred pictures of the painters of his own day,—such a work as the editor of a magazine is said to have recently demanded of a well-known writer, a "Life of Christ up to date and snappy."

He sketches into the picture with rapid strokes the popular stories of the apocryphal gospel of the infancy, like the birds of clay made to fly by the Infant Jesus. He tells in detail the story of Christ's descent into the under world. He expands the incidents which seem apt to excite the interest of his readers. He gives a description of the feast of the marriage at Cana and reports a long discourse of Christ to the young couple on the dangers of the married state. He is particularly pleased with the incident of Mary Magdalen, describes a splendid banquet served in her house and gives two pages to a full description of the toilet she makes when persuaded by her good sister to go and see Christ. The Master receives her with a speech precisely like a paragraph from the sermon of one of the popular preachers of the day; several of whom Aretino admired very much. Some of the sayings of our Lord recorded in the gospels, Aretino reproduced clearly and with vigour. Indeed, the vivid and nervous style he occasionally uses in his letters and comedies, was well fitted to translate the gospels. Aretino had found it where Luther found the words for his translation of the gospels, in the mouths of the common people who "heard Christ gladly." But Aretino tries to emphasize Christ's words by diluting them into his other style—the style of his complimentary letters to the scholars of the time like Bembo and Molza, or to the kings and captains who paid him. Here, for instance, is the way he begins the Sermon on the Mount,—"Blessed are they whose spirit, poor in power of argument, is content in Thy belief, considers what it sees, what it hopes and what it possesses as the gift of God and does not make confusion for itself in doubt suggested by the temerity of the sciences. The Kingdom of Heaven is of him who nourishes the intellect with the simplicity of faith. Blessed are they in whose bosom beats the heart of a lamb and not of a lion, because meekness is the manna of the soul, and pride is the poison which puffs up the body. The meek have power to make the earth fertile with blessings. Therefore their humility surpasses the heights of the mountains." [1] Here is the way he makes Christ begin the model prayer,—"Our father who art in heaven, our country for we travel like pilgrims in these bodies until the hour Thou dost appoint for us takes us from this vale of tears, and, recalling us from earthly exile, replaces us

[1] Edition of 1545, page 62.

in the bosom of paradise; hallowed be Thy name in everything that comes to pass. Because whether we are called by Thee through grace, or punished by Thee through justice, both results are to Thy glory," etc.[1]

Instead of illustrations the book is provided with little reproductions in words of such pictures as the artist friends of the author were painting from the Life of Christ; the Nativity, with the background of "the ruin of an ancient edifice with broken columns and many pieces of living stone which storms and ivy taking their own way had made their own;" or the Descent from the Cross, with the fall of the limbs of the dead body and the muscular action of those lowering it minutely described from canvases Aretino remembered; or the Angel descending from Heaven to comfort Christ in the Garden, "his wings coloured like the rainbow letting him sink to earth gently as a pigeon into its nest." In all these features the book appealed to the taste of the day, and although of far less literary value than his comedies, his pious writings were equally admired. Religious literature suited to popular tastes was as yet little known in Italy, and in it the famous satirist scored a great success. Nor is there anything in this Life of Christ, judged by lasting standards, more foreign to the spirit of the gospels or more shocking to taste, than that paragraph of one of the most celebrated lives of Christ of our own day, which makes "the vision of a lovesick woman give to a world a risen God." Everything indicates that Aretino had no sense of incongruity in publishing during the same year the Life of Christ and the Ragionamenti. He prints the dedicatory letters to his

[1] Edition of 1545, page 64.

Ragionamenti, his Sonnets on Marc Antonio's engravings and his Life of Christ side by side in the first volume of his letters.[1] Nor did any of the thirty odd Cardinals to whom he wrote or from whom he received letters, suggest that the collocation was infelicitous.

In the publication of his letters Aretino showed again his originality. He was the first Italian to print his own letters in the vulgar tongue and a crowd of imitators proved the success of the experiment. Five years after their appearance he spoke of plenty of volumes of "learned elegances of all the best wits of the century," being in print. But he comforted himself for the poor showing his might make among these learned imitators, by the reflection that, though "the types of Aldus are like pearls, one would much sooner have made the first rude characters which began the art of printing." [2]

The men of the sixteenth century seem to have been ceaselessly engaged in correspondence. More than three thousand of Aretino's letters have survived. And there is every reason to believe him when he says that a number at least as great has perished. The conscientious reader is often tempted to wish that time had been a little more severe. For the scattered pages in which, with quick and sure strokes, he draws pictures full of life, are surrounded by interminable successions of pompous and complimentary phrases, laboriously repeating the same idea. As the reader can see by the extracts already given, Aretino could write straightforwardly and naturally. But, to please his

[1] Aretino, Lettere, I, 258, 259, etc.
[2] Aretino, Lettere, III, 19.

public, he uses for most of his letters the sort of writing he employed in his religious works. The decadence of taste which was to show itself in the love of baroque art was beginning to appear in a liking for the bombastic in literature, and Aretino fed this nascent liking to the full in foretastes of the sort of rhetoric Shakespeare parodied in Love's Labour's Lost. In sentences fairly smothered in the exuberance of their own rhetoric he reiterates his thanks for gifts or letters, his excuses for not having written before, his sense of unworthiness of such favours, and rises above the pitch of Japanese politeness in compliment and self abasement. According to his own account he burst into tears of joy on receiving many letters. He cannot force himself to the impertinence of writing to one who has deigned to notice him. For example, he tells the Cardinal Pisani,—"If the vileness of my condition could approach as close to the nobility of yours as the nobility of yours is superior to the vileness of mine, I would say that the astonishment I have felt in finding myself obliged to write to you, would be equal to that you will feel at sight of the letter I address to you." [1] He tells Messer Ugolino Martelli that he loves him because he has "the tree of genius entirely covered with the flowers which produce the fruits that the sun of glory ripens." [2]

It is difficult to see why there was any demand for hundreds of pages of this sort of collocation of words, and future generations may wonder at the vogue of writers who appear to us perfect. One thing is certain, Aretino wrote in this way not because of the infection of literary

[1] Aretino, Lettere, II, 240.
[2] Aretino, Lettere, I, 152.

fashion, but from choice. We can tell this because his style is direct, whenever he sets it free, and because of the flashes of shrewd common sense which break into the long drawn passages of rhetoric. If at one time he spends a page of strained eloquence praising the virtues of clemency and its usefulness in government, he is able to condense it all into a phrase when he writes—"the city of Perugia is like a hard-mouthed horse which, ridden with an easy hand, seems to be quite gentle." [1]

He is full of contempt for the two most powerful literary affectations of his day, the idea of the Pedants that the perfect writers of classic antiquity had left nothing for succeeding ages except comment or imitation, and the similar idea of the Petrarchists that all possibilities of Italian style and diction were contained in the poetry of Petrarch and the prose of Boccaccio. He frankly confesses more than once that he cannot read Latin,—"I hardly understand the language with which I was born and I talk in it and write in it, and so Plato and Aristotle, Demosthenes and Cicero, Homer and Virgil talked and wrote in their native idioms." [2] "If the soul of Petrarch and Boccaccio," he burst out in disgust, "are tormented in the other world as their works are in this, they ought to deny their baptism." [3] For we find two kinds of writing among Aretino's letters; one which frankly expresses what he thought and felt at the moment, the other related to the chief purpose for which he wrote half his letters and printed them all. That purpose was to coin his fame into gold.

[1] Aretino, Lettere, I, 49.
[2] Aretino, Lettere, II, 242.
[3] Aretino, Lettere, I, 21.

Aretino was a born spendthrift. Money burned in his pockets and leaked through his fingers. And like so many men with the gift of language, he claimed the right of genius to have every desire satisfied. In 1537 he was spending, according to his own account, about a hundred ducats a month, and in 1542 he reckoned his receipts at eighteen hundred ducats a year.[1] A small part, if any, of Aretino's income came from the sale of his books. He nowhere alludes to such gain, and when he issued his first volume of letters, printed in it the following letter to his publisher, Marcolini:—"With the same good will with which I have given you the other works, I give you these few letters which have been gathered by the love which my young men bear to what I have written. The only profit I wish is your testimony that I have given them to you. * * * For a man to print at his own cost and to sell the books he produces by his imagination seems to me like feeding on himself. * * * God willing, I wish to get my pay for the fatigues of writing from the courtesy of princes and not from the poverty of those why buy my books, preferring to bear poverty rather than lower my genius by bringing the liberal arts down to the level of the mechanic arts. And it is clear that those authors who sell what they write become servants of their own infamy. Let him learn to be a merchant who seeks material gain and practising the trade of a book-seller, lay aside the name of a poet. * * * So print my letters carefully and well, because I do not want any other return from them. On the same terms, from time to time,

[1] The income of the contemporary Venetian nobles ranged from seven hundred to four thousand ducats of gold.—Molmenti.

you will be the heir of what comes from my brain."[1] This letter was omitted in later editions, and one may suspect that Aretino changed his views of "the mechanic baseness" of selling his works and sometimes eked out his income from the book-shop.

For that income he depended on the "cortesia" of Princes returned by him in "servitù." "Cortesia" is a magnanimous readiness to promote in every way the pleasure of a man of ability. It belongs to the character of a prince. Without it the monarch is lower than the merchant who has it. "It is a noble thing," he writes, "to love a woman; it is a divine thing to wish well to a man of genius, because the love of genius is related to the love of God." And his pages are full of praises of this divine trait of liberality to genius and invective against meanness. By "servitù," which repaid cortesia, he meant the moral duty of the man of genius to repay his patrons by immortality. He asserts that "the road of Cortesia leads to eternal glory." [2] He writes to the Grand Duke of Florence: the volumes produced under the patronage of Princes are "to the aspect of their serene names like torches gleaming in that perpetual splendour which renders testimony to the merits which fortune cannot leave behind nor time bury in oblivion." [3] For he believed that his writings would give eternal glory to those mentioned in them and he called himself "the secretary of the world." [4] The belief was not too fatuous in one who was told in various forms by dozens of correspondents "your

[1] Giornale Storico, Vol. 29, page 239. Pietro Aretino e il Franco.
[2] Aretino, Lettere, I, 54.
[3] Aretino, Lettere, Dedication to, Vol. III.
[4] Aretino, Lettere, I, 206.

benefits are of such a nature that they render immortal those who receive them."[1] And the world of great men treated him like its secretary, with splendid garments, heavy gold chains, splendid plate and streams of ducats. The man who was pensioned and complimented simultaneously by Henry VIII of England, Francis I of France, and the Emperor Charles V, might not unreasonably claim to hold a position of international authority in the world of letters.

For all the favours he received from his patrons Aretino paid to the best of his ability. It is difficult to see how adulation could be raised to a pitch higher than the tone of some of his letters. He writes to Antonio da Leyva,—"It is not to be doubted that Antonio is more God than man, because, if he was more man than God, he would not have risen from a private position to be a prince and from a mortal to an immortal. Everybody knows how much dignity Alexander gained from being born of a king and how much was added to Cæsar because he was not descended from an emperor. For which reason virtue and not fortune crowned him in the same way in which she will crown you. And very justly, because you have gained of yourself all that is in you. Therefore the fortunate emperor ought to count the chief of his felicities the possession of his good Leyva."[2]

It was rather difficult, of course, to keep on this scale in a letter to da Leyva's master, printed almost next to it. Aretino was equal to the task. He tells the Emperor that "if the scroll on which he writes had a soul, it ought to

[1] Lettere al Aretino, II, part 2, page 113.
[2] Aretino, Lettere, I, 46.

prefer itself to all the glorious scrolls of the ancients just because it is not read but merely touched by the friend of Christ, Charles Augustus, before whose merits the universe ought at once to bow. And certainly as God has enlarged the world to give room to your merits, it is necessary for Him also to raise the sky because the space of the entire air is not large enough for the flight of your fame." [1] And to be sure that the flattery has the needed personal touch he adds in another letter,—"Truly, O Augustus, the miracle of miracles which makes you miraculous is you yourself." [2]

He has variants on this same theme; as when he writes to the Duke of Urbino that—"he prays God to keep him in the world two or three centuries because for the need it has of your virtù any other term of life will be short." [3]

He is able to touch the harp of flattery with a firm hand for private patrons also. He writes to Signor Severino Boner, who has shown towards him the royal virtue of magnificence in every sort of "cortesia," that—"He is worthy of being deified in the eternity of memory as a terrestrial Jove." [4]

He tells Signora Ginevra Malatesta, that "everybody celebrates her, everybody admires her, everybody watches her, and in so doing they watch, admire, and celebrate the visible divinity of this entire age." [5] And he bids Signora Beatrice Pia,—"exulting in the thought of the graces with which the grave qualities which make you

[1] Aretino, Lettere, I, 49.
[2] Aretino, Lettere, III, 53.
[3] Aretino, Lettere, II, 55.
[4] Aretino, Lettere, II, 195.
[5] Aretino, Lettere, II, 17.

illustrious shine in splendour, feel certain that you abound in such great perfection of your essential nature that you could, with the mere superfluity of such a divine gift, change into goodness the imperfections of the being of all your sex."[1]

He is not appalled even by the difficulties of writing to Barbarossa, the pirate ruler of Algiers, who had wasted Italy with fire and sword. He tells him "the sun envies you because the glory of the fame which crowns you with eternal praise goes into those parts of the world where the light of the flame which he offers, cannot go." "So that your name is known to more nations, to more people, to more races than his. And hence it comes that all tongues learn it, reverence it and spread it."[2]

But perhaps the masterpiece of the vast collection of flattery, of which the reader has only a few scattered specimens, is found in Aretino's dedication of his second volume of letters to Henry VIII. "O supreme arbiter of peace and war, temporal and spiritual, do not be indignant that the universe does not dedicate to you temples and erect to you altars as to one of the more sublime Numi, because the infinite number of your immense deeds

[1] Aretino, Lettere, II, 5.

It must not be supposed that this sort of writing was invented by Aretino. He only practises well a common style. His contemporary, Agrippa of Nettesheim, a native of Cologne, thus addresses Marguerite of Valois in the dedication of his Treatise "On the Nobility and Excellence of the Feminine Sex."

"To you, Divine Marguerite, whose like the five divinities of light have never illumined among all the illustrious women there ever have been, there are, or there ever will be on the earth, either for the glory of beautiful deeds, or nobility of blood, or for excellence of virtues to you I say Princess incomparable and truly unique in your kind * * * I dedicate this book, as by the distinction of your life and manners you have mounted to a pinnacle of merit which elevates you infinitely above all the good which could ever be said of the feminine sex," etc., etc. Leiden, 1726. Vol. I, page 35.

[2] Aretino, Lettere, II, 201.

keeps it confused, just as the sun would confound us if nature, taking it from its place, should place it close to our eyes."[1]

In this exchange of "servitù" for "cortesia," Aretino was simply carrying into literature the relation of the mercenary soldier to his patron. As the Swiss guards of the Tuileries two centuries later felt bound to die for their bread, so Aretino felt bound to exalt and defend the glory of those who sustained his genius. He writes to Signor Luigi Gonzaga,—"I was always, Signore, and always will be as faithful to my patrons as to my friends and unless I am given cause of offense, would rather die than attack the honour of another."[2]

He had written three letters to Cromwell, the all powerful minister of England.[3]

He reminded Cromwell how much his pen could do for his fame. Cromwell has left in one of his memoranda a note, "To remember Pietro Aretino for some reward."[4] But death surprised him before he could carry out his purpose. He had, however, been useful in urging Henry VIII to send a large present to Aretino, and Pietro hearing of his fall and execution writes,—"I am sorry for such a misfortune because I had some benefit from him and well would it have been for him if the 'cortesia' shown me by commission of the illustrious Henry, had been mixed with his own personal liberality. As it is, I

[1] Dedicatory Epistle to Vol. II, Lettere.

[2] Aretino, Lettere, I, 76.

[3] One is in Lettere, Vol. II, 137. One is calendared Letters and Papers of Henry VIII, Vol. XIV, part 2, No. 712. The other is an Italian fragment printed without signature, Vol. XIV, part 2, number 716. Any one familiar with Pietro's style can recognize these fragmentary sentences as his.

[4] Letters and Papers of Henry VIII, Vol. XV, page 71.

will never put out of my memory that I was once grateful to him."[1]

In thus hiring himself out as a giver of immortality, Aretino was playing on the common weakness of the men of his day, an insatiable desire for fame. This craving for glory, which possessed the age like an infectious disease, was not the desire to be praised by those who knew, for doing well things worth doing,—but a passion largely vulgar,—a thirst to be known among one's fellows for anything and everything, a material pride that made all ears itch for even the coarsest flattery. This liking for applause beset the men of the Renascence. One has only to glance at a book which shows the best side of the society of the first generation of the sixteenth century, the Cortigiano of Castiglione, to see that he advises the perfect gentleman to be always, in every act of his life, playing to the gallery.

Aretino has given perhaps the most striking description of this characteristic passion of his age—this thirst and hunger for praise which made fame seem almost like a material thing to be eaten and drunk. "I do not know the pleasure misers feel in the sound of the gold they count, but I know well that the blessed spirits do not hear music which is more grateful than the harmony which comes out of one's own praises. One feeds on it as in paradise the souls feed on the vision of God."[2] He writes to the Cardinal of Trent at the baths,—"Although it may be that crowds of friends, a swift succession of pleasures, harmony of instruments, the sight of jewels,

[1] Aretino, Lettere, II, 151.
[2] Aretino, Lettere, I, 100.

the suavity of odours, the delicate folds of drapery, the pleasantness of books, the joyfulness of songs and agreeable conversations, may not seem to you suited to your pious dignity, you can enjoy instead of such pastimes, the thought of your own merits, recreating your senses and spirits with the goodness which all people perceive in you, for which grace all men bow before you, praise you, and watch you. Certainly there is no joy which surpasses the joy of him who is not only known as good but is approved as the best." [1]

It was the shrewd choice of a man who knew his public which led Aretino to give up the small gains of bookselling to levy heavy tribute on the vanity of the great men of his day. And he would not sell flattery at retail. He writes Signor S. G.—"I have sent back the ten ducats to your friend, begging him on receiving back your gift to return the praises I gave you. Because it does not seem to me the part of an honest man, to honor one who vituperates me as you would have vituperated me, if I had accepted what is rather an alms given to a beggar than a present to a man of genius. Certainly those who buy fame must be generous minded, giving not according to the rank of their souls but as the condition of him to whom they give demands; because the poor ink has a hard task in trying to exalt the name which is weighed down as if by lead by every sort of demerits." [2]

The passion for fame had another side, and the audacious cleverness of Aretino's scheme for coining his reputation cannot be appreciated until we have looked at it.

[1] Aretino, Lettere, II, 70.
[2] Aretino, Lettere, II, 263.

The love of flattery seldom fails to breed an extreme touchiness. The man greedy of adulation, shrinks with an agony of dislike from dispraise. If the Italian of the Renascence was apt for satiric speech, he paid for his evil tongue by a thin skin, sensitive to every malicious breath. Even to-day among the Latin races where the Renascence flourished in its vigour, there is a lasting sense of wrong for verbal insult "injures," "oltraggi," which the English-speaking race, used to a word and a blow, or to words forgotten, finds it hard to appreciate. And Aretino counted on this shrinking hatred of mordant words to bring in his tribute from those who thought the price of his praise too high.

When he came to Venice he had won by his pasquinades and his comedy a great reputation, and his specialty was "maldicentia." It was admitted that he had the worst tongue in Italy. In his Giudizî his running comment on events, his irregular newspaper mixing news with editorials, he found a field for his power of satire. It became the object of every prince in Italy to keep out of the giudizî the facts of his career or the traits of his character which would bring cynical laughter instead of applause. From the time he went to Venice until his death, Aretino asserted that he had a divine mission,—to punish the vices of princes and expose the hypocrisy of priests. This is what he meant by calling himself "the fifth evangelist."

One cannot turn over five pages of his letters without finding vague allusions to the crimes which haunt princely courts, and the vileness by which prelates rose to power at Rome. For example, promising to write regularly, he adds,—"And in case I fail, put it down to the fault of a certain beastly desire to resemble princes. And not being able to do so with any other mask than that of lies, it may be that I make this promise keeping it in the way they keep theirs." [1] Asked by a preacher to define "charity," he answers,—"A friar's hood, because the shadow of its sanctity covers the multitude of the vile progeny of your hypocritical actions." [2] A certain transaction, he says, would be dishonest "even among cardinals." "If," he writes to the Spaniard Don Luigi d'Avila, "from being Italian one could change into a Spaniard, as from being a Christian one can change into a priest," etc. Through all his letters runs a stream of such allusions to the meanness and bad faith of princes or to the hypocrisy of all ranks in the church. These allusions in his published letters are for the most part vague. Occasionally, indeed, where the pay of one of his patrons had been too long delayed, he becomes more pointed. He writes to Signor Giovanni Dandalotto: "The fact that the gift which, through the influence of your excellency, was promised to me by the distinguished brother of the Emperor, has not materialized, lessens the dignity of his crown, injures your intercessions and dishonours my virtù." [3] He goes a little farther with Count Massimiano Stampa: "It is so difficult to decide, O Marchese, which is greater, the praise with which I exalt your honours or the trick with which you deride my hopes, that I keep silent about it,—and in my silence I am

[1] Aretino, Lettere, I, 48.
[2] Aretino, Lettere, II, 258.
[3] Aretino, Lettere, I, 50.

sorrier for myself who believe in you than for you who trick me,—because my trustfulness comes from a certain stupid simplicity of nature and your cheating me comes from princely malevolence, wherefore in such a matter I am more worthy of excuse than you of blame.[1] And sometimes he names prelates who for him incarnate the hypocrisy he denounces in the church. But these passages, though not few among his published letters, would hardly have maintained, amidst the strong competition of the day, his reputation of having the most dangerous tongue in the world. This reputation, absolutely necessary for keeping at its highest figure the income he drew from his profession, he maintained in his Giudizî, his satiric verses and in unpublished letters; pieces circulated for the most part in manuscript. By these less public writings he could cause fear without giving deadly offense. If necessary, he could disavow them.

The choice which Aretino presented to kings and great men was a very simple one. An eulogistic letter assured them of his desire to spread their fame and make them immortal. Not to accept the offer was to run the risk of being pilloried for the laughter of Italy. This literary mill, whose upper stone was flattery and its lower satire, squeezed from the vanity of men a steady stream of gold for its ingenious author. The plan was not entirely original. In the fifteenth century the sale of eulogy and invective had been common among the humanists, but Aretino first assembled and arranged the rude and elementary devices of his predecessors. And he drew from his machine a large income which enabled him to live in

[1] Aretino, Lettere, II, 184.

far better style than Erasmus, the acknowledged king of letters.

From the seventeenth century on, writers have expanded in severe epithets on the infamy of this system. One obvious thing seems to have escaped them. If the system had seemed in its own day too infamous it could not have been so successful. The utterances of a ribald blackmailer, looked down on by all honest men as infamous, could not have steadily flattered pride nor stirred fear. Nor did Aretino try to hide his practices. On the contrary, he made so clear an explanation of his system in letters he printed that we trace it entirely in them.

He claims as his proudest title the inscription stamped on one of his medals, Flagellum Principum, the Scourge of Princes. He is never tired of asserting his readiness to shake the lash over vice, and the divine blessing on his task, and he boasts of the gains of satire.

His letters abound with passages like the following: "Believe me I am the same good companion I was in old days, and my joyful amiability has grown with my growing reputation and ease of life. The weight of years would seem light to me if I were not fat. The fault of my increase of flesh many attribute to the happiness with which God has surrounded me, and the talents he has showered on me by His grace. And I confess it, because mummies would be restored to life if the world continually visited them with tribute. And for that I render thanks to Christ, because certainly these things are His gifts and not our merits."

"If I were not worthy of any honour for the originality with which I give life to style, I merit at least a little glory for having forced truth into the ante-chambers and the ears of the great ones of the world, to the shame of adulation and falsehood. And not to defraud my rank I will quote the words which fell from the sacred mouth of the great Antonio da Leyva: 'Aretino is more necessary to life than sermons, for they direct towards the right way only simple people, but his writings men of birth and power'." [1]

He writes to his publisher Marcolini,—"In case you hear it said again that great men give me money every day for fear and not for love, consider it a sign of my greatness. Certainly if I were a prince I should choose to be loved rather than to be feared. As I am Pietro, I think it better for lords to fear me than to love me. The judgment you report is nothing but ignorance and malignity. The envy of many really exalts me while it tries to abuse me. In very truth, I must be a terrible man since kings and emperors give me presents out of fear. So compose yourself in peace about it without getting angry." [2]

He is equally frank in showing the gains of his service and his willingness, to rent either silence or speech.

He speaks of "one of those presents which princes often give me, I hardly know whether to say out of fear or out of liberality," [3] etc. "Oh, if princes (who do not drive me to despair by giving nothing that I may not vituperate them, and do not console me by giving me enough in order that I may not fear them), could only

[1] Aretino Lettere, I, 254.
[2] Aretino Lettere, III, 89.
[3] Aretino Lettere, II, 187.

take the middle path,"[1] etc. He points out that "the gifts of kings ought to be not only quick, but frequent like drops of rain. Their majesties ought to remember continually a man of talent; otherwise they give him reason to talk too much; whence their fame and their courts get a bad reputation."[2] He often threatens "the vendettas of ink more eternal than the offenses of blood."[3] "The stinginess of promises and the tenacity of avarice are a reason for acting badly, not simply for speaking badly; and if they don't look out, I will put an ornament on the face of the name of somebody which shall stand for a sign until the day of judgment."[4] One of his medals shows on the reverse Aretino seated while figures bring him gifts, and the inscription is "Princes supported by the tribute of their people bring tribute to their servant."

He thought he had done a great service to literature in systematizing this commercial use of invective and eulogy, and calls himself the "Redeemer of Genius who has restored her to her ancient place!" "Her glory was dimmed by the shadows of the avarice of men of power, and before I began to lacerate their names, men of genius begged the honest necessaries of life. And if some one rose above the pressure of necessity, he did it as a buffoon and not as a person of merit. My pen armed with its terrors has brought matters to such a pass that the Signori, coming to themselves, have cherished great intellects with enforced 'cortesia.'"[5]

[1] Aretino, Lettere, II, 244.
[2] Aretino, Lettere, II, 76.
[3] Aretino, Lettere, II, 254.
[4] Aretino, Lettere, II, 14.
[5] Aretino, Lettere, I, 85.

Conscious of this great service, he was convinced that the world owed him the splendid living he drew from the vices and merits he praised or blamed. For he naively writes in thanking the new Duke of Florence for money, —"The cortesia shown me is an augury of felicity for the reign of his Excellency, because none give to me but true princes who reign by the choice of God and by the counsel of good men." [1]

This easy conscience about his work is the more emphasized by the pious phrases which run through his letters. Aretino considers himself an excellent churchman and a good Christian. To attack the corruptions of the clergy and the Roman court was not of course in the least incompatible with piety and orthodoxy. Some of the saints had done it in the past; some of the apologetes of the Church against schism did it in his own day. Heresy Aretino always hated. He makes many hostile allusions to Luther. Writing to a young friend at the University, he reproves him for eating meat all the time; because Fridays and Lent are the days of God, the rest of the year belongs to man. But he adds, that he feels sure this only comes from careless willingness to imitate bad example, and not because of any "belief you give to Luther, that diabolical spirit." [2] He congratulates the Cardinal of Trent on the services of Vergerio, who has "not only become a trumpet of the gospel and a key to the doors of the Holy Scriptures, but thunderbolts and lightning flashes against the head of the heresy of Luther. * * * He has composed three homilies on the subject

[1] Aretino, Lettere, I, 126.
[2] Aretino, Lettere, III, 99.

of the heresy of Germany, whose object is to uncover the poisonous intent of those who, under the veil of religion, are bringing about the ruin of states, of princes and of souls, overthrowing laws, customs, loyalty and peoples." [1]

He is a great admirer of strong preaching, and often speaks of the pleasure or profit he had gained in listening to this or that "trumpet of the gospel." [2] He wanted to hear practical and simple sermons. He is very strong against those "Reverend Fathers who keep shouting in the pulpits about how the divine word became incarnate in Mary, or in what way the dust and flesh and bones thrown to the winds or scattered through the sea can come together and rise again to life. Certainly the temerity of such themes is a reproach to Christ for having said nothing about them. * * * We go to church free from doubts which the perverse raise in questions of religion, and expecting to hear the preaching of the gospel. We hear strifes and disputes which have nothing to do with the gospel or with our sins."

The interest Pietro took in religion, an interest shown in repeated passages in his letters, cannot be better illustrated than by a letter he wrote to a parish priest of his neighborhood,—"The dignity of the higher offices of the church, the mitre and the cardinal's hat, would become you, Reverend Father, because you neglect nothing which is for the praise and honour of that little church of which you are the worthy custodian. Therefore, you have the name of a good priest. And this is confirmed with loud voice by all the people who see how you study to enlarge

[1] Aretino, Lettere, II, 66.
[2] Aretino, Lettere, I, 178.

the present building. Meanwhile you divide the small salary which comes from the parish among strangers, the sick and the poor, until one might wonder how you can buy bread to eat, let alone providing the other necessaries of life. However, the grace of God beholding such charity transubstantiates itself into what you need. You are so much the fervent and careful father of everybody who lives in the parish, which obeys you in Christ at the temple which decorates you with its title, that everybody feels like a son towards you; and I for my part not only love you with the zeal of a son, but reverence you with the purest sincerity, because I consider you a model of that spiritual care which belongs to all those who have the oversight of our souls. You who control the income of the treasury of the merits of the crucified Jesus, must dispense it in the benefits of the altar, of masses, of the divine offices, of offerings, of incense and lights, of sacerdotal ornaments, of baptisms and of communions; and loving your neighbour with pure purpose, aid with what you spread before them the cravings of the spiritual hunger of those whose pastor you are. Religious privileges must be shared in a holy way, and the food of Christ distributed according to His teachings. And woe to him who uses them differently. But what shall I say, O honest and excellent man, of the reputation you have gained by your goodness in inviting every preacher of good fame, holy life and sound doctrine to come and expound the divine word in your pulpit? Which is to you a source of clear commendation and to us of evident salvation. Twice, thanks to you, we have heard Fra. Bernardino da Siena—

twice, I say we have heard him, thanks to you, and for that alone you deserve to be remembered. Because his Apostolic voice, his catholic words, make the guilty good and the perfect justified. Therefore, rejoice in yourself, thanking the Saviour for the power you have with his creatures, and while you do this, take pleasure also in the gentleness of your affable profession, whose human kindness opens the very bottom of every one's heart." [1]

These various traits of Aretino, his lack of shame for pornographic writing, the brutal immorality of his life, his sense of high moral service to the world, his thanks to God for the gifts he used in that service, his interest in religion, his self complacency and his frank exposition of willingness to praise the virtues of the princes who paid him not to denounce their vices, are hard to unite into a consistent character. And most writers have solved the problem in portraiture by the easy device of labeling him a blatant hypocrite. But to see him set forth in his own letters as we can see Benvenuto Cellini in his autobiography, is to perceive that Aretino, while not without a tinge of hypocrisy, took himself on the whole at his own high valuation—and one who does not believe that this may be true, has not begun to know the men of the Renascence.

Italy of the early sixteenth century was in a strange condition, at once fecund and decadent. She produced miracles of art and praised extravagantly puerilities and obscenities in literature. She sang hymns to love and looked on woman as the prey of the senses. Her men joined a passionate desire for fame to an atrophied sense

[1] Aretino, Lettere, II, 299.

of duty. Her proud cities hated and betrayed each other, while France and Spain wasted her fields, and the Turk swept thousands of slaves from her coasts. The rulers of the institutions she held in trust for the world spent their thought and the church treasure in Italian politics, their leisure in watching Raphael and Michael Angelo, while Europe, north of the Alps, was breaking from the unity of Christ. That brilliant blooming time of human genius we call the Italian Renascence, gave to all nations a new impulse in art and learning, strengthened in the world the desire for truth and beauty, but the atmosphere it bred in Italy at its height, was at once glorious and shameful,—stimulating and corrupting. If we wish to know it we must look at the men it bred as they were, and not at descriptions of what we suppose them to have been, arranged under the rubrics of our own moral categories.

To account for the success of Aretino's masterly organization of the crude methods of the humanists for the sale of eulogies and invectives, writers have pointed out that there is a resemblance between his Giudizî and the modern newspaper. It is suggested that Charles V, who paid Aretino more than he paid Titian, knew what he was about in subsidising a rising power—the power of the press. It would be easy to spend several malicious and partly true pages, suggesting certain similarities between Aretino's methods and style and those of some newspapers, and there is truth in the comparison, but not enough to make us attribute too much force to the motive. Charles V may have shrewdly calculated that the pen of Aretino might arouse or allay certain hostilities to his policy, but we know that when his ambassador first advised him to put Aretino on a pension, it was for fear he might publish a particular private scandal about the Emperor's life which was already talked about and thought to be true.

And in addition, the power of the press has risen with the power of democracy. Now, while Aretino was living at Venice, the democracy everywhere throughout Italy was either dying or dead. Public opinion in the sense of a general moral judgment producing political effects, did not exist in the Peninsula. Charles V, who made a bastard Medici Duke of Florence, and built a fortress in Siena to hold a Spanish garrison, had little reason to fear the political effect of public opinion.

Aretino's letters did not always bring golden answers. Little unpleasantnesses occasionally arose. He found it hard to hold his insolent tongue even about his patrons. His greed kept him in intermittent irritation over the smallness or delay of their payments, and they resented things he said not intended for their ears. Here, for instance, is a letter received in 1530 by the Ambassador of Mantua in Venice,—"His excellency understands that Pietro Aretino cannot stop talking evil about his servants and his court, and that he threatens to say more. Give him to understand that if from now on he opens his mouth to talk, or his hand to write about the smallest personage, not simply of his excellency's court, but of Mantua, the Duke will be as much offended as if the words applied to his own person; and that, by the body of Jesus Christ, he will have him given ten dagger thrusts in the middle of the Rialto. He has had enough of his evil tongue; let him look to himself. The Duke does not feel like bearing it any longer, and even though he does send him the copyist he asks for, it is not because he is afraid of his threats." [1] As the last sentence suggests, this letter did not need to be taken very seriously. These quarrels, though they often arose, seldom broke finally the relations of Aretino and his patrons. He needed their gold pieces; they knew that flattery masked universal envy eager to laugh or sneer. The scratch of Aretino's quill calling the harpies to the feast of scandal, turned their self complacency into an agony of mortified vanity. Aretino might well sign himself—"Free man by the grace of God." In an age when all men feared princes, his keen mastery of their common weakness made all princes fear him. At the same time it must be true that genuine admiration had a large place in the motives of Aretino's tributaries. In the Bibliothèque Nationale in Paris, there are five of Aretino's works bound with the arms of Francis I.

Even in Venice, however, where justice was often firmly done and assassination comparatively dangerous, Aretino did not always come off with idle threats. The pension promised him by Henry VIII was not paid as promptly as Aretino wished, and he said that Harwell, the English agent, kept the money. Harwell, walking with his servants, met Aretino on the street and gave him a sound thrashing. Against this violence Aretino appealed successfully to the sympathy of his contemporaries. The incident unquestionably suggests the difficulties with which any one trying to carry on his trade in countries north of the Alps, would have found the path to fortune beset. The Italian of the sixteenth century thought ven-

[1] Luzio, Pietro Aretino nei primi suoi anni, etc. Documenti XXXVIII.

geance the sacred duty of a gentleman, but only a refined and deliberate punishment was worthy of a man of culture. If Harwell had hired another Achilles della Volta to stab Aretino, there would have been no shock to public opinion. To give him a public thrashing seemed to Italian society coarse and brutal. Which of these two views is the less objectionable is a question of taste on which Latin and Teuton will be apt to differ to the end of time.

There is another story about a man who knew how to treat Aretino, so good that the student is sorry to find his suspicion that is too good to be true, confirmed. Tintoretto was a man with whom it was ill jesting. His manners were at times unconventional. When a self elected critic was explaining to a crowd of visitors who infested his studio, that though other artists painted more slowly than Tintoretto, they painted more correctly, he broke into the discourse, "That is, because they haven't a lot of bores around them as I have." Tradition has it that Aretino had been talking about Tintoretto. The young painter meeting the too talkative man of letters in the street, invited him to his house. He said he wanted to paint his portrait. Aretino went, and when he was about to sit down, Tintoretto suddenly produced a long pistol. The frightened Aretino, thinking the time was come to pay old scores, commenced to cry out—"Jacopo, what are you going to do?" He answered—"Oh be quiet and let me take your measure;" and going from head to foot he said—"You are just two pistols and a half long." Aretino merely answered—"Well, you are a great lunatic and never act like anyone else." But he was not anxious to backbite him again and became his friend.[1]

The path of Aretino was not always strewn with compliments. Several of his contemporaries attacked him with tremendous bitterness. Two of the most determined of these denouncers were young men he had befriended and kept in his house. Franco had been rescued from misery by Aretino, who employed him as secretary and in the first edition of his letters praised him highly. After he had been driven out of the house, Franco waged a desperate fight against his former patron, chiefly in sonnets, many of which rival in obscenity the worst of Aretino's lines. One of them in praise of the murderous Achilles da Bologna, ends: "He is worthy of fame even though he failed, for at least he longed to free the world of its shame." Another on Titian's portrait of Aretino, congratulates the "brush more than divine," on the triumph of having "enclosed with a little square all the infamy of our age." [2] Early in the quarrel, another of the young men of Aretino's household stabbed Franco in the face on the street. After Franco had fled from Venice, Aretino wrote a few letters in which he handled him without gloves. But on the whole, he did not try to keep up his side of the literary warfare. In one of his letters he uttered the careless vituperation—"You are destined by your own sins to the gallows * * *." [3] Time made it a prophecy; twelve years after Aretino's death, Pope

[1] Quoted from Carlo Ridolfi, Vite de'Pittori Veneziani. Venezia, 1648, by Mazzuchelli in Vita di Pietro Aretino, Edizione Seconda, Brescia, 1763, page 75. Ridolfi quotes no authority for the story.

[2] Quoted by Mazzuchelli, page 163, from Delle Rime di M. Niccolo Franco contro Pietro Aretino. Terza Edizione, 1548.

[3] Aretino, Lettere, V, 312.

Pius V hanged Franco in Rome as punishment for a rabid attack on his predecessor.

Antonio Francesco Doni had been a close friend and a warm admirer of Aretino. In 1538 he wrote Aretino the following letter,—"I hope to tell you in four words what fame says of your good nature * * * Listen: Five gentlemen, all litterati, illustrious and worthy of entire confidence, undertook to cross the sea of your fame with the prosperous wind of your conduct. One pointed out how you are blessed of God with the gift of charity, because you give what you have to the enjoyment of all the good, and receive men of talent in the arms of the riches God and your own gains have given you. The second affirmed and swore to it, that he had been in a gondola with you, and that the poor ran to the front of the houses while you, like a banker of mercy, gave money to all saying, 'God has given it to me and for love of Him I want always to distribute it.' A third confessed to having experienced from you an act of divine goodness. He said he had offended you. Fortune gave him into your hands and you could have returned the offense with heavy interest and you, like a Christian, embraced and forgave him saying,—'I am sorry the offense was not greater that I might forgive you even more willingly.' The fourth said that your house supports secretly twenty-five poor people and you do not know it. Think then how good a master you are, since those who serve you give away without any permission as those who think it a duty to follow your steps; and do it without saying anything about it. The last prophesied that you would have money and titles of service and honour from all the princes of the world.

The reason is this, that the good God wills to have it so, in order that, since they want to give genius and poverty misery for daily bread, you may atone for their defects, and be able to supply by your prodigality enough to satisfy everyone who asks. And I say that the goodness of God has given you one hand to write and subdue princes and the other to receive gifts, in order that with both you may give. And you who recognize that divine gift, give and will give to whoever asks, and even to him who does not ask, if you only know of anyone in need.

"Your Doni, without other phrases, friend and servitor from the heart." [1]

Of this saintly, God-gifted person, Doni promised in 1552 to write the life. He kept his promise in 1556. But meantime he and Aretino had quarrelled, and the life which appeared was entitled "Earth-quake of Doni the Florentine with the ruin of a great colossal beastly anti-Christ of our age—work written to the honour of God and the defense of Holy Church as well as of good Christians." It was addressed to "The vituperative and scoundrelly Pietro Aretino, source and origin of everything bad, stinking limb of diabolical falsity and true anti-Christ of our century." [2] The work surpasses the promise of the title and the address. As we have already seen, filth seemed to drop into the ink of writers of the day, and least of all in controversy were their pens clean.

Several others of less note attacked him. But a certain pride in crossing swords with the dreaded Scourge of

[1] Lettere al Aretino, I, part 2, page 347. Compare II, part 2, page 352.

[2] Il Terre moto di M. Anton Francesco Doni Contro M. Pietro Aretino. Secondo la copia dell' anno, 1566.

Lucca, 1861. Per Bartolomeo Canovetti.

Princes, can be seen between their bitter words. Aretino had several of the fashionable stock literary quarrels, which the combatants sometimes ended by reciprocal complimentary letters; much as two attorneys after belabouring each other in court will lock arms and go off to luncheon together. We may think what we choose of Aretino; in his own lifetime the men who, over their own signature, expressed the very highest opinion of him, were, in dignity and numbers, fifty to one compared to the men who spoke evil of him. The dilemma is clear; either the literary world was terrified by a man of his stamp who openly made a rich living by blackmail, or else they admired him. Of all his assailants only one can be put in the same class with dozens of his admirers,—that was Francesco Berni. Berni's hostility was so well known that the most rabid of all the attacks on the Scourge of Princes, was printed under his name. Scholars are now agreed that he did not write it. A closing note to Pietro says—"you are dying of hunger," and ends, "whatever you do you will always be an ass, a pig and a blockhead." Three of these four statements are manifestly false. And the same proportion would probably hold true of the alleged facts in the rest of the work.

On the whole, Pietro did not take much trouble to answer what his enemies said about him. He affected towards them a lofty contempt which was perhaps more clever than sincere. When Captain Gian Battista, marshal of the camp of the Company of Pietro Strozzi, killed a Signor da Monte Albaddo, who spoke ill of Aretino, Pietro thanked him but expressed his regret; because "we are Christians" and because the "license of free speech is not to be punished by the cruelty of fatal violence." [1] But in another letter he suggests that bloodshed was superfluous in any case of the sort because "it is wonderful that such enemies don't hang themselves for envy at the success of my writings and the shame of theirs." [2] He bids Dottore Cavallino, who was troubled at some assaults on him, not to be disquieted: "His enemies will find his name a diamond which breaks the teeth of those who try to bite it." [3] One of his medals shows on the reverse a nude figure over whose head a winged Victory holds a laurel crown. The demon of envy struggles under its foot and Jove in the clouds above poises the thunderbolt. The inscription reads "Veritas parit odium."

It was fair enough for Aretino to use such an inscription, for the subtlest trait of his art in wielding an evil tongue was that he rarely lied. Luzio, who has tested the statements of the only one of his Giudizî which has survived, says,—"The Archives of the Gonzaga prove that Aretino rarely calumniates and invents. Ninety-nine times out of a hundred he does nothing but propagate accepted scandals, put in circulation malignant assertions of others, giving them a sharp and striking form." [4] When one of the characters in Aretino's Cortigiana asks: "How can I best say evil of men?" He receives the answer,—"By telling the truth—by telling the truth." For Aretino discovered very early that in his business of literary blackmail truthfulness was the best policy. This

[1] Aretino, Lettere, III, 65.
[2] Aretino, Lettere, III, 66.
[3] Aretino, Lettere, III, 106.
[4] Un Prognostico Satirico di Pietro Aretino. Torino, 1888, page XXXI.

crafty truthfulness gave him a great superiority over his adversaries. And he further disarmed them by proclaiming as virtues those things in his life they denounced as infamous. It was useless for Franco to call him "an angry cur to whom men fling bones in order not to be bitten." Aretino had already in letters and medals proudly announced himself the Scourge of Princes, drawing tribute from their fears by denouncing their vices. And the boasts had not checked the intimacy of great artists, dropping into his house as if they belonged to the family, nor prevented his aristocratic neighbours from sending fruit and flowers from their gardens, nor stopped the rain of gold chains that fell upon his neck from all quarters of the world.[1]

It is not to be supposed that Aretino's manipulation of vanity was invariably successful. In Michael Angelo, for instance, he found a difficult subject. For many years Pietro was accustomed to use phrases of the utmost flattery, devotion and admiration in writing to Michael Angelo and also in writing about him. According to his usual custom he expected something in return. In 1538 Michael Angelo had acknowledged one of his letters in the most complimentary terms.[2]

But Pietro expected something more than compliments, and he kept writing with growing insistence to Michael Angelo and to common friends for some drawings from the master's hand to be added to his art collection. When the drawings did not come, Pietro became annoyed. In 1544 he asks Michael Angelo, in a most flattering letter,

[1] Aretino, Lettere passim.

[2] See the letter quoted on page 76.

—"Why don't you reward my constant devotion in reverencing your heaven-given qualities, with a remnant of those sketches which you care least for?"[1] A little later he tells a friend to ask Michael Angelo "how long he thinks that I can suffer the continual torment of waiting for the sketches promised me?"[2] The next year, he says,—"In case there is any longer delay I shall be forced to give up the faith I have placed in so great a man."[3] A month later he asks the same common friend, in a brief letter without any of the admiring adjectives he has been wont to apply to Michael Angelo's name,—"In short, tell me frankly whether I ought to put confidence in Buonarroti or not?" "If you say no, I shall understand that you wish me to turn my affection for him into disdain."[4] This veiled threat proved ineffective and Pietro showed how dangerous he was in the character of indignant friend; and what Michael Angelo might expect if he did not send the sketches. Four months later he wrote a letter intended for circulation, in which he attacked the painter for showing the world in his Last Judgment,—"no less impiety in religion than perfection in painting. He has placed in the greatest chapel in the world, above the first altar of Jesus, before the eyes of the Vicar of Christ, figures of angels and saints entirely nude." He speaks of this action with grief, shame and indignation as sacrilege and suggests that it is the Christian duty of the Pope to destroy the picture. He adds that he does not feel astonished that Michael Angelo has not kept his

[1] Aretino, Lettere, III, 45.
[2] Aretino, Lettere, III, 52.
[3] Aretino, Lettere, III, 122.
[4] Aretino, Lettere, III, 131.

promises. For even the treasures left by Julius for a tomb, could not make him keep his promise to finish it. "A failure to do your duty which is looked on as your theft."

In this letter according to his usual method, Aretino used truth as his most reliable weapon. The nudities in the Last Judgment did shock the religious sensibilities of the day. As we have already seen, Aretino had a good deal of religious sensibility and he also may have felt the shock. For some members of Italian society bore the spectacle of a Pope and his Cardinals chuckling over the obscene allusions of the Suppositi and the Calandra, with more complacency than the idea of the unclothed figures of Michael Angelo's fresco in the Sistine Chapel. But the motive which made Aretino express this feeling in his mordant letter, is unmistakably plain in the postscript. "Now that I have a little blown off my anger against the cruelty you show towards my devotion, and have, I think, shown you that if you are divine (di-vina) I am not of water (d'acqua), tear up this letter which I have also torn up and make up your mind that I am the sort of man whose letters even emperors and kings answer."

Perhaps Pietro did tear up his copy of this letter, but he repeated the most damaging part of it without the postscript and with extraordinary similarity of phrase, in a letter written the next year, and then printed it. The reader will probably be glad to be told that, so far as we know, Michael Angelo never sent any sketches.

In another direction also, Aretino's system of literary blackmail failed to work to his satisfaction. All through his writings runs a series of damaging and denunciatory allusions to the Papal court, the clergy and monks. These allusions are vague and general, and not at all incompatible with his equally continuous professions of loyalty to the orthodox faith and the ancient church. They do not prevent the exchange of highly complimentary letters with a large number of prelates and monks nor the receipt of favours from popes. His attacks are generally by way of slurs, as when he writes to the Cardinal of Trent that "he is as truthful as every other man of his habit is full of lies," [1] or says that a certain thing "would be shameful even among cardinals let alone among cavaliers," [2] or tells Cardinal Hippolito de' Medici "that as others show the honours, incomes and favours gained in the Roman court by their vices, he will show the offenses he has received for his virtues." [3] Sometimes he repeated a story like that of Julius II rushing out of his room in fury at five o'clock in the morning to pursue a careless singer in the corridors of the palace, not heeding one of his attendants, who kept calling "Holy Father, go to bed," and finally giving a terrible rap over the head to his luckless steward who came to see what the row was and was taken for the rash musician.

But on occasions he made more direct and deadly assaults. Just after the sack of Rome, he wrote a satiric address to the Roman clergy, called the "Pax Vobiscum." The scorching sentences struck Pope Clement in the midst of his ruined city so cruelly that he let the book fall from his hands and burst into tears.[4] In the presence of Aretino's friend, the painter Sebastiano del Piombo, he

[1] Aretino, Lettere, I, 69.
[2] Aretino, Lettere, II, 192.
[3] Aretino, Lettere, I, 30.
[4] Lettere al Aretino, I, page 309.

said with a sigh, when in the castle of Saint Angelo,—"If Pietro had been with me I should not be here worse than a prisoner," and went on to explain that the representatives of the Emperor would not dare to treat him so shamefully if the dreaded pen of Pietro were on his side.[1]

In this attack as in others, Pietro was cleverly using for ignoble ends what was generally thought to be the truth. It was the universal opinion, expressed by many whose fidelity to the Church could not be questioned, that the sack of Rome was the divine judgment on the sins of the Curia. But the impelling motive of Pietro's criticism of the Church was not prophetic wrath, nor were his temporary reconciliations with the popes entirely the result of that readiness to forgive injuries of which he often boasts, and not without truth. In the case of the corruptions of the Church, as in the case of the corruptions of princely courts, he was using, sometimes without being conscious of it at the moment, a not altogether ungenuine indignation to gratify revenge and greed. And the man to whom that seems impossible does not know the curious anomalies of character that flourished in the air of the Italian Renascence.

The justice of this judgment on the chief motive of his slurs on the clergy, and his willingness to exchange invective for eulogy if he was paid for it, are made perfectly plain by his own pen. Soon after Paul III became Pope, Aretino wrote to a newly-made Cardinal—"Miserable men of genius everywhere fallen into need, hope to rise again and with the piety of your aid to ob-

[1] Lettere, al Aretino, I, page 12.

tain from the best of popes their daily bread. And when they have obtained it, you will be the cause of making their spirits give breath to the trumpet of Holy Scripture, instead of sounding the horns of the defects of others with the voice of desperation. What miracles will issue from that genius and intellect when they are given not bishoprics * * * but a proper income and a decent competence by means of which they can study, and honour God with the results of study. * * * Why not aid them? Why not use them? If one of them has a biting tongue extract it with 'cortesia.' Close his mouth with a gift. See how the great Cæsar * * * has done this in honour of my free virtue giving me reason to talk and write good. See further how Our Redeemer entered into the heart of Saul with His grace in order that he might become a bell sounding His name, as I would become a bell to sound the virtues of the ministers of His temple, if the imperial 'cortesia' were imitated."[1]

He made this offer more plain in the Giudizio for 1534, the only one which has survived. He asks the King of France to induce the Pope to reward his servitù. And the "necessities of Aretino being met, the name and works of priests will not be lacerated. Whence, sire, you will acquire no less glory by freeing from true and eternal disgrace the clergy, now become the fable of the vulgar because of my most just anger, than your predecessors have acquired by having freed them from the hands of their enemies. And obtaining such favour I will not only keep silent about every signore and monsignore, but I

[1] Aretino, Lettere, I, 75.

will turn my natural style to speaking well," etc., etc.[1]

Six years later, he struck another note on the same string he so often sounded. He writes to the Apostolic Legate with a copy of his "Life of the Virgin Mary." "* * * Happy the ink, happy the pen, happy the paper which are used, which are spread for the praise of Mary. Now most reverend Monsignore, reputation of the honour of the clergy, how long ought I to wait that Rome should consider, not the many years which she robs from my servitù, but the many books I have composed to the honour of God? Think of the Psalms of David, The Genesis of Moses, the Humanity of Jesus. See how the Life of His Mother is overlooked by the church because I am not set down as approved in the catalogue of hypocrisy. But where are the writings about Christ made by those who receive so many honours, so many properties, so many solid returns from the Church? But if I, driven to despair by the cruelty of the court, do not fail to show myself to be a Christian, what do you suppose I would do if she should show herself grateful?" [2]

When the imperial pension had been granted, no one had any further fear that Aretino would publish the whispered scandals about the life of Charles V, and utterances of which these are specimens, seem to show that the red hat, or some reward less onerous to a man of his temper and habit, would have kept the most "dangerous tongue" in Italy from repeating what he heard about the Court of Rome. Across the Alps, there was a contemporary of the dreaded Venetian whose mastery of words

[1] Un Pronostico Satirico di Pietro Aretino, page 34.
[2] Aretino, Lettere, II, 168.

was greater, and whose power of denunciation was even more terrible. Aretino always spoke of him,—and, unless this essay has failed, the reader must see he spoke without hypocrisy—as an enemy of the church, of society and of God's truth. It would be far easier to sustain an indictment for libel against details of Luther's utterances about the Roman Curia, than against those of Aretino, but of the lofty passion which made the German monk refuse to sell his copyrights for a large sum Aretino could not have the smallest understanding.

It was during the bitterest part of his attacks on the papal court, that this bravo of the pen received his hardest and most damaging blow. It came from the same household that furnished the assassin's dagger that drove him from Rome. The Datario Ghiberti, afterwards bishop of Verona, had as secretary Francesco Berni, who wrote burlesque poetry with such success that he has given his name to the Bernesque style which Byron used in Beppo and Don Juan. Soon after the publication of the "Pax Vobiscum," Berni wrote a famous sonnet in answer. It contained at least one malicious libel, the story about Aretino's sister, and enables the reader to judge of the malodorous flowers that bloomed in the controversial pages of Aretino and many of his contemporaries. A simple prose translation is the needed relief from the impossible task of reproducing its rollicking measure and easy rhyme:—

"Will you go on saying and making lie after lie, O, rotten, putrid and unsalted tongue, until a dagger shall be found better and luckier than that of Achilles?"

"The Pope is pope and you are a rascal who lives by

the bread of others and evil speaking. You have one foot in the brothel and the other in the hospital. You miserable maimed thing—ignorant and arrogant. Giovomatteo (The Datario) and those he has at hand, who by the grace of God are safe and sound, will drown you some fine day in a privy vault. May the hangman punish thy panderous manners. And if you want to go on chattering, look out for yourself! Take care of your breast, your head and your hands. (Achilles had wounded him in these three places.) But do you behave like the dogs who, after they have shaken off a good beating, are better than ever. Have the grace to be ashamed of yourself, presumptuous pig, infamous monster, image of vituperation and starvation. A dung-heap waits for you, O rogue, where you can die beside the two, your sisters, who do you so much honour in the brothel at Arezzo, dancing to the tune 'What does my love?' * * * Traitor, you ought to write your ballads and stories about these and not of Sanga,[1] who has no sisters. These are they who by their evil life shall pay your expenses and their own, and not the Marquis of Mantua, because now you are a stench in the nostrils to every country, every man, every animal. Heaven, God and the devil wish you ill. Those ducal garments, the fruit of begging and cheating which, fallen into misfortune, like morning weeds weep for you and your back to the sound of the drubbings you get, will be stripped off you before you die, by the Reverend Father, Mr. Hangman, who will take you out of the world by a halter and for a further favour, quarter you;

[1] A Roman attacked by Aretino. See Virgili's Life of Berni, note to page 248.

and your parasites, panders of your vices, tavern loungers will sing for you the eternal requiem. Now live and behave yourself, or a dagger, a cesspool or else a noose will shut you up somehow." [1]

It is a typical instance of the way in which Aretino has been made the scapegoat of his time, that Berni's biographer, Virgili, who cannot be stern enough about the coarseness and irresponsibility of Aretino, should speak of this sonnet as a "frank and loyal" attack on that unique monster of wickedness.[2] Its tone and method are the more illuminative of the manners of the age because Berni was apparently not a man ready for any dirty work a patron might ask of him. Those who had reason to know asserted, that after he became a canon of the church, he was suddenly taken ill while dining one day with his friend and patron, Cardinal Cybo, and died in a week, poisoned by the orders of his host. The cause of the alleged crime was that Berni had sharply refused Cybo's command to poison Cardinal Salviati.[3]

There was only one Pope from whom Aretino received anything like what he thought his due. After having vainly written such letters to the court of Paul III, as we have quoted, Aretino turned again to attack, and even ended one poem by invoking the Turk to come and reform with cannon balls the horrible corruptions of Rome.[4] At the death of Paul III, Julius III became Pope. He

[1] Berni, Rime, edited by Virgili, page 62.

[2] Virgili, Life of Berni, page 543.

[3] Virgili, Life of Berni, and Staffeti, "Il Cardinale Innocenzo Cybo." Firenze, 1894.

[4] Quoted from MSS. by Luzio, Giornale Storico della Letteratura Italiana, XIX, page 102.

was from Arezzo and the brother of one of Aretino's friends. Aretino saluted him at once with complimentary writings. Julius made him a cavalier of St. Peter and invited him to Rome, saying he would make a second jubilee because every one would flock to Rome to see him.[1]

Aretino felt this was what he deserved, but he claimed something more. And two years later we find him pointing out to a friend in Rome from whose intercession he had failed to obtain more solid benefits, that his "tongue is pestiferous to those it does not admire, for example, Leo and Clement, whose diabolical holinesses instead of wiping off the sweat of my servitù with the ready hands of reward, dipped them in my blood for no other reason than that I am without guile—that truth is my idol, that etc., etc." He goes on to brag of his services to the church, his widespread fame, the rewards given by all princes, and to ask why the clergy, for their own honour and the safety of the church, do not also "gild his pen?"[2]

In 1553 the Duke of Urbino, made Captain General of the Church, took Aretino to Rome with him. The Pope in audience rose from his seat to greet Aretino with a kiss of "fraternal tenderness" and assigned him magnificent apartments in the palace. He sent back to Venice laudatory descriptions of what he had seen and complimentary letters about the Pope. Julius' brother, who had been enormously advanced in wealth and power, had promised Aretino a pension of ten scudi a month.

[1] Aretino, Lettere, VI, 160.
[2] Aretino, Lettere, VI, 113.

But for some reason or other, perhaps because Aretino could not keep from evil speaking, this was suspended. Aretino burst out in savage utterances against the Roman court, but thought better of it and wrote most abject letters, begging to be forgiven and have his pension again. He had only bitten like "a family dog whose bone has been snatched away;" "for men of virtù ought to be compared to lean mastiffs who lick the feet of him who gives them food and tear the legs of those who refuse it to them." [1] When all his prayers could not obtain pardon, he wrote a sarcastic letter of thanks to Baldovino, thanking him "for relief from the disgrace of accepting so vile a guerdon." [2] And far from being ashamed of letters through which we know of this last vendetta with Rome, the writer published them himself.

They are among the last we have from him. On the 21st of October, 1556, he died of a stroke of apoplexy, in the sixty-fifth year of his age. Slander became busy soon after his death in forming the legend that he died an atheist. His native city of Arezzo, which made him a patrician, gave him the title "Salvator Patriae," hung his portrait in the council chamber, still preserves his house, and made, in 1581, inquiries about his death. The sworn attestation of Aretino's pastor found some twenty-five years ago in the archives of Arezzo, has disposed of the legend that he died an atheist. The priest sends a deposition, sworn before a notary, that, shortly before his sudden death, Aretino confessed to him and took communion with tears that showed great feeling.

[1] Aretino, Lettere, VI, 215.
[2] Aretino, Lettere, VI, 261.

When death had removed him from attack, war was made on his works. Ten years before his death, an attempt had been made to persuade the Pope to have his religious works burnt.[1] The year after his death some of his writings, two years after, all, were placed by the Church on the index of prohibited books. The need of stopping their circulation if they were heretical, is suggested by one account of the officers of the Inquisition. They seized the stock of Cappello, a bookseller of Naples, who was agent for Gabriel Giolito, a publisher and bookseller of Venice with shops in Bologna, Ferrara and Naples. In the stock of seven hundred and twenty-nine books, one hundred and twenty-six were by Aretino; the next best selling author, if we can test by this standard, was Erasmus, of whose works seventy-one copies were found. There were in stock thirty-nine copies of Aretino's dramatic works, thirty copies of his letters and forty copies of his religious books. Of his pornographic writings only nine copies were found.

It has been assumed that Aretino's works were put upon the index, because of his pornographic writings. This assumption seems to be mistaken; the very slight references which have survived to suggest the motives for that condemnation refer to heretical tendencies. There are things in his religious writings on which a charge of departure from orthodoxy could have been based. And when the influence of the Council of Trent was being felt in reforming the abuses and restoring the discipline of the church, Aretino's freedom in criticising the clergy became offensive.

[1] Aretino, Lettere, III, 105.

That this was the motive for putting Aretino on the index is strongly suggested by the way in which the redactors treated other lascivious writers. The Council of Trent ordered that books should be placed on the index which "intentionally narrate or discuss lascivious and obscene things," because it was necessary to defend "morals as well as faith." But the "Redactors of the Index, the official correctors of profane literature, almost all forget the interests of morality, and think only of reëstablishing the honour of the ecclesiastical body." The works of Straparola, Bandello and Firenzuola, extremely licentious and coarse, escaped condemnation. The expurgated edition of Bandello, published in 1560, lacks little of the obscenity of the original, but the stories which centered on scandals of clergymen are omitted. In 1573 the Pope ordered an edition of the "Decameron," which Catholics might read without disobeying the index. This edition, authorized by the inquisition, left lascivious passages unchanged, but lacks words like "devil" and "hell" and all obscene phrases which contained the names of saints. And whenever a clergyman was the hero of a scandalous adventure, the expurgator left the adventure unchanged, but made the hero a layman, and the abbesses became citizens' wives. In addition every passage which sounded like the phrases used by heretics, such as the suggestion that "the grace of God comes without merit," was cut out.[1] In a similar spirit the Spanish Inquisition in 1619 erased from the original edition of Don

[1] The foregoing paragraph is in part quoted, in part summarized, from the valuable work of M. Dejob. De l'influence du Concile de Trent sur Literature et les Beaux Arts, Paris, 1884.

Quixote the playful remark of the Duchess when advising Sancho to scourge himself for the release of Dulcinea from enchantment,—"Remember, Sancho, that works of charity done in a lukewarm and half-hearted way, are without merit and of no avail." [1]

These and similar comparisons suggest that Aretino was condemned not for obscenity but for heresy, and more particularly because of the sneers and derogatory remarks against the clergy, which were scattered so freely through his works.

He was buried in the church of San Luca, but his tomb was destroyed when the level of the floor was changed. His epitaph was not the fabled one which accused him of never having known God, but probably the one a German traveller reports at the end of the sixteenth century:—

"From a lowly origin, Pietro Aretino rose to such height by denouncing impure vice that, through the fear he inspired, he levied tribute from those to whom the world paid tribute." [2]

[1] Don Quixote, etc. A translation, etc., by John Ormsby. London, Smith, Elder, 1885. Vol. III, page 399, note.

[2] Quoted Carlo Bertani, Pietro Aretino, etc. Sondrio, 1901. (237.) From Shrader Monumenta Italiæ Helmaestadii, 1592.

III

THOMAS CROMWELL

Two men have risen to larger power in England than has been wielded by any other Englishman not connected by birth or marriage with the royal line. They were of the same blood, for Oliver Cromwell was descended in the fifth generation from the sister of Thomas Cromwell, who under Henry VIII wielded the highest authority in Church and State.[1] They were very unlike in character, but had common traits: unusual capacity for the affairs of government, tact in dealing with men, an iron will and the gift of foresight.

Fame has been unfair to both of these great men. In giving judgment upon each in turn she has stood with eyes bound, not to weigh more evenly good against evil, but to take with blind confidence the opinion of his bitter enemies as a just estimate of his work and character.

The opponents of Oliver Cromwell hung his coffined body on the gallows, and then flung his bones into a shallow grave at its foot. But they buried his memory under obliquy so deep that, more than two hundred years afterward, the city government of Leeds dared not accept the gift of a statue to him because they feared the people. A saner judgment has at last prevailed. It was

[1] Milton in his "Second Defense of the People of England," refers to this descent of Oliver Cromwell "from illustrious ancestors distinguished for the part they took in restoring and establishing true religion in this country."

voiced five years ago by the man who held at death the almost unquestioned primacy among the writers of history in the English tongue. "It is time for us to regard him as he really was, with all his physical and moral audacity, with all his tenderness and spiritual yearnings, in the world of action what Shakespeare was in the world of thought, the greatest, because the most typical, Englishman of all time." [1]

For the older but the smaller of these two kinsmen the ebb and flow of the tide of injustice has been reversed. Within two generations of Thomas Cromwell's death on the scaffold at the hands of a priestly cabal, Fletcher or Shakespeare put the popular estimate of his work and character into the prophetic adjuration of the dying Wolsey:

"Cromwell, I charge thee, fling away ambition.
. . . . Be just and fear not.
Let all the ends thou aim'st at be thy country's,
Thy God's and truth's; then if thou fall'st, O Cromwell!
Thou fall'st a blessed martyr."

But modern writers, particularly during this generation, have presented him as the importer of the unknown vices of Italian politics, a mere tyrant's hireling and flatterer, the light of whose intellect displays no large aims, but, as by infernal fires, only illumines the cruelty and greed of an adventurer. This peculiarly sinister atmosphere comes chiefly from the *Apologia,* a long rhetorical letter written the year before Cromwell's execution to the Emperor Charles V, urging him to invade England

[1] Samuel R. Gardiner, *Oxford Lectures on Cromwell.*

and force it from schism to obedience. Its author was Cardinal Reginald Pole, an Englishman of the blood royal, outlawed for treason, who had tried to bring Papal money into England to back an insurrection which menaced the throne and demanded Cromwell's head.[1] This attempt Cromwell answered by sending to the block the chief of the Pole family and their intimate friends. It is as unreasonable to base a final estimate of Cromwell upon such a document, as it would be to base a final estimate of the character and purposes of Abraham Lincoln on a letter of Jefferson Davis, written during the Civil War to gain the alliance of a European power for the Confederacy.[2]

An historical sketch of Cromwell must judge him, not by the ideals of his opponents, but by his own; test him by the moral average of his times, and take account of the qualities his friends truly praised, as well as the vices his enemies justly condemned. This attempt is based chiefly on the seven thousand letters, by, to or about Cromwell, calendared in the *Letters and Papers of Henry VIII*. There is nothing in it which cannot be supported by citations from that collection or other contemporary writings. The writer believes he has never differed from the opinions of modern historians without being aware of it, and every such difference implies a dissent which seems to him justified by evidence drawn from the primary sources.

[1] *Letters and Papers,* XII, part 1, 123, 1141. Pole denied this. The article in the appendix shows by documents that he did not tell the truth.

[2] In addition to this reflection, sufficient for the present purpose, the writer has found the *Apologia,* after critical examination, erroneous in detail. The article in the appendix of this volume, reprinted from the *American Historical Review,* gives the grounds for this conclusion.

Henry VIII had that eye of a king which sees capacity while yet in obscurity. Under his favor two men, unaided by birth or money, rose to high positions which became the background to display remarkable talents—Thomas Wolsey and Thomas Cromwell.

Thomas Cromwell, born toward the end of the fifteenth century, was the son of Walter Cromwell, who was descended from two generations of people of wealth and importance in burgher society. He owned at various times a blacksmith shop, a fulling mill and a brewery, but in his later years lost most of his property.[1] The only contemporary accounts of Cromwell's youth contain several demonstrable mistakes, and have therefore been perhaps unduly discredited. But it is certain that, while still a lad, he traveled abroad and led a rough and adventurous life. In Italy he fell into great poverty, and for a time served as a soldier. During this wandering life he gained skill in business affairs, and acted as clerk, or bookkeeper, in the two great commercial cities of Antwerp and Venice. At some time in his early life he acquired Latin, French, Italian and a knowledge of law. According to a story told by a man who would be apt to know the facts, he developed, while still young, tact in managing men. The town of Boston wished to obtain some favor from the Pope, and Cromwell went with their agent to Rome. The request was reasonable, but Cromwell was delayed by a great crowd of suitors. In this situation, he used his wits instead of the usual presents to attendants to get an audience before his turn. Wait-

[1] See the summary of evidence in *Thomas Cromwell,* by Roger B. Merriman. Macmillan, 1902.

ing for the Pope as he came home from hunting, Cromwell's company, when the cavalcade drew near, sang an English "three-man song." The novel music attracted Julius' attention, Cromwell clinched the favorable impression by the gift of some English jellies or sweetmeats, and in the audience he got obtained the favor Boston sought.

Between the ages of twenty-five and thirty, he came home, settled down and married the daughter of a shearman, an old neighbor, who had perhaps coöperated with his father's fulling mill in the manufacture of cloth. For a time he carried on the business of the fulling mill, to which he added the profession of a notary and business agent. His connections with the Italian and Flemish merchants living in London evidently helped him, and prosperity followed hard work. In 1524 he seems to have given up the fulling mill and devoted himself to his profession as a lawyer. He gained a good practice, and increased his earnings by loaning them among the merchants and gentry whose affairs he managed.

About ten years after he returned to England, he bought land in a good quarter of London. He had already become a person of position in the burgher society in which he moved. In 1522 he was put down in a joint power of attorney alongside of Poyser, grocer, London, as Thomas Cromwell, London, Gent.[1] In 1523 he sat on the inquest of wardmote for his ward. It was an energetic committee. It presented Hanchok and Bonyfaut for a defective pavement in front of their doors, and some twenty other owners had similar complaints lodged

[1] *Letters and Papers*, Dom. Series, III, 2447.

against them. There was a "noisome goose house in Scalding Alley." William Delke had threatened members of the inquest—probably for doing their duty. The wives of Spencer, Harrison and Badcoke were presented for scolding, and the wife of Andrew Forest for being a common scold. The draft of the committee's report is partly in Cromwell's hand.[1]

The same year he sat in the House of Commons. Among his papers there is a draft of a speech in Parliament, in the handwriting of his clerk, which doubtless represents what Cromwell said or intended to say. The King had declared war against France and her ally Scotland. Wolsey, yielding when he must, presented the need of the throne and asked for a large grant of money, because the King intended to invade France in person. The speech of Cromwell combines most skillfully an appeal to patriotism, readiness to support the King, and the suggestion, conveyed so subtly that Henry could not have been offended, that the plan was a poor one. He denounces the treachery of France and the wrongs her King has done to England, but he is alarmed by the idea that Henry should put his person in danger across the sea. He points out the difficulty of bringing the Frenchmen to meet in open battle the forty thousand men to be sent, the risk of pushing on to Paris, leaving fortresses in the rear, and the impossibility of England's finding coin and bullion enough to feed so great an army, "seeing that the inhabitants of Flanders" (where provisions would have to be bought) are so anxious "to have much of our money for little of

[1] *Letters and Papers*, III, 3657.

their victuals." These campaigns might prove more loss to England than to France, and reduce the realm to coining leather. The true object of English arms was Scotland. "Who that intendeth France to win, with Scotland let him begin." It is folly to think of holding possessions across the sea when Scotland obeys another Prince. Scotland once united to England all other possessions are safe.[1]

It was after sitting in this Parliament that he wrote one of the very few purely personal letters which have survived, and the only one which suggests the flavor of the pleasant conversation for which he was famous: "Supposing ye desire to know the news current in these parts, for it is said that news refresheth the spirit of life, wherefore ye shall understand that by long time I amongst others have indured a Parliament which continued by the space of seventeen whole weeks, where we communed of war, peace, strife, contentions, debate, murmur, grudge, riches, poverty, penury, truth, falsehood, justice, equity, deceit, oppression, magnanimity, activity, force, attempraunce, treason, murder, felony, and also how a commonwealth might be edified and continued within our realm. Howbeit in conclusion we have done as our predecessors have been wont to do, that is to say as well as we might, and left where we began." [2]

The habit of not taking himself too seriously, the friendly and familiar atmosphere out of which this comes, was evidently the atmosphere of Cromwell's house. And he seems to have early displayed that ready gratitude for

[1] *Letters and Papers,* III, 2958.
[2] *Ibid., III,* 3249.

kindness, that fidelity to those who had helped him, for which he became noted at home and abroad. People liked to go to his home and remembered their visit with pleasure. John Creke addresses him from Bilboa as "the dearest man in the world," and says that the recollection of walking with Cromwell in the garden and talking of spiritual things, makes him desperate with loneliness.[1] Three different men within the year choose, among the customary superscriptions for letters, such forms as "my right loving friend, right faithful friend, heartily beloved friend." And several letters end with words of greeting to common friends. In the little circle which gathered round Cromwell, his wife and his mother played their part. Correspondents ask to be remembered to them. One wants the good housewife "to send another plaster for his knee," and another desires to be commended "to your mother, after you my most singular good friend.[2] These are slight instances, but everything in the few letters which have survived from this early period points toward a merry and gentle house, visited by good friends and "gossips," with whom the Cromwells shared the pleasures of life down "to half a fat doe." And it was a prosperous house, for in 1524 Cromwell bought a sapphire ring worth in modern value some £40 and a gold bracelet with a jacinth worth £80.[3]

For most of his correspondents Mr. Thomas Cromwell became during the next five years "The Right Worshipful Thomas Cromwell." Though those who possessed, or desired to claim, intimacy choose the more familiar of the

[1] *Letters and Papers,* III, 2394.
[2] *Ibid.,* III, 2624, 3015, 3502; IV, 1385.
[3] *Ibid.,* IV, 166; IV, App., 57.

usual formal addresses, as when Lord Berners addressed his letter to "my well-beloved friend," or Lord George Grey endorses his "to my fellow and friend." The reason for this greater social consideration appears plainly from 1528 on, for his full title then becomes "The Right Worshipful Mr. Cromwell, Councilor to my Lord Cardinal's Most Honorable Grace."

Wolsey, the first man in the kingdom, whose wealth rivaled that of the King, employed him as the manager of the revenues of his diocese of York, and gradually a large part of the Cardinal's legal business fell into Cromwell's hands. As he trusted Cromwell's capacity, Wolsey naturally came to employ him in the project nearest to his heart—the establishment of his two colleges, one of which survives at Oxford, a monument to the love which could plan such a palace for learning, and the pride which blazoned his own insignia on every coign and chief stone of its walls. It was a visible evidence of the secret forces which were undermining mediæval institutions by changing scholastic habits of thought, that Wolsey obtained in Rome a bull permitting the suppression of smaller monasteries in England and the diversion of the funds to the establishment of his two colleges. For, as a man of the New Learning which had spread in his day from Italy over Europe, Wolsey shared the humanists' dislike of the ascetic ideal, and was prepared to make war on the results of that exaggeration of it which had left Europe covered with thousands of monasteries, whose inmates no longer played any very useful part in the changed life of the world.

In this conversion of ancient foundations, which turned

monasteries into colleges and substituted professors and students for monks, Cromwell was Wolsey's most active agent. And in this service he gained hatred. In any suppression of the kind there must be suffering to those who lose an assured living. Hatred is apt to follow, even in the gentler atmosphere of this century. The sixteenth century was anything but gentle, and therefore it is not surprising to find a letter to Wolsey in France at the end of August, 1527, telling him that "incredible things are reported about Allen (Cromwell's coadjutor) and Cromwell, as I have heard from the King and others."[1] What these "incredible things" were does not appear. Cromwell, like most men in subordinate positions, from royal ministers to the pages of a Baron's waiting-room, took, from the needs of suitors, fees and presents for such influence as they might have with their superiors.[2] And it is more than probable that, during this suppression of monasteries and the pensioning of their inmates, Cromwell made money which, to one of more delicate feelings of honor than those of the average man of his day, would have seemed to soil the hand that took it. But there are indications that the things reported were "incredible" and, to a large extent, the result of the hatred of the sufferers by the suppression, and its opponents.

In the first place, we know of these charges only from letters which express disbelief in them, the one quoted above, the one quoted below, and

[1] *Letters and Papers,* IV, 3360.

[2] "Es lag im Geist dieser und auch noch der folgenden Zeit das ungescheut fürstliche Diener sich die Hände schmieren liessen." Ulmann, *Maximilian,* I, page 813. A dozen similar citations from men who know the period might be given.

one from John Rushe, a helper in the work, who wrote to Cromwell, "You would be astonished to learn what lies are told about us in these parts." [1] In the second place, an investigation evidently took place, for, in the beginning of November, John Cheking wrote Cromwell that various reports were spread in Oxford about him, which he is glad to know proved false.[2] And the next year, when Wolsey had fallen from power, Stephen Vaughan, a servant and friend, who did not hesitate to write a letter of stern warning and reproof when he thought it needed, writes: "You are more hated for your master's sake than for anything which I think you have wrongfully done against any man." [3] At Wolsey's fall Cromwell was naked and open to his enemies. The London burghers and the House of Commons were apt to involve him in their vengeful feelings toward Wolsey, the incarnation of the idea of the temporal power of the clergy against which they so strongly protested. Cromwell stood day after day in the House of Commons as the chief obstacle to bar that vengeance. If charges of unusual peculation or extortion could have been supported by any sort of evidence, it would have been easy to use the hatred of the master to overwhelm the man. And even if Cromwell, as seems probable,[4] had obtained privately the royal assent to defend Wolsey, this would not necessarily have saved him from assault. Henry was unable to defend Wolsey against his enemies, and had to send se-

[1] *Letters and Papers,* IV, 6110.
[2] *Ibid.,* IV, 4916.
[3] *Ibid.,* IV, 6036. Compare VI, 1385.
[4] *Ibid.,* IV, Appendix, 238.

cretly to assure him that he was not altogether abandoned.

Wolsey fell from the very faithfulness with which he had served his King. He had opposed the war which rendered heavy taxes necessary, and then, when the storm of unpopulariy which frightened even Henry arose, he shouldered all the blame.[1] And he had laid himself open to that indictment for the crime of præmunire, under which he was stripped of most of his property and power, by bringing into England his commission of Papal Legate at Henry's own desire. The King would not stand by his unpopular minister. Henry had the temperament of a tyrant, but he had also the Tudor instinct for kingship, and though he might disregard the opposition of this or that class, he never risked too firm a resistance to any feeling he had reason to believe common to the mass of his people. And the bulk of the nation wished for Wolsey's fall.

The King was displeased with the great minister because he had failed to get from the Pope permission to set aside the Queen and crown another. But apparently Henry, while he wished Wolsey's fall, did not desire his utter destruction, and so when Cromwell, faithful in adversity, became the prop of his master's falling house, he saved it from ruin. He succeeded, by skillful bribery of Wolsey's chief opponents and by open defense before Parliament, in preventing his attainder for treason. Cavendish, Wolsey's gentleman usher and biographer, writes: "There could nothing be spoken against my lord in the Parliament House but he would answer it incontinent or

[1] Hall's *Chronicle.*

else take until the next day, against which time he would revert to my lord to know what answer he should make in his behalf; insomuch that there was no matter alleged against my lord but that he was ever ready furnished with a sufficient answer; so that at length for his honest behaviour in his master's cause, he grew into such estimation in every man's opinion, that he was esteemed to be the most faithfullest servant to his master of all other, wherein he was of all men greatly commended."

No doubt he used the turn of the tide of feeling which drifted his master out of danger, to further his own fortune. But they who in these most recent times assert that he was faithful merely in the selfish hope of winning praise, not only choose to attribute the meanest possible motive to an action, but forget that he could not have been sure of success when he began the perilous task of defending his hated patron. Wolsey trusted him, and writes often in such phrases as "mine only aider in this mine intolerable anxiety and heaviness."[1]

Wolsey did not take Cromwell's advice to submit and return to the affairs of his archbishopric. He sought French influences for his reinstatement. The Spanish Ambassador reports that he sent messages suggesting forcible outside interference with Henry's divorce.[2] He seems to have written to Rome to cause pressure to be brought on the King for his own recall; at all events he hoped for Papal influence.[3] The Duke of Norfolk, his successor in the State, feared and Anne Boleyn hated him. They got hold of Wolsey's physician, who could give ev-

[1] *Letters and Papers,* IV, 6098.

[2] *Calendar State Papers, Spanish,* Vol. IV, pp. 601, 619, 692.

[3] *Ibid.,* page 805.

idence that was quite enough to excite the fierce anger of Henry against any one who opposed a cherished plan. The physician perhaps distorted what he knew or added to it.[1] Wolsey was summoned to London, and his death on the journey probably saved him from the scaffold.

In the beginning of 1531, about a month after Wolsey's death, Cromwell became a Royal Councilor,[2] an appointment which made it possible for him to be present at Councils of State, but did not necessarily give him any influence upon State policy. This, by the testimony of the foreign ambassadors, was largely determined by the Duke of Norfolk and the other relatives of Anne Boleyn. That Cromwell should have passed from Wolsey's service to the King's is nothing extraordinary. Large numbers of the Cardinal's "men," from yeomen of the guard up, did the same thing, and the careers of Bonner, afterward Bishop of London, and Gardiner, afterward Bishop of Winchester, were helped rather than hindered by the fact that the one had been Wolsey's chaplain and the other his secretary. Gardiner, as one of Cromwell's intimates wrote with disgust, refused to lift a finger to help his former patron.[3]

Of the way in which Cromwell became the King's man we have two contemporary accounts. Ten years afterward Reginald Pole wrote to the Emperor to prove that Henry VIII had become Antichrist through the seductions of the diabolically inspired Cromwell. He says that on one occasion, after Henry's at-

[1] *Calendar State Papers, Spanish,* Vol. IV, page 819.

[2] A letter, dated January 10, is addressed to him as "One of the King's most gracious Council."

[3] *Letters and Papers,* Dom. Series, Vol. IV, 6112.

tempted divorce had brought him into conflict with the Papacy and the Empire, "when he saw the strongest men of the State drawing back from the affair to such an extent that even Wolsey, smitten with dismay, had begun to withdraw his service, being very much disturbed in mind, he observed with a great sigh that he had sought a divorce from Rome in the hope of getting it, but if the Roman Church was determined to deny it, he would not go any further in the matter. He remained in that state two days, and then began to renew his efforts more sharply than ever." [1] Pole says he got the King's remark from one who heard it, and thus far he is probably telling facts.

He then goes on to explain the cause of the change by relating what, from his own account, is conjecture. He says Satan sent to the King a messenger "whose real name was that of the demon by whose impulse he acted," "but to begin with the name he received from his family before he fell into the hands of demons and degenerated into their nature;" it is Cromwell. Pole gives a long speech (thirteen hundred and fifty words) which he supposes Cromwell delivered to Henry. It is an attempt to prove that a king may do as he pleases, without regard to the laws of God or man, and that therefore Henry ought to declare himself head of the English Church and deny all authority to the Pope. Pole gives no authority for believing that Cromwell had any such interview, and says expressly that he did not hear Cromwell's speech or know what he said, but there is nothing in the speech as he gives it which "he has not heard either

[1] *Apologia ad Carolum Quintum,* page 116.

from that devil's nuncio himself or, at different times, from his friends."

Pole expressly tells us elsewhere that he had only spoken to Cromwell once[1] in his life, and gives an account of the interview. It makes no mention of the very point of Cromwell's advice to the King, the headship of the English Church and the denial of Papal authority. Nor did Henry's first assumption of the title of Head of the English Church, in January, 1531, necessarily imply the denial of Papal authority. It seems evident that Pole, in the account of this interview of Cromwell with the King, which he gives as the cause of his becoming a Royal Councilor, is making a conjecture based on Cromwell's subsequent activity in passing and defending the Act of Supremacy of 1534, which did separate England from the Papacy. And, as he tells the story, the conjecture is a violent one. He represents the King as in despair because Wolsey had drawn back from the attempt to secure the divorce. This scene must therefore have taken place before the fall of Wolsey, in October, 1529. Cromwell was not appointed to the Royal Council until 1531, and it was two years later before the Spanish Ambassador became aware that Cromwell was of sufficient importance to mention his name in a dispatch. If this interview with the King ever took place, why was the man who suggested the policy of England kept so long in the background? And how did Pole find out what the Spanish Ambassador, whose business it was to know the intrigues at Court, was ignorant of—the im-

[1] *Ex illo uno congressu et colloquio.*

portant fact that the King had a new all-powerful secret councilor?

The other contemporary account of the way in which Cromwell entered the King's service is not a conjecture, made in a highly rhetorical polemic by a man who in all his life had only a single talk with Cromwell, but a plain statement of fact by one who saw him often. Cavendish, Wolsey's gentleman usher, writing his master's life, points out that Cromwell, at the time of Wolsey's fall, not only won men's respect by faithfulness to fallen fortunes, but also, having occasion to see the King frequently in connection with the Cardinal's property, by "witty demeanor" and capacity for business "enforced the King to repute him a very wise man and a meet instrument to serve His Grace, as it afterward came to pass." And this fits exactly into the fact that for a long period after his reception into the Royal Council, Cromwell had merely legal and business affairs to manage. The only exception was a disastrously unsuccessful attempt to induce the King to employ in his quarrel with the Pope the pen of William Tyndale, then abroad to avoid the laws against heresy. Cromwell became a Privy Councilor as he had gained wealth, by being, in the phrase of Tacitus, "equal to business and not above it."

He had accumulated a comfortable fortune before he entered the royal service. In July, 1529, he made a will in which he left about £1660 and real estate yielding in 1534 and 1535 an income of some £163 a year. As Cromwell considered five per cent. a safe and procurable rate of income from land, this represents a total property of some £5000, equal in modern purchasing power to £50,000 to £60,000.[1] He had added to the sapphire ring and gold bracelet a number of rings, plain jewels, intaglios or enameled stones. He shared the prevalent taste for silver plate and owned a number of spoons, goblets, flagons and cups.[2] [3] His wardrobe was that of a well-to-do gentleman of what might be called the upper middle class. He dressed, usually, in black or russet, but occasionally put on a coat of dark blue, or a green coat "welted with green velvet." He sometimes wore the orange tawny which was the dress of gentlemen servants of Wolsey. He owned three rings, one set with a rock ruby, one with a table diamond, and one with a turquoise. He had three swords, one of them by a good maker in a black velvet scabbard. His hats and caps were black satin or velvet.[4]

There is nothing in the State papers to indicate that he had any particular weight within the Council until the latter half of 1532, eighteen months after he entered it. The Parliament of 1532 passed thirty-four bills. Drafts of three acts for that Parliament, written or corrected by Cromwell, have come down to us—one the germ of the future Act of Supremacy, one for the Improvement of Seaports, one for the Improvement of Husbandry. Only one of these was passed, which indicates that as yet he

[1] *Letters and Papers,* IV, 5772; IX, 478; VII, 1610; IV, 5772.

[2] *Ibid.,* IV, 3197.

[3] It seems to have been the ambition of all English families to have silver. An Italian traveler of 1500 records his astonishment at the amount of plate to be seen in the houses of ordinary people. "In one single street named Strand there are fifty-two goldsmith shops, so rich, and full of silver vessels, great and small, that in all the shops of Milan, Rome, Venice and Florence put together I do not think there would be found so many of the magnificence that are to be seen in London."—*Camden Society,* Vol. 37, page 43.

[4] *Letters and Papers,* IV, 3197.

was not employed in the more important affairs of the Crown. But by the middle of the year he was "in the high tide of prosperity and overwhelmed with affairs."[1] And in October he crossed to France, the only commoner appointed for the train of twenty-five men of title who accompanied Henry to an interview with Francis I at Calais.[2]

On his return his influence is evident. His correspondence, which had been increasing during the year, now began to rise to enormous proportions. From this time until his death, on the average, forty per cent. of the documents calendared for each year in the governmental series of *Letters and Papers of Henry VII,* are addressed to Cromwell. In April, 1533, the Imperial Ambassador perceived his importance, and mentioned him in a dispatch as "Cromwell who is powerful with the King."[3] This late perception of the importance of Cromwell in the Royal Council was not due to the fact that his power had been artificially concealed.[4] The testimony of the State Papers points to the more natural conclusion that the growth of his influence had been so gradual as to escape notice until it was well established. Wolsey possessed great ability and a power of work which enabled him on one occasion to write twelve hours on a stretch without food or exercise.[5] Norfolk was incapable of the tact, work and insight necessary in the crisis through

[1] *Letters and Papers,* V, 1210.

[2] *Ibid.,* V, Appendix, 33.

[3] *Ibid.,* VI, p. 168. There is a previous simple mention of his name in a dispatch of February 15 (*Calendars of State Papers, Spanish,* Vol. IV, part II, p. 601).

[4] The hypothesis of Mr. Merriman.

[5] Cavendish, *Life of Wolsey,* page 96.

which England was passing. Henry openly regretted his great minister's death and rated the leading councilors for their lack of skill.[1] The King promoted Cromwell because of proved capacity. A list of his chief titles shows the offices conferred upon him and marks his rise in dignity and power. Privy Councilor, Master of the Jewels, Clerk of the Hanaper, Master of the King's Wards, Principal Secretary to the King, Master of the Rolls, Vicar General and Visitor General of Monasteries, Lord Privy Seal, Vicegerent of the King in Spirituals, Baron Cromwell, Knight of the Garter, Earl of Essex.[2] And his actual power was greater than his official authority. For eight years the internal affairs of England passed through his hands.

No English statesman has ever had a more difficult task. The age was pregnant with disasters to the leading states of Europe. Germany was consolidating the power of scores of petty princedoms undermining the basis of central authority, destroying the sense of national unity. Among her people there was forming that fierce hatred about religious opinions which the greed of her princes was to use as an excuse to make her the fighting ground of all the nations of Europe. Italy, bleeding at every vein from the struggle of France and Spain over her conquest, lay helpless before the foreigners who wasted her fields and sacked her cities. In the Netherlands fear and hate were getting ready to turn the revolt against Spain into one of the bitterest of civil

[1] *Calendars, Spanish,* IV, part I, page 819.

[2] See Merriman's list, Vol. I, p. 143. He also gives a list of Cromwell's minor appointments, Vol. II, p. 183.

strifes. Wise Frenchmen saw ominous signs of the outbreak of those intermittent Huguenot wars which filled France with fire and blood for forty years and threatened to put a Spanish dynasty on the throne. Spain was falling under that Hapsburg absolutism, supported by national pride, defended by the money of the New World and the pressure of the Inquisition, which, after stimulating a wondrous bloom of literature and art and guiding a marvelous output of energy, crushed the race for centuries into national nervous prostration.

England was to escape all these evils. She alone was to be free from protracted civil war about religion, from the misery and shame of foreign armies trampling her soil, from a kind of absolutism which destroyed the standing ground of future liberty.

Cromwell could not have foreseen these miseries which befell England's neighbors after his death, but he could perceive, and set himself to fight, the tendencies which produced them. The most dangerous of them appeared to be the separatist influences of feudalism. In the disorders of the ninth and tenth century a method of land tenure had bred a bastard government, the child, not of power and consent, but of power and circumstance. The scholastic theology had given divine sanction to this progeny by a scheme of the world in which God figured as a supreme over-lord. During the last half of the fifteenth century the critical spirit of the Renascence had, to the minds of many men, destroyed belief in the divinity of the mediæval scheme of the world. Some time before this weakening of the mental habits which helped to support feudalism, it had ceased to be the necessary alleviation of a bad situation. Barbarian invasions had come to an end. Trade and manufactures enabled landless men to live outside of serfdom or the profession of fighting. Money exchange, replacing barter, decreased the social, political and economic weight of landowners. Barons who feared not God neither regarded man, trembled when siege guns were leveled at the walls of their ancestral castles. The fierce rush of Swiss mountaineers, the unbroken phalanx of the Flemish artisans, the arrow flight of English yeomen, had proved to the astonished knights that a horse is a vain thing for safety. The day of chivalry was gone. The rough game of the tournament long survived as a fashionable amusement; but it lost its meaning. The ideal of chivalry went to seed in the formal phrases of gallantry, and few knights even tried to remember, like Bayard, that privilege implies duty.

But feudalism had struck its roots too deep into selfish passion and local pride to be exterminated easily. It was a tremendous task for Ferdinand and Isabella in Spain and the Valois in France to beat it into subjection to the Crown, as the symbol of the new sentiment, almost unknown to the middle ages, the sentiment of national patriotism. In England, at the very time when it seemed to be dying, feudalism had revived in a hybrid form. Edward Third's marriages of his children to the heirs and heiresses of great landed estates, had produced nobles uniting feudal influence to the authority of royal blood, and the aristocratic factions of the White and Red Rose had for two generations marred the peace of England in a struggle for the Crown. Henry VIII, whose favorite emblem was the Red Rose imposed on the White, was the first King for more than a century who inherited an undisputed title to the throne. He followed the policy, mingling ruthlessness and craft with wisdom, by which his father had won the nation's loyalty to a crown picked up on the battlefield of Bosworth. Like his father, he tried to fill his Council with men of great ability rather than men of high birth. He realized that the support of the Tudor dynasty was the middle class, so strong in England that, to the astonishment of the French chronicler, the barons had not dared to plunder and slaughter the people, even in the merciless days of the wars of the Roses. These strongest of England's children dreaded the fires of civil war, and were willing to commit her destinies to a powerful, if need be a tyrannical, throne. Henry VIII continued the work of suppressing the remanent abuses by which the aristocracy used their influence to wrong their weaker neighbors. He employed the power of the Crown, which his father had made efficient to enforce common law in the Court of Star Chamber, to break the power of the little great men of different localities. "Bearing," or the aiding of evildoers to continue crime or escape its punishment; "maintenance," or the willingness of a lord to stand by his "man" though thick and thin; "livery," which was usually the symbol of an expectation of maintenance and the willingness to back the quarrel of the maintainer; "embracery," where bearing showed itself in the attempt to coerce or bribe a jury —all felt the pressure of the king's justice.

The power of feudalism was broken when Cromwell became the chief man in England under the King, but the instincts and habits bred by it survived. Into the Tudor struggle to suppress them Cromwell threw himself with an energy which recked not of obstacles. His zeal for the support of the general authority of law tended to make him not too solicitous for justice to the individual. Most men who have fought deep-rooted traditions and habits of lawlessness in feudal, brigand or frontier communities, have been driven toward the temper of the lyncher. The epithet of "sinister," which modern historians are so fond of applying to Cromwell, is not well chosen; but his aims, and the opposition to them, constantly strengthened in him some of the characteristics of the type which the Italians label *"nomo terribile."*

There was no one left who could openly resist the King or the national law. The Duke of Buckingham, last of the great nobles of the old style, who kept solitary state almost royal, had died on the scaffold in 1521. But everywhere the forces of disorderly local privilege needed the strong hand of a master. Men were quick on the dagger.[1] A justice of the peace reports a quarrel with a courtier. "He said, 'I lied like a fool,' and I that 'He lied like a knave.' Then he drew his dagger and struck me on the head, and I drew mine, but the other gentlemen stepped between us." [2] Strong bands of men broke into parks, killed the deer and set the law at defiance.[3] As when, on one occasion, the parson drank at the inn with the young bloods of the neighborhood until they sallied out at two in the morning, some in harness, all with cross-bows or long-bows,

[1] *e.g., Letters and Papers,* XII, part I, 129.
[2] *Ibid.,* XIII, part II, 578.
[3] *e.g., Ibid.,* XIII, 318, and Appendix, 7.

to hunt in the neighboring park, threatening to kill the keeper unless he kept quiet about their poaching. The great lords near Winchester dammed the streams, made a marsh and destroyed the salmon fishing, and tried to stop those who broke down the "waterworks" in obedience to statute. Latimer wrote from Hartlebury: "Here is much bolstering and bearing, and malefactors do not lack supporters. What is needed is a good Sheriff, and that is not easy to find." [1] The country squires of the borders oppressed their humble neighbors. "A poor man, following the tread of an ox that had been taken, found him lying in a petty gentleman's floor, and durst not say a word for fear of his life." [2] On the Welsh border things were so far out of order that the Bishop of Chester reported "by the common law they will never be redressed."

Cromwell supervised the enforcement of law without fear. The most disorderly parts of England were on the marches of Scotland and Wales, where the ideas and habits of feudalism were little affected by social and economic changes. He induced Parliament to extinguish the feudal courts of the Bishopric of Durham [3] and, according to memoranda in his notebook, wished to extinguish all franchises under which powerful wrongdoers might take refuge from the heavy hand of the King's justice. He continued the work of limiting, and he wished to abolish the right of sanctuary, by which criminals who reached the liberties of certain churches, might dwell there untouched of law, or, if they wished,

[1] *Letters and Papers,* XIII, part I, 1258.
[2] *Letters and Papers,* XIV, Appendix, 7.
[3] *The County Palatine of Durham,* Lapsley, pp. 1, 99, 197-254, note 255.

withdraw unarrested from England. The five counties of the North were put under a permanent Royal Council, as the King said, "for the conservation of those counties in quiet, and the administration of common justice."

Wales and its marches were placed in charge of a similar Council, whose decrees were executed by a bishop with a strong sense of injustice. "Two outlaws were brought in. We have sent them for trial, and tomorrow they shall have justice done them. God pardon their souls. Two days later four other outlaws were brought to us. Two had been at large for sixteen years. Three were alive and one slain, brought in a sack trussed on a horse. We have had him hanged on the gallows here as a sign. All thieves in Wales quake for fear." [1] And he adds as a postscript a "list of thieves slain." By December, 1537, this bishop, with a halter for crozier, could write from Shrewsbury: "All is quiet here, save now and then a little conveying amongst themselves for a fat sheep or a bullock, which is impossible to be amended, for thieves I found them and thieves I shall leave them." [2] The good work in the Welsh borders was rendered permanent by the incorporation of Wales into England and its division into shires.

It is evident that Cromwell liked to be known as a promoter of stern and equal justice, for a series of letters have survived written by suppliants, who either believed him to be a defender of the rights of the weak or, at least, hoped to please by calling him so. Edward Beck, of Manchester, whom he sent to Ireland in 1535, writes:

[1] *Letters and Papers,* X, 130.
[2] *Letters and Papers,* XII, part II, 1237.

"The country is in good peace and quiet, and in greater fear of justice than it has been these forty years." Cromwell made many enemies by his administration of England. None of his modern biographers has been at the pains to point out that he also made many friends. In his character there was joined to that unscrupulous severity which marked all the efficient governments of his time, a trait of humanity not so common. A man suspected of offenses in the North appeals to Cromwell. Sir William Goring writes: "He would rather die than appear before my Lord of Norfolk, he is so extreme. And he trusts you will hear him." [1] Latimer, commending a poor man's cause, writes that he thinks Cromwell was set up "to hear and help the little ones of God in their distress;" [2] and Maude Carew, in a grateful letter, "prays God to prosper and continue his Lordship to the comfort of all poor widows." A prisoner gladly answers Cromwell's agent, sent to look after poor prisoners, by a complaint of evil treatment.[3] Another, asking for further help, quotes his charitable pity in delivering him from Ludgate Prison.[4] The widow of the Marquis of Dorset writes to thank him and ask for more help, because she has "no other succor in all her troubles." [5] She commends to his care her son at Court, to whom he has already shown kindness. "Whenever you shall see him in any large playing or great usual swearing or any other demeanor unmeet for him to use, which I fear me

[1] *Letters and Papers,* VII, 1534.
[2] *Ibid.,* XI, 1374.
[3] *Ibid.,* IX, 431.
[4] *Ibid.,* IX, 1133.
[5] *Ibid.,* V, 926.

shall be very often, I pray you for his father's sake rebuke him." [1]

He evidently had a sympathetic ear for love troubles. Mary Boleyn, the Queen's sister and former mistress of the King, had made a clandestine marriage with Sir William Stafford. The anger of the King and Queen and her powerful relatives of the families of Boleyn and Norfolk was great. In her troubles she writes to Cromwell, saying that her sister, father, brother and uncle are so "cruel against us" she dares not write to them. She knows that her marriage displeases the King and Queen, "But one thing, good Master Secretary, consider: that he was young and love overcame reason. And for my part, I saw so much honesty in him that I loved him as well as he did me; and was in bondage and glad I was to be at liberty; so that for my part I saw that all the world did set so little by me and he so much, that I thought I could take no better way than to take him and forsake all other ways and live a poor honest life with him. For well I might a had a greater man of birth and a higher, but, I ensure you, I could never a had one that should a loved me so well. * * * We have been now a quarter of a year married, * * * but if I were at liberty and might choose, I ensure you, Master Secretary, for my little time I have tried so much honesty to be in him, that I had rather beg my bread with him than to be the greatest Queen christened." And she begs Cromwell, as he has "the name of helping all that need," that he will help them.[2]

[1] *Letters and Papers,* VII, 153.
[2] *Ibid.,* VII, 1655.

At least one other pair of lovers turned to him for help. An unsigned letter has survived, thanking Cromwell for renewing his goodness "in writing to my father for us, as I understand by my dear friend. If I did not trust in you, I would soon tire of life to find my father no better to me than he is. My mother, that was wont in such matters best to persuade him, being taken to God's mercy. * * * As he whom my heart resteth upon regards you more as a father than a master, I will ever as one body with him bear a daughter's affection to you. Your Lordship's most bounden handmaid." [1]

Almost all who give an account of this age allude to the harsh letter Cromwell wrote to the Princess Mary when he was trying to induce her to avoid her father's brutal treatment by accepting the decrees that declared her mother's marriage void—a submission which brought her the Crown of England by her father's will. The letter was hard, but Mary came to feel that Cromwell had stood her friend. The Spanish Ambassador reports: "The King has been all the time furious and Cromwell himself in some danger of his life * * * owing to his having shown sympathy for the Princess." [2] He says that after Mary submitted to her father Cromwell paid his respects to her, begging her pardon for the harsh terms and rude conduct of his former visit. "This she was glad enough to grant, knowing, as she now knows, Cromwell's good intentions and affection toward her, and that he has been, and still is, working for her welfare and the settlement." And the Duchess of Norfolk, whom

[1] *Letters and Papers,* XII, part II, Appendix, 26.
[2] *Calendars, Spanish,* V, part II, pp. 184, 185.

her husband abandoned for another woman, wrote to ask Cromwell's help, "because she has trust in him," having heard "how good he was to the King's daughter in her trouble."[1] The year before Cromwell's death Mary chose him "for her valentine,"[2] which she would hardly have done if she had felt in regard to his conduct toward her as many modern writers have felt.

One of the charges in his attainder was that he had set at liberty persons convicted of misprision of treason and others suspected of treason. Lord Herbert of Cherbury, writing three generations after his death, says: "He was noted in the exercise of judicature to have used much moderation." And the French Ambassador, who despised him because of his humble birth and who disliked his policy, wrote just before his fall: "He shows himself willing to do justice, especially to foreigners."[3]

To exalt the authority of the King as the incarnation of common law, in order to subdue the lawless tendencies bred by feudalism, was the least difficult thing Cromwell helped to do. In that he only had to finish what was begun in the generation before he came to power. When he undertook to free England from connection with an Italianized Papacy, and to limit the political power of the clergy, he began a task harder and more dangerous. The Papacy was Italianized; that is to say the Popes again and again sacrificed the spiritual interest of Christendom to Italian politics or family ambition. When, at the beginning of the fifteenth century, three Popes claimed the tiara, and the strife threatened to destroy the Church,

[1] *Letters and Papers*, Vol. XII, part II, 143.
[2] *Ibid.*, XIV, part II, page 329.
[3] *Ibid.*, XV, 486.

Christendom had met in the Council of Constance, deposed all three Popes, elected another by a conclave where representatives of the five chief nations sat with the Cardinals, decreed that the supreme power of the Church was in a General Council, not in the Pope, and solemnly charged the new Pope with the duty of reforming the Church in head and numbers, reporting as a responsible executive to regularly assembled Councils. That responsibility the succeeding popes had refused to acknowledge, that duty of reform they had failed to carry out in a hundred years. This is no longer a controverted statement. It is conceded by the ablest Roman Catholic historians, and its truth can be seen with unmistakable plainness in the contemporary writings of loyal Churchmen. Such a strictly orthodox clergyman and obedient Churchman as Jacob Wimpheling (1450-1528) has left, in sermons and writings, not only unqualified denunciations of corruption in the Church, but detailed accounts of particular scandalous abuses.[1]

One thing the popes since Constance had done. They had ably restored the temporal power of the Papacy over the States of the Church. This task had absorbed their energies. And it lies on the surface of lives like those of Sixtus IV, Alexander VI, Julius II, Leo X, Clement VII, that they had little enthusiasm for the magnificent ideal of the Pope as the Vicar of Christ, the visible representative of the justice and mercy of God. They used their authority as spiritual heads of Christendom, and the wealth which came from it, largely to gratify the

[1] See Wiskawatoff, Jacob Wimpheling, and Histoire Litteraire de la Alsace—Charles Schmidt.

ambitions and tastes they shared with other princes of the Italian Renascence.

The spectacle of this corrupted and Italianized Papacy had been denounced again and again by Italian writers of all shades of religious opinion from Savonarola to Machiavelli. The world north of the Alps had long watched it with an impatience foretelling exasperation. It was taken for granted by most intelligent laymen that the Church needed a thoroughgoing reformation. In 1495 a friend of the Emperor wrote to tell him of the presence of the King of France in Rome and of his own fear that the King will reform the Church "and so win through all Christendom praise, honor and reputation, which, on grounds both of human and divine right, belongs more to your Imperial Majesty than to him." [1]

As a result of this condition and the prevalent opinion about it, the general loyalty of Christendom to the splendid ideal of the Papacy, which had stood the strain of so many bitter disappointments, was seriously weakened. Biting epigrams were circulating through the world. Like this on Alexander VI, who had been elected Pope by notorious bribery, from which only five out of twenty-three Cardinals were thought to have been free:

"Vendit Alexander cruces, altaria Christi
Vendere jure potest, emerat ille prius."

(Alexander sells Christ's crosses and altars for pelf.
He has a right to sell them—he bought them first himself.)

When an Imperial Ambassador, in a letter which ex-

[1] Chmel Urkunden, etc., zur Geschichte, Maximilian I. Stuttgart lit. Verein, Vol. X, page 56.

presses horror at the iconoclasm of the Lutherans, writes that some of the Cardinals have "sneered at a General Council to reform the Church, and offered to wager ten to one it will never take place;" [1] when another Ambassador writes from Rome to the High Commander of Leon, "since Cardinals sell themselves so cheap, your Lordship ought to consider that it would be impolitic to defer rewarding those who are our friends," [2] it seemed to some minds no longer a question of a theory of the Church, but of an impossible situation.

There were only two things to do: make another attempt to reform the Church, and secure the election of a Pontiff with spiritual enthusiasm, or else decide that the last two hundred years had shown the ideal of the Papacy to be unworkable, abandon it, and establish a series of national Churches, appealing for justification to another Council of Christendom as really representative as that of Constance. All those who believed that the "fullness of power" was given by God to the Pope, stood by the ancient ideal for conscience' sake. And they were joined by people whose conservative temper suggested the fear that truth would perish if traditional institutions were destroyed. On the other hand, men whose radical habits of thought led them to hope that truth and order would survive the fall of ancient institutions to create new forms of expression and guarantees of law, were inclined to destroy the one remanent universal institution of Christendom as no longer fitted to the needs of the world.

A feeling common to those classes of the English peo-

[1] *Calendars, Spanish Papers,* IV, part I, page 835.
[2] *Ibid.,* IV, part II, page 887.

ple who possessed political power enabled the men of radical temper to sway English policy on the question of obedience to the Pope. There was a growing dislike of foreign interference with English affairs, rapidly crystallizing around the throne of the Tudors into the national sentiment which was to be the background of the great output of English energy under Elizabeth. The feeling was old and had been shown before. In the fourteenth century, when Wycliffe, not yet guilty of the crime of heresy, had voiced England's refusal of Papal tribute, he had been the hero of the majority of Englishmen who were neither priests nor monks. When Cromwell came to power, five generations later, this dislike of foreign control was very strong. Circumstances enabled him to evoke and shape it into legislation.

In 1527, Henry VIII had made application to the Papal Court for a divorce from his Queen, Katherine, widow of his older brother Arthur, to whom he had been married eighteen years. There were reasons of state for such a divorce. Henry had but one legitimate child, Mary. No woman had ruled England except Matilda, four hundred and fifty years before. And her reign had been a long anarchy, ended only when she ceded the throne to her cousin Stephen, on condition that at his death her son Henry II should succeed. Henry VIII might well have doubted whether any woman could carry on the policy of the Tudors, for it was impossible to foresee the strength of that loyalty of the mass of the nation to the Tudor dynasty as the guarantee of peace, which afterward sustained the repeatedly shaken thrones of Mary and Elizabeth. And in addition, only the single life of a delicate girl stood between England and the horrors of a certain renewal of civil war over a disputed succession.

If Henry desired to avoid this danger to his dynasty and England, he must obtain from the Church permission to put away his wife and take another who might bear him heirs. He believed that he could obtain this from the Pope. The Church maintained in theory the noble attitude toward the sacredness of the marriage tie which is now enforced upon the adherents of the Roman Catholic communion. But the unreformed abuses of the administration of the Curia rendered it possible for people of wealth and influence to obtain facile divorce. Henry's brother-in-law, the Duke of Suffolk, had two living wives beside the King's sister. And this complicated matrimonial situation had been made legal by Papal bulls and dispensations.[1]

In 1528, Henry's sister Margaret, Queen of Scotland, obtained a divorce from the Earl of Angus on such flimsy grounds that Henry bade Wolsey write her that "the shameless sentence sent from Rome plainly discovereth how unlawfully it was handled," and warn her of the "inevitable damnation of adulterers." [2] Twenty-nine years before the Pope had granted a divorce, which Louis XII of France asked for reasons very similar to those which lay behind Henry's request. When Louis came to the throne in 1498, he had been married for twenty-two years to Joan, daughter of Louis XI, noted for her goodness and the dignity of her character, but unattractive and without children. Louis wished to marry Anne of Brit-

[1] *Anne Boleyn,* by Paul Friedmann. Macmillan, 1884.

[2] *Letters and Papers,* IV, 4131.

tany, his predecessor's widow. Strong reasons of state as well as inclination suggested the match. The throne needed direct heirs, and marriage with the Queen Dowager would keep her hereditary Duchy of Brittany closely bound to the Crown of France. The Pope appointed a commission which granted the divorce, with his approval. Louis immediately married Anne of Brittany. The people resented the injustice to Queen Joan and nicknamed the three commissioners Caiaphas, Herod and Pilate.[1]

Henry had very good reason to expect that the Pope would enable him to put away his wife in order to take another. In his application for divorce he chiefly emphasized spiritual reasons. He said that the French Ambassador, while conducting negotiations about the marriage of the Princess Mary, had suggested that her title to succeed to the English throne was not beyond question, because Henry's marriage to Katherine, his brother's widow, although resting on special Papal dispensation, was against the laws of the Church and the Word of God.[2] This remark, Henry said, had produced increasing torments of conscience for living with his brother's widow, in disobedience to the Word of God. The intimates of the English Court suspected, with good reason, that the most acute motive impelling him to seek this divorce was a passion for one of the Court ladies, Anne Boleyn, a woman of noble blood and vulgar nature, who was skillfully dallying with Henry in order to be-

[1] *De Maulde la Clavière Procédures Politiques du Règne de Louis XII.*

[2] Such a dispensation to marry a brother's widow was not unexampled. Heinrich Deichsler in his Chronicle records under the year 1489 that a Nuremburg patrician married three brothers in succession, sending to Rome to obtain a dispensation. Chroniken der deutschen Städte, V, 352.

come Queen of England. Self-indulgence and flattery had bred in Henry a desperate selfishness and the temper of a tyrant. It is a Nemesis for these sins that his most active motives, which were generally his most unworthy motives, have often seemed to posterity his only motives. The facts, however, indicate beyond a question that Henry's eagerness to marry Anne Boleyn was not all passion, but partly statecraft, clearly seeing the need of male heirs to the throne. When her power over him was failing, Anne felt that the birth of a son would reinstate her in his favor. And her enemies openly rejoiced as soon as it became known that her child was a girl.

It is a superficial view of the complicated character of Henry and the subtle, morbid character of his depravity, to see in his professions of torments of conscience nothing but bold, conscious hypocrisy. French literature has made us familiar with the type of woman at once *galante* and *dévote*. Henry's conscience, too weak to control his conduct, was acutely sensitive. He thought himself to be religious, was proud of his training in theology, and possessed skill as a casuist. Whenever he did a bad thing, he usually succeeded in persuading himself that he had a good motive for it.

However much England might need heirs to the throne, the divorce was a most blatant injustice. Since an indiscretion of her youth,[1] Katherine had lived a life above reproach. By her husband's own saying, she had been a most patient and faithful wife. It is to the credit of the Papacy that Henry, neither by bribes nor threats, could induce the Curia to consent to the divorce. Clement VII

[1] *Calendar of State Papers, Spanish,* supplement to Vols. I and II.

was in great fear of Katherine's nephew, the Emperor Charles V, whose Spanish and Lutheran regiments inflicted on Rome in 1527 a frightful sack, in which all the world, whether they rejoiced at it or deplored it, saw the punishment for the sins of the Curia. But it is unjust to assume that fear was the only motive for refusal. Even shifty and worldly Clement VII, using his office of Pope chiefly to advance his family, probably shrank from dishonoring one of his predecessors and disregarding the appeal of a wronged woman to the visible judgment seat of Christ.

When Cromwell began in in the middle of 1532 to acquire influence in the Royal Council, he found the King trying to force the Pope to grant a divorce from Katherine that would enable him to marry Anne Boleyn. The fate of Wolsey told any man of discernment that the necessary condition of power was to help the King to get what he wanted. The original motives, England's need of more children of the royal blood, and the inclination of passion turned by self-deceiving casuistry into the torments of conscience, were now reinforced by the dominant trait of Henry's character. That habit, called by those who approve of the objects toward which it is turned strength of will, by those who disapprove of them obstinacy, had mastered him. Opposition to a purpose made him more bent on its accomplishment. Cavendish heard the dying Wolsey tell Kingston, the lieutenant of the Tower: "He is sure a prince of a royal courage and hath a princely heart, and rather than he will either miss or want any part of his will or appetite, he will put the loss of one-half his realm in danger. For I assure you I have often kneeled before him in his privy chamber on my knees for the space of an hour or two to persuade him from his will and appetite, but I could never bring to pass to dissuade him therefrom." Cromwell, years afterward, described to the Spanish Ambassador how "the King's whole Council were assembled for three or four hours, and there was not one of them but remained long on his knees before the King, to beg him for the honor of God not to lose so good an opportunity of establishing a friendship so necessary and advantageous, but they had not been able to change his opinion." [1]

Only one thing ever made Henry give way—the clear perception that he was in danger of destroying that consent of the English middle class on which he was basing his throne. He now judged, and the result showed he was right, that the openly expressed sympathy of large numbers of the people for Katherine would not take the form of an irrepressible rebellion aiming to dethrone him, in order to prevent her from being uncrowned.

Whether Cromwell felt the injustice done to Katherine cannot be known. If he did, like many statesmen of his own and succeeding generations, he was not capable of the moral heroism of sacrificing the need of the state to the rights of an individual. No one would be apt to feel more strongly England's need of male heirs to the throne than this hater of disorder, born of that very burgher class to which the Tudor policy appealed.

He also saw in the situation an opportunity of doing something which would please the King, and at the same time be, from his point of view, of great service to Eng-

[1] *Letters and Papers,* X, page 298.

land. That was to make two changes in the English Church. First, to remove it from the overlordship of popes, spending the money they drew from England in wars to create princedoms for their relatives, and, second, to destroy the independent political power of the clergy. The first intent was finally expressed by making the Church of England a national Church, using in service the vernacular instead of the universal Latin, constituting its own Primate, without the authority of the representative of Christendom. The second intent was carried out by subjecting the clergy to the efficient control of the Crown.

Before Cromwell attained influence in the Royal Council, Henry may have thought of revolting from the traditionally established Papal authority. But if he had thought of schism from the body of Christendom, he had not yet determined upon it. In 1531 he had compelled the Convocations of the English clergy to acknowledge him as Supreme Head of the English Church, "so far as the law of Christ allows." But that title was not entirely new. It was unpleasant to the defenders of the Papal "fullness of power," but it did not necessarily imply a denial of the authority of the Pope, nor was its assumption taken by the Papacy as a declaration of schism. Practically it was quite consistent with a method of ecclesiastical management which the Papacy had conceded to nations by Concordats. Henry had induced Parliament to vote that annates, *i. e.*, the whole or a part of the first year's income of certain ecclesiastical offices, paid to the Papacy by custom which had become law, should be withheld. But this did not necessarily imply schism, for the

Pragmatic Sanction of Bourges, under which the French Church was managed from 1438 to 1516, forbade, under penalties, the payment of annates to the Pope. And the English act against annates was not final. It would only become law in case the King failed to come to an agreement with the Pope. Henry sent word to Clement that the usual annates would be paid if they could agree. And Henry and Francis, at an interview, promised to stand together to force the Pope to do what each wanted. The Acts of Parliament were as yet only threats to bring the Pope to terms with the King.

But, soon after Cromwell's rise to great influence in the Royal Council, this policy of threats and pressure, which had often been tried before by kings who had no intention of seceding permanently from the Papal obedience, was changed for a policy recently used by some cantons of the Swiss Confederacy and some princes and free cities of Germany. The English nation through its constituted heads denied the right of the Bishop of Rome to exercise any jurisdiction over the Church of England.

This withdrawal from Papal obedience did not then imply in any supporter of it who professed willingness to submit to a general council, the denial of the traditional creeds. It was many generations before the dogma of the infallibility of the Pope was made de fide. It had been most strenuously and explicitly denied, at some time during the last two centuries, by each of the leading countries of Christendom. Even the doctrine of the Papal fullness of power, the theoretical base of the conception of the Church as an absolute monarchy, though long asserted, might still be freely attacked on canonical grounds. At no time since the earliest suggestion of it had the idea been fully accepted by all Churchmen. And in the early fifteenth century, the Council of Constance, the most widely representative assembly of Christendom ever held, expressly denied it, and asserted that the Pope was responsible to the hierarchy and the representatives of the nations of Christendom. Schism was a sin, but it did not become heresy unless it was accompanied by the refusal to submit to a general council of the Church. Neither was the idea of a national Church a novelty among men who had no quarrel with dogma. For example, in 1495 when Henry VIII was yet a boy, and long before Luther and other organizers of heretical churches had appeared, a South German nobleman wrote an open letter to the Duke of Saxony, suggesting that the political intrigues of the Pope in support of the King of France would be sufficient ground for the Diet, "because of such wickedness, to withdraw obedience for a time from the Pope, and set up in the place of the Pope a national patriarch.[1]

We cannot conclude, therefore, from his action that Cromwell had adopted at this time any of the new theological opinions. As a patron of the New Learning he probably disliked some traditional practices like pilgrimage, the veneration of relics and the sale of indulgences. But men who did not secede from the Roman Communion, men like Erasmus and More, had denounced the abuses which had gathered round those pious customs.

[1] Der Traum Hans von Hermansgrün. Ulmann. Forschungen zur deutschen geschichte, XX, page 187.

The mediæval ascetic ideal seemed to him, as it did to most men of the New Learning, to fetter the human spirit. But those most active servants of the orthodox creed and the traditional Church system, the Jesuits, were soon to break away from it. His conduct is not sufficient reason for assuming that he sympathized with the new theological opinions. And we know at least two things which indicate plainly a lack of sympathy with heresy. His will made in 1529 leaves ten marks a year, equal to some three hundred and fifty dollars, "to hire a priest to sing for my soul for seven years." [1] And in May, 1530, he wrote to Wolsey, "the fame is that Luther has departed this life. I would he had never been born." [2]

As to the question, since so ingeniously and warmly debated, whether the withdrawal from the Roman obedience was a schism, or the lawful assertion of the rights of the English Church against Papal usurpation, it is not probable that Cromwell took the smallest interest in it one way or the other. When a thing had to be done, he was not the sort of man to care much what it was to be called. Moreover, his mind was probably little affected by ideals of the Church. The intimate friends he made in his days of obscurity, and kept in his days of splendor, indicate that he cared for the things of the soul as well as for those of the mind; but he was a lawyer, not a clergyman; a politician, not an ecclesiastic. His habitual mood made him more actively interested in the glory of England than in the glory of the Kingdom of God.

In addition, he seems to have gravitated by natural in-

[1] *Letters and Papers,* IV, 5772.
[2] *Ibid.,* IV, 6391.

clination toward an opportunist point of view. His perception that something ought to be done and his decision as to what was best to do, were not apt to be obscured by theories. Some of the rulers of men who have been most useful in dealing with problems of politics complicated by hatred arising from discussions about religion, have been subject to this secular temper or have been inclined toward the opportunist view point. Under Elizabeth, England escaped the dangers of feudal reaction and civil war about religion which ruined France because the Valois could not master them. Under Henry IV, who thought "Paris worth a mass," France laid down the torch and the sword for the plough and the loom. And it seems probable that the essential teachings of Jesus Christ about the Father in Heaven, had freer course under the opportunist peace of secular-minded Elizabeth and Henry than amid the fanatic hatred of the Huguenot wars. But, useful as these rulers of secular mood and opportunist temper have been in times of intense hatred bred by differences about religion, certain minds find it difficult to be just to them. The man whose strongest emotions turn him toward the service of the church, is only too prone to conclude that he who in times of religious strife looks first to the safety of the state, must be an infidel. The man who holds that a given form in church or state is of divine origin, thinks the opportunist must have no ideal, because his ideal is not definite. And the conservative, whose reverence for institutions outweighs his hopes of progress, is always apt to accuse the radical of undermining the moral foundations of human society. This was the attitude of Reginald Pole, Cardinal for England. He denounced Cromwell as an incarnate devil, denying the very distinction between right and wrong.[1]

But no mood defends a ruler against the temptations of the power to do great things. If the patriot is tempted to forget God, the ecclesiastic seems to be tempted to hate man, which, according to John, makes him unable to love God. The rule of ecstatically and sincerely devout Mary was certainly no less cruel than that of her father. And the maxim, "One may do evil that good may come," has been labeled in common speech as having belonged to the practice of Machiavellians and of Jesuits. Cromwell gained power by helping the King to do what he wanted, and, like almost all men of ability in politics, he was ambitious. But there are reasons for what he did, which millions of her people of his own and succeeding generations have thought to be connected with the best good of England. It is as superfluous to accuse him of being moved only by the base ambitions of a greedy and flattering adventurer, as it would be to assert that Pole, in standing by the Roman obedience, was bribed by the red robe or a cardinal and the income equivalent to $100,000 which came to him from his benefices.[2]

For his plan of breaking from the Papacy, Cromwell could count on no assistance from the higher clergy, a body very distinct from the parish priests. It is true that only three of the twenty-six English bishops were now absentee Italians. But many English bishops, abbots and members of the cathedral chapters, believed that the Pope's authority was given by God. All preferred it to

[1] *Apologia ad Carolum Quintum.*
[2] Philip's *Life of Pole,* Vol. II, page 294.

the rule of the laity. Both these grounds of scruple were expressed in the protest of the Archbishop of Canterbury, Primate of the Church, that no concessions made by Convocation were to be understood as implying any restriction of the power of the Roman Pontificate, or any infringement upon the liberties of the Province of Canterbury. And many things indicate that the clergy gave a grudging assent to the revolt from the Papal authority, which left them without shelter against the power of the King.

This reluctance of the clergy to submit on equal terms with the laity to the control of the laws, was one of the strongest reasons why Cromwell thought it best for England to separate from Rome. And the control of the laws meant to him the control of the King, the guarantee of peace and order, the symbol and defender of the nation. American ecclesiastical establishments are entirely voluntary, they have almost no endowments, and this puts them so entirely in the hands of the laity whenever they choose to use their power, that it is difficult for an American to appreciate the situation in England at the beginning of the sixteenth century. The clergy were a corporate body, freed from the ordinary jurisdiction of the common law, deciding matters connected with marriage and wills by courts constituted by themselves, having sanctuaries where the criminal who entered was free from arrest, enjoying an income two and a half times that of the Crown, owning real estate estimated at one-third the total of the kingdom, casting in the persons of the twenty-six bishops and the twenty-seven mitred abbots almost two-thirds of the votes in Henry VIII's first House of

Lords, and able as great landed proprietors to exert influence on elections to the House of Commons. And this formidable body confessed supreme allegiance to a ruler living in Rome whose predecessors had repeatedly claimed the divine and unquestionable right to dictate to kings and nations about the conduct of their affairs.

A corporation legally so independent and politically so powerful would not be suffered to exist in any modern state. Large numbers of men of all shades of religious opinion, thought this temporal power and political independence of the clergy, appealing to the irresponsible divine authority of the Pope, to be injurious both to Church and State. The same attitude under modern conditions has been taken in our own day by the Roman Catholic people of Italy. They have felt it to be intolerable that an ecclesiastical jurisdiction independent of the laws of Italy should exist at Rome. Henry VIII expressed the views of numbers of statesmen in all countries of Europe, when he wrote to James of Scotland: "What more intolerable calamity may there be to a Christian prince than unjustly to be defeated of the righteous jurisdiction within his own realm, to be a king by name, but not in deed? To be a ruler without regiment over his own liege people?"

Cromwell, a man of the Renascence, who had thrown off mediæval ideals, was trying to form out of England a modern state, by that process of unification under an absolute throne through which all the states of Europe which early achieved nationality passed. He wanted, therefore, to make the King the efficient head of the Church. He determined to loose upon the clergy the dislike of their independence and the jealousy of their power felt by a part of the people of England.

Unmistakable instances of this feeling appear in contemporary writings. In 1514 Richard Hunne was arrested for heresy. In reply, he brought a criminal charge against the clergy who accused him. He was found hanging in his cell in the ecclesiastical prison, and the Chancellor of the Bishop was accused of murdering him. The Bishop wrote to Wolsey, asking that the prisoner might be tried by a commission of the Royal Council. "Assured am I that if my Chancellor be tryed by any twelve men in London, they be so maliciously set in favour of heresy that they will condemn my clerk though he be as innocent as Abel."[1] A popular pamphlet of 1527, in the form of a petition to the King reciting the abuses of the clergy, asks rhetorically: "What remedy? Make laws against them? Are they not stronger in your own Parliament house than yourself? What law can be made so strong against them that they, either with money or else with policy, will not break or set it at naught?"[2]

On the 8th of November, 1529, the Imperial Ambassador writes: "Sure as I am that your Imperial Majesty does not care for mere speculation as to the future, which after all is an art for which I am not at all fitted, I will not venture upon predictions. * * * Respecting the clergy of this kingdom I may say, without having recourse to the said art of divination, that they will be for certain both punished and reformed, fined and mulcted: for they are generally very rich, from which circumstance

[1] Hall's *Chronicle*, page 579.
[2] *Supplication for Beggars.*

and hatred of the Cardinal (Wolsey) they are an object of envy to the nobles and commoners of this country." [1] A month later he writes that the reform of the clergy will be pushed: "First in the hope of plunder by sale of Church property, second because they hope by antagonizing the clergy to persuade the people to consent to this marriage, because nearly all the people here hate the priests." [2]

This dislike of the wealth and power of the clergy, had been expressed in laws before Cromwell gained great influence.[3] In 1529 Parliament had passed an act about the oppressions and exactions of the ecclesiastical courts in the probate of wills, which, in spite of promises, "be nothing reformed or amended, but greatly augmented and increased against right and justice and to the great impoverishment of the King's subjects." [4] It had also been enacted, for the increase of "devotion and good opinion of the laity toward spiritual persons," that no spiritual persons "should farm or buy or sell for lucre;" and that an ordinary priest might not hold more than one "benefice with cure of souls," and must live in the place where his duty as a pastor was.[5] A third act had been aimed at what the anti-clerical chronicler Hall calls "the great polling and extreme exaction which spiritual men used in taking corpse presents or

[1] *Calendars, Spanish,* IV, part I, page 325.

[2] *Ibid.,* IV, part I, 367.

[3] Mr. Lea has pointed out that the cahiers of the Spanish Cortés for two hundred years show a similar dislike of the Spanish people, caused by clerical privileges before the law and jurisdiction over civil matters. Camb. Hist. Reformation, page 675.

[4] *Revised Statutes,* I, 247.

[5] *Statutes of the Realm,* III, 292.

mortuaries, for the children of the defunct should all die of hunger, go a-begging rather than they would of charity give to them the silly (simple) cow which the dead man ought, (owed to the priest) if he had only one."

Cromwell, from his first entry into the Royal Council, appears to have been anxious to express this feeling against the clergy in the form of a general attack upon the clerical abuses under which many of the laity groaned. This was finally done in the form of a petition of the Commons against the Ordinaries (judges of the spiritual courts), presented to the King 18th of March, 1532. Hall says the petition was presented after a long debate over "the griefs of temporal men caused by exactions of the spirituality." Four drafts of this "Book against the Clergy" are among the English records. Two are written in the hand of Cromwell's chief clerk; two in a strange hand; three of them are corrected and interlined in Cromwell's hand.[1] Hence several writers on the period conclude that Cromwell was the author. It is not improbable. He was one of those London citizens among whom the feeling against the clergy was exceedingly strong. He had done business for many of them and they knew his capacity. He understood the clergy from his relations to Wolsey. Whether this complaint against the clergy originated among the representatives of London, or, as was often the case with petitions, was sent down by the Crown, it may easily be true that Cromwell was asked to write or revise it. The recently made suggestion that he artificially created the discontent it expressed, is a conclusion not only superfluous but against the facts. There is abundant reason

[1] *Life and Letters of Thomas Cromwell,* Roger B. Merriman.

to believe that the majority of those English citizens who possessed political influence, felt what Sir William Fairfax wrote to Cromwell: "There will never be peace in England so long as spiritual men have so much temporal power."[1]

It is more than probable that Cromwell was the framer of a series of Acts of Parliament which did four things—defended the Crown against wars over the succession, cut England from the Papacy, stripped the clergy of wealth and political power and subjected them to the King, conferred upon the Crown powers finally rising almost to summary court-martial to meet the attempt of Papal Curia to force England back to obedience. The vigor and unity of this legislation, and the skill and energy of its administration, indicate a single mind at the centre. The contrast between the eight years of Cromwell's power and the years which preceded and followed them, strongly suggests him as the author of this policy; subject always to the powerful will, the tyrannous temper, the selfish impulses and the exceedingly able judgment of Henry.

To accomplish this fourfold purpose Cromwell used Parliament. Henry had consulted Parliament comparatively little before Cromwell came to power. During the first twenty years of his reign statutes were passed only in eight. Wolsey feared or disliked Parliament. It met once between 1515 and 1529, and was soon dissolved after a reluctant grant of money. On the contrary, there was legislation during six out of the eight

[1] *Letters and Papers,* XII, part I, 192.

years of Cromwell's power, and the laws passed during his administration fill nearly forty per cent. of the pages which record the legislation of the thirty-eight years of Henry's reign. It must be remembered, of course, that the Parliament of Henry VIII was not the Parliament of to-day. Very few writers on Henry VIII's reign for the last twenty years permit their readers to forget that. We are told repeatedly that it was a "packed" House of Commons. So it was. One of the complaints of the Northern insurgents of 1536 was that "Parliaments ought to have knights of the shire and burgesses at their own election, not such men as the King will appoint." [1] But the reign of Henry VIII was not the only time when the members of Parliament did not represent the free choice of large numbers of the English people. The House of Commons was chosen under greater or less pressure from the Crown or the territorial aristocracy down to the nineteenth century. An over emphasis on Cromwell's activity in elections, as if his conduct had been uniquely tyrannous, may easily produce a false impression. The facts are these: He was in power during two general elections. Concerning those elections there have survived two electioneering reports, one from the Duke of Norfolk,[2] the other from the Earl of Southampton,[3] and letters in regard to six elections.[4] These letters and reports show that divergent opinion was not entirely suppressed for there was opposition to the Court candidate in at least three places, and, with one exception, the often quoted

[1] *Letters and Papers,* XI, 1244.
[2] *Ibid.,* XIV, part I, 800.
[3] *Ibid.,* XIV, part I, page 224.
[4] Compare *Ibid.,* X, 903; XIV, 564, 598, 672, 695, 706, and others.

case of the Canterbury election, they could be duplicated again and again in the election correspondence of the seventeenth and eighteenth centuries. And even the Canterbury election is not unparalleled for the next two hundred and fifty years.

Cromwell did his best to fill Parliament with the King's friends. It was not too difficult a task for he was able to find a large body of King's friends to choose from. And members opposed to the royal policy could be to a large extent controlled. For a century and a half later, strong opposition to the Crown was dangerous. And it was much more dangerous in the sixteenth than in the seventeenth century. Wolsey had told the citizens of London that to oppose the royal loan might "fortune to cost some their heads." The policy of suppressing opposition in the councils of the nation by fear, was freely used by Cromwell's opponents. A single example will make this plain. Cromwell disliked the Bill of Six Articles. The approval of Henry for it marked the rising influence of that alliance between his deadly enemies, Gardiner, Bishop of Winchester, and the Duke of Norfolk, which was to bring him to the scaffold. When it came down from the Lords, he sent a message to his friends in the House of Commons, "that if any man should stand against the bill earnestly the same should put himself in great danger of his life." Thomas Brook, Alderman of Calais, spoke against it, and Cromwell sent a personal message to him telling him as he loved his life not to speak against the bill. Brook continued his opposition, and Cromwell, meeting him afterward, said, "he never knew man to play so desperate a part as to speak against that bill, unless he made a reckoning to be either hanged or burned; but God," said he, "hath mightily preserved thee, whereof I am glad." On his return to Calais, Brook was arrested for heresy, as Kingston, the lieutenant of the Tower, had threatened in open Parliament. He would undoubtedly have perished but for his bold and skillful defense and an order from Cromwell that he should be sent to London for examination.[1] Cromwell had no objections to this pressure upon electors and members, common then and, by other methods, for generations afterward; except that he did not want it successfully used by his opponents.

But the conclusion that such unscrupulous terrorizing of opponents reduced Parliament to a negligible quantity is mistaken. Even under Henry VIII packing and controlling Parliament had its limits. Bills supported by the Crown were withdrawn and amended, and Henry found there were things he could not do.

That Cromwell, when it was necessary, tried to force Parliament to do what the King wanted done is not so much a thing that can be proved, as a conjecture supported by scattered facts and strongly suggested by probable inference from the political opinions which must have underlaid his policy as Chief Minister of the Crown. The modern ideals of Parliamentary government were unknown. To the Lancastrian constitutionalism which had worked so badly in the fifteenth century,[2] Cromwell

[1] Catley's *Foxe's Book of Martyrs,* Vol. V, 502-519. This narrative finds support in the *Letters and Papers,* and Foxe could easily have known about it. Foxe is a strong partisan. It has been shown that he is inaccurate in some instances. But the present habit of disbelieving everything he says for no particular reason except that he says it, is not judicious.

[2] It will be sufficient to cite the opinion of Stubb's *Constitutional History,* Chap. XVIII, sections 363-373.

preferred a Crown as powerful as possible. He believed that the will of the King was the best safeguard for the interests of the nation. But the nature of the absolutism he promoted ought not to be overlooked. The Tudor absolutism crushed opposition ruthlessly, but while breaking the two chief pillars of the mediæval state, the nobility and the clergy, it was forced to find a base in the national consent. The potential of liberty destroyed under Hapsburg, Valois and Bourbon increased under Henry VIII and his children. "The House of Commons, down to the electoral reforms of the nineteenth century, was the House as they created it." They added or revived about ninety boroughs and the twelve shires of Wales, nearly doubling the strength of the lower House.[1]

Cromwell used the royal power to flatter or dragoon members of Parliament, but he appealed, by printing press, pulpit and in Parliament, to national support for his bold policy, and the result shows that he must have obtained it. No English King was ever threatened by greater dangers than those Henry incurred in 1533 and 1534. He had no standing army, and was obliged to depend for defense on the levies raised by commissions issued to loyal gentlemen. His regular expenses were exceeding the Crown income. No one could say of him as was said of the King of France that he could tax "as much as he pleased." Wolsey's experience with the Amicable Loan had warned him not to repeat the experiment of heavy taxation without grant of Parliament. A throne cannot rest on nothing. If the mass of the nation did not support Henry's throne, why did it not fall?

[1] Poole's *Atlas,* Vol. II, Map XXIII.

Nor was Henry trying to disarm his people and reduce them to the helplessness of the peasants who were slaughtered by the nobles in the French Jacquerie, or massacred by the princes in the German peasant revolt. Legislation five times repeated forbade the use of the crossbow and the hand gun, those facile but as yet less efficient foreign weapons which were causing the "decay of the ancient artillery of England."[1] Every man between seventeen and sixty must keep a bow and shoot regularly at the butts. He was forbidden to practice at less than two hundred yards. For every boy between seven and seventeen his parents must provide a bow of elm or hazel. And bows must be sold cheap that every one might buy.[2]

It was not by overriding the feelings of the mass of Englishmen who had political power that the ends of the Crown under Henry VIII were accomplished. It was by using and directing them.

Events gave Cromwell opportunity to move toward the accomplishment of his purpose.

February 22, 1533, the Pope confirmed the election of Thomas Cranmer as Archbishop of Canterbury, Primate of England, to succeed Warham. In May the new Archbishop secretly cited the King to answer a charge of living unlawfully with his brother's wife, and declared his marriage to Katherine null and void. He followed the sentence by the declaration that the King's marriage to Anne Boleyn, privately celebrated four months before,

[1] Tract on *Decaye of England*. In 1541, when guns had improved, every inhabitant of a city, borough or market town was expressly freed from this prohibition, allowed to keep a long gun and practice at a mark.

[2] *Statutes of the Realm;* also *St. Paul's Magazine,* Vol. V, page 330.

was lawful. On June 1st, Anne was crowned Queen in Westminster Hall with great splendor. This whole procedure had been planned by the Crown, and was defended beforehand by an act of Parliament, passed in February, prohibiting "appeals to Rome in causes of matrimony, divorce, etc." The Pope answered by a sentence declaring the marriage to Anne null and her children illegitimate, and threatening the King with excommunication unless he repudiated her and took back Katherine (July 11, 1533).[1]

Henry made every preparation to meet the threatened excommunication and defend the succession to the throne. He tried vainly to persuade the obstinately honest Katherine to withdraw her appeal to Rome, offering, if she did so, to recognize Mary's right to succeed to the Crown in case he left no children by Anne Boleyn. Then he appealed in the ancient formula, "from the Pope ill informed to the Pope better informed," and a pamphlet appeared containing an "address from the King's Council to the residue of his loving subjects." It exhorted them to "despise the Pope" and stand by a marriage which "sets this realm in the way of true heirs." The Parliament sessions of 1534 and 1535 produced the legislation necessary to carrying out the intentions of the Government. It was contained in several bills which may be grouped with two chief acts, Of Succession, and Of Supremacy. Succeeding supplementary acts fell under the same heads.

The Act of Succession, "calling to remembrance the great divisions which in time past hath been in the realm by reason of several titles pretended to the Crown of the

[1] Pococke, *Records of the Divorce*, II, App. 677.

same . . . whereof hath ensued great destruction of man's blood," declared the issue of Henry and Anne heirs to the Crown, adjudged the penalty of treason to any one obstinately and maliciously impugning their right, and required an oath from every subject to keep the whole contents of this act. A refusal of the oath was equivalent to a denial of the act.[1]

The Act of Supremacy, repudiating the authority of the laws of any foreign prince, potentate or prelate, made the King Supreme Head of the Church of England. The clergy might pass no canons without his assent. He was authorized to appoint a commission of thirty-two, sixteen clergymen and sixteen lay members of Parliament, to revise or repeal existing canons with their help and advice. From these two groups of acts concerning the Succession and the Headship of the Church, the threads of Cromwell's legislation and administration lead out to the accomplishment of his fourfold purpose—to avoid the danger of civil war over the Crown, break with Rome, destroy the political power of the clergy, and defend what was done.

For it needed defense. There were in England men whose devotion to the ancient ways would not permit them to see the power of the clergy and obedience to the Pope destroyed without a struggle. On Easter, 1532, Peto, a friar of the Franciscan Observant Monastery at Greenwich, was invited to preach before the King. He denounced the marriage with Anne and warned Henry to repent lest he receive the punishment of Ahab, whose blood was licked up by dogs. When the preacher was

[1] *Statutes of the Realm.*

answering Peto, the next Sunday, two friars interrupted the sermon by denouncing him as one of "the four hundred prophets into whom the spirit of lying has entered, seeking to establish the succession of adultery." [1] Peto and one of his supporters were reprimanded and sent out of England. About a year later the Warden of a Franciscan convent in Southampton preached in defense of the Papal authority, exhorting the people to stand and suffer martyrdom for it. Cromwell had him brought to London for examination, and then sent him back to his convent.

In 1533 many of the clergy, in the pulpit and the confessional, denounced the King's marriage and the denial of the Papal authority. The most effective of these appeals to popular sympathy for Katherine and devotion to the Pope, was made by the Holy Maid of Kent, a nun who for many years had great influence because of her visions and miracles. She was thought to be connected in some way with a letter from heaven written by Mary Magdalen to a widow in London, with Jesus, Maria, in gold letters at its head. And those associated with her related, among other things, how the devil, when she resisted his temptations, had spat in her face, and that she showed the napkin with which she wiped it, "black and stinking," to her confessor.[2] She prophesied that the King would in a short time lose his kingdom, and said she had "seen the place prepared for him in hell." [3] She, two monks, two friars and two priests, accused of

[1] Harpsfield (1519-1575), *The Pretended Divorce*, etc., page 202, Camden Soc., 1878; also Stow's *Annals*.

[2] *Letters and Papers*, VII, 72.

[3] *Ibid.*, VI, 1419.

having circulated her prophecies, were attainted of treason by Parliament and executed in May, 1534. On the scaffold the two friars were offered their lives if they would acknowledge the Act of Supremacy The nun had publicly confessed, in the presence of the others, that she had deceived the people by false miracles. This confession may have been made in the hope of saving her life. But one of those who died with her sent word to Cromwell that he had been "miserably deceived by that false and dissembling woman." [1] And Sir Thomas More wrote: "Cromwell has done a very meritorious deed in bringing to light such detestable hypocrisy, so that others may take warning and be afraid to set forth their own devilish dissembled falsehood under the colour of the wonderful word of God." [2]

Together with Fisher, Bishop of Rochester, the most distinguished and respected of the English bishops, Sir Thomas More, ex-chancellor of England, had been arrested for misprision of treason in concealing the nun's prophecies. He said that he had been skeptical about her revelations, refused to listen to anything she said about the King, and warned her of danger. No steps were taken against him, but Fisher was attainted and condemned to the loss of all his property and imprisonment during the King's pleasure. The confiscation was remitted on payment of one year's revenue of his bishopric and he was not kept in prison.

When the Oath of Succession, by which all subjects were to be sworn to obedience to the King and Queen and

[1] *Letters and Papers,* VII, 138.
[2] *Ibid.,* VII, 287.

their heirs, and not to any other within this realm, nor to any foreign authority nor potentate, and to defend the whole contents of the Act of Succession, was offered, every Englishman asked to take it did so; except some of the Franciscan friars, the ex-Chancellor Sir Thomas More, Fisher, Bishop of Rochester, and a few others of less note.

The Government closed the convents of the Franciscans, and in June, 1534, threw about two hundred of their members into prison. Most of them were soon permitted to go either to Ireland, France or Scotland, but thirty-two were sent to prisons in various parts of England. The jails of England then, and for generations afterward, were cold and haunted by infectious diseases. Few survived a long confinement in them. Three years later only eight of these brave monks remained alive, and they were at last allowed to go to Belgium.

Sir Thomas More and Bishop Fisher offered to take an oath to the succession of the children of Henry and Anne, but not in the form prescribed; nor would they swear to the whole contents of the Act implying a rejection of the Papal sentence annulling the marriage. They were committed to the Tower, April, 1534.

Their refusal to take the oath was a dangerous incident. The English clergy had voted in Convocation in accordance with the legislation of Parliament, but there was great opposition among them, not only to lay control, but also to the denial of the Papal authority. The Government began to be aware that in the confessional, in the pulpit, in private conversation, the nation was being urged to stand by the Pope and resist the King. They felt it necessary to take strenuous action.

It was the duty of a pope to extirpate heresy and subdue schism. Previous popes had again and again appealed to all good Christians to do this by the sword. And the temper of the modern Curia had not changed. The College of Cardinals wrote to the Emperor in March, 1524, telling him: "that former Emperors did not earn their great reputation by expelling the French, conquering the English nor subjecting Italy, but by making war on the Jews, putting heretics to death and subduing Africa to the Christian obedience. They exhorted him to follow their example by concluding peace with France, making war with the Turks and trampling under foot and extirpating the Lutheran heresy."[1]

Cromwell wished to meet the attitude frankly expressed to him by the Imperial Ambassador, "that if the Pope were to fulminate censures * * * which would deprive the King of his title and deliver his kingdom to those who took possession, it would be the most just and catholic title that any prince could have."[2] An Act of Parliament was passed in the end of 1534 making it treason to deny any of the King's titles, or to pronounce maliciously by words or writings that the King was heretic, schismatic, tyrant, infidel or usurper.

Under this Act, the Carthusian monks were required to acknowledge expressly that Henry was Supreme Head of the Church of England. The result was one of the pitiable tragedies which continued intermittently down into

[1] *Calendars, Spanish,* Vol. II, page 609.
[2] *Letters and Papers,* VIII, page 371.

the seventeenth century, because the conscience of some Englishmen made them traitors in the eyes of others. The Carthusian monks were honored of all men until religion and patriotism came into conflict, and they had proved the honesty of their convictions by their lives, before they sealed them with martyr's blood. The priors of these convents finally pleaded guilty to declaring that "the King is not Supreme Head on earth of the Church of England." They were executed May 4, 1535, by the awful method of the legal punishment for treason, their leader declaring at the gallows that he was there because "Holy Mother Church has decreed otherwise than the King and Parliament, and rather than disobey the Church he was ready to die." Six weeks later three more were executed on the same charge. For two years the other brethren were confined in their convent, and every effort was made by sermons and books to persuade them to give up their allegiance to the Pope. Under this treatment and the pressure of harsh discipline, twenty of them took the oath acknowledging the royal supremacy in May, 1537. Twelve recalcitrants went to prison, where nine of them soon died. The remaining three were sent to the gallows.

Their fate moved little pity in the minds of those who approved the policy they opposed. Executions were very common. Scores of men were hanged for petty offenses against the common law. Death, therefore, did not seem so severe a penalty as it does now.

Cromwell appears to have had a strong trait of humaneness in him, but it is probable that he thought of these executions for the safety of the state as calmly as his opponents, Gardiner and Pole, when they came to the head of affairs, took the burning of nearly three hundred men whose conscience forbade them to consent to the destruction of the church established during Cromwell's administration.

Fisher was found guilty of treason by a jury and beheaded in June, 1535. He ascended the scaffold meekly and bravely, as became an honest old bishop dying for conscience' sake.

Sir Thomas More was condemned to death on the 1st of July. An acknowledgment of the Royal Supremacy or a denial of the Pope's power to depose the King or invalidate his marriage, would at once have procured his liberty. There was difficulty about the legal evidence to convict him, for he was a skilled lawyer, and had kept silence about his opinions. The testimony of Richard Rich, the Solicitor General, to a private conversation in the Tower was used to justify a verdict, and More denounced Rich in open court as a perjurer. More was the most celebrated of living Englishmen, the worthy intimate of Erasmus. His virtues were as well known as his learning, and all men loved him, except the friends of heretics whom he had pursued to the death with conscientious severity and thought "worse than murderers." [1] Everybody, including his own family, tried to persuade him to conform, but he smilingly refused. In the writings of his youth he had rejected the ascetic ideal, pilgrimage, fasting and the use of relics, questioned the exclusive priesthood of the clergy, impugned the good faith of the popes, and satirized their influence upon political moral-

[1] *More's Works*, page 901.

ity.[1] But when reform deepened into revolution he, like most of the older humanists, took alarm. His hopes for the progress of truth gave way to a fear for the stability of institutions, and the bold advocate of religious liberty and the abolition of private property, persecuted heretics fiercely and died in defense of the Papacy. In earlier years he advised Henry not to print that treatise for the Supremacy of the Pope which had earned the royal title of Defender of the Faith. But his study of the question under the stress of revolution converted him into a believer in the Papal Supremacy, even as similar study changed Luther from an adherent into an opponent of the Pope, and More died for his convictions with such beautiful simplicity that it seemed easy. When he laid his life on the altar of God he did not think too highly of the offering or take himself too seriously even as a martyr. Kneeling on the scaffold, the last gleam of his sunny humor played over the uplifted axe. He swept aside his long beard, saying, "Pity that should be cut; that has not committed treason."

To modern judgment the execution of these men seems both a crime and a blunder. It must be remembered that in the sixteenth century the killing of men for opinions was practised by all governments and approved by religious teachers of almost all types. Lutherans, Calvinists, Zwinglians, Anglicans, Roman Catholics were agreed that it was the right and, if needful, the duty of the state to repress false opinions by the sword. When More urged that he should not be put in peril of his life for opinion, Cromwell replied it was as just to put men in

[1] Utopia.

peril before the law for opinions dangerous to the state as for opinions dangerous to the church, and More, when in office, had sternly enforced the laws against heresy. More could only reply that the opinions for whose denial he had condemned men to death were old and held in many countries; this opinion which he denied was new and held in one country.[1]

More and Fisher, like the Carthusians, were appointed to be tried because they were the most conspicuous defenders of the Papacy. When the Government felt it had made clear its determination to suppress without faltering all attacks upon the succession to the throne, executions stopped. More's son, condemned also for refusing the oath, was pardoned.[2]

Cranmer felt that the execution of More and Fisher was a blunder. He advised that their offer to swear to the succession in their own words should be accepted. Cromwell wrote to him that the King could not agree, because he felt "that manner of swearing, if it should be suffered, might be an utter destruction of his whole cause and to the effect of the law." This letter only expresses what the King wanted to give out as the reason for severity. It does not necessarily show either Cromwell's own feeling or the real though perhaps unconscious motives of Henry.

There are no signs of Cromwell's feeling about Fisher, unless this is one. Antonio Bonvisi, an Italian merchant living in London, sent meat, wine and jelly regularly to the two prisoners; and More wrote him with charcoal on

[1] *More's Examination.*

[2] *Life of Sir Thomas More,* by Cressacre More.

the eve of execution a beautiful letter of gratitude and friendship. It was shown in court that he had done this kindness to Fisher. He had long been a close friend of Cromwell and the friendship continued intimate.[1] Fisher was a sincere ecclesiastic, unable to conceive of the English State as existing outside of the Roman Church. There was good reason to believe that he had not concealed his opinions from friends. The upshot of those opinions makes evident to us what Cromwell suspected, that, if excommunication produced either insurrection or invasion, Fisher would not stand by the Crown against the adherents of the Pope. He had frequent secret conferences with the Spanish Ambassador as to the best means of thwarting the royal policy. At a time when Chapuys was urging Charles V to forcibly interfere in the affairs of England, "A work as pleasing in the eyes of God as war upon the Turk," he writes: "Bishop Fisher advises prompt action on the part of your Majesty, such as I recommended in one of my last dispatches. Indeed, not many days ago he sent me word to say that strong measures must now be taken." [2]

More, on the other hand, maintained silence on the Royal Supremacy, would neither affirm nor deny it when questioned in Court and had no dealings with any foreign ambassador. There are strong indications that Cromwell deeply regretted his death. When he heard he had first refused the oath, he cried out, "He would rather his own son had his head stricken off, for displeasure and suspicion would now be aroused in the King's mind."

[1] *Letters and Papers,* VIII, page 329; X, No. 439.
[2] *Calendars, Spanish,* Vol. IV, pp. 812, 813, 821.

In a note from the Tower More tells his daughter that when he offered, if he had the King's license, to give his reasons for refusing to answer, Cromwell interrupted him, pointing out the legal danger of doing this even with the King's license. "In this good warning he showed himself my especial tender friend." And he writes that when he finally refused the oath "Cromwell seemed greatly to pity him." [1]

Fisher's fate, which was so closely bound to More's, was sealed when the Pope appointed him a Cardinal. Henry took this promotion of a man under the charge of treason as a challenge to touch him. When the divine right of kings was objected to Oliver Cromwell, who felt that the life of Charles endangered the Commonwealth, he answered, "I tell you we will cut off his head with the crown on it." To "throw the mantle of the Church" over Fisher was to draw the same fire from Henry. It brought out the question underlying the whole controversy, whether an Italian Pope or her own King was supreme ruler of England. Henry swore that when Fisher's red hat arrived he should have no head to wear it. It may be conjectured that the real cause of More's death was the jealous egotism of the King, now so inflamed that one word of criticism gave more pain than fifty of flattery could cause pleasure. Henry VIII was not satisfied to be allowed to do as he wanted. His morbid conscience played into his vanity, and all his intimates must also say on demand that what he wanted to do was right.

The Bull of Deprivation, long threatened against

[1] *More's Works.*

Henry, was now (August 30, 1535) prepared but not issued. It forbade his subjects to obey the King or his officials or magistrates. It absolved all princes from every oath to him and commanded them to break every treaty with him. All princes were commanded to rise in arms against him and all who obeyed him; all Christians were to seize wherever found the money, ships, credits and goods of any one who acknowledged his authority. And by the "fullness of power" given to the Pope, these became the absolute property of whoever seized them. All who refused to enforce this sentence became subject to the same penalties. Every clergyman in the world was to proclaim this curse before the largest possible concourse, and a lighted candle was to be cast down and extinguished, even as the souls of Henry and his supporters were condemned to hell.[1] But the publication of the bull was suspended.

Such a sentence would readily suggest to Cromwell, even if there were no other motive in his mind, that the defensc of his policy required the suppression of the monasteries. This act earned Cromwell's familiar name, "The Hammer of the Monks," and the worst traits of his character, traits common to most men of the day, show so plainly in the transaction that the solid reasons for it which appealed to a man of his type have been obscured. The monastic orders were corrupt. Cromwell sent commissioners to investigate the condition of the monasteries. Their sweeping denunciations were based on hasty investigation and probably exaggerated for a purpose. The so-called "Black Book" which presented to Parlia-

[1] Wilkins' *Concilia,* III, 792.

ment the reports of this commission to investigate the monastic houses, has perished. It is safe to conclude, however, that it was not drawn up in a judicial frame of mind. But there are unquestionable judgments on the general corruption of the monastic orders of the day.

Gasparo Contarini, afterward Cardinal, writing in 1516 on "The Duties of a Bishop," said: "Unfortunately in some of the chief and celebrated cities most cloisters have become almost lupanaria." [1]

Bembo, Papal Secretary to Leo X, afterward Cardinal, wrote: "I have often found, under the affairs of friars, all human wickednesses covered with diabolical hypocrisy." [2] In 1536 the Pope appointed a commission of the ablest and best men around him to draw up a report on the reform of the Church. There is no language in any of the English reports or discussions stronger than that in which they denounce the condition of the monastic orders.

"Another abuse to be corrected is in the religious orders, because many have departed from God to such an extent that they are a scandal to secular Christians and do much harm by their example. *We think all the conventual orders ought to be abolished*; not, however, in such a way as to do injury to any one, but by prohibiting them from admitting novices. For thus, without any wrong, they might be swiftly swept out of existence and good religious could be substituted for them. But for the present we think it would be best if all boys who have not taken vows of any sort should be kept out of their

[1] *Opera Parisiis,* 1571, page 426.
[2] *Letters, 1520, Opere Venezia,* 1729, I, III, page 385.

monasteries."[1] This report was, quite properly, intended to be private, but the Protestant apologetes having by some means procured a copy, its publication was forced. It was forwarded to Cranmer from Louvain, with the report that the monks of that place "fear their houses will perish. They have faith in the Provincial of the Carthusians who lately came from Italy, prophesying all rules of religion to be annulled."[2] Cranmer forwarded this letter to the Government, probably to Cromwell, adding, "The book he sent me was *Concilium delectorum Cardinalium de emendenda ecclesia*," and copies out the passage quoted above.

There is reason to believe that the monasteries of England were not as bad as those in some other parts of the world. There are satires and attacks on them in English popular literature, but they are less numerous and bitter than in Germany or Italy. During the destruction of the English monasteries there were no outbreaks of popular hatred against them, while several counties rose in arms to defend them. On the other hand, the insurgent German peasants, in 1525, though they killed no monks, destroyed monastic buildings with a careful fury that indicates hatred coming out of a long smouldering sense of wrong. But though the English monasteries were probably neither as corrupt as monasteries in other parts of the world nor as bad as they were reported to be by their enemies, it would be possible to collect, out of the remanent

[1] *Concilium delectorum Cardinalium de emendenda ecclesia*, British Museum.

[2] *Letters and Papers*, VIII, 739. This letter is assigned to the wrong date, 1535. The *Concilium* was first published in 1538. The letter also alludes to an answer in preparation to the King's *Epistle to the Emperor*. The Epistle appeared in 1538.

material from which the Black Book was prepared, a formidable body of definite evidence to show that in many of them the ideal of their own order did not control the lives of the inmates. The Jesuit apologete Sanders wrote, in 1575, of "the publication of the enormities of the monasteries, partly discovered and partly invented." [1] This judgment by an orthodox Roman Catholic churchman of the next generation after their fall, agrees with the testimony which survives and is probably fair.

Whatever the degree of their guilt may have been they menaced the state. There were in England more than seven hundred monastic establishments and they owned enormous stretches of land. Ninety monasteries of Gloucestershire had an average of sixty-five thousand acres apiece. Twenty-seven abbots had seats in Parliament. The bishops could not control the monks, whose vows bound them to allegiance to their superiors, generally foreigners. They were directly connected with the Papacy, and the monastic orders came to be spoken of as the Pope's standing army. Cromwell was afraid of them. The schismatic governments of Europe—the Lutheran states, the Scandinavian kingdoms and the Zwinglian cantons of Switzerland—suppressed the monasteries in the sixteenth century. Most of the Roman Catholic countries limited the power and wealth of the monasteries under different conditions in the nineteenth—Portugal, 1834-64; Spain, 1835-51; Italy, 1866; Prussia, 1875; France, 1880. The United States is a country whose Constitution and practice exclude any suspicion of religious intolerance, but her Commission in the Philippines

[1] Sanders' *Anglican Schism,* Ed. David Lewis, page 130.

reported that the landed possessions of the monastic orders were an obstacle to good government. And steps have been taken to destroy their political power by buying their great estates. There must be some reason, plausible to say the least, for so universal an action.

At the beginning of the sixteenth century monastic institutions seemed to many people an anachronism in the modern world coming into being. The ascetic ideal was outworn. Cromwell, as a man of the Renascence, shared that repulsion of the humanist for the monk which appears in Renascence literature from the *Decameron* to the *Utopia,* and led the Jesuits, who used the new learning in the service of the Church, to abandon the ascetic ideal. The loss of its power over men's minds went far deeper than appears in controversy. In the twelfth century four hundred and eighteen monasteries were founded in England. In the thirteenth, one hundred and thirty-nine. In the fourteenth century only twenty-three. In the fifteenth century only three.[1] The monks were no longer the conservators of learning, but the strongest defenders of scholasticism against the humanist revival of letters. On the Continent they were the bitterest opponents of Reuchlin and Erasmus. Nor were they more intellectually progressive in England. Pole says that Reynolds was the "only monk in England who knew the three languages (Latin, Greek, Hebrew) in which all liberal learning is contained." [2]

Beyond all this, in the opinion of many men, the monks did too little and got too much. A contempo-

[1] Pearson, *Hist. Atlas,* page 61.

[2] *Letters and Papers,* X, page 405.

rary writer expresses their feeling roughly when he writes of the "nourishing of a great sort of idle abbey lubbers, which are apt to nothing only to eat and drink." [1] Sir Thomas More, in his critical youth, wrote of "those holy men, the abbots, who, not thinking it enough that they living at their ease do no good to the public, resolve to do it harm instead of good" [2] (by turning tillage fields into pasture). And Sir Richard Gresham, Lord Mayor of London, gave the criticism practical form when he asked the King to put three hospitals in the city under the rule of the Mayor and Aldermen, because they "had been founded and endowed for the aid of poor and impotent people, not to maintain canons, priests and monks to live in pleasure."

Early in 1536 an Act of Parliament gave to the King the property of all religious houses having a yearly income below £200 (equivalent to $10,000-$12,000), because "of the vicious, carnal and abominable living of small monasteries." Their superiors, if they did not try to conceal the jewels of the houses, were to be pensioned. The monks might be assigned to the greater monasteries, "wherein, thanks be to God, religion is right well kept and observed." Any monk who wished to return to the world was to receive eight gold pieces.

But this last change in the ancient order caused the cup of wrath against Henry to overflow. That there was discontent in England and danger to the throne is sufficiently shown by the legislation passed to defend it and the nine executions under these laws. Observers dif-

[1] *Dialogue between Pole and Lupset.*
[2] *Utopia.*

fered as to the extent of that discontent. The Spanish Ambassador, who spoke no English and heard only what the opposition faction of the nobility told him, thought the great majority of the people were against the King and waiting to welcome the Emperor when he should come to punish Henry's rebellion from the Pope. This judgment, so far as we can judge from what happened fifteen years later, when the marriage of Mary to the Emperor's son almost cost her the crown, was very much mistaken.

The opposition faction of the nobility were, it is true, engaged in forming a conspiracy against the throne. They had long been begging the Spanish Ambassador to persuade Charles V to invade England, and promising to support him in arms if he came. As early as the end of 1534 Lords Hussey and Darcy offered, if imperial troops were sent to the North and the mouth of the Thames, to rise under the imperial banner with a crucifix attached. They promised the support of large numbers of noblemen and gentlemen of the North. From several quarters advice came to the Emperor to centre this discontent among the nobles around Reginald Pole, an heir to the Yorkist claim to the throne and intimately connected with three families in the Southwest who had great wealth and influence. "In two counties alone they might easily raise twenty thousand men under arms, the best soldiers England can boast of." The Ambassador told his master that many people thought Pole's title better than Henry's,[1] and said Reginald's brother Geoffrey continually urged that if Reginald came with an imperial army England could easily be conquered.[2]

[1] *Spanish Calendars,* IV, part II, page 813.
[2] *Letters and Papers,* VII, page 520.

His elder brother, Lord Montague, was reported ready to take arms, and his neighbor, the Marquis of Exeter, "only regrets that he has no opportunity to shed his blood for Katherine and Mary. If anything were doing, he would not be among the laggards." But the threads of this conspiracy could not be drawn together, and it was surprised by an unpremeditated outbreak against the throne arising among the common people of the North.

England, north of a line drawn from the Wash to the mouth of the Humber, has until recent times differed much from the remaining two-thirds of the kingdom. It was always conservative, standing for things as they were or had been. In the civil wars of the seventeenth century it became the stronghold of the Crown. During the sixteenth century, it rose intermittently against the Crown in attempts to restore the pillars of the old state, the aristocracy and the mediæval Church. It was thinly settled and the inhabitants lived by raising grain and cattle, with very little trade or manufactures. The instincts bred by feudalism lingered in the North long after they had perished elsewhere in England. The influence of the priests over the people was stronger than in the South, and the habit of fighting with the Scots and each other, made the inhabitants apt to take to their weapons.

The monastery of Hexham stood near the debatable land of the border. Its stout walls and bold canons were a defense against the raids of the Scots, a refuge to retreating English raiders. In September, the commissioners for its dissolution found the gates shut, the inmates in full armor standing on the roof, and the people of the neighborhood pouring in armed at the sound of the alarm bell. One of the canons, holding an arrow on the string of his bent bow, called out, "We be twenty brethren, and we shall die all ere you shall have the house." Before any steps could be taken to subdue these bold monks, Lincolnshire rose in rebellion. By the 6th of October, "ten thousand well harnessed men, with thirty thousand others, some harnessed and some not," were reported to be marching on Lincoln. "And the country rises wholly before them as they go." [1] They cursed Cromwell, and a false rumor said they had hanged one of his men, sewed up another in a bullskin and then baited him with dogs. Their banner, displaying a plough and a chalice, and their demand for the expulsion of "vile blood" from the royal councils, indicates the mixed motives, agrarian, feudal, religious, which roused them.

Steps were at once taken to raise the royal levies. A list of two hundred and thirty-eight gentlemen and noblemen who were to muster from two men to a thousand, has survived. But there was no need to put forth the strength of the kingdom. As the van of the King's forces approached, the insurgents began to break up and return to their homes.[2] On the 13th of October, one week after the issuing of the commissions of array, Lincoln, the centre of the rebellion, was defenseless, and the gentlemen, who claimed to have been forced to join the Commons in this rising, were offering to come into the royal camp.

But on the same day that this news arrived in London, a message came from York, the second city of the King-

[1] *Letters and Papers,* XI, 567.
[2] *Ibid.,* XI, 658, 694, 701.

dom, asking aid against a new rebellion. It was far more serious than the first. On the 17th of October 40,000 men were reported under arms.[1] The leaders made every effort to organize the movement and force the whole North into it. The commons were called to arms on pain of death. And if any gentleman refused the oath of the insurgents, he was to be put to death, the next of his blood put in his place, "and if he deny it, put him to death likewise, and so on." [2] This notice was to be posted on the doors of all parish churches.

In the mind of the lawyer Aske, who was its active leader, the movement was aimed against the statutes of Succession and Supremacy and the Act suppressing the smaller monasteries.[3] The commonalty rose in defense of the old institutions they loved and against the men who had changed them. "I trust to God," cried out a priest when the insurrection was in full swing, "we shall have the old world again." Their oath bound them to enter into "The Pilgrimage of Grace for the Commonwealth . . . . . for the maintenance of God's faith and Church, preservation of the King's person and issue, purifying the nobility of all villains' blood and evil counselors to the institutions of Christ's Church, and suppression of heretic opinions." [4] Their songs demanded that the innkeeper (Cranmer) should give place to the ancient nobles in the Royal Council and the shearman (Cromwell) be hanged high as Haman.

However much power Henry might delegate to his

[1] *Letters and Papers,* XI, 692, 758.
[2] *Ibid.,* XII, part I, 163.
[3] *Ibid.,* XII, part I, page 405.
[4] *Ibid.,* XI, page 272.

ministers, he was always King of England—a strong-willed man and an able ruler of men. From the time when the trouble began in the North until it ended, letters and reports came, not as before to Cromwell, but to Henry. And the orders of Government issued directly from the King. This was not simply to avoid irritating the rebels, one of whose chief demands was Cromwell's head. In the hour of danger the master wanted the helm in his own hand. There are no signs that Henry lost courage before the storm. There is in all his letters no trace of any intention of yielding one bit to an insurrection raised, like most rebellions, in the name of the throne it attacked and to free the King from evil counsels. He was angry with the Duke of Norfolk for making a truce with the insurgents,[1] because, Norfolk said, his army was without fuel or provisions and the pestilence had begun among them. Henry sent commissioners to meet the rebel leaders in December, with instructions to grant a Parliament to assemble when he should appoint, and a pardon. If they demanded anything else, the commissioners must ask twenty days' respite, secretly levy the forces of the nearest shires, of which 8000 men were to be ready at an hour's warning, hold the fords of the river Don, and wait till he advanced in person with the entire force of the kingdom at his back.[2] The royal terms were accepted, and a letter sent from the King invited Aske to London.[3] On his return he issued in January a manifesto that the King would order his sub-

[1] *Letters and Papers*, XI, 1226.
[2] *Ibid.*, XI, 1227.
[3] *Ibid.*, XI, 1306.

jects' petitions in a Parliament to be shortly held at York.

But the North did not trust these promises. Two futile risings followed, and the Council of the North advised Henry to exercise great severity. He took their advice. These, as well as the two previous insurrections, were punished with the rigor which marked the suppression of rebellion in England down to the eighteenth century. Norfolk had been suspected by others beside the King of not wanting to fight the rebels. The Spanish Ambassador, writing to advise that the Pope should send Reginald Pole with money and musketeers to aid the insurrection, had reported that Norfolk sympathized with their demands. And the Pope, in telling the Spanish Ambassador at Rome that he had sent the money, said the rebels had found a new leader whose name ended in "folc."[1] Norfolk was anxious to disprove the reports about his lack of zeal of which the King had informed him. He executed seventy-four by martial law, induced Aske and other leaders to go to London, and wrote advising that they never come back. "Hemlock is no worse in a good salad than I think the remaining of any of them in these parts should be ill to the Commonwealth."[2] Cromwell was not inclined to show mercy to those who had asked his head and threatened England with civil war. Henry had always insisted on force and punishment, and accepted reluctantly the temporizing policy which Norfolk and his Councilors advised. None of the leaders came back to the North, except in chains

[1] *Letters and Papers,* XI, 1159.
[2] *Ibid.,* XII, page 311.

to be hanged. Aske, in private, just before his death (July, 1537), acknowledged that they had expected help from abroad, and accused the King and Cromwell of having promised him life if he would confess.[1] There is other reason to believe that the treachery of which the age was full, mingled with severity in the punishment of the insurrection.[2]

It made evident that the forces which desired a return to the old Church and State were not strong enough in England to stay the progress of the revolution which was destroying the institutions of the Middle Ages. Even in the northern counties, part of the gentry and nobility could not be dragooned into joining the insurgents by the threat of death. The great families had stood aloof, and some country gentlemen had held their houses for the King by arms. The doubtful counties of Lancaster and Cheshire had offered 3000 men each for the King. Only seven out of the thirty-seven counties, and those the most thinly populated ones, were affected at all. Nor could the utmost inquiries of the Government find any dangerous signs of widespread sympathy in the rest of England. If the southern counties had backed the North the throne of Henry must have fallen.

The motives of the revolt were mixed, but it was predominantly religious, led by the priests and monks, or due largely to their influence. The Government answered by ordering the pulpits everywhere to attack the suprem-

[1] *Letters and Papers,* XII, part II, page 121.

[2] Es ging ein zuttiefer verlogenheit durch die welt und Jeder hielt es für erlaubt, selbst seinen verbundeten in Jedem Augenblicke zu verraten. Huber Geschickte Oesterreichs, Vol. III, page 280.

acy of the Pope and defend the new Anglican Church. And Cromwell did his best in every way to replace the scholastic learning, which underlay mediæval institutions and ideas, by the New Learning of the Renascence. A clergyman of Bristol felt this strongly and denounced the "new preachers, preaching new learning with their new books. Their new learning is old heresy new risen, like unto old rusty harness new furbished. And whereas they say they have brought in the light—no—no—they have brought in damnable darkness and endless damnation." [1]

Just before this Northern rebellion, a new Parliament had been called, June, 1537, to secure the work of the Parliament of 1529. In a session of six weeks it established two new oaths; on the Supremacy and the Succession. The first was to be taken by every ecclesiastical and temporal officer. It solemnly renounced the Bishop of Rome, his authority and jurisdiction, and promised support to the King as Supreme Head of England in Church and State. The second oath was appointed because the "whole peace, unity and greatness of realm and subjects depends upon the surety in the succession to the Crown." It promised to hold the marriage with Anne Boleyn invalid and to defend the succession of the children of Jane Seymour (made Queen May, 1536), or failing children by her, the right of the heir named by the King in his will. To refuse either oath was treason.

The tragedy of Anne Boleyn had been foretold by Wolsey because he knew Henry's brutal fickleness, by

[1] *Letters and Papers,* XII, part I, page 528.

Thomas More because he knew Anne's vulgar levity. And only one child, a girl, had been born of her to meet the kingdom's need of heirs. As Henry's passion cooled into neglect Anne struggled desperately to hold her power. Cromwell told the Spanish Ambassador she was doing her best to get his head. She angered the King by hysterical reproaches for his infidelities. In the spring of 1536 a new divorce was talked of in Court circles, because of the lack of a male heir and the King's dislike for his wife. There would have been small difficulty in getting it from the subservient Archbishop for the same grounds on which he declared Anne's marriage null and void, May 17, 1536. But in the end of April, Anne was accused to the King of adultery and desiring his death. Together with her brother, three courtiers and a court attendant, she was arrested, tried before the peerage of England, the Mayor, Council and representatives from the trade guilds of London, declared guilty in the presence of a great crowd of spectators, and soon after executed.

All of the prisoners but one asserted their innocence. The distinct and definite charges which have survived in summary are very difficult to reconcile with Anne's innocence of the entire indictment. The chief reason for doubting her guilt on all the charges, is that some are too bad to be credible. The modern hypothesis that she was the innocent victim of a diabolical plot, is not supported by the evidence. If the object had been simply to smooth the way for another marriage, Anne's death, and certainly the death of five men, was unnecessary. And the hypothesis is therefore not only unsustained but superfluous.[1]

Cromwell knew that the "Pilgrimage of Grace," the rising of the North for mediæval ideals against the new state, national and lay, independent of the Universal Church and the power of the clergy, had been connected with a Papal conspiracy to force England back to obedience. Of the nobles who had plotted with the Spanish Ambassador, only Lords Hussey and Darcy had been involved in the Northern rebellion, and Cromwell did not know that the houses of Exeter and Pole had offered to serve the Emperor against the King. But he had gotten hold of the thread of conspiracy from the other end. Secret information from Rome told him that the Pope had made Reginald Pole Cardinal for England, with the express purpose, as the Pope himself said, of sending him "to Flanders, publicly to admonish the King to return to the Church, secretly to aid the Northern insurrection" with money and Church authority.[2] He knew that Pole had written a most terrific indictment of Henry's policy, appealing for insurrection and foreign invasion, and that, on arriving in Flanders too late to help the insurrection, he threatened, unless England returned to the Papal obedience, to publish his attack, together with the suspended Papal excommunication calling on all Christians in or out of England to drive Henry from his

[1] This opinion is also suggested by Mr. A. F. Pollard, in his recent small but exceedingly strong *Life of Henry VIII*.

[2] *Letters and Papers*, XII, part I, 123, 1141. The last reference reports that the Pope does not want Pole to take priest's orders. The reason for this wish is that he may be ready to marry Mary and replace Henry on the throne.

throne, and denouncing upon the disobedient outlawry in this world and damnation in the next.

Cromwell had tried to trapan Pole and bring him to England. Pole had slipped away to Rome, and Cromwell had written him a savage letter, hinting "that ways might be found in Italy to rid a treacherous subject;" a threat that greatly alarmed Pole, though a careful review of existing evidence implies that Cromwell did not try to carry it out.[1] Two subjects of the Emperor, who were trying to do precisely what Pole was trying to do, stir up war against their former sovereign, were assassinated in Italy by the Viceroy of Milan in 1540, certainly with Charles' approval, probably by his orders. And fanatic zeal was soon to make the assassin's arm a common weapon of the great hatred bred by disputes over religious opinions. But assassination does not seem to have been Henry's way. Not because it involved either treachery or cruelty. He shrank from those as little as most contemporary sovereigns. But Lord Herbert of Cherbury wrote, two generations after his death, "I do not find him bloody but where law, or at least pretext drawn from thence, did countenance his actions."

Though it is doubtful that Cromwell tried to assassinate Pole, he did make every other possible preparation to defend his policy against assault from Rome, which was using Pole as its chief implement. During the year 1538, he renewed his attack on the monk, that most characteristic product of the ancient world whose institutions he was destroying. Over three hundred monasteries had

[1] The editor of the *Letters and Papers* thinks differently.

been suppressed under the Act; two hundred friaries still surviving were now swept away.[1]

There remained over two hundred large monastic establishments, which had been, as a whole, excepted from the charges of immorality presented against the smaller ones. The abbots of some of these were executed for complicity in the Northern rebellion; in which, Cromwell was informed, the priests and monks were the chief "doers." A process, not completed for three years, then began by which the heads of these large monasteries were induced to surrender their establishments to the King. The way for this course of action had been opened by the Act of Suppression, which, in addition to all monasteries under £200 annual income, had given to the King the property of any which might be granted to His Majesty by their abbots. It looked for some time as if there would be little difficulty in getting rid of the last corps of this class of men, among whom were to be found the most devoted adherents of the Pope. In many monasteries some monks wanted to abandon the monastic life. Six of the White Friars of Stamford, for example, signed a surrender, "considering that Christian living does not consist in wearing a white coat . . . . ducking and becking . . . . and other like papistical ceremonies."[2] Many abbots were willing to take the pensions or afraid to refuse surrender. Most of them doubtless simply yielded to the inevitable.

But while thus steadily moving in a policy which destroyed the centres of support for any invasion to carry

[1] Gasquet, *Henry VIII and the Suppression of the Monasteries*, Vol. II, page 239.

[2] *Letters and Papers*, XIII, part 2, 565.

out the bull of excommunication Pole had dangled like a sword of Damocles over Henry's head, Cromwell was watching for an excuse to strike hard at a certain section of the nobility which, if the threatened blow fell, would be still more formidable. These were the Yorkist nobles, the Marquis of Exeter, Lord Montague, Cardinal Pole's elder brother, and Sir Edward Neville. He was the son of Lord Abergavenny, whose father-in-law, the Duke of Buckingham, had talked of his claims to the throne, and revealed a mind to renew the War of the Roses if the death of Henry should leave the infant Mary, an unprotected little girl, as his heir. For these incautious words Henry had sent him to the block in 1521. This was the knot of nobles—Exeter, Montague and Neville's father—which had been pointed out to the Emperor by his ambassador as able to put 20,000 men into the field, and to be depended upon to do so if they were given the centre of an invading force. Cromwell did not know this. But he knew they were dangerous to his plans, and he used without the slightest scruple the first chance to indict them for treason.

He heard that a certain Hugh Holland had carried letters from Lord Montague to his brother, the Cardinal. Holland was arrested and carried to London. Sir Geoffrey, the youngest Pole, frightened out of self-control, immediately volunteered confessions which threw the net around the men Cromwell wanted. There was no evidence of any overt act of treason, but there was stronger evidence of a will to destroy the Tudor monarchy than that by which Henry had executed Buckingham seventeen years before.

Executions because of verbal attacks on a government were not confined to England. In 1517 the City Council of Ulm executed a weaver in the market place for talking against the Council.[1] The celebrated Strasburg preacher Geiler of Kaysersberg, who died in 1510, used this argument in favor of punishing blasphemy by death: "If any one speaks evil of the burgomaster or of a member of the City Councils he is cast into prison and does not come out except to be hung or drowned." An insult to God, he argues, ought to be as severely punished.[2] And Claude Haton tells of a canon who made scandalous remarks about Catherine de' Medici, was arrested and only escaped the law by bribery.[3]

And to read accounts of state trials is to become aware that the modern presumption of the law among English-speaking people, that a man is innocent until he is proved guilty, did not obtain in trials for treason for more than five generations later. In 1614 a manuscript sermon, attacking the government and denouncing a death like that of Ananias or Nabal for the King, was found among the papers of Edward Peacham, a rector of Somersetshire. It had never been preached. But, with the approval of Francis Bacon, he was tortured to extract evidence of a conspiracy, tried and condemned to death for treason. At the end of the seventeenth century Algernon Sydney died on the scaffold for opinions in an unpublished manuscript which Charles II and a Tory jury thought dangerous to the monarchy.

There was current in England under Henry VIII

[1] *Chroniken der deutschen Städte,* XXV, 78.

[2] L'abbé L. Dacheux, Un réformateur catholique à la fin du XVe siècle.

[3] Documents inédits. VIII, 330.

a cant phrase to label the attitude of those whose opinions threatened the throne. As men spoke of the malicious "obstinacy" of heretics who dissented from the orthodox Church, so the adherents of the "new world" in England spoke constantly of the "cankered hearts" [1] of those who longed for the ancient system in Church and State. Of such "cankered hearts" there was good evidence in the case of the prisoners. The breaking of the power of nobles and clergy, a career open to talents, the revolt from Rome, an indisputable succession to the throne—these things were against their feudal instincts and their religious feelings. "Knaves rule about the King," Sir Edward Neville was wont to sing, "but lords shall rule again one day." And Exeter, shaking his fist, said, "I'll give these knaves a buffet some day." Montague said, "The Northern rebels were fools to strike only at the Council. They should have struck at the head." Letters had been carried to Cardinal Pole and brought from him. At the news of the arrest some of these had been hastily burned. "They liked not the proceedings of the realm, they approved the opinions of Cardinal Pole." "The King will die suddenly," said Montague, "then we shall have jolly stirring." [2] As remorselessly as they would have killed him and destroyed his work, Cromwell had them condemned for treason, executed in December, 1538, and their execution confirmed by Parliament in a bill of attainder. Montague's mother and Exeter's wife were included in the

[1] See *Letters and Papers, passim.*

[2] See the depositions against Neville, Montague and Exeter, *Letters and Papers,* XIII, part II.

attainder, but they were not touched during Cromwell's lifetime.

On the 17th of December, 1538, the long-suspended Papal excommunication, condemning Henry and all who obeyed his magistrates to hell, making them outlaws and calling upon all Christians to attack and despoil them, was published.

Cardinal Pole was sent from Rome on a mission to the Emperor and the King of France. It was suspected, in spite of Pole's denials, that his errand was to persuade them to make peace and unite in a crusade against England. The suspicion was correct, as appears in Pole's *Apologia,*[1] written at the time, and in Charles' report of his conversation to the Venetian Ambassador. For the Emperor told Mocenigo that Pole tried to persuade him to defer the Turkish expedition in order to attack England, and related his own answer, pointing out the danger of leaving Italy open to Turkish attack if he withdrew his forces to attack England.[2] Henry and Cromwell did not know that Charles would take this view of the matter. In the middle of 1538 they had seen the war between France and Spain closed in a personal interview of Charles and Francis, in which they showed the most pleasant relations and swore eternal friendship. If France, Spain, Scotland and Ireland should attack England she would be ringed about by foes. Such a combination in support of a papal bull of deposition, though difficult to form, was not impossible. The danger was

[1] See Appendix.

[2] This conversation is reprinted in *The Emperor Charles V,* by Edward Armstrong, M.A., Vol. II, page 21.

not a paper one. The same threat fifty years later materialized into the great Armada, flying the banner of a crusade and bringing a Spanish army to drive excommunicated Elizabeth from her throne. The same spiritual power gave its chief strength to the Holy League and compelled Henry IV to be reconciled to Rome in order to gain peace for France. It is not "reading history backward" [1] to perceive that what caused and maintained war in the end of the sixteenth century, was capable of causing it at the beginning of the century. Contemporaries did not think the danger imaginary. The Spanish Ambassador writes from Venice, that it is common talk throughout the city that Spain and France are to attack England.[2] And the Venetian Ambassador at Paris had reported to the Senate some time before that the Emperor was disposed to obey the Pope by attacking England.[3] It would have been reckless indeed for the King and his minister to take this danger as lightly as some modern historians insist they ought to have taken it. Henry wrote instructions to enforce Cromwell's readiness to put England in a state of defense, adding as a spur to his work, "Dilligence passe sence." [4]

Four thousand sets of armor and supplies of powder were bought in Germany. And the King tried to engage there 100 expert artillerymen.[5] Government ordered a general muster of the kingdom, and the rolls show that it was carried out, at least in part, for Wales and two-

[1] William Stubbs, D.D., *The Study of Mediæval and Modern History.*
[2] *Letters and Papers,* XIV, part I, 372.
[3] Documents inédits, Vol. 47, pte. 71.
[4] *Letters and Papers,* XIV, part I, 529.
[5] *Ibid.,* XIV, part II, App. 14.

thirds of England. The following entry in the records of the Corporation shows what the capital did: "His Highness was lately informed that the cankered and venomous arch traitor Reynold Pole, enemy to God's word and his own natural country, had moved diverse great princes of Christendom not only to invade this realm of England with mortal war, but also by fire and sword to extermine and utterly destroy the whole generation and nation of the same. . . . Thereupon His Highness in person took many journeys toward the sea coasts and caused many bulwarks to be made. He also caused towers to be built from the Mount to Dover and so to Berwick. He caused the Admiral to assemble all the navy at Portsmouth, and directed commissions throughout the realm to have his people mustered. . . . But when the Lord Mayor and his brethren were informed by Lord Thomas Cromwell, Keeper of the Privy Seal (to whom the city is and has been much bounden), that the King himself would see his loving subjects muster before him, they decided that no alien, even though he were a denizen, should muster, and that Englishmen who had jacks, brigandines or coats of fence should not go out, but only such as had white harness and full accoutrements."[1] The parade took place on the 8th of May, 1539, and the French Ambassador estimated fifteen thousand men in the ranks, for those days a large force.

The surrenders of the greater monasteries had stopped with April, when two-thirds of the number had been surrendered, and from then until the 1st of November they did not average one a month; whereas for the previous

[1] *Ibid.*, XIV, part I, 940; *Reprint from Archæologia*, XXXII. 30.

sixteen months they had averaged about six a month. And the unsurrendered included a number of those most dangerous from the Crown's point of view. There were twenty-five mitred Abbots in England with the right to sit in the House of Lords; only seven of them had surrendered by the 1st of November, 1539. And the Government had reason to believe they were in communication to encourage one another in resistance. Cromwell determined to break their opposition. After his manner, he struck at the tallest heads. The Abbot of Glastonbury was, by virtue of his office, a great noble. The broad acres of the monastery lands were rated to supply from among their laborers and tenants twenty-five hundred men to the royal muster, and brought in one of the largest incomes in England. November 15th, 1539, the Abbot was executed on a charge of robbing the monastery church. On the same day the Abbot of Reading was hanged. Two weeks later the Abbot of Colchester went to the gallows. Both were charged with treason for having supported the authority of the Bishop of Rome over the King, desired the success of the Northern insurrection, and wished Cromwell and the other Councilors at Rome or in the North, *i. e.,* at the stake or on the gallows. The hiding of plate to keep it from the spoiler, talking against the changes in the Church and the Councilors who made them, these were doubtless being done in most of the monasteries left in England. They do not seem serious offenses. But the same Parliament which imposed the penalty of death for night fishing in a private fish pond, imposed the death penalty on them. Cromwell, who with all his lack of scruple was not inclined to bloodshed, might have let these offenses go. But he needed an example, and he made it. So far as we can judge, the evidence of the charges was quite sufficient to justify a verdict according to the laws made to defend the revolution in England against the plots of those within and without her bounds who wanted the "Old World" again.[1]

The hard stroke broke the last resistance of the Orders. Within six weeks twenty-nine monasteries surrendered, among them ten mitred abbots. In another month the "standing army of the Pope" was entirely disbanded in England.[2]

It has been estimated that the seven hundred and odd conventual establishments thus suppressed yielded to the royal treasury in gold and silver vessels, estimated simply at their melting value, a sum equal to about five millions of dollars. Of the large quantities of jewels set in sacred vessels or shrines, no estimate can be found. The sale of monastic lands realized between forty and fifty millions. The income of monastic estates during the eleven years from the beginning of the suppression to the death of Henry was between twenty and twenty-five millions. Miscellaneous profits amounted to some three to four millions more. The last included the sale of everything in the monasteries down to the lead of the roofs.

[1] See letters on the subject in *Letters and Papers,* Vol. XIV. This judgment is made after full consideration of Gasquet's able special pleading for the victims. It is, perhaps, needless to remark that these laws, like most laws motived by fear, were cruel.

[2] A justification of the use in this connection of this common phrase is found in the memoir which the zealous, orthodox preacher Wimpheling sent to Maximilian in 1510. He warns him to be cautious in reforming the manifest abuses of the church, lest "the mendicant monks, those devoted servants of the Holy See, should preach against you, and the Pope should deprive you of your crown." Hist. Lit. de la Alsace, I, 448.

Cromwell was determined to make it difficult to restore monasticism. The great churches, the stately buildings which an Italian visitor in the beginning of the century described "as more like baronial palaces than monasteries," were carefully swept out of existence. From the church of Lewes, four hundred and twenty feet long, supported by pillars ten to fourteen feet thick, to the tiny house of Wilton, with its church thirty-four feet by fourteen, a cloister twenty-four feet long, a dortour sixteen feet by twelve, a little garden and meadow-ground of three acres, wherein dwelt one friar,[1] all went down in ruin; an enormous destruction of beautiful creations of past generations. Of the eight thousand monks and nuns supposed to have lived in them, some who were priests received benefices, and about one-half were pensioned. Abbots of large monasteries received, on the average, from five to six thousand dollars a year; monks, on the average, about three hundred a year. Heads of smaller houses got less, ranging down to nine hundred dollars a year. Of the fifteen hundred friars and the fifteen hundred monks in the smaller monasteries who preferred going out into the world to transference to larger houses, some received a present of from ten to fifty dollars.

Henry was subject, like most monarchs of his day, to the vice of reckless extravagance, and like all selfish men, when he needed money, he was exceedingly greedy for it. This latter vice was exaggerated by popular report. And the Abbot of Colchester doubtless expressed the opinion of many when he said: "The King and his Councilors were driven into such a covetous mind that if

[1] *Letters and Papers*, XIII, part I, 590.

the Thames flowed gold and silver it would not quench their thirst."[1] Henry did not, however, take the greater part of the vast profits of the suppression of the monasteries for himself. In the many cases of suppressing monastic and ecclesiastical foundations during and since the sixteenth century, the privileged or influential classes have always tried to make their profit out of the situation. On the whole, perhaps as large a proportion of monastic property in England was devoted to public uses, as in other suppressions when public opinion was unorganized and the people powerless to control and revise. Henry used in building and for personal and household purposes about twenty millions of dollars. Four or five millions went in pensions and expenses. The foundations of six new bishoprics used up five or six millions more.

The bells of the monasteries were melted into cannon, and about forty millions, over half of the royal profits from the dissolution, were spent on the fleet, coast defenses and military preparations to resist the invasion threatened by the papal excommunication. Of the estates of the monasteries the King probably did not keep more than a quarter.[2] He distributed the rest for nothing, or at a very low price, to the ancient nobility, to country gentlemen or to the "new men" he was raising to greatness by his service. For Cromwell's policy used greed as a factor, and his knowledge of human nature told him

[1] *Letters and Papers,* XIV, part II, 458.

[2] This account is condensed from Father Gasquet, who bases his reckoning on books of the Augmentation Office. The sums are roughly transferred into modern American values. It is held by most English writers that the purchasing value of money was then ten to twelve times what it is now.

that the sharers of the spoils would never consent to the reversal of that by which they profited. From the Dukes of Norfolk and Suffolk, the Marquis of Exeter, etc., down to the cooks in the royal kitchen, every one scrambled for a share in the spoils.

Cromwell took his share with the rest.[1] He accumulated a great estate in monastery lands. Its exact value cannot be estimated, but in rough numbers it brought him in between £2000 and £3500 a year, equal in purchasing value to between $120,000 and $200,000. His income from all sources was large. In 1536 it was between $130,000 and $150,000. During the years '37, '38 and '39 he received what is equivalent to between $2,250,000 and $2,500,000. His expenses ate up more than half this. But his accounts show that he invested some $600,000 to $700,000 in lands and annuities, and put over $100,000 into a diamond and a ruby, probably because they were portable. His steward's books show a balance in his favor of £7000 ($350,000 to $400,000 modern value), which agrees with the account of the ambassador who wrote at his fall that people were surprised because much money was not found in his house, the total sum being only about £7000.

Cromwell made all he could out of his office and influence. The English of the sixteenth century seem to have given presents very much as the modern Chinese do, and the list of things Cromwell received is most incongruous. It ranges from "twenty apples good to drink wine with" and "ten bags of sweet powder to lay

[1] This summary account of Cromwell's finances is the result of a careful examination of all letters and accounts bearing on the subject in *Letters and Papers,* checked, so far as possible, by the *Valor Ecclesiasticus.*

among cloths," through a toothpick and a gold whistle, four live beavers, seeds from Barbary, a complete Innsbruck harness and six Bibles, to a thousand-weight of tin to make pewter vessels, and 18,000 slates to roof his new house. He took fees and bribes very commonly, and those possessed of any means who asked his help or influence, generally sent money or a promise of money. Sometimes the gift was delicately conveyed in a pair of gloves, left under a cushion or elsewhere in the house. Much of this would be recognized as illegitimate at the time, for Sir Thomas More, who as Chancellor astonished his contemporaries by refusing to take any presents, was greatly praised for uprightness. But the condemnation was so formal that people did not lose caste by a practice which was universal and taken for granted. Wolsey received a huge pension from Francis I; and other nobles of Henry's Council, the Duke of Norfolk, the Bishop of Winchester, Earl of Worcester, etc., Cromwell's enemies as well as his supporters, received pensions from the Kings of France or Spain to look after their interests. The Councils of Switzerland, Germany and Flanders were equally, if not more, corrupt. The Fuggers were used to convey into Spain the foreign pensions of Councilors. When Francis Bacon, Chancellor, was condemned in 1621 for having taken bribes, he wrote: "And howsoever I acknowledge the sentence just and for reformation sake fit, I am the justest Chancellor that hath been in the five changes since Sir Nicholas Bacon's time" (1559).[1] Practices so deeply condemned by modern opinion as to ruin those guilty of them persisted with small conceal-

[1] *Spedding*, Vol. II, p. 518. Boston, 1878.

ment and no rebuke among English State officials into the eighteenth century. Pitt created a great sensation and won an unmatched reputation for honesty in 1746 by refusing to accept commissions on foreign subsidies or to appropriate the interest of balances in his hands. Cromwell's bribes and fees are not in the least to be defended, but it is unhistorical to separate his greed from its background and represent it as unusual in kind or even unique in degree.

This wealth Cromwell spent freely. He built a stately house opposite where the Stock Exchange now stands in the heart of London.[1] The eight lots and four gardens of the building plot he bought for the equivalent of $12,000 from his friend Antony Vivaldi.[2] The ward was then a good residence quarter on the outer edge of the city. The house, though stately, was not one of the magnificent palaces built in the Tudor age. A rough sketch which has survived indicates the heavy square gate tower common to contemporary architecture; a good specimen of which can be seen at Coughton, the seat of Sir Nicholas Throgmorton, whose false testimony brought Cromwell to the block. The building has since been destroyed by fire, but we have a description of the interior, made after Cromwell's death. It had a large banqueting hall, and ample kitchens well fitted for hospitality on a large scale. And Cromwell considered buying in Flanders for 40 crowns ($500) a carved dinner table "of such size as there are few in England." We do not know whether he got it. But we know that his house was finely

[1] See description in Herbert, *Twelve Great Livery Companies of London*, under Drapers' Company.

[2] *Letters and Papers*, VII, 944.

furnished by one who showed the tastes of the Renascence. A mutilated list of his furniture at the time of his death shows that he had twelve pictures. No list of his books has survived. But there are scattered notices of them among his papers from the beginning of his power, when we find a poem, "Amongst all Flowers the Rose doth Excel," jumbled up with the "Estimate of charges of the King's house for a year;" "A Dialogue between Pasquillus and Marforius" next to "A list of wastes done by divers persons to the King's forests of Dean," and Italian verses between the "Supplication of the inhabitants of Rompney Marsh" and "The answer of the King of Denmark and his Secretary." [1]

Cromwell had attracted before he became great the friendship of men of literary tastes. Miles Coverdale, translator of the Bible; Henry Morley, author of a large number of works on Biblical criticism; Thomas Elyot, author of the Book of the Governor, a Latin Dictionary and a number of other books; Richard Morrison, author of several treatises and translations; Thomas Starkey, one of the best writers of his generation on affairs of church and state; John Palsgrave, who did much for the knowledge of French in England and wrote one of the earliest French grammars and dictionaries—all these were more or less intimate with him in his early days of law practice. And they made a circle very large in comparison to the limited number of literary men in England. These and other friends he made before his rise to power he kept after he became great.

[1] *Letters and Papers,* VI, page 135.

The contemporary Italian novelist, Bandello, afterward titular Bishop of Agen, made him the hero of one of his tales. It presents Cromwell in the most odious light, as a destroyer of the Church, who killed "an infinite number of monks, decapitated many great prelates of the holiest life and extinguished almost all the nobility of England." But it relates and praises his gratitude and magnificent liberality to a Florentine merchant who had helped him in his poverty-stricken youth and, having lost his fortune by the chances of trade, was in misery in London. The fact that this Italian monk, supporter of orthodoxy, chose the great heretic and schismatic for the hero of his tale on gratitude, is a proof that Cromwell had the reputation that cannot be earned except by deserving it. Richard Morison wrote: "You are the only man in your place who has never forgotten his old friends." [1]

Cromwell entertained largely, dining the King and foreign ambassadors. And his varied and witty conversation added to the pleasure of his guests. He kept a large household and took care to have men among them who could play on various instruments and make up a band.[2] He was evidently fond of music, for his steward paid a poor woman for bringing a nightingale, and "Mr. Reynolds' servant for bringing a cage of canaries," sums equal to over seventeen and twenty-five dollars.[2] He kept a fool to amuse his guests,[2] and played bowls,[3] cards and dice,[3] losing at the latter Court amusements sums ranging from $50 to $1,200. He shot with the long bow

[1] *Letters and Papers,* XIII, part I, 1297.
[2] *Ibid.,* XIV, part II, 782.
[3] *Ibid.,* VIII, page 433; also above note.

and hunted. But his favorite sport was hawking.[1] The gifts that pleased him best were hawks, spaniels or greyhounds. The Spanish Ambassador went out hawking with him, to find a good opportunity for a private talk, and his favorite sport colored his speech, for the ambassador reports that he said: "The Emperor and his agents, like hawks, rise high to come down faster on their prey." [2] Just before his fall Parliament reënacted laws to prevent the destruction of hawks' nests and eggs. He kept nearly a hundred horses, but rode a mule to and fro between his house and Court.[3] A bitter enemy said of him: "He was a great taker and briber, like his brother the Cardinal (Wolsey). No lord or gentleman in England favors him, because he will do for no man except for money, but he spent it honorably and freely like a gentleman (though he were none), and helped many honest men and preferred his servants well." [4] Nor was his hospitality limited to his friends. His steward's accounts show many entries of gifts to the poor, as, for instance, £6 *20d.*, equal to some $350, "to be distributed in alms in the prisons about London." And Stow, no friend of Cromwell, whom he thought guilty of an act of injustice to his father, says that when a boy he had seen more than two hundred poor fed twice a day at Cromwell's gate.[5]

Around the house of Cromwell, with its filled banqueting hall and open gates, there centred not only friendship and gratitude but hatred. The hospitalty which has any

[1] *Letters and Papers*, V, 1281; VI, 1164, etc.
[2] *Ibid.*, XII, part II, 629.
[3] *Ibid.*, XIV, part II, 337.
[4] *Ibid.*, XIII, part I, 471.
[5] Stow, *Survey of London*, Ed. 1618, page 139.

of its roots in extortion is apt to make more enemies than friends. And there were other reasons beside the way in which he gained part of his money, which suggests to us how much he was disliked. The sincere and intense antipathy of extreme conservatives for a radical and opportunist, the malignant hatred which some members of any privileged class always feel toward the man who destroys their privileges, the honest indignation of religious men who believed that the mediæval Church was the divinely authenticated form of the Kingdom of God on earth—these varied motives engendered in the hearts of a large section of the English clergy a terrible anger against him.

The nobility also disliked Cromwell. Even those who may have come to acquiesce in the Tudor policy which had destroyed their feudal independence, did not like the prominent instrument of that policy. Almost all the English nobles of ancient descent were men of small capacity. A paper is extant, found among the archives of the Papacy, in which some one has given a brief account of the heads of the English nobility—probably as a basis for judgment about the possibility of exciting successful religious war against the Crown. It passes favorable judgments on "The Duke of Norfolk, 72 years, the chief and best captain;" "The Marquis of Exeter, lusty and of great power, specially beloved, diseased often with gout, next to the throne," and "The Marquis of Dorset, 26, with little or no experience, well learned and a great wit." But the more characteristic entries are: "The Earl of Oxford, 66 years, a man of great power, little wit and less experience"; "The Earl of Derby, young, and a child in wisdom and half a fool"; "The Earl of Cumberland, a man of 50 years, without discretion or conduct"; "The Earl of Sussex, of little discretion and many words"; "The Earl of Bath, old and foolish"; "The Earl of Worcester, young and foolish"; "The Earl of Huntingdon, of great power, little discretion and less experience."[1] The new nobles advanced by Henry received more favorable judgment. "The Duke of Suffolk" (Henry's brother-in-law), "a good man and captain, sickly and half lame"; "The Earl of Wiltshire, wise and little experienced, Queen Anne's father"; "The Earl of Hampton and Admiral of England, made by the King, wise, active and of good experience; one of the best captains in England"; "The Earl of Hertford, young and wise, brother unto the last Queen deceased."[1]

The pride of an hereditary aristocracy degenerated in ability often bears an inverse ratio to its capacity, and its members resent particularly the rise of capable men to the influence and positions once wielded by their class. The new blood which the Tudors infused into the highest classes of English society was greatly to the advantage of the English nobility. The families they founded became the great families of later times. But the members of the played-out old lines did not welcome the newcomers, and they hated Cromwell more than the rest because his influence was greater, and he was not of gentle blood. Idle courtiers, who could not have led a company in war without disaster or managed the simplest affairs of state without confusion, had sneered at Wolsey as "the butcher's dog." Cavendish wrote of Cromwell "as

[1] *Letters and Papers*, XIII, part II, 732.

a kite flying with royal eagles, a jay chattering in a golden cage." And in the same spirit the Marquis of Exeter, forced from the Royal Council, had shaken his fist at the "knaves" (base-born men) "who ruled about the King." The story, often repeated, that in 1536 he struck Cromwell with his dagger, which was turned by a secret coat of mail, is not very authentic. Cromwell may indeed have worn a secret coat of mail. For at the end of 1533 the Duke of Norfolk had asked the Venetian Ambassador to get five impenetrable coats, of the kind made at Brescia, for himself, the father and brother of Queen Anne, the Lord Treasurer and Cromwell.[1] They probably had some reason to fear a plot to assassinate them, though there does not appear to have been any. And the Spanish Ambassador reports the delivery of five coats of scale armor as a present from the Venetian Senate.[2] But it is highly improbable that the dagger of Exeter ever discovered one of these coats on Cromwell's body. The story rests only on the malicious denunciation before a Somersetshire magistrate of the boastful words of a butcher, said to have been spoken six months before they were denounced. But we do not need this anecdote to tell us that most of the nobility, like the orthodox clergy, were enemies of Cromwell for reasons both good and bad.

It has been so frequently repeated that Cromwell was generally hated because he filled England with spies, that it is a little surprising to find how slight ground for the charge is found in the State Papers. If Cromwell sustained a general spy system throughout England, or had

[1] *Calendars, Venetian,* Vol. IV, pp. 374, 382.
[2] *Calendars, Spanish,* Vol. V, part I, page 74.

a regular establishment equivalent to the secret service men of modern governments, it would plainly appear in their reports made to him of arrests for seditious and treasonable words. The ancient laws of England made "tale-bearing" against "the great men of the realm" a serious offense. A statute of Edward I,[1] twice confirmed under Richard II, ordered the imprisonment of any one repeating "such scandalous reports until he had brought into court him who was first author of the tale," to be punished by the Royal Council. The new law making it treason to call the King heretic, schismatic or infidel, or to deny the legitimacy of his heir or impugn his title of Head of the Church, had commended to all magistrates the enforcement of the old as well as the new law. I have examined in the Calendars reports, made to Cromwell between 1533 and 1540, of ninety odd arrests under these laws, practically all that exist. In none of them is there any suggestion of a system of spies to watch the people or report their incautious words. A King's commissioner, a yeoman of the Crown, a commissioner of subsidy, each report one case; several county magistrates, evidently seeking to curry favor, report a few cases; in five cases a constable or bailiff seems to be the chief accuser. Even this does not indicate any "spy system." And the overwhelming majority of the cases are denunciations before the local magistrates by ordinary inhabitants of town or village—tinkers, ironmongers, fullers, weavers, butchers, etc. They show that numbers of the people throughout England believed in the laws or were freely willing to use them. Some fifteen or twenty

[1] III, Edward I, 34.

cases are the denunciations of parsons by their parishioners, who evidently want an incumbent of the "New Learning." In ten cases priests denounce another priest. This also probably was the "New Learning" against the "Old Learning." Some ten cases look like simple malicious false witness growing out of a quarrel; and most of these are so commented upon by the magistrates who report them. The examination of these hundred cases is very far from suggesting the presence, or the need, of a body of spies to keep down the people.

In the year 1540 Cromwell suddenly fell before his enemies. April 17th he was made Earl of Essex; July 28th he was beheaded. He had long foreseen his misfortune. He told the Spanish Ambassador in 1536. "He had admitted to himself that the day might come when fate would strike him as it had struck his predecessors in office; then he would arm himself in patience and place himself for the rest in the hands of God."[1] During the year 1540, Cromwell's foreign policy had brought him into disfavor with his master for two reasons. It crossed the theological beliefs of the King and it made him personally uncomfortable.

Cromwell prepared to resist the possible foreign invasion in support of the Papal bull excommunicating Henry, not only by fortifications and musters, but also by alliances. Against a combination of France and Spain, England must obviously seek allies in the North. Cromwell did his best to form an alliance with the anti-imperial and anti-Catholic princes of Germany. In this he found one practically insurmountable obstacle—the theological

[1] *Calendars, Spanish,* V, part II, p. 82.

differences between the Lutheran and English Churches. Most of the Lutheran divines received from Luther himself a great tenacity of theological opinions and a strong intolerance for dissent. They had refused to join a defensive league with the Zwinglians; many of them were to refuse fellowship with the Reformed of France. After examining the doctrines of the English Church, they advised their princes not to make alliance unless the English accepted the true Word of God—namely, the formulas of the Lutheran Church. But, far from doing that, an Act of Parliament in June, 1539, made the Six Articles the test of religious orthodoxy in England. These denounced the penalty of death against all who spoke or wrote against transubstantiation, communion in one kind, the need of celibacy in the clergy, the perpetual obligation of monastic vows, private masses or auricular confession.

For some years Cromwell had been encouraging in England the spread of Lutheran opinions. Between 1536 and 1539 two books were printed containing *The Augsburg Confession* and *Melanchthon's Apology*, "translated by Richard Tavernier at the commandment of Lord Thomas Cromwell." He had not only licensed Coverdale's translation of the Bible, but, as he told the French Ambassador, spent six hundred marks (equivalent to some $20,000) in getting it printed. It finally appeared in 1539 with Cromwell's arms upon the title-page, and a Preface setting forth a "Summary and Content of Scripture" quite Protestant in tone.[1] He must have used

[1] In the title-page of the subsequent editions under the royal patronage the arms of Cromwell have been cut out of the plate, leaving a blank in the engraving. See copies in the British Museum.

his influence to promote clergymen of anti-orthodox opinions, for the heretical Bishop Latimer wrote him in the end of 1538, saying: "Your Lordship has promoted many more honest men since God promoted you than any of like authority have done before you." [1]

By the beginning of 1539 Cromwell was regarded by all who wished to see England advance rapidly toward the position taken by the Protestant princes of Germany or the Zwinglian cantons of Switzerland as the hope of "the gospel" in England. Their opinion of him may be fairly represented (making due allowance for the tone usual in prefaces to patrons) by the dedication of Richard Morison's *Apomaxis,* published in the middle of 1538: "Who that knows anything is ignorant that all things depend on you? Who does not wonder at your bodily strength, broken by no labours? It is incredible that the strength and memory of one man can suffice for so many and such divergent affairs. You receive all suppliant letters, you hear all complaints, you send few from you without help, either in the trouble itself or, next best, by counsel. Is there any one distinguished by virtue or learning or any of unusual mental powers whom you have not aided? All, except very few, gladly see conquered and bound by you Popes, heaps of indulgences, pounds of lead, wax easily moulded to evil (Papal seals), a thousand stratagems of fraud, huge armies of rapine and finally the bodyguards of Papal rule—Force, Terror, Cruelty, Flames, Threats, Thunders—captive, sad and hopeless, following the triumphant chariot.

[1] *Letters and Papers,* XIII, part II, 1036.

"May Christ long keep you safe to ornament our state and make plain our gospel."

How far Cromwell was moved by conviction in thus promoting Protestant opinions is difficult to determine. His early literary friends, with the exception of Lord Morley, had moved toward heresy as well as schism, and Cromwell may have moved with them. In any case we may assume that he thought more of England than of theology. Probably he concluded that, if England was to be kept from connection with Rome, she must not only break with the mediæval Papacy, but also with some doctrines of the scholastic theology, for the two hang so closely together that it is hard to separate them. And he understood that if any permanent alliance was to be formed in Germany, some concession must be made to the doctrinal prepossessions of the Lutherans.

Now the King was not at all inclined to rapid divergence from old theological opinions. He piqued himself on his knowledge of theology. He hated Luther, who, in controversy some years before, had handled him without gloves. And he was so adverse to heresy that Cromwell had not been able in 1531 to get him to have any dealings with Tyndale, in spite of the strong support to theories of absolute power given to kings by God contained in Tyndale's book. In protecting men who held opinions denounced by the Act of Six Articles, Cromwell was playing the dangerous part of forcing the hand of the King, a thing which Henry always deeply resented.

In addition, Cromwell's policy had made Henry uncomfortable, and that had come to be in his eyes the worst possible offense. To cement the German alliance, Henry, a widower since 1537, had married Anne, sister of the Duke of Cleves, whose rich and fertile domains in the Rhine country, on the borders of the Netherlands and Germany, made him a sort of diplomatic centre for any anti-imperial European alliance. Before Cromwell came into power the advantages of marriage into this family, whose eldest daughter was wife of the Elector of Saxony, head of the defensive League of Lutheran Princes, had been laid before the King in a memorial of Herman Ring (May, 1530). The King had been told that Anne was very beautiful and, satisfied with the reports and a portrait painted by Holbein, had agreed to the marriage. When she came to England, a glance made plain that she was not at all beautiful. The King at first sight took a great dislike to her, and tried hard to get out of keeping his promise to make her his wife. Cromwell pointed out how impossible this was, and he reluctantly went through the ceremony. But woe to the man who forced him to do what he disliked. An intense irritation gathered in his heart. And the desire to get rid of Anne was increased by his liking for Katherine Howard, a pretty young niece of the Duke of Norfolk. Gardiner, Bishop of Winchester, head of the orthodox clerical party and Cromwell's bitterest opponent, gave the King opportunity to meet Anne's rival in his palace.[1] Cromwell was aware of his danger, but saw no way to avoid it. Sir Thomas Wriothesley, one of the King's secretaries, deposed that five months after the marriage, "He asked Lord Cromwell to devise some way for the relief of the King, for if he

[1] *Letters and Papers,* XVI, page 114, and *Letters from Richard Hillis, Zurich Letters,* Vol. I, page 200.

remained in this grief and trouble they should all one day smart for it. To which Lord Cromwell answered that it was true, but it was a great matter. 'Marry,' said Sir Thomas, 'I grant, but let the remedy be searched for.' 'Well,' said Lord Cromwell, and broke off."

The French Ambassador perceived that a fight for the control of the state had begun. The party of reaction, with Gardiner and Norfolk as its leaders, and the radical progressive party, under Cromwell, had locked arms for a battle to the death. The orthodoxy of Henry, his dislike for Anne, his growing passion for pretty Katherine were strong cards held by Gardiner. But Cromwell was an old player and it looked for a moment as if he would win. On the 1st of June, the French Ambassador reports the Bishop of Chichester in the Tower on a charge of treason and adds: "A trustworthy person says he heard from Cromwell that there were still five bishops who ought to be treated thus, whose names, however, cannot yet be learned; unless they are those who lately shook the credit of Master Cromwell so that he was very near coming to grief. Things are brought to such a pass that either Cromwell's party or the Bishop of Winchester's must succumb. Although both are in great authority and favour of the King, their master, still the course of things seems to incline to Cromwell's side, as Winchester's chief friend, the Bishop of Chichester, is down."[1]

On the 7th of June the Bishop of Chichester wrote to Cromwell a letter from the Tower showing an inclination to be used against the leaders of the clericals.[1] Then the frightened opposition struck a blow which they must have

[1] *Letters and Papers,* XV, pages 351, 360.

plotted some days before. On the 10th of June Cromwell was arrested for treason at the meeting of the Royal Council.

He recognized in an instant that the ground was countermined beneath his feet by some false but plausible witness. A charge of treason against Cromwell, who lived to exalt the throne, was ridiculous. As he saw his work undone by the tricky but incapable Norfolk and the able but reactionary Winchester, he flung his cap on the ground in sudden wrath, appealing to their consciences whether he was a traitor, and bidding them not let him languish long in prison. The French Ambassador understood it perfectly as a faction fight "between this King's ministers who are trying to destroy each other. Cromwell's party seemed the stronger lately, but it seems quite overthrown by the taking of the said Lord Cromwell, who was chief of his band." [1] The King sent the ambassador word that: "He wished by all possible means to lead back religion to the way of truth. Cromwell, as attached to the German Lutherans, had always favored the doctors who preached such erroneous opinions, and that recently, warned by some of his principal servants to reflect that he was working against the instructions of the King and the Act of Parliament, he said that the affair would soon be brought to such a pass that the King with all his power could not prevent it, but rather his own party would be so strong that he would make the King descend to the new doctrines even if he had to take arms against him." [2]

The King's irritation, caused by dislike for Anne and

[1] and [2] *Letters and Papers,* XV, 766, 767.

liking for Katherine, had increased, while at the same time the peace of the Duke of Cleves with the Emperor, and a truce between Charles and the French King made Henry fear that the marriage he hated was a political mistake. His distaste for heresy deepened. And at the psychological moment, when the unconscious dislike for the minister who had been the means of making him uncomfortable was ready to burst into the fury of a selfish man who is crossed, a sudden false accusation evoked the terrible pride of the King. Rich, Chancellor of the Court of Augmentations, and Nicholas Throgmorton, with whom Cromwell had long been at odds, accused him of having said two years before: "If the King would turn from it (the promotion of the Protestant doctrine), yet I would not turn; and if the King did turn and all his people, I would fight in the field in mine own person with my sword in my hand against him and all others." They added that he pulled out his dagger with the words: "Or else this dagger thrust me to the heart, if I would not die in that quarrel against them all."

To have desired insurrection against the Crown was against all Cromwell's ideas, to have plotted a hopeless rebellion was utterly at variance with his sagacity, to have expressed his intent before a personal enemy like Throgmorton was a lack of caution impossible in one who had so long walked with firm step the slippery corridors of Henry's palaces. A son of Cromwell's grandchild informed Fuller that, when told by Rich and Throgmorton that he had an accuser of want of fidelity, he had replied, "Were he here now I would strike my dagger into his heart."

Cromwell might have said this. He was not fool enough to have said the other before such witnesses,[1] even in the highly improbable event of feeling it. Like Sir Thomas More, Cromwell accused Rich of plain perjury.

Whether distortion or sheer invention, the false witness served its purpose. The King at once believed it, though later he came to think it false. Cromwell had forced him into a hated marriage. He had encouraged heresy when the King loved orthodoxy. Henry had unconsciously wanted an excuse for a nervous discharge of rage which might relieve his irritated egotism. He stripped his favorite of all his dignities, and every incapable scion of a noble house in England rejoiced that the "base knave" who had risen to the head of the English Government, because he was the most capable man of affairs in it, was, in accordance with royal edict, to be spoken of as "the shearman." The contemporary chronicler tells us that "many lamented" his arrest, but "more rejoiced, and especially such as had been religious men or favored religious persons, for they banqueted and triumphed together that night, * * * and some, fearing lest he should escape although he were imprisoned, could not be merry. Others, who knew nothing but truth by him, both lamented him and heartily prayed for him." A Spaniard long resident in London, who thought Cromwell "had better never been born," wrote of his execution: "He was brought forth with a thousand halberdiers as a revolt was feared, and if all who formerly

[1] He had been on bad terms with Throgmorton, and he knew perfectly the part Rich had played in the conviction of More.

wore his livery and called themselves his servants had been there they might easily have raised the city, so beloved was he by the common people." [1]

At the Courts of France, Spain and Rome the news of his fall was received with great joy, which, curiously enough, has been taken by some modern writers as an indication of the injury his ministry had done to England. From France came accusations apt to insure his death—that he had plotted to marry the Princess Mary and seize the Crown. No pretense was ever made of sending the promised proofs when the King asked for them after Cromwell's death.

From that death nothing could save him. For many generations later little stood between a fallen minister and the scaffold. A threat of the axe was the ancient equivalent of a vote of want of confidence. From Wolsey, who died on his way to death, the list is long of fallen rulers of England who saw the scaffold on their path. More, Cromwell, Norfolk, Seymour of Sudeley, Somerset, Northumberland, Norfolk, Buckingham, Strafford, Charles I, Sir Henry Vane, Clarendon, Danby, Shaftesbury and the Councilors of James II, all met death or looked hard upon the axe. During a century and a half, on the average, once in ten years a leader of the English state died on the scaffold or was in danger of it. None of these men, with the possible exception of Northumberland, could be convicted or attainted of treason by a modern jury or Parliament. Cromwell was therefore only one in a long list of those who came to the steps of

[1] A chronicle of Henry VIII of England, translated by M. A. S. Hume. London, 1889.

the scaffold by the violence of English political parties.

He understood that his one hope of mercy lay in the will of the King, and tried by the most abject efforts to placate the diseased egotism he knew so well. It was his last card in the game of life, and he played it with the same lack of dignity which his antagonist, the Duke of Norfolk, head of the English aristocracy, showed when his turn came. Cromwell got nothing by his abject appeal, except that the title and estates were left undisturbed to his son, which was, perhaps, all he hoped.

The men of the sixteenth century often died better than they lived. There is no particular reason to doubt the essential authenticity of Cromwell's prayer on the scaffold, in which he humbly repents of all his sins, trusting in the mercy of God, and asking that the righteousness of Christ might hide and cover all his unrighteousness. Those sins were many. But, to put his career against the background of his times, and look at it with the eyes of a man who believes in God and righteousness rather than with those of an ecclesiastic who believes that the world gets at God and righteousness only by a church establishment, is to see that there was in them no peculiar tinge of sinister wickedness. He was the most active servant the Tudors found in destroying mediæval institutions. He stood for a career open to talents and the energies of England, going out in the light of the new learning and the new patriotism, into those paths of thought, of industry, of adventure, which have brought the men who speak the English tongue into their inheritance. Therefore the distant North and the ancient nobility hated him. But those who knew him best liked him most. His gratitude was proverbial. Prosperity did not make him forget the friends of his adversity. He struck without scruple at those who opposed his plans, but he did not willingly shed blood which seemed needless, and he helped many of the weak. He took bribes and sold his influence, but it is nowhere recorded of him that he ground the faces of the poor. He did not die, like Wolsey, unlamented. He was "beloved of the common people." His arrest had been secret and sudden because of fear of trouble in the city. His scaffold was guarded to prevent a rescue. A war of broadside ballads arose over his death which had to be suppressed by the council.[1] The joy at Madrid, Paris and Rome was broken by laments from Germany and the Netherlands over the deeds of "the English Nero" and the martyrdom of the friend of "the Gospel." For in those days *nobody* judged a man by what he was or what he did, but by his attitude toward their faction in religion and politics.[2]

It was easier for the King to get rid of a good servant than to find another. Wolsey, More and Cromwell were the ablest men he raised to high office in the State. Within a year of Cromwell's death, the Spanish Ambassador wrote: "The King has no confidence in his ministers, and sometimes even reproaches them with Cromwell's death, saying that upon light pretexts, by false accusation, they made him put to death the most faithful servant he ever had." [3] The last part of Henry's reign was the least successful. He began to shed blood which, from any point

[1] Publications of Society of Antiquaries, London.

[2] It is impossible to write the history of the sixteenth century fairly until this fact is more clearly and widely recognized than it has been.

[3] *Letters and Papers,* XVI, 590, page 285.

of view, was superfluous, so that the French Ambassador reports: "Cromwell was reckoned the sole deviser of the death of so many people, but it appears since that he was not altogether author of that piteous tragedy, but rather played his part as it was rehearsed to him."[1] No one could be found to manage the English finances. The debasement of the coinage, continued during Henry's reign before Cromwell came to power, suspended as long as he had influence, went on again worse than ever, until Elizabeth made her generation pay for the mistakes of their forefathers by returning it to purity and beginning to build up again the ruined credit of England.[2]

Cromwell left no account of his motives and no description of his policy. He shed without remorse the blood of men who, if they could have gained the power they asked the Spanish King and the Italian Pope to help them gain, would have killed him without an instant's hesitation and thought it God's service to destroy all his work. He increased by every means the power of the throne, because, in common with many of the ablest statesmen and writers of the age, he believed an absolute prince to be the only security for national peace and national prosperity. But he did not try to strengthen the throne by creating a standing army or disarming the people. He defended his policy by the pulpit and the printing press. He used the arts so long familiar to English ministers to manage Parliament, but he appealed to the consent of the nation through it, and increased the potential of liberty. He broke England from all connection with the Papacy. He fostered

[1] *Letters and Papers,* XVI, page 289.

[2] Schanz Englische Handelspolitik, etc. Vol. II, Abtheilung, II, IV.

the Renascence against mediævalism, the New Learning against the Old Learning. He reduced the Welsh and Scotch borders to order. He helped the destruction of local jurisdictions and made it possible to bring them under the common law. He maintained the stability of the succession by a policy which defended the loyalty to the throne that carried England through the sixteenth century without a great civil war. He finished the breaking of the feudal nobility, eager to renew the War of the Roses, and kept the path open to talents. He aided trade, retrieved the finances and stopped the adulteration of the coinage. He swept monasticism from England as an anachronism which had outgrown its usefulness, and used half its wealth for national purposes. He broke the temporal power of the clergy and put the national Church under the same control as all other national affairs.

Much of this is so opposed to certain theories of Church and State that it seemed to their advocates a diabolical work, even as it seemed to their opponents a blessed work. The truth is that Thomas Cromwell was neither martyr of Protestantism nor Satan's agent to attack the Church; but a statesman working hard to give England an efficient government, and to guide her safely during the difficult transition from the mediæval to the modern state. Close mouthed and unscrupulous as he was, there was nothing particularly mysterious about his methods nor uniquely sinister about his personality. He sought to advance his own fortune, but evidently he had larger aims. Surely labors so consistent and efficient must have been inspired by some other motive and reason than the greed of a crafty adventurer flattering a tyrant.

And if, without theological prejudice or ecclesiastical bias, we judge him for what he was, a person whose ideals were predominantly secular, we find him morally neither better nor worse than the average man of his age; if we judge him by what he did, it seems difficult to deny him a place among the most capable statesmen of all ages.

MAXIMILIAN I

AFTER THE ENGRAVING BY LUCAS VAN LEYDEN

IV

MAXIMILIAN I

The map of the present Empire of Austria shows at a glance that it consists in the main of three quite distinct lands. The first is a group of seven provinces containing the Alpine ranges east of a line drawn from the Lake of Constance to the Lake of Garda. Tirol, the most mountainous of these provinces, extends toward the west between Italy and Bavaria and is shaped, to the complaisant imagination, somewhat like the handle of the figure of the spade on a playing card. At the eastern extremity of Tirol, the border of the Empire runs sharply north and south and the six other provinces of this group cover the foothills until they reach the banks of the Danube on the north and the lowlands on the east. The figure of the spade is completed chiefly by two provinces,—Hungary, a vast low plain stretching from the edge of the Alps to the Carpathians and drained by the Danube; Bohemia, a high plain sending its waters by the Elbe toward the northwest. The distinction between this low plain drained into the Black Sea, this high plain drained into the North Sea and this mountain land to the south and west, is made more marked by a glance at the names of the towns on the map. In Tirol and the provinces which cover the Alpine foot-hills, they are German. In Hungary, they are for the most part, Magyar. In Bohemia, two-thirds of them are Czech, for the population of this triple empire is about a quarter German, a half Slav and a quarter Magyar.

The combination of these three lands under the power of one ruler whose descendants took the name and state of Emperor of Austria, was to a great extent the work of Maximilian I, Duke of Austria from 1493-1519. And at the same time that he assured to his descendants the base for the future Empire of Austria in the east, his matrimonial diplomacy won for them in the west the provinces of the Netherlands, the crown of Spain, South America and the dominant influence in Italy. Thus, east and west, he saw his two grandsons, Charles and Ferdinand, heirs of a vast group of possessions artificially combined by war and dynastic marriages.

Between these two groups of the possessions of the House of Hapsburg, lay the German Empire, to whose crown Maximilian was elected. Its position and population destined it to be, not an artificial state, bound together merely by the right of its head to rule the several parts, but a real state, resting on the desire of its people to have a common organ to work out the national destiny, a supreme ruler who might incarnate common aspirations. But it was three hundred and fifty years after the death of Maximilian before the Germans living in the plains and valleys draining into the North and Baltic Seas, became a nation. It is hardly fair to say that the blame for the weakness of Germany lies at the door of the Emperor Maximilian in the same sense that the credit for the splendor of the dynasty of the Hapsburgs must be given to him. True, he seemed to have a great opportunity, for he was chosen as leader of the Germans at a time when all classes of the people wished a reformation of the Empire, an anachronism too much affected by modern conditions to remain mediæval and too mediæval to be easily transformed into a modern state. But the hearts that turned towards him were not single. Great numbers of Germans, however much they might talk about the glory of Germany, were, when the test came, willing to barter for a mess of pottage mingled of local pride and petty jealousy, their national birthright. The task his office laid upon him was perhaps too hard for any man to accomplish, but not too hard for any man to try. And Maximilian did little that was wise or efficient to unify the inchoate confederacy of the Empire into a German nation. When his interests as hereditary Duke came into conflict with the advantages of Germany, he set no example of self sacrifice. He turned his craft, his energy, his skill into the channels of dynastic gain. He never poured them out with manifest devotion for the good of Germany. And to read through the mass of his writings and letters, is to receive an ineffaceable impression that he would rather have been the forefather of a splendid dynasty than the ruler of a nation whose greatness narrowed the limits of the power of his house. To one in whose mind the interests of a nation take precedence of the interests of a dynasty, it seems that Maximilian gained his dearest desire at the expense of his plainest duty.

It is not to be supposed, however, that this was a conscious dereliction. In spite of the fact that he had received a smattering of the new ideas which, during his lifetime, were spreading from Italy over Europe, Maximilian always remained in his tastes and instincts a man of the old order. Whenever the superficial polish of his humanism was scratched, the knight of the fourteenth century showed beneath. When egotism plunged him into war, he always fought with a good conscience for his "rights," and it is doubtful whether it ever crossed his mind that any who opposed him might have had wrongs.

When he acceded to the Empire in 1493, he had victoriously defended the great possessions of his son against France on the west and reconquered the lands of his father from Slav and Magyar on the east. When he died a quarter of a century later he was a pathetic figure without influence or authority. His grandson, Charles, was manifestly to become the most powerful ruler Europe had seen for seven hundred years, but for Maximilian himself, the founder of this greatness,—there was none to do him reverence.

And the last state of the German Empire was worse than the first. Her soil was ready for the seeds of the selfish greed of petty dynasties and the brutal hatred bred by controversy over religious opinions. The ruler Maximilian's policy had left for the Empire, was too busy managing Spain and the Netherlands and Italy to meet these evils with an eye single to German interests. They sapped the very roots of patriotism, and finally a century after Maximilian's death, the harvest of the dynastic policy of the Hapsburgs was reaped by the German people as it had before been reaped by the Spaniard, the Dutchman and the Italian. The sense of German brotherhood was lost in thirty years of savage civil war. While from every side greedy adventurers, Slav and Magyar, Swede, Dane, Dutchman, Englishman, Frenchman, Spaniard, Italian and Swiss, poured into the German Empire for plunder and bloodshed.

The causes of this splendid success and this marked failure, are not all to be found in Maximilian's capacity and character, and his success is due more to himself and less to fate and circumstance than his failure. A great mass of literary work helps one who can read between the lines, to estimate his ability and perceive his purposes, and the light his writings throw upon his deeds, seems to show that his weaknesses conspired with circumstances to work out failure and his capacities moulded events to lead to triumphs. This brief sketch attempts to set what he did against the background of what he was.

Maximilian's mother was Eleanor, Princess of Portugal. At the time of his birth in 1459, his father, Frederick III, Duke of Austria, had been for nineteen years Emperor of the German Empire, an honour to which he was chosen by the electors after the death of his distant cousin, Albert II. Frederick III prized the title of Emperor, for he clutched at every mark of distinction with an ambition which seemed more like an avarice for dignities than a desire for power. But nothing except a powerful personality wielding great resources could make the office anything but a splendid burden of anxieties. The bonds of the mediæval Empire were decayed and no new ones took their place. "The Holy Roman Empire of the German Nation" gave its Emperor neither a treasury nor an army. There was no common law and no force to impose order upon a large class of people who deemed plundering and killing for private revenge a right of freeborn Germans. The imperial crown brought to him who wore it no power to fulfil its duties. He must either neglect the tasks for which it stood or rely for their accomplishment on his own resources. Frederick chose the easier way of neglect. For Frederick always took the line of least resistance, except when he showed the obstinate tenacity of a turtle which seizes something it wants and then retires so far as possible into its shell.

Even with the desire to rule the Empire, it is doubtful whether he would have had the capacity. He could not remain master of his own hereditary dominions, and at two years of age the infant Maximilian was shut up in Vienna besieged by his uncle. The first memories of the child thus cradled in the lap of war with cannon shots for lullabies, were of the hardships and perils of a soldier. In later years Maximilian often recalled a second siege he endured in the castle of Vienna. The boy, charmed by the noise of the cannon, ran out to join his father who was overseeing repairs to the walls, and the huge stone of a bombard, breaking at that moment through the repairs, barely missed both.[1] The coarse bread to which even the Emperor and Empress were reduced, was very distasteful to the pampered lad. He begged his mother with tears for something nice. Word of the little prince's distress reached a young man from Transylvania, a student of the University in the insurgent city, and, at the peril of his life, he smuggled into the ditch around the fortress some partridges and other game. Thence

[1] Latin Autobiography Jahrbücher der Kunst historischen Sammlungen. Vol. VI, page 423 (35).

he was drawn up into the castle by a rope and gave his dainties to the young prince.[1] Maximilian, as grateful for benefits as he was unforgetful of injuries,[2] rewarded and always remembered the kindness.

The boy's thoughts and ambitions all turned toward war. The glimmer of armor and weapons was the first thing that drew his attention and, while still in his nurse's arms, whenever he saw a dagger he cried until he could touch it with his hand. His favourite playthings were little figures of jousting knights, two of which are still to be seen in the New Museum at Vienna.[3] When he was larger he begged successfully for some play cannon. Refused ammunition, he formed a conspiracy with one of his comrades to steal it. The two lads smuggled it out of the powder magazine in folds of their clothes, crammed the play cannon to the mouth and were ready for a grand celebration. Their smutted faces excited the suspicion of an attendant, the celebration was suppressed and, as Maximilian afterwards thought, his life was saved.[4]

So much in love was he with the life of a soldier and hunter that it was hard to get him to stick to his book. He hung around the stables and took fencing lessons from the guards. He organized the boys of the court into opposing bands and fought mimic battles. Sometimes, fetching a horse from the stables, he led a wild band of youngsters in and out through the courts and even the

[1] Cuspinian Opera, page 602.

[2] Alberi Relazioni degli ambasciatori Veneti al Senato. Firenze, 1839. Serie I, Vol. VI, page 27.

[3] Reproduced in Jahrbücher der Kunsthistorischen Sammlungen, etc., Vol. XIV, page 10. Also shown in a picture of his boyhood made by Maximilian's order for Weiss Kunig and reproduced in Vol. VI with that work.

[4] Latin Autobiography Jahrbücher der Kh. S., etc., Vol. VI, page 423.

halls of the castle. He slipped his hounds on the cats and calves and his father's pet animals. Nothing short of threats of a sound thrashing would break him of a persistent fancy for stalking the castle chickens with bow and arrows.[1]

The lad promised to be worthy of the name Maximilian, which was given him in the hope that he might unite the skill and success of Fabius Maximus and Paulus Æmilius.[2] And in all the exercises which became a knight, Maximilian developed considerable, in some, remarkable skill. An able horseman he could hold his own with other princes in contests of the tournament, though one does not find, outside of his own books or poems written to please him, a record of his supreme skill in those dangerous games. He could drive the shaft of an arrow without any iron on it through two finger breadths of larch plank.[3] One of his captains tells how, finding the Nuremberg contingent drawn up for exercise and review during the Swiss war, the Emperor got off his horse and beat all the gun masters in shooting with the cannon.[4] He was a noted hunter, killed huge boars single handed with the sword and followed the chamois to the topmost crags. And in all these accomplishments he used brains as well as strength and skill. Like the great Italian soldier of fortune, Jacopo Sforza, he appreciated the danger of a hard-mouthed

[1] Grünpeck Die Geschichte Friedrichs III und Maximilian I. Geschichtschreiber der Deutschen Vorzeit. Zweite Ausgabe Fünfzehntes Jahrhundert. Band 3, page 40.

[2] Weiss Kunig, page 49.

[3] Weiss Kunig, page 86.

[4] Pirkheimer Schweizer Krieg. Herausgegeben von Karl Rüch. München, 1895.

horse and invented a new bit.[1] When someone who knew that he supervised the stables himself asked him why he did not leave things to his master of horse, Maximilian answered,—"A nail holds the shoe, a shoe holds a horse, a horse holds a man, a man holds a castle, a castle holds a land, a land holds a kingdom." [2]

He had a knowledge of casting cannon and invented several types of guns.[3] He practised powder making and showed an armorer in Innsbruck how to fit a new sort of screw to a cuirass.[4] He was never content to stupidly follow accepted methods but tried eagerly and often successfully to improve them. As a boy he seems to have been less apt at his books. At the age of twenty-seven he spoke to the Reichstag at Frankfort. His father was very much astonished at his ability, and said to those around him, "I don't know how he can read or talk Latin for certainly at the age of twelve years I was afraid he would turn out either a mute or a fool." [5]

Maximilian himself had mingled memories of his first learning: When a man he wrote to Innsbruck asking to have the Latin grammar he used as a boy, found and sent to him together with his blank book of Latin exercises,[6] but he had a severe judgment for his first teacher. One of his biographers says he heard him wish Peter were alive and he would make him repent of having been a

[1] Cuspinian, page 614. The elder Sforza brought up his more celebrated son, afterwards Duke of Milan, on three precepts. One was, "Never ride a hard-mouthed horse."

[2] Weiss Kunig, page 106.

[3] Max. I vertraulicher briefwechael mit Sigmund Prüschenk. von Krauss Innsbruck, 1875, page 90.

[4] Jahrbücher der Kh. Samm., etc., Vol. XIII.

[5] Cuspinian, page 602.

[6] Jahrbücher Kh. S., etc., Vol. I, part 2, XXXVII.

bad teacher. "We owe much," the Emperor continued, "to good tutors but bad tutors ought to be soundly thrashed for making us waste the precious hours of youth and teaching us what it takes great pains to unlearn." [1]

In later years he made up for his early sluggishness and his mind became active like his body.

The influence of the Renascence was just beginning to reach Germany at the time of Maximilian's birth. By the time he became a youth new ideals were influencing methods of education. The time was drawing near when all the strongest German students were to look longingly toward Italy as the promised land of scholars; an Eldorado of learning where new and untold treasures were to be found. Already the suspicion was rife that a better training than the traditional one was to be had and that it was useful to those who were born to wealth and station. Princes and rich merchants who had travelled began to desire this "New Learning" for their sons instead of the "Old Learning" of the scholastics.

Maximilian did not receive a training in this New Learning according to the ideals of its advocates, the humanists—such a training as Lorenzo de' Medici had for example. At eighteen Commines thought him very badly educated. A better Latin was of course a most intimate sign of the New Learning as opposed to the Old. Guarino, Vittorino da Feltre, or any good Italian master of the new school, would never have sent Maximilian out capable of composing the Latin he dictated. For to get away from what poets and court scholars wrote about Maximilian's Latin and read it, is to see at once that "a

[1] Cuspinian, page 602.

more perfect monk's Latin could not be conceived."[1] But though Maximilian did not receive a humanist education, his quick mind was much affected by the stirring in the air of thought which the Italian Renascence was producing in Germany. The most unmixed triumph of his life was his management of the University of Vienna. He reorganized it so as to subject it to his own control, put men of the New Learning into many of the chairs and left it at his death with five thousand students and a very high reputation for scholarship.[2] And the account of his education given in Weiss Kunig shows plainly that, from the time when he abandoned the cloddish attitude of his boyhood, the widening of the circle of human interests which produced the New Learning and was fostered by it, appealed with constantly increasing force to his mind. These influences did not change Maximilian. He always remained a mediævalist and never became a man of the Renascence. The name "last of the knights," applied to him is open to no objection except that there were many more like him long after his death. The result of the education he worked out for himself was to graft into the stock of that mediæval mind, producing by its chief thoughts results like those of his ancestors, some bizarre fruits of the New Learning, and to stimulate in him that thirst for every and any sort of distinction, which was the dominant passion of the men of the Italian Renascence.

Throughout his whole life Maximilian hated idleness. When he was not working or actively playing he was

[1] Hermann Klaje. Die Schlacht bei Guinegate. Griefswald, 1890.
[2] Aschbach Geschichte der Wiener Universität, etc. Wien, 1865.

learning. He took an interest in everything with an energy which suggests restlessness and perhaps accounts for some of his shortcomings. A restless mind lacks grip and trains itself away from the patient reflection which makes a man wise and efficient.

Whether Maximilian suffered from over activity or not, certain it is that out of his hatred of idleness there came a versatility worthy of note even in a generation noted for versatile men. To inventive skill in mechanic arts he added competence as a draughtsman. He was proud of his ability to design mummeries or costume dances, in which he delighted to join. He left a record of his success in managing the kitchen and the preparation of great banquets. He planned over one hundred books[1] on every possible subject from prayer to fencing and, with the assistance of his secretaries, wrote thirty. He attended to the details of the work of his councilors until he drove at least one of them to the verge of distraction.[2] It is said he could talk to the captain of his mercenaries in Wendish, Flemish, English, Spanish, French and Italian, and dictate letters to his scribes in several languages at once. A number of letters written in French to his daughter Margaret have survived, and if his other languages were no better than his French, his captains must sometimes have found him hard to understand. But it was a time when a little knowledge of a foreign language went a long way, and Maximilian's linguistic accomplishments were

[1] See the account of various MSS. notes and memorandums of Maximilian in Das Fischereibuch Kaiser Max. I. Dr. Michael Mayer. Innsbruck, 1901, page 1, note b.

[2] Prüschenk vertraulicher briefwechsel, etc. Letter from Cyprian von Serntein to Paul von Liechtenstein.

perhaps as sound as those of most of the princely prodigies of the sixteenth century. Germany possessed no capital and her Emperor no palace. Therefore, these activities of mind and body were interpolated among ceaseless journeys, and the energy they implied survived the hardships of repeated campaigns.

Maximilian's active career as a governor and leader of men, began in his nineteenth year with his marriage to Mary of Burgundy. Her father, the Duke of Burgundy, had, by inheritance, marriage and conquest, joined a number of territories to form a triangular principality based on the North Sea and driven like a wedge between France and Germany. He created a fine army and planned to dismember France and become the dominant ruler of Europe; king of a state reaching from the North Sea to the Mediterranean; father of a dynasty more powerful than his cousins, the Valois. A mediævalist, he could not foresee the conditions of a modern state and, when in three battles against the Swiss he annihilated his army and lost his life, the elements of his future great kingdom threatened to dissolve at once.

His daughter Mary, was at her father's death in 1477, twenty years old. The richest heiress in Europe, her hand had been sought by many suitors. Two months before his death, her father had written to her that he had promised her hand to Maximilian, and already the duchess had given him her heart. The young couple had never met, but they exchanged pictures, and it was noted by the Duchess' attendants that she took her medallion out twenty times a day to look at it. The death of her father added a heavy burden of trouble to the rich dowry of

Mary. Louis XI, King of France, was her father's rival and bitter enemy. On the ground that the King of France was her feudal overlord, he claimed the right to appoint her bridegroom, announced that she must marry the dauphin, and proceeded to seize the Burgundian cities. The burghers of the Netherland cities had been heavily taxed by Mary's father to support the army with which he served his boundless ambitions. They refused to continue to pay the old rates, and demanded the restoration of certain rights of self government which had been forcibly taken from them, extending them for better defense in the future. Mary, left without the means to continue her father's tyranny, was obliged to grant their demands. The helpless girl immediately became the center of intrigues woven by greedy men who wanted her dowry. The King of England pressed the suit of his brother-in-law. The King of France bribed two of her ambassadors to back the cause of his son. The council of Ghent promptly condemned them to death for falsehood and treason, and their heads fell on the scaffold in spite of Mary's earnest plea for mercy. Then the burghers tried to force Mary to marry Duke Adolf of Cleves.

If Maximilian wanted his bride, it was the hour for action. But never in his whole life did Maximilian move quickly in great affairs. That Hapsburg's unwillingness to reach a sharp decision and express it in action, appearing in his father Frederick III, noticeable in his grandson, Charles V, reaching the point of disease in the slow moving great grandson Philip II, beset Maximilian. On the second of April, 1477, Frederick III issued a call to the Princes of the Empire to meet at Easter and follow his son to the Netherlands. The lagging lover had just received this letter from his promised bride. It was brought by a messenger whom he had sent back to Mary with a jewel and a request for her colours to wear on his helmet:—"My dear and friendly lord and brother,—I greet you from my whole heart. . . . You must not let yourself doubt that I will yield obedience to the arrangements made between us by my lord and father, now in glory, and will be to you a true wife, and I do not doubt that you will do the same. The bearer will tell you how I am hemmed in and God, may He give us both what our hearts desire, knows that I cannot talk to him as I would like. I beg you not to remain away—because of the comfort and help you can bring to my lands when you come—and if you don't come, my lands can expect no help or aid from you—because I may be compelled to do things that I should never want to do because I am forced to do them and abandoned by you." On the twenty-first of April there was a marriage by proxy, but still the husband did not come, though the children in the street cried out "Emperor, Emperor," and demanded their prince Maximilian to save them from French conquest. At last in the end of May the Prince was under way for the journey. Two months later he had not gotten beyond Cologne. Two causes helped this delay. The sluggishness of the princes of the Empire in fulfilling their duties and Maximilian's lack of money. His rich bride sent money to meet him at Cologne and at last followed by three of the Electors and many of the princes and nobles, he set off on a slow ride of eighteen days across the lowlands to Ghent.

The city received him with ceremony and enthusiasm. Fifteen hundred white clad burghers met him in stately procession carrying two banners inscribed—"Thou art our Prince and our leader, fight our battle, and all that thou sayest we will do." Mary, standing at the head of the palace steps, received him with a kiss as he ascended by torchlight. At five o'clock the next morning Maximilian, in silver armour, rode again into the castle. In the chapel his bride met him. She was clad in damask embroidered in gold, and girt with a golden girdle set with jewels. She wore a little ermine cloak over her shoulders and a rich golden purse hung at her waist. On her head was the ducal crown of Burgundy blazing with jewels. A papal legate read mass. Then he took a bite from a baked cake and Maximilian and Mary divided and ate it. Then they both drank from the same beaker of red wine and stood man and wife.

The bride whom politics had brought to Maximilian, won an empire over his heart she never lost. This is the way he describes her and his own life in a letter, written four months after marriage, to his comrade left behind in Vienna:— "I have a pretty, virtuous wife that I am satisfied with and give God thanks. She is as tall as the Laxenbergerin but slender of body, much slenderer than Rosina, and snow white. She has brown hair, a little nose, a little head and face, brown eyes mixed with gray, clear and pretty. The underlid of her eyes is somewhat relaxed as if she had slept, but it is not very noticeable. The mouth is a little high but clear and red. And besides there are many girls prettier than I have ever seen together in my life and merry. The women are not kept shut up in the day time but only at night. The whole house is full of women and girls, about forty of them. They can run about the house everywhere all day long. The old lady, our mother, is a fine old woman, very pleasant and good. If we only had peace it would be a garden of roses. . . . . My wife is a thorough sportswoman with hawk and hound. She has a wind hound that is very swift. It sleeps generally all night in our room. Here everybody goes to bed about twelve and gets up about eight. I am the most miserable man in the world that I can't eat, sleep, walk or joust because I have so much to do."[1]

He might well complain of having much to do. The Netherland cities were perhaps the richest in the world outside of Italy. But though the burghers were able to bear heavy taxes, they were not disposed to do so. Their forefathers had been used to a voice in the use of public moneys and the conduct of government, and the Flemings were not so willing as Mary, to let the German boy who had married her do as he pleased. Louis XI, with a treasury and a powerful army at his command, was ready to seize any portion of Mary's inheritance along the north-eastern border he could get by force or bribery. War in defence of these was a great injury to the trade of the Flemish cities of the south, who not unnaturally objected to spending their blood and money on a struggle which brought them nothing but loss. In the northern provinces two cruel factions, the Hooks and the Codfish, were engaged in an obstinate feud. Each demanded Maximilian's unreserved support to exterminate the other. And in addition, the inhabitants of the Duchy of Guelders on the east-

[1] Prüschenk vertraulicher briefwechsel, etc., page 27.

ern border of the Netherlands had only submitted out of fear to the rule of Charles, who bought the Duchy from the noble who claimed to own it. The inhabitants, who had never ratified the sale, preferred at Charles' death a Duke of their own choosing and supported him against Maximilian.

For two years after Maximilian married Mary, the war with France over her inheritance came to nothing but skirmishes and surprises interrupted by truces. It was the summer of 1479 when the two armies met in pitched battle. A council of war decided to attack the French border fortress of Therouanne, and Maximilian started on the invasion with a mixed force of English, Netherland, Burgundian and German troops, amounting to twenty-eight thousand. The bulk of the army was made up of Flemish infantry, militia of the cities; a good part of the remainder were mercenaries. Scarcely was the siege begun, when word came that the French army was within three miles of Therouanne, evidently meaning to give battle. It was difficult to receive an attack with a well garrisoned hostile fortress on the flank; and an assault upon the advancing enemy meant the passing of the Lys. While the artillery and baggage crossed on the pontoons, the infantry waded the river and mounted the hills of the other bank to find themselves face to face with the French drawn up in battle order, "their corselets and head pieces glittering in the sun." They were about twenty-five thousand strong. Maximilian formed his army with the English bowmen and German Schützen in front. Behind them he placed the field guns, and in their rear the masses of his pike-men in two columns. He took his own position with his following of nobles in the last rank. He addressed his captains, bidding them fight bravely; and the French leader also seems to have indulged in a flight of oratory. All these arrangements took up the time until two o'clock when artillery opened the battle. The French answered by a flanking movement of the cavalry. The inferior Burgundian cavalry tried to check it, and were driven from the field in rout. Meantime the first lines of Burgundian infantry had attacked, and the main body of the French, whose leader was in hot pursuit of the routed cavalry, left their strong position to meet them. Charging down the hill, they drove the English bowmen back, took the cannon and charged the two columns of Flemish infantry. They trembled and threatened to break. Then Maximilian sprang from his horse and calling on his nobles to follow, rushed into the ranks. The pikemen rallied, rolled the enemy back through the guns and up the hill, until they broke and fled, leaving their camp at the mercy of the victors. Nearly half the French army and many of their captains fell in the fight or were slaughtered by the peasants in the rout. Maximilian made no further use of the victory so gallantly won. Five days after the battle he dismissed his army and withdrew into Flanders with his booty. His wife rode out to meet him and Maximilian, taking his infant son in his arms, rode with her in triumph through the streets of Ghent amid the shouts of the crowd.

Triumph brought him little rest. Louis XI continued to inspire a border warfare, and factions, the Hooks in the Dutch provinces, the native party in Guelders, French partisans and democrats in Flanders, gave Maximilian few chances during the next three years to lay aside his armour. Then in March of 1482 the great misfortune of his life befell him. As they rode hawking in the meadows near Bruges, the Duchess put her horse at a ditch, the animal fell and she received a fatal hurt. Maximilian broke into such despair when Mary told him,— "I feel we must part," that she begged him to leave the room. "For so it would be better for them both." She summoned the knights of the Golden Fleece, the leading nobles of the Netherlands, and solemnly swore them to be loyal to her husband and support him as regent for her infant son. Maximilian married twice afterwards but never forgot the wife of his heart. In the great picture he planned to show the triumphs of his life, his boyhood's bride and not the wife of his maturity appeared at his side, and several of his intimates have testified that to the time of his death he could never mention Mary's name without the tears springing to his eyes.

The loyalty she showed in the reception of her lover had only increased during the five years of marriage, but the loyalty with which the people of Flanders and the other provinces greeted their young Duke had vanished. The difficulties of government increased with Mary's death, and for years Maximilian, either in person or by lieutenants, waged almost ceaseless war against rebellious peoples he claimed to rule in the name of his son.

To rule the Netherlands well was a difficult task for anyone. Local pride and factional jealousy were rampant everywhere. The provinces were an unassimilated mass of separate administrative entities. Their various privileges clashed sharply with the needs of any common executive. It was a confederation, not a union, and its strongest bond was that the same ruler wore the different crowns. All the blame for these continuous civil wars with his subjects ought not to be laid at the doors of Maximilian, and yet certain qualities which limited his ability to cope with the task, appear with great plainness; nowhere more plainly to the discerning eye than in his own brief account of his troubles in the Netherlands.

This is found in the Weiss Kunig, one of a stately series of works Maximilian composed with the help of artists and secretaries, to record his virtues, capacities and triumphs for the instruction of his descendants and the admiration of posterity.[1] All of these four works, Weiss Kunig, Teuerdank, The Triumphal Arch, The Triumphal Procession, were planned and overseen in every stage of execution by Maximilian himself. The interpolations and revisions of the manuscript of Weiss Kunig and Teuerdank, the drafts dictated or written by him, have made plain to their latest editors that Maximilian is their real author. Even where some of the words are those of his secretaries, all the thoughts and many of the phrases are his own.[2] Whether these four works in which he recorded what he wished remembered of his life work, use prose, poetry or engraving as the medium of expression, they are allegorical. Maximilian, though trained in the New Learning, kept like many of its votaries, the mediæval taste for allegory, and besides, that vague literary form enabled him better to mould to his purpose hard facts

[1] For an account of the Literary Activity of Maximilian, see an article by the writer in the *American Historical Review,* October, 1905.

[2] Jahrbuch des Kunsthistorischen Sammlungen dee Allerhöchsten Kaiserhauses, etc., Vol. VI, page 12. Vol. VII, page 5.

whose cold record might not have given to his descendants just that impression of his transcendent virtue and capacity in meeting them, of which Maximilian himself felt so sure. It takes very little comparison of Weiss Kunig with other accounts of events there spoken of, to conclude that Maximilian felt entirely justified in adjusting or suppressing facts, in order to produce upon the minds of his readers the impression of the great truth of his own supreme tact, courage and skill in meeting adversity. Weiss Kunig therefore is not history, and no one can rely on it for any accurate account of what happened.[1] But this only makes more certain the unconscious disclosures of his motives for action and his attitude toward conditions.

The most significant of these, is the absence of a suggestion of the slighest suspicion that there might have been any justification for the complaints brought against his captains and councilors. For instance, he records that the Flemings said,— "His councilors and captains were thieves. . . . That was a lie for his councilors and captains were pious and honourable." Now it is certain that the mercenaries Maximilian maintained pillaged the people of the Netherlands, friend and foe, in the most shameless and brutal manner. It would indeed have been difficult for Maximilian to restrain them. He was always at his wits' end for money to pay their wages, and to have maintained too strict a discipline would have brought the danger of mutiny among the unpaid troops. That difficulty he could not meet by any remarkable personal

[1] Jahrbücher der K. H. S., etc., Vol. VI, preface, page xxviii.

influence. It is true that soldiers admired Maximilian for the strength that enabled him to break the haft of a great landsknechts spear by the unaided movement of his hands,[1] and the reckless courage which always plunged him into the thickest of every fight, but his court biographer is mistaken in the assertion that those who served him were always full of love and loyalty. Seven marked instances can be cited where his inability to command the loyalty of his unpaid troops betrayed his fortunes to the most dangerous losses.[2] And in the Netherlands he kept the loyalty of his troops largely by losing the loyalty of his people.

His unwillingness to entertain complaints against his councilors came from noble traits of character; generosity, which made money run through his fingers to reward those who served him, and an habitual desire to stand by his friends. But however amiable in a private person, an overwillingness to stand by one's "friends" has always, whether under a monarchy or a republic, been a weakness in a ruler, as fertile for the oppression of the people as deliberate injustice. And a mass of concurrent testimony renders it certain that Maximilian's confidence in his officials was terribly abused. Almost all councilors were at that time in receipt of pensions from foreign potentates, fees to look after their "interests." By the witness of ambassadors of all nationalities, Maximilian's councilors were particularly venal. The English ambassador reports: "The Emperor has councilors as corrupt as possible and plunderers in every way of their

[1] Grünpeck.
[2] Ulmann, Kaiser Maximilian I. Stuttgart, 1884. Vol. I, page 863.

master's goods."[1] Another English agent reports that those of Charles V's councilors who had served under Maximilian, "are hated by all in Almayne."[2] Indeed the Electors had made it a condition of Charles' election that all Maximilian's councilors should be excluded from the new Imperial Council. And at Maximilian's death the people of his Austrian Duchies immediately made a clean sweep of all his officials, and appointed new ones.

This exaggerated corruption of Maximilian's servants continued all his life, until it became proverbial and passed into anecdotage. Erasmus tells in his Colloquies [3] the story of a young nobleman who, having collected fifty thousand florins, returned only thirty thousand to the Emperor. Maximilian took it without question, but the councilors induced him to summon the nobleman again to give an account. The young man, looking around on the assembled council, expressed his willingness to do so if some of those present, "very ready at making up such accounts," would show him how. According to Erasmus, the Emperor smiled at the wit of the reply and asked nothing further.

Another reason beside this willingness to stand by his friends through thick and thin, brought Maximilian into trouble with the burghers of the Netherlands; that was a deep rooted instinctive dislike to political power in any but noble or princely hands. In spite of his popular manners when he mingled at Augsburg or Nuremberg in

[1] Letters and Papers of the Reign of Henry VIII. Domestic Series, Vol. IV, part I, number 1447.

[2] Letters and Papers of the Reign of Henry VIII. Domestic Series, Vol. III, part I, page 134.

[3] Colloquies of Erasmus, translated by N. Bailey. London, 1900. Vol. II, page 177.

city dances, and a sincere desire to do justice to the common people, Maximilian had no confidence in peasant or burgher. This appears in every brief account given in the Weiss Kunig, of different rebellions in the Netherlands. Germany needed nothing more than the hanging of a score of robber barons, but the only executions pictured by Maximilian's orders among the nearly two hundred and fifty wood cuts of Weiss Kunig, are four showing the executions of rebellious peasants or burghers. One shows a block house surrounded by armed men, on one side are wheels on posts; on top of each wheel is a man broken, around the circumference is a fringe of men hung. The note tells how he took a fort of the insurgent Flemings and "whatever of the garrison was not shot or stabbed, he had strung up."

When Maximilian entered Ghent in 1577, the people hated France and hailed him with joy as their defender against French conquest. Five years later on the death of his wife, they threw themselves into the arms of France to be rid of Maximilian's rule. However great the provocation they may have given to their regent, it is hard to apologize for such a fact. People do not usually exchange a hatred for an affection unless they are driven to it.

Maximilian was a constructer of day dreams in which he played a glorious part as restorer of the Empire, or as the head of a crusade driving the Turk from Europe, or as a restorer of the Church, or the founder of the greatest line of kings Europe had known, but his literary works show a most dreary lack of any real power of imagination, and it is probable that he never once succeeded in seeing his rule in the Netherlands from the Netherlander's point of view.

He forced them to take his point of view. He was a merciful man, but war was very cruel in those days. He records that when he invaded France, he made so great a burning that the smoke covered the sun and "for three hours harness did not gleam."[1] He let his troops do their best at destruction around Ghent, which was the center of resistance to his authority, and, in the beginning of the summer of 1485, he entered the city in triumph, accompanied by his young son, who had been kept from him by the insurgents for years. His authority as regent was fully acknowledged, and the leaders of the opposition were sent to the scaffold.

But on almost the same day when the house of Hapsburg thus vindicated by force control over the rich lands of the west, disaster came to it in the east. All of the reigning European houses run back to Adam through two German Countesses, half sisters, who, in the middle of the fourteenth century, married Princes of the houses of Austria and Baden.[2] The desire of the German princes to marry heiresses, which this implies, was a marked characteristic of the Hapsburgs, and their luck in getting rich wives is recorded in the saying,— "Tu felix Austria, nube."

Frederick III's distant cousin and predecessor in the Empire, Albert, had married Elizabeth, who was daughter of Sigismund, Emperor of Germany and King of Bo-

[1] Weiss Kunig, 146.

[2] Lorenz O. Reichskanzler und Reichskanzlei Preuss. Jahrbücher, Vol. XXIX, Introduction IX.

hemia, by Maria, Queen of Hungary. Albert's son, Ladislas Postumus, therefore received the crown of Bohemia through his grandfather and of Hungary through his grandmother. At his death his guardian, Frederick III, advanced a claim to Hungary and Bohemia. But it was not very strong even when supported by his assertion that Bohemia, as a fief of the Empire, was, in default of a male heir, at his disposal. And when Bohemia elected as King, George Podiebrad who had ruled with great skill in the name of the boy-King Ladislas, Frederick, after Austria had been wasted by King George's armies, made peace, and gave a half promise to confirm him in the fief of Bohemia and grant him the title of Elector of the Empire.

The throne of Hungary was claimed by William, Duke of Saxony and Casimer, King of Poland, husbands of Ladislas Postumus' sisters. But the Hungarian nobles were very unwilling to have an outsider for their ruler. They chose Matthias, son of John Hunyadi, who had occupied in Hungary the same position George Podiebrad held in Bohemia, and driven a great Turkish army from the walls of Belgrade.

A rebellion against Matthias offered the crown of Hungary to Frederick III and the civil war was closed by an agreement that Matthias should be King, but if he died without a son, Frederick or one of his sons should succeed to the crown of Hungary. A war between George of Bohemia and Matthias of Hungary, was closed by the offer of George to acknowledge Matthias as heir. Shortly after George died and the Bohemians, disregarding the agreements between Matthias and George, chose Prince Ladislas of Poland, King. Matthias' persistence in fighting for his claim to the Bohemian crown when the Turks were threatening to destroy Hungary, produced a rebellion among his nobles, who elected another King. Matthias subdued the rebellion, and forced Ladislas of Bohemia to surrender the greater part of his possessions, with the privilege of redeeming them on Matthias' death for a huge ransom. The Emperor Frederick intrigued against Matthias' plans, and the outcome of the ill feeling was that, in 1485, Matthias overran Austria and entered Vienna in triumph while the Emperor Frederick fled from his duchy to ask help from the German princes.

Their answer was to elect his son, Maximilian, King of the Romans, a title which made him heir apparent to the Empire. On the ninth of April, 1486, the three archiepiscopal Electors of Cologne, Treves and Mayence crowned him at Aachen. Maximilian promised to take up the burden of the war in Austria,[1] but no sooner was he crowned than he returned to the Netherlands, and took the first opportunity of beginning a war of revenge on France. By the summer of 1487 Flanders was plunged into disorder and discontent. Maximilian's unpaid mercenaries again plundered his subjects, and the burghers of Ghent and Bruges saw no reason why their money should be spent in a war whose only effect upon their fortunes was the ruin of their trade with France.

The discontent was not long in finding expression. In 1487 a general assembly of the guilds of Ghent voted unanimously that peace with France ought to be main-

[1] Pruschenk vertraulicher briefwechsel, etc., page 58.

tained, and ordered an inquiry into the causes of the deplorable condition of the finances of the city. They deposed the city officials and appointed new ones. Maximilian replied to this revolt by putting a price of six gold pieces on the head of each insurgent and twelve for each prisoner. Bruges refused to vote troops to attack Ghent, and sent a deputation to inquire into the causes of the discontent in the sister city. Ghent replied by complaining of the war with France, the maladministration of the finances, the filling of the offices with foreigners, and the protracted refusal to give any accounting for the expenditure of the extraordinary taxes they had voluntarily voted to the government.

Meantime, trouble had arisen between Maximilian's mercenary troops, hated on account of their pillaging, and the people of Bruges. It was increased by the report of a plot to seize the gates and let in the army outside to master the city. The alarm bell rang, the burghers assembled in the market place, overawed the men at arms and the regent became a prisoner in his own city. A number of his officials accused of peculation were executed after summary trials.

Vain attempts were made to free Maximilian. The Pope threatened the maledictions of the Church on Bruges. The Emperor summoned the forces of the Empire to march to release the King of the Romans. His partisans ravaged the country and rode round the walls. One of the many adherents, whose loyalty he kept through good and bad fortune, Kunz von der Rosen, a nobleman who was in court half as friend and half as licensed jester, got into Bruges in the robe of a monk to beseech Maximilian to take his disguise and steal out, leaving him to bear the fury of the outwitted burghers. Maximilian refused the stratagem as unworthy of his royal dignity. Despairing of aid after four months' imprisonment, he yielded to the insurrection. On the 16th of May, 1488, he solemnly swore in the market place to dismiss his mercenaries from the Netherlands, to give up the regency of Flanders and allow a council to rule them in the name of his son. He also promised to maintain peace with France. In the other provinces he was to remain regent, but deputies were to meet every year in a common assembly of the Netherlands, and neither peace nor war was hereafter to be made without the vote of this assembly. In return, he was to receive a sum of money to pay his mercenaries before dismissal and a considerable yearly income from Flanders. Maximilian left hostages in Bruges and Ghent for the keeping of this oath, and took it with mention of the penalties of the church on perjury, and he promised to persuade the Pope, the Emperor and the Electors to confirm these agreements.[1]

Scarcely was he free when he heard that his father, with an army of twenty thousand men, was on the banks of the Rhine. Arrived in the camp, he tried to induce the army to turn back, but was finally persuaded to break his oath and fight with them; probably on the ground that the citizens of Bruges had treacherously imprisoned him and compelled him to swear to the dishonour of the Empire.[2]

[1] De Smet Memoire Historique de La Guerre de Maximilian Roi des Romains Contre les Villes de Flandre. Mem. de l'Académie, Bruxelles, Tome XXXV.

[2] Ulmann, Kaiser Max. I. Vol. I, page 30 ff.

He himself wrote that he made the campaign not in his own quarrel, but only as a Prince of the Empire bound to follow its banner. At the same time he demanded the payment of the sums of money which had been part of the agreement he was breaking; an instance of the way in which Maximilian's tenacity in holding to his own rights, limited his power to put himself in another's place and was unmitigated even by a sense of humour.

But the army could not take Bruges, and by the autumn was back in Germany. In the end of December, Maximilian said farewell to the Netherlands where he had spent twelve years of almost continuous fighting, and followed it. His own authority in his infant son's provinces was far from strong. Flanders and Brabant in the south, Guelders in the east, were in the hands of his opponents backed by the French and The Hooks were stirring in Holland and Zealand.

He left his affairs in strong hands, Albert Duke of Saxony was one of the most efficient of living Germans, and in three years, by cruel war and bold diplomacy, he had allayed or crushed opposition.

While Albert of Saxony was thus maintaining Maximilian's fight to remain regent of the Netherlands, the King of the Romans was very busy with those troubles of his house in south and east which his father had been unable to master. In this he employed what was undoubtedly his greatest power,—an ability to conciliate opponents. Skill in conciliation was in those days, and probably has been in all days, rarer than power to fight, and Maximilian seems to have possessed a high degree of it. He was an exceedingly amiable personality with tactful manners, based on real thoughtfulness for others.[1] One of his biographers called him the most affable prince of his age. People embittered by wrongs were often appeased by a meeting with him. And he always tried to put everyone, prince or peasant, at his ease. Frederick the Wise said, that "during his whole life he had never met a more polite man than the Emperor Maximilian."[2]

He employed this skill now in three directions—to reconcile King Matthias, the conqueror of the Austrian lands, with his father Frederick III,—to reconcile Frederick III with his son-in-law, Albert of Bavaria,—to reconcile his distant cousin, Sigismund of Tirol, to the estates of Tirol.

He agreed to meet Matthias at Vienna in August, 1489, and though the meeting never took place, an exchange of ambassadors brought the King of the Romans and the King of Hungary very near to an agreement for the peaceable restoration of Austria upon payment of an indemnity. Maximilian had reckoned without his old and suspicious father, who, though powerless to recover his domains, refused all compromise. But a truce until September, 1490, was finally established.

Maximilian immediately moved westward to arrange the affairs of his house in Tirol. At Innsbruck he found an exceedingly strained situation. Duke Sigismund of Tirol, a man of some parts and cultivated tastes, was too weak and selfish to be even a tolerable ruler. He had fallen com-

[1] In his last hour, when the clergy gathered in his room to chant the penitential psalms, unable to speak, he made a sign with his hand for them to be seated. Funeral Oration by Faber. Freher Struve, Vol. II, page 741.

[2] Friedrichs des Weisen Leben und zeit geschichte nach Spalatins handschrift herausgegeben. Neudecker und Preller, page 45.

pletely into the power of unworthy favorites and greedy councilors. They had squandered the public money, and finally induced Sigismund to declare in March, 1487, a useless war on Venice. This ruined the trade by which Tirolese merchants lived, and his incompetent commanders met disaster in the field. An assembly of the Estates practically deprived him of the exercise of the powers of government by putting affairs in the hands of a council chosen by him out of their nominees. They added to the decrees which established the new order, that, if the agreement was broken, they should feel justified in calling another prince of the house of Austria to become their Duke. Sigismund quarrelled with his new council and a dangerous deadlock was referred to the assembly. Maximilian, coming to Innsbruck, persuaded his cousin to break it by assigning to him the authority over Tirol and the lands which went with it. The astonished assembly gladly hailed Maximilian as Duke and he ratified all their rights and privileges.[1]

The third reconciliation was the most difficult. The Dukes of Bavaria had long been rivals of the Hapsburgs, and they had played on the weakness of Sigismund to the utmost. Flattering his vanity, they had exploited his needs, until, by sale or pledge, they had obtained large portions of the Hapsburg lands between Tirol and Bavaria. The older branch of the house found their opportunity to protest against this when Albert of Bavaria, a handsome and brilliant Prince of thirty-eight, saw at Sigis-

[1] Jäger Albert. Der Uebergang Tirols und der österreich ischer vorlände von dem Erghergoge Sigmund an den römischen König Maximilian, Archiv für österreich ische Geschichte LI.

mund's court the beautiful Kunigunde, the Emperor's twenty-year-old daughter. He promptly fell in love with her. Frederick was not unwilling to make the match if the House of Bavaria would give back the lands they had gotten from Sigismund. If this were done, he would give his daughter her mother's jewels and a small dowry in lands. The bankrupt Sigismund, with his usual generosity, also offered a dowry for Kunigunde. But in the midst of these negotiations, the wooer took another good piece of Hapsburg territory. The Imperial City of Regensburg was deeply in debt. Albert offered to pay this debt and grant privileges which prophesied prosperity. The council accepted his offer, ceased to be a Free City owing direct allegiance to the Emperor, and became subjects of Albert. The Emperor at once withdrew his consent to the marriage. But Albert evidently intended to get lands and bride too. He forged a letter from the Emperor consenting to the match, and the willing Sigismund and Kunigunde hastened the marriage. And, far from giving back to the house of Hapsburg the lands he held in pledge, he followed the marriage by the largest purchase of lands he had yet gotten from the good natured spendthrift who had helped him to his bride. At his sister's request, Maximilian now tried to remove their father's anger with his son-in-law. It was naturally very difficult. But after he had made the house of Wittelsbach willing to return, in exchange for the money advanced on them, the lands sold or pledged, he finally succeeded in effecting an outward reconciliation between the old Emperor and his children.

These three successful efforts at pacification were,

however, interrupted by war. King Matthias of Hungary died in April, 1490. He left no legitimate son and according to the old treaty with Frederick, made in 1463, a Hapsburg was to succeed. The situation gave Maximilian a chance not only to reconquer Austria but to seize the crown of Hungary. The magnates of Hungary were not disposed either to carry out the old treaty, by which the crown went to Maximilian, or the wishes of their dead King, that his illegitimate son, John Corvinus, should wear the crown. They elected Ladislas of Bohemia, as their King. He marched promptly to secure the possession of the Hungarian conquest of Austria. Unexpected difficulty met him, for Vienna was tired of foreign rule. The burghers rose, shut the Magyar garrison up in the citadel and prepared for defense. Maximilian pushed the enlistment of mercenaries and in the end of July, began a swift re-conquest of the lands his father had lost. On the nineteenth of August, 1490, he entered Vienna amid the shouts of the people, greeting one whose entry a leading physician, in the joy of his heart, recorded in his diary thus: "Omnipotent God of his grace gave to the people the most just, most chaste, most strenuous, most warlike, Maximilian (in black ink), Maximilian (in red ink), Maximilian (with green ink)." [1] By the end of the month the Hungarian was driven from the Hapsburg lands.

The University of Vienna had solemnly voted that Maximilian was rightful King of Hungary. The curse of the age was senseless war, denounced by all its ablest men from Erasmus to Machiavelli. It was a rare ruler

[1] Fontes Rerum Austriacum, Vol. I, page 53.

who could resist the temptation to assert a paper claim upon foreign territory in campaigns which could bring nothing but loss to the country of which he was the natural sovereign. Many years were needed before Henry VIII outgrew the day dream of adding the crown of France to the crown of England, and three successive Valois squandered blood and treasure upon Italian invasions denounced by their wisest counselors as promising more present loss than future gain. Maximilian could hardly be expected to be cleverer than the bulk of his contemporaries, especially since his father's reluctance to make war, had seemed so much the outcome of weakness rather than of wisdom. In October, 1490, he crossed the Hungarian border with a strong army. His march was a triumphal procession. In November he stormed the rich Stuhlweissenburg where the Hungarian kings were crowned and buried, and the whole kingdom lay helpless at his feet. The mercenaries celebrated the victory with slaughter and plunder, and still demanded extra wages. Maximilian, as usual, had no money and without payment his men positively refused to move forward. In December he was compelled to march back to Vienna. Six months later his conquests were lost, and the only result of his attempt to gain the crown of Hungary was a heavier debt for himself and the wasting of the farms of Hungarian peasants with fire and sword. Nothing remained but compromise and, in the end of 1491, the Peace of Pressburg, ratified by the Hungarian magnates, acknowledged Ladislas as King of Hungary and his male children as heirs, on condition that, failing a male heir, the crown should go to Maximilian and his descendants.

To celebrate his success in unifying the possessions and enlarging the prospects of the Hapsburgs, Maximilian had a medal struck in the spring of 1490. One side shows his head. The reverse displays the arms of Hungary, Austria and Tirol with the arms of Burgundy below.

Maximilian was glad to be set free from trouble in the east. For many months he had longed to hasten toward the west. His efforts for internal peace had for their strongest motive a plan which promised at once revenge on France and an extension of Hapsburg territories. He had long been an ally of the Duke of Brittany, last of the great semi-royal feudal magnates, who had so long hampered the Valois in their efforts to make France a nation. In 1488 the Duke had been defeated by the forces of the crown, compelled to surrender his fortresses and to promise not to marry his daughter and heir Anne without the consent of the French King. Anne was fourteen years old and like Mary of Burgundy, besieged by suitors. Among them she preferred Maximilian; strong, warlike, able to champion her distress. The French crown offered Maximilan free hand in Flanders if he would let Brittany alone. Maximilian apparently accepted, but, in the end of 1490, was secretly married to Anne by proxy.

His bride, little more than a clever child, was surrounded by enemies. He knew he must help Brittany, which he loved more than his Duchess, by the sword. He was therefore compelled to come before the Reichstag asking men and money for two enterprises; against Hungary in the east, and France in the west. They reluctantly voted eight thousand men and, in August, Maximilian announced to his father the intention of marching into Brittany with such a force as he could gather. His father gave unwilling permission to carry the banner of the Empire, but warned his son of disaster. The smallest knowledge of men ought to have told Maximilian that, whatever his enemies said, they were leaving nothing undone to break his marriage. And the smallest knowledge of women should have warned him that they would surely succeed if he kept too long away from the young girl who had turned to him in distress. But impulsive as Maximilian was in making a plan, he was very slow in carrying it out, and he seems to have laboured under the delusion that to form the idea of a stroke of state-craft, was the same as accomplishing it. Lack of enough men and money and the commands of his father to let Brittany alone until he had attended to Hungary, may have made it impossible for Maximilian to go to Brittany. But in that case he ought not to have been surprised to hear, a week after the agreement of Pressburg had made him heir to the throne of Hungary if the dynasty failed, that the young girl who for a year had vainly called for his help, flattered by his enemies, attacked by her own, insulted by his neglect, had given way. The Pope annulled her marriage and in November, 1491, Anne of Brittany, became Queen of France. Maximilian's daughter Margaret had for years been in France where she was being educated as the affianced bride of Charles VIII. At one stroke, therefore, the Valois had taken Maximilian's bride and jilted his daughter.

The fact that he had given the chance for this double insult made Maximilian feel it the more. The slow burning Hapsburg hate never died out of his heart and during all his life, it was hard for Maximilian to free himself long from the instinctive desire to get even with the Valois. At the moment he could do but little for vengeance. The princes of Germany would not give him forces fit to invade France, and his allies, Henry VII and Ferdinand of Aragon, allowed themselves to be bought off by the French crown. He made a successful invasion of the ancient Burgundian lands, and at Senlis, May, 1493, received back the greater part of his daughter's dowry.

Both sides were ready for peace because Charles and Maximilian were drawn from the war over Brittany and Burgundy by larger plans. The young King of France wanted to use the great power won for him by his keen and unscrupulous father and his clever sister, in some undertaking which should give him the pleasures of adventure and the sense of glory. He mustered his soldiers and called his nobility to follow him over the Alps and Apennines to assert his claim upon the crown of Naples. At the end of August, 1494, with the greatest army at his back Europe had seen for a generation, he poured down into the Lombard plain and opened a long series of wars in which Frenchman, Spaniard, German and Swiss slaughtered the Italian peasant in his field or plundered the shop-keepers of the cities, to decide who had the right to wear the crowns of the Italian principalities.

Maximilian was not able to keep out of this conflict, into which he was called by duty, inclination, ambition and hate. But the plan which made him eager to put aside even his war upon France, looked to a larger prize than the control of the destinies of Italy. The crusading impulse, so far as it affected the people of Europe, was dead. The enthusiasm which had swept thousands from their homes, careless of life and property, to assoil their sins and wrest the tomb of Christ from the infidel, could not be roused again. For a century, popes who took their office seriously had tried in vain to light that old flame and for a generation, popes who looked on the office of Vicar of Christ as a means to gratify taste or satisfy family ambitions, had used the duty of checking the Turk as a pretext for raising money. The duty was a plain one, and rested no longer on fanatic hatred of the infidel but on the need of self defense. The Turk, firmly established on the lower Danube, and entrenched at Constantinople, had made evident his intention of conquering Europe if he could. He was not really a menace. Asia never was a match for Europe, and the forces of Mahomet II were less able to beat the men who said their prayers in Latin than the army of Xerxes was to master the men who called on Zeus in Greek. The Teutonic and Romanic peoples could have driven him back over the Armenian mountains even without the help of Slav and Magyar. But their eagerness to fight each other made the Turk a menace. His galleys swept the shores of the Mediterranean, his horsemen ravaged the banks of the Danube and, by a diabolically ingenious circle of evil, war fed war. Thousands of Christian children, whose parents had died vainly defending their homes, bred up as Mohammedans, menaced the cities of Europe in the ranks of the Janizaries. Thousands of Christian captives laboured at the oars which bore blood and fire and slavery along the coasts of Italy.

The crusading impulse was dead, but the dream of pouring an army down the Danube, breaking the gates of Constantinople and driving the terror and shame of Christendom across the Bosphorus was still to fascinate the minds of many a European ruler. Over none did it exercise a stronger sway, than it held from boyhood to age over the romantic mind of Maximilian, always starting to build the towers of his castles in the air before he sat down to count the cost. He recorded in his autobiography that his mother wanted him named Constantine because he was to recover Constantinople,[1] and, two years before his death, he told the Earl of Worcester that he had never cared for the title Emperor of the Holy German Empire, because he had intended to take the title Emperor of Constantinople, of which he was rightful heir.[2] Although an assault on Constantinople was an undertaking beyond Maximilian's ability, a man of his capacity might have defended Styria and Carinthia from the ceaseless plundering of raiders. But while Maximilian dreamed of storming Constantinople, the Turkish horsemen were sweeping his people into slavery, and he took the field against nearly everybody else in Europe except the Turks.

The Emperor Frederick III had for several years withdrawn entirely from public business. There are no indications of any particular affection between him and his son. They seldom met and Frederick did little for his successor's plans except to hinder them. The old

[1] Jahrbücher de Kh. S., page 423 (14).

[2] Letters and Papers of the Reign of Henry VIII. Domestic Series, Vol. II, part II, page 1022.

man had suffered for some time with decay of the bones of one leg. He refused an operation so long as possible, and even in the agonies of amputation at the knee, called out,—"Alas, Kaiser Frederick III, that you must carry to all posterity the nickname of the 'Halting'." He had not to bear his lameness long. He was passionately fond of fruit, and ate in the early morning a huge quantity of melons. The result was death in the seventy-eighth year of his age (1493).

The magnificent funeral of his father only interrupted for a time the plans of Maximilian against Constantinople. In all probability, his third marriage was related to these. Lodovico Sforza, heir presumptive of the Duchy of Milan, which he ruled as regent for his nephew, was not of noble descent. His grandfather, Jacopo Attendolo, was a peasant who had become one of the celebrated mercenary generals of his day. His father, a great soldier, had married the daughter of the Duke of Milan and seized the Duchy at his father-in-law's death. It is difficult to see why the match with the pretty young daughter of this house, Lodovico's niece, was accepted by Maximilian. He never cared for her in the least, and her plebeian descent was the object of scorn from the German princes. It is probable that he thought he could use against the Turk her large dowry of three hundred thousand ducats, and her father, whom he promised to invest with the Duchy of Milan, would protect him from trouble in Italy and send troops for his crusade. Five months after this marriage, he solemnly joined in Antwerp the Order of St. George, and two weeks later, he sent out an appeal to all princes of the world to join the Order and thus become sworn soldiers of the cross against the crescent.

In November, 1494, he issued a call for a Reichstag next year at Worms, to make preparations for a stately journey to Rome, that he might receive the crown of the Empire at the hands of the Pope and then march at the head of Europe against the infidel.

Before the Reichstag assembled in March, his plans had changed. The young King of France had swept all before him in Italy. Naples lay at his feet and he began to dictate to the rulers of Italy like a master of the world. It was reported that he intended to realize Maximilian's daydream to drive the Turk from Europe and re-establish the Roman Empire in the East. But the hegemony of Italy was easier to gain than to keep. The states which had invited his expedition against Naples, now frightened at his power, drew together. Naples, Milan and the Pope, formed in the end of March, the Holy League, ostensibly against the Turk, but secretly against France. Maximilian and Ferdinand of Spain were its allies.

Maximilian's entry into this League was in every way natural. Most of the North Italian states were nominally fiefs of the Empire, whose crown, according to custom, must be taken at Rome. It was difficult for him to keep out of any fight. An expedition across the Alps promised change, adventure, glory and it was hard for him to see the rival who had taken his betrothed wife, threatening to assume that central position in the world's stage which he felt belonged by divine right to himself.

Nor was he singular in this opinion. One of the most interesting literary remains of the age is a "Dream" written in Latin in 1495 by Hans von Hermansgrün, a nobleman who had studied in Rome under the distinguished humanist Pomponius Lætus. The manuscript was circulated at the Reichstag and read by its members. It relates how the writer, returning to Saxony, spent the night with a friend, Henry of Amensdorff, in his castle at Rothenburg on the Saale. After dinner they talked late of the dangerous situation of the Roman Empire. When Hans retired, soothed by the good bed and the pleasant murmur of the river which bathed the castle walls, he soon fell into a deep sleep. He saw in his dream the splendour and strength of the Roman Empire assembled in the great church of St. Mauritius at Magdeburg. No one presided over the assembly. While all stood in expectation, three men of superhuman size, wearing imperial diadems, entered the church. All bowed to the ground as they took their place on raised seats. One of them arose and, introducing his comrades as Charles the Great and Otto the Great, named himself as Frederick Barbarossa, "who restored the falling state of the Germans and bore the victorious eagles over land and sea throughout the world." Checking the murmurs of applause with a wave of his hand and looking sternly on them, he addressed the assembly. He pointed out that the Empire was threatened by two wars, on the east from the Turks, on the west from the French. Germany could meet both these dangers if it were not for the decay of German spirit. Luxury had imperiled the courage and ambition of her princes and nobles. Military discipline was undermined. Justice was no longer administered. The strength of the nation was wasted in petty civil wars. Let them wake from their sloth and disorder to remember the ancient glories of the Empire. They ought not to attack the Turk leaving France in the rear. France had seized Italy, and they must hold it for certain that they could not retain the orb of Empire unless they wrested Italy from France. And France, after she had securely subdued Italy, could with the wealth thus gained conquer Germany. Let them make a close alliance with Venice and Spain, call England to share in the spoil and destroy France. It is true that their King, Maximilian, was more fitted for the distaff than the spindle. Sunk in slothful pleasures he had let the King of France conquer Bungundy, Piccardy, Brittany, and the Duchy of Milan, insult his daughter and seize his wife. Let the princes, in spite of this weak and spiritless King, join in counsel and save the Empire. While the assembly stood astonished and ashamed at this oration of Frederick Barbarossa, Hans was awakened by his servant.

Such writing, from the pen of one of the few humanists who have written anything but praise of Maximilian, shows that the Imperial idea and its expression in the two great wars of which Maximilian dreamed so long, was in the air.

But the bulk of the Germans with political power did not share this desire to make great exertions in order that a German Emperor might control the Italians, dictate to the Dutch and destroy the prestige of France. The motives for this lack of practical enthusiasm for the ideal of the Emperor as the master of Christendom, were both good and bad. Some of the princes were envious of the

Hapsburgs and ambitious for the glory of their own dynasties. Some princes did not want a strong Emperor lest he might curtail their own independence. The cities hated war which destroyed their trade and weakened them before the princes and barons, always ready to humiliate or oppress them. Everyone shrank from taxation, and nearly everyone felt that certain reforms in those German speaking states, lying between the Alps and the North and Baltic seas, which formed the core of the Empire, ought to precede any great expenditure of energy toward the west, the east, or the south.

Maximilian could not be unaware of the need of internal reform, which had been ceaselessly discussed among Germans since he was born. He hoped, and not altogether unreasonably, to lay the foundation for it in a revival or an increase of the control of the Emperor over the different parts of the loose confederation of which he was nominal head. Centralization around the imperial throne was his solution for the problem of reform. He felt that to get the Germans to follow him in fighting for the glory of the Empire against men who spoke another tongue, was the best way to bring Germany into order by bringing it to union.

He failed to persuade the Germans to adopt his plan and the reasons for his failure seem to have been in himself. They may be stated under two heads: First,—in spite of his marked abilities, certain traits of his character roused a suspicion, which his conduct steadily nourished, that he was not capable of conducting large enterprises; though the difficulties which lay before him were so increased by this very suspicion that his admirers suggest as the chief reason for his failure, the unwillingness of small-minded German princes to follow him in large enterprises. Secondly,—the suspicion, also nourished by his conduct, that he regarded the glory of the Empire as an appendage to the glory of his dynasty. It is impossible to read through the letters and books of Maximilian without seeing that this suspicion was just. The unconscious self-betrayals of his writings show so clearly that he who runs may read, that Maximilian was Hapsburg first and German afterwards.

The Reichstag, or great assembly of the representatives of the states of the Empire, was a very difficult body to lead to any conclusion, and the task of reform was prodigious. In the beginning of the sixteenth century, the ambassador Vincenzo Quirini, writing to the Venetian Senate, says the sovereign states of the Empire consist of two kingdoms, about thirty duchies and an archduchy, four marquisates, a great number of countships, five arch-episcopates, twenty-five bishoprics, twenty abbeys, fifteen priories, five knight's orders holding sovereign rights, one territory and a hundred free cities. He estimates that the united incomes of three of these great princes would exceed that of the Emperor; the incomes of ten of them would be more than double Maximilian's revenues. He believes that the total income of the free cities exceeds that of all the princes of the Empire, spiritual and lay, put together. From these political units four hundred and seventy-five representatives were summoned to the Reichstag. All those summoned never assembled. One hundred delegates, many of them holding proxies, made a large Reichstag. The great cost of the meetings, where delegates rivaled one another in the size of their trains and the display of their life, kept many from coming. The tedium of the disordered, complicated and ineffective procedure of the three chambers, electors, princes and cities, made all who came anxious to get away. Nor was everybody always summoned. Therefore the Reichstag which met at Worms in 1495, sometimes called the great Reichstag, with five electors, one hundred and six princes, counts and lords, and the representatives of twenty-four free cities, was a large diet.[1]

All Maximilian really cared about was a grant of men and money to attack Charles VIII. What the enormous majority of the Reichstag chiefly cared about, next to their own territorial interests, was the reform of the Empire. The need of reform could hardly be exaggerated. It appeared most acutely in two closely connected disorders; the lack of any proper administration of justice, and the feud right which filled Germany with plundering and killing. Each of the political units of the Empire from the smallest count to an elector, thought it a natural right to avenge injuries by war upon a neighbour. And the lack of a proper administration of justice or of any force to compel obedience to the imperial courts, put temptation to vengeance in the way of the just and gave an excuse for highway robbery to every lazy and rapacious knight who could hire a dozen mercenaries to serve in his petty "war" against a neighbouring city. Some of the princes maintained order in their own borders, but in whole sections, particularly in South Germany, the roads were unsafe because of noble highwaymen. Occasionally one of these

[1] Alberi Relazioni, etc. Series I, Vol. VI.

was taken and had his head cut off in the market place of Nuremberg or Augsburg. But usually when the burgher militia marched out to attack these pests of the industrious inhabitants of town or country, they defied attack from the walls of their castle on the crags, or took refuge in the hills still thickly covered with forests. The frequent feuds of the greater princes and the cities poured out little armies killing and burning. The Empire was seldom free from at least one of these feuds raging or smouldering.

The lesser nobility regarded them as profitable and legitimate means of livelihood. Götz von Berlichingen was a robber baron with a sufficiently good conscience to conclude in his memoirs recording how he plundered the burghers, that "Almighty God had been with him, wonderfully with His grace, help and mercy and had done more for him than he had for himself." He tells how, riding in the night with a prisoner held for ransom, he saw wolves suddenly attack a flock of sheep. "In this sight I took great pleasure and wished luck to them and to us. Good luck, good comrades," I cried, "good luck everywhere. I held it for a good omen that we had thus attacked at the same moment."

He was not without a rough humour and describes how he waylaid some burghers going to the Frankfort fair. "I caught five or six of them, among them a merchant whom I took for the third time in six months, besides once getting some of his goods. * * * I pretended I was going to cut off all their heads, or at least their hands. I made them kneel down and lay their hands on a block. Then I caught the first with my foot in the stern and gave the second a good one on the ear; that was the only punishment I gave them and then I let them go." [1]

Some of these human beasts of prey were less good humoured, for a popular nobleman's song was,—"Wilt thou get a living, young nobleman? Then follow my advice. Lurk in the greenwood. When the peasant drives through, rush out at him, grab him by the collar, rejoice thy heart, take what he has, cut loose his horses, be quick and hardy. If he hasn't a penny, then slit his throat." [2]

We must not exaggerate this evil. The German cities had grown rich in spite of it. It did not prevail in all parts of the land, and blackmail would usually bring protection. Nor did a certain chance of plundering seem as great danger to a generation used to arms as it would now. The prospect of giving or taking death was not intolerable to a large part of the community, for the world was used to violence and the brute in man nearer the surface. But while public robbery and private war was being repressed in most other European lands toward the close of the fifteenth century, Germany was going backward. "The German people loves its laws," wrote a Frenchman in 1493, "but the complaints are universal that justice is deeply sunken in the imperial and other courts and that even when verdicts are rendered, there is no quick and strict fulfilment of them. Therefore, feuds have long been a dreadful plague and robber knights make the roads unsafe and care nothing for right and justice." [3]

[1] Lebensbeschreibung des Ritters Götz von Berlichingen.

[2] Quoted by Lamprecht, Deutsche Geschichte, Berlin, 1896, Vol. V, Erste Halfte, page 80.

[3] Pierre de Froissard Lettres, 5-6. Quoted Janssen, Geschichte des deutschen Volkes, Freiburg, 1881, Vol. I, page 457.

Maximilian could not have felt that the reform of this condition was his first care, for he had planned to stay only a couple of weeks in Worms, and then to carry off the princes from the Rhine to the mountains of Tirol; where he hoped to rouse such a "sound of horns and hunting calls that the Turks and all other bad Christians should hear them echo."[1] This was time enough to get men and money. It was not time enough to arrange a reform of the Empire. His fiery call to meet the French in defense of their honour and freedom, was coldly heard by the princes to whom the danger did not seem so pressing. And in the demands he made upon them Maximilian laid bare one of his worst traits,—a certain changeableness, which grew upon him until his enemies came to count on it as an ally. Often he made a plan of action, only to suddenly lay it aside and take another, not because circumstances changed, but because his lively fancy had slipped the control of will and reason and borne him headlong in some other direction. He kept continually altering his demands upon the Reichstag at Worms, now asking for men and now for money, now bidding the princes follow him in person, now pointing toward France and now toward Italy. The answer of the Reichstag was firm and practically unanimous. It would not make any grant for war until complaints were redressed. And it would not discuss a new military organization of the Empire, unless provision was made for better courts and the preservation of public peace. The members presented to Maximilian plans for an imperial court, a permanent

[1] Prüschenk vertraulicher briefwechsel, etc., page 102.

"landfriede" or prohibition of private war, and an imperial council.

He finally agreed that a new imperial court should be created, to sit permanently at Frankfort instead of following the Emperor. It was to be composed half of knights and half of doctors of law. The Emperor was to name the chief judge. For the other places nominations were to be made by princes, assemblies and cities, and a committee of the Reichstag was to choose among them. He also accepted an "ewige landfriede," or lasting prohibition of private war, in place of the suspension for ten years then ostensibly in force.[1] But the Imperial Council Maximilian absolutely refused. The proposition was to put the executive power of the Empire into the hands of a Council of seventeen; he was to name the president; each of the six active electors to name a member, the other ten members, four from the archdioceses, four from the civil divisions of the Empire, two from the cities, were to be chosen by the Reichstag, and the council thus constituted was to fill vacancies. Such a plan made the Empire an oligarchy where the electors or greatest princes held the chief power. It was perhaps not to be expected that Maximilian would accept such a change. But it must be remembered that the Empire was then nothing but a name, and the rights he indignantly refused to yield only paper ones. Indeed, at that very moment, the titular Emperor of Germany was vainly begging the representatives of his subjects for a few thousand men and a couple of hundred thousand florins. The evils of which his

[1] Ausgewählte Urkunden, etc. Altmann und Bernheim. Berlin, 1895, page 254.

subjects complained were patent and undeniable. He must either accept this plan to destroy them, or propose another which was effective. Two hundred years later, William III, no lover of constitutional government, granted all the parliamentary privileges of England in order to secure her support in his war against France. If Maximilian had been a great ruler, consulting facts rather than his desires, and with any foresight of the way men would act, he ought either to have done the same, or else, abandoning his war with France, have devoted all his energies to crushing the oligarchical opposition by proposing a reform effective enough to do what needed to be done, and thus rally a party round himself. What he did do, was to accept the proposed landfriede and imperial court, take the vote of a special aid and the establishment of a regular imperial tax, half poll tax and half property tax, and propose an Imperial Council dependent on himself and acting only in his absence. The notorious corruption among Maximilian's ministers, and the lack of financial skill which left him at the opening of the Reichstag unable to pay the inn bills of his wife in the Netherlands, made the Reichstag afraid to trust the expenditure of the new taxes to such a body. They finally agreed to substitute for an Imperial Council, a yearly meeting of the Reichstag to see that the reforms were carried out. This failed to give Germany the stronger executive she needed, but the radical reform party was tired of the long discussion; split up by jealousy and selfishness. Maximilian thought seriously of nothing except raising enough money to cross the Alps.

The money came in very slowly. The tax was voted

but not paid. Maximilian called a new Reichstag to meet in the Summer of 1496, and reached Italy in August, 1496, with only four thousand men and not a single German prince behind him. The French King had left Italy, and his easy conquest of Naples had been lost before the troops of Spain and Venice. It was therefore enough for Maximilian, as protector of the fiefs of the Empire in Italy, to bar the Alpine passes against his return and subdue his ally, Florence. But Maximilian proposed the largest plans. He was to embark a great force and attack France from the southern sea coast, while the German princes, under the lead of the Elector of Mayence, the head of the Reform party he had disappointed in Worms, was to invade France from the west. Another imperial army was to descend into Italy over the Alps. This was great strategy, but for the tactics to express it Maximilian had only four thousand men, reserves not mustered except in his own mind, princes who did not want to fight France, allies some of whom wished him back over the Alps. His treasury was so empty that he was obliged to beg a loan of two hundred or three hundred ducats to pay his table expenses. A risky dash to take Livorno, the sea-port of Florence, failed. Maximilian, discouraged and disgusted with the insubordination of his allies, suddenly gave up the attack on Florence, and, in a humour so bad that he even refused his beloved sport of hunting, withdrew over the Alps in the end of December, 1496. The four months of his campaign in Italy had only confirmed the unwillingness of the German princes to see in him another Frederick Barbarossa, sent to restore the glory of the Germanic Empire, and greatly injured the reputation as a soldier he had gained in the Netherlands and Hungary.

It was eighteen months later before he again addressed the German princes on his duty to fight France. He summoned the electors and some of the other princes of the Reichstag to his presence, at Freiburg, in June, 1498. Charles VIII had died in April, 1498, and Maximilian thought it an excellent time to regain his rights. In the name of his son, Philip, he peremptorily demanded the return of the duchy of Burgundy, seized by the French King at the death of Philip's maternal grandfather. He raised seven thousand men and threw them across the border of France for a demonstration, but his allies of the League did not want to back this war upon the new ruler of France, and Maximilian's son Philip, in whose name he waged it, agreed to do homage to the King of France for Flanders and Artois and leave the question of Burgundy to be settled, without war or law process, by common agreement.

Maximilian was not turned aside from his intention by the fact that no one except himself wanted to fight France about Burgundy. He made to the princes he summoned to his presence, a most impassioned address. It was now impossible, he said, to recover the heritage of the House of Hapsburg his son had surrendered, but he meant to give France a slap in the face which should be remembered for a century. He had been betrayed by the Lombards and misled by the Germans. He would say that, if he had to throw the crown from his head and tread it under foot. If he was really deserted by the Empire, he would renounce his imperial oath, for he had sworn also to defend the interests of the House of Austria. He peremptorily demanded an answer, "yes" or "no," whether the Empire would back him in punishing France. In vain, Berthold, Archbishop of Mainz, pointed out that the Reichstag had the right to be consulted about the use and need of a war before they voted supplies for it. Maximilian answered he would not be bound hand and foot and hung up on the wall like Gunther on the Nibelungenlied. To this mood the princes yielded somewhat, very much as men yield to quiet an excited woman, but though he might thus have his own way to some extent, Maximilian, in the long run, only weakened his ability to lead Germany.

He was certainly not leading Germany in the direction of reform. The financial basis of the whole scheme adopted at Worms in 1495 was the common tax, and when inquiry was made about the collections, it appeared that in the Hapsburg Netherlands the subjects of Maximilian's son, for the most part, bluntly refused to pay, and, in Maximilian's Austrian lands, the collection had not been proportionately as successful as in several other principalities of the Empire. Maximilian had been engaged for months in skillfully reorganizing their administration, but he had taken no effective steps to force payment from recalcitrants. This inevitably suggested to the princes that he took no deep interest in anything except the filling of his war chest. This suspicion was increased by the obvious fact that his attention could not be diverted from demands for an advance on the uncollected tax, to discussions of methods which might make its future collection surer and easier. For Maximilian often appears like an excitable child when it dashes toward the object of momentary desire, reckless of obstacles and, falling, rises again to continue the impetuous run.

Two campaigns, one to repulse a French raid on Franche Comté, the other a vain attempt to reconquer the revolted Duchy of Guelders for the Hapsburgs, engaged him in the Autumn of 1498, and, before the latter was finished, Maximilian had on his hands the first war in which his armies met continued disaster and defeat.

The people who lived in the mountain lands lying between the French border, the angle of the upper Rhine with the lake of Constance, and the Italian slopes of the Alps, had long been estranged from other Germans and independent of the Empire. Neither Emperor nor Reichstag could easily exercise any efficient control over the larger states of Germany, and this independence had been increased by defensive Leagues among the political units of the Empire. For generations, many cities of the north coasts and a part of the watershed of the Rhine and Elbe, had been united in the Hanseatic Union. Frederick III had founded the Swabian League. In the same way the Swiss cantons were bound together in a league. And as time went on, this Swiss League had become practically an independent Republic owning merely nominal allegiance to the Emperor. This situation was to a great extent based on a complete estrangement of feeling. The peasants and burghers who pastured cattle, tilled land, manufactured and traded in those mountain valleys, had destroyed feudalism as a governmental system, rejected its fundamental ideas and established, either democracies or commercial oligarchies with democratic features in their government. The German nobles, clinging to their feudal rights, the German princes trying to build absolutism on the ruins of feudalism and the liberties of the cities, had for the Swiss that dislike of aristocrats and absolutists for republican neighbours which seems in the long run to be inevitable. Among some of the nobles this dislike was changed to hatred by fear. The idea of questioning the "right" of one family to tax other families was contagious, and some inhabitants near the borders of the Swiss League, saw in it a ready means to escape the claims of their feudal lords. In some places the bitterness spread to the population because of border raids. It was expressed on the northern side by insults, surviving in songs and proverbs, hard for any one to bear. Mountaineers are apt to be quick of their hands, and the descendants of the people who, at Morgarten and Sempach, at Granson, Morat and Nancy, had rolled the horse and his rider under foot, were none too apt at taking the disdain of men who had not yet waked up to the fact that the time was past when knights could treat all peasants and burghers as they choose. And pride of arms and the commercial spirit, made them eager for gain, and not more scrupulous than their neighbours how they got it. There was a feeling, therefore, that the Swiss were troublesome and disloyal members of the Empire who ought to be put down.

They had beaten Maximilian's ancestors and killed his father-in-law, but he wanted to be at peace with them. Not out of fear. Maximilian never was afraid of anything. He dashed alone into a strangling swamp to kill a savage boar, or led a handful of men onto the locked shields and great pikes, with the same reckless courage.

Maximilian disliked the Swiss war because he did not want to be diverted from his hopes of getting revenge on France and wresting glory from the Turks. The men of the Alpine valleys were the best mercenaries in Europe. He needed them behind his banner, and he disliked to increase their tendency to take the prompter pay of France. The cultivated patrician, Willibald Pirkheimer, a great friend and admirer of Maximilian, commanded the Nuremberg contingent in the Swiss war. In his account of it [1] he lays the responsibility for its outbreak at the doors of "those who were dear to Maximilian." Their injuries and exactions provoked it against his will. And it broke out when he was absent in another vain attempt to compel the people of Guelders to give up a native dynasty and acknowledge the house of Hapsburg. The cities, Pirkheimer says, sent their contingents unwillingly to follow the imperial banner because they knew that the war had been brought on "not of necessity, but only by impotence and arrogance." The nobles who had done so much to provoke it were "not so bold in resisting an army as apt at robbery and the plundering of travellers, for they were strenuous in that exaction, which they had inherited from their ancestors, thinking it no small proof of courage and nobility to live like a thief from plunder and on the misery of others." He gives the most unbounded praise to the Swiss militia. They were sworn under penalty of death to instant obedience, to silence in fight, never to leave the ranks or begin flight, touch the

[1] Willibald Pirkheimers Schweizer Krieg herausgegeben von Karl Rück. München, 1895. Quoted in following citations, pages 67, 83, 89, 72, 110, 98; and elsewhere summarized.

spoils or burn buildings without orders, to abstain from all dishonour to churches or violence to non-combatants, to kill all captives made during battle and not to hold them for ransom. In consequence of this oath and their discipline, Maximilian's offer of a hundred gold pieces for a prisoner to examine, was vain. "They could be killed, but in no way could they be captured."

The contest was fearfully bloody and wasteful. Pirkheimer says: "In a large mountain valley whose villages were burnt and deserted," he met "two old women driving about forty little boys and girls like a flock of sheep. All were starved to the most extreme emaciation and, except that they moved, looked not unlike corpses, so that it was horrible to see. I asked the old women whither they were leading their miserable flock. They, astonished and hardly able to open their lips for sorrow and hunger, answered I should soon see whither they led their wretched herd. Hardly had they replied when we came to a meadow. They turned in and falling on their knees began to eat grass like cattle, except that they picked it first with their hands instead of biting it from the roots. They had already learned the varieties of the herbage, and knew what was bitter or insipid, what sweeter or pleasanter to the taste. I was horrified at so dreadful a sight, and stood for a long time like one who can not trust his senses. Then the old woman asked,—Do you see why this wretched crowd is led here? Well would it have been if none of them had been born. . . . . Their fathers have fallen by the sword, their mothers have died of starvation, their property has been carried off as booty, their houses burnt; we two wretches, tottering with age, are left to lead this miserable herd like beasts to pasture and, so far as we can, keep them alive on grass. We hope that a short time will release them and us from our miseries. They were twice as many, but in a brief time they are reduced to this number, since daily some die of want and hunger, far happier in a quick death than in longer life." When I had seen and heard these things I could not restrain my tears, pitying the pitiable human lot, and detesting, as every true man ought, the fury of war."

For six months, disaster crowded upon disaster to the imperial arms. The undisciplined levies badly led, could not stand against the Swiss. At Dorneck, for example, four thousand confederates surprised fifteen thousand imperialists, killed three thousand men and put the army to utter rout with the loss of their banners and cannon. Maximilian returning from the Netherlands with six thousand troops, faced his losses like a man. Pirkheimer, his companion in evil days, says that in the midst of "irreparable misfortunes . . . he could never see the smallest sign of perturbation in the Emperor." But he could not turn the tide, impose order upon his armies or put sense or spirit into his worthless generals. In September, 1499, he accepted the good offices of his father-in-law, the Duke of Milan, for a peace. The treaty assured the practical independence of the confederates; though they remained nominally subject to the Empire until the peace of Westphalia in 1648. Within two years the cities of Bale and Schaffhausen entering the league of the Swiss, gave them fortresses and gates toward the east and the north, and their reputation for fighting became so great, that, from the day of her reception as a member of the league, Bale "substituted for the usual guard of her gates an old woman armed with a distaff."[1]

Louis XII of France had taken advantage of the Swiss war to make himself stronger in Italy. He had made an alliance with Venice which freed his path for an attack on Milan, whose ducal crown he claimed by the poor title that his grandmother had been a Visconti. He took the city with little trouble, for Maximilian could not help his father-in-law, nor could Ludovico hire Swiss mercenaries to defend himself. He could only flee to the mountains of Tirol. When he had made peace between the Swiss and Maximilian, he raised an army and came down to attack Milan. The people had found the plundering of the French worse than the taxes of Ludovico. They threw open their gates to him with an enthusiasm equal to that which had welcomed his enemies. But he was to feel one more turn of the wheel of fortune. Two months later, as he stood prepared for battle with a new French army, his Swiss mercenaries revolted and refused to fight their compatriots who followed the lilies. Ludovico, attempting to escape, was handed over to his enemy by some of his own men, and carried to France, where he died, ten years later, a prisoner in the castle of Loches.

Maximilian again appealed to the Reichstag for an army to repress the insolence of France in seizing Milan, which was a fief of the Empire. Instead, the Reichstag adopted a plan for a regular army of about thirty thousand men. It was to be raised by every four hundred inhabitants with

[1] Daguet Histoire de la Confédération Suisse. Septième édition, Paris, 1879. Vol. I, page 401.

property contributing to the pay and equipment of one infantry man. In addition the pastors throughout Germany were to make collections in the churches for the defense of the Empire. For this army, Maximilian's brother-in-law, Duke Albert of Bavaria, was named general, and the Emperor's command, even when he was present on the field of battle, was much limited by the authority of the general. The Emperor no longer felt strong enough to decline the Reichsregiment or governing council he had declined at Worms in 1495, nor could he persuade the Reichstag or the Regiment to interfere in Italy for the protection of the nominal vassals of the Empire against France.

There is some reason to suspect that he was not quite as determined as his speeches declared, to make war to the end on France. He hated the house of Valois. He had fought it; but he now hoped to enter into alliance with it for the gain of his own family. His son, Philip, was very anxious to avoid further contest between the Hapsburgs and Valois. Three deaths in three years had made his wife heiress to the thrones of Castile and Aragon. To secure her heritage and her claim on Naples, he joined her father Ferdinand in seeking the friendship of France. On the 10th of August, 1501, a marriage treaty was signed engaging Philip's infant son, Charles, to marry Louis's infant daughter, Claudia. In October of the same year, Maximilian enlarged this into a family compact between Hapsburg and Valois; the first of a series of such agreements between the two houses. The marriage of Carl and Claudia was to be matched by a marriage between the Dauphin and Philip's daughter. The King of

France promised to favour so far as he was able, the expedition of Maximilian to Rome to obtain the imperial crown, and also bound himself to support the claims of the Hapsburgs on the thrones of Spain, of Hungary and Bohemia. Within three years, he was to join the other rulers of Europe in making under Maximilian, an expedition against the Turk. In return, Louis, after taking the oath for Milan as a fief of the Empire, was to become its Duke. The deposed Ludovico was to have the freedom of five miles around his prison and be generously entertained.

This agreement, like those which followed it, skillfully flattered Maximilian's two ruling passions. It promised to increase the glory of the House of Hapsburg, and held out the prospect of gratifying that desire to march on Constantinople at the head of Europe, which was a compound of his instinctive longing to hold the center of the world's stage and his sense of duty as the first layman of Christendom; the only one who communed in both kinds, the God appointed protector of the church.

The peace thus won, Maximilian tried in vain to use in his long continued attempt to conquer the Duchy of Guelders and in preparations for crossing the Alps to be crowned in Rome. From these enterprises he was diverted by a war in the heart of Germany, during which, by skillfully taking advantage of events, he gained for the first time in his life a large measure of control over the Empire of which he was the titular head.

On the first of December, 1503, Duke George of the Bavarian house of Wittelsbach died. The possessions of the house had been divided about a century before between three lines. One of them had died out, and George had inherited from his father and his cousin. He left therefore great possessions in land and treasure which had gained him the surname of the "Rich." By an old law of the house, excluding women from inheritance, his cousins Albert and Wolfgang of the Munich line, were heirs. But George had made a will leaving everything to his only daughter outside of a nunnery, Elizabeth, who was the wife of Rupert, son of the Elector of the Pfalz. Maximilian considered this will and the house law of the dynasty of Wittelsbach it violated, encroachments upon his rights as over-lord of the fiefs of the Empire. Albert was married to his sister, Kunigunde, and Maximilian saw his chance, on the ground of his right to dispose of vacant fiefs of the Empire, to increase the power of the Hapsburgs at the expense of the quarreling heirs of their great rival, the house of Wittelsbach. He immediately acknowledged Albert and Wolfang as heirs of George, in exchange for an agreement signed by Albert to come to a friendly settlement of Maximilian's claims upon the inheritance. The Assembly of the Estates of the lands in dispute, also begged Maximilian to avoid civil war by deciding the question of inheritance. Maximilian appointed a day when he would hear all interested at Augsburg. To the assembled claimants and representatives he announced that George the Rich, by making a will in spite of his warning and against feudal laws, had forfeited to his over-lord all his property in land and people, artillery, provisions and furniture. In short, everything the Duke had, except cash and jewels, was now by law the property of Maximilian. His previous investure of

George and Wolfgang only extended, therefore, to what they were legally entitled to receive. He did not propose, however, to enforce his rights, and would take only two cities, four castles, three count ships, about one hundred thousand gulden of taxes and crops and all the debts he owed to the late Duke. The remainder he proposed to divide between the two brothers and Elizabeth. Her husband, Rupert, refused to accept this award and, after vain attempts to arrange a division acceptable to all claimants, both parties left Augsburg to prepare for war.

Rupert began it by seizing, with the help of the inhabitants, several cities which had been consigned to regents until the dispute was settled, and Maximilian launched the ban of the Empire, which made him and his wife outlaws. Rupert's father, the Elector, backed him, and he used his dead father-in-law's treasure to hire mercenaries from Bohemian noblemen. The war was a slow one, fought castle by castle and raid after raid. Brother faced brother, and the poor peasant was slaughtered and plundered by both sides. In the midst of it all Rupert died, and his wife followed him to the grave about a month later. Their faithful captains vainly tried to keep up the contest for the claims of their children. And their hopes depended on the arrival of a strong body of Bohemian mercenaries. By forced marches Maximilian fell unexpectedly on this force. They stood fiercely at bay behind their great wooden shields. Maximilian led his men at arms against the mass, and, after a desperate fight where he was saved from being unhorsed and trampled to death only by the devotion of one of his followers, broke into their phalanx. Four-fifths of the Bohemians were killed on the spot or in flight, the rest were taken prisoners. This fight decided the war. It dragged along in places, but Maximilian's decision was enforced; the children of Rupert and Elizabeth received the treasure and the lands north of the Danube, while Albert and Wolfgang received the lands south of the Danube. Maximilian took for himself what he originally claimed, and rewarded some of his faithful followers out of the estate he had thus administered with fire and sword. The only people who got nothing but loss out of the contest, were the peasants whose labour gave value to the lands which these nobles and princes fought over.

In the summer of 1505, Maximilian entered into Cologne in triumph, marching in the party-coloured costume of a landsknecht, the great eighteen foot-spear over his shoulder. Nearly a thousand princes and noblemen followed him, and sat down to a banquet in honour of the victory which Philip, aided by Maximilian's skill in handling artillery, had just won in Guelders. The stronghold of the dynasty supported by France and the people, had fallen, and the Duke was driven out, leaving Guelders in the possession of the Hapsburgs.

Then began a period of four years when there was no open and active party of opposition to Maximilian in Germany. Berthold of Mayence, the head of the reform party, had died in December, 1504. Many of the generation of princes which supported his attempts to bring Germany to law and order, as an aristocratic confederation in which the oligarchy of the electors should hold the chief power, died within a few years, and, just as the partisan war over the succession to George the Rich, gave a field for Maximilian's best qualities as a soldier, his flashes of energy, his skill in personal fight, his reckless daring, his cunning, so the situation in the Empire gave a chance for his talents for politics. He never forgot a face, if he had seen it only once, twenty years before, at a Reichstag.[1] He knew how to put the most awkward at their ease; he had great self-control, and, even when the veins of his neck swelled out in wrath, he bit his lip and kept from harsh words. His politeness was unfailing even to opponents, and few who came to court with complaints could resist the charm of his talk. These qualities aided him in a policy thus described to the Senate by the Venetian Ambassador.[2] He points out that at the death of his father, Maximilian found himself with little credit and a lack of money, little feared or obeyed by the princes of the Empire. These, under the lead of six, were so strong that the Diet never voted what Maximilian wanted,—"And because time always brings occasion, the King, seeing he could not do anything he wanted because of the resistance of these princes, determined to advance by temporizing, and commenced, little by little, every time a prince-bishop of the Empire died, to use his influence in support of the election to the bishopric of some trusted friend or even a relative of his own. And he did this not only with ecclesiastical princes, but also tried always to favour and flatter the eldest sons of secular princes, so that, when their fathers died, they would follow his wishes. After this, four years ago, the death of George of Bavaria caused

[1] Friedrichs des Weisen Leben und zeitgeschichte nach Spalatins handschrift herausgegeben. Neudecker und Preller.

[2] Alberi. Series I, Vol. VI, page 32 ff.

the war between Duke Albert of Bavaria and the Elector of the Pfalz (Rupert's father). Maximilian favoured Duke Albert his brother-in-law, and, with the bishops and princes he had already made his friends, destroyed the power of the Elector of the Pfalz. About the time of this destruction there died also the Archbishops of Mayence and of Treves. In place of Treves there succeeded a near relative of the King, and in place of Mayence another prelate, not at all like his predecessor either in mental ability or in power, who is very dependent on his majesty. Thus little by little, the King of the Romans, having destroyed the Elector of the Pfalz, the powerful princes his adversaries being dead, and the friends he had raised to positions of power having increased, has grown so influential that he has made himself almost omnipotent among the princes of Germany, to such an extent indeed that there is not one who is anxious to oppose him in anything. This has come about not only by the fear inspired by his destruction of the Elector of the Pfalz, but also by the favour which the young princes and newly elected bishops show him."

In other words, Maximilian had, by the beginning of the year 1507, formed a party from which he could expect support. In addition his son Philip had died in September, 1506, and the regent who ruled the Netherlands for Philip's young son Charles, was Maximilian's daughter Margaret; an able woman very fond of her father and much more apt to take his advice than her brother Philip had been. Maximilian's correspondence with her shows that he often directed the foreign policy of her government, and constantly used the patronage of the Dutch and

Flemish states to reward his adherents and friends.[1]

This power, based on prestige and personal influence, Maximilian, in the next ten years, lost entirely. And it is difficult to avoid the impression that he lost it because nothing ever seemed to him important compared to the glory of the house of Hapsburg, and because of an overmastering itch for distinction always driving him to play a showy part in affairs. These two feelings, continually tempting him out of the path leading to greatness, were helped by palpable blunders in his chosen games of war and diplomacy, where he thought himself supremely skillful. For no one can read the Weiss Kunig without seeing that Maximilian thought himself a very great ruler of men, a soldier comparable to Julius Cæsar, a complete master of state craft.

He first appealed to his backing among the members of the Reichstag to support the claims of the house of Hapsburg to the crown of Hungary. If the sickly King Ladislas died, as was probable, without heirs, Maximilian according to the earlier agreement between the houses, was to succeed. But the Hungarian nobles wanted one of their own number for ruler, and they swore an oath in case of a failure of the succession to elect none but a Hungarian king. The assertion of a national right against a dynastic right, was always meaningless to Maximilian. Indeed no ruler of the age gave any true response to that note. War in defense of his right was his instinctive reply. The Reichstag voted the troops he asked, but Maximilian succeeded in using that weapon of marriage

[1] Le Glay, Correspondance de l'Empereur Maximilian Ier et de Marguerite d'Autriche. Paris, 1839, passim.

which brought him far more gain than arms. The daughter of Ladislas was pledged to marry one of Maximilian's grandsons, Carl or Ferdinand and, if Ladislas had a son, he was to marry Maximilian's granddaughter Mary. Maximilian marched an army to the border, and demanded that the national assembly ratify this agreement which secured the succession to the crown of Ladislas to the Hapsburgs. The answer was a summons of Hungary and Bohemia to arms. The birth of a son to Ladislas interrupted the fighting. So long as this boy lived, the continuance of a Hungarian government seemed assured. The magnates, therefore, made a peace which neither denied nor acknowledged the Hapsburg claims (July, 1507).

Maximilian had created a party, it now remained to be seen whether he could manage it. The plan for which he asked the support of the Reichstag of Constance was one which appealed to every German,—a march to Rome to receive from the Pope the crown of the Holy Roman Empire of the German Nation.

But Maximilian desired no mere peaceful possession. He proposed the restoration in Italy of the conditions the Hohenstaufeus had perished in trying to maintain. Milan must be recovered,—the prestige of France must be broken and the princes of Italy taught to look up to the eagle instead of the lilies,—French control of the papacy must be destroyed, lest, at the next vacancy, French cardinals should choose a French pope who would crown Louis XII Emperor to the dishonour of Germany. For these ends he asked thirty thousand men. The Reichstag voted fifteen thousand, and Maximilian assured them he would withdraw his attention altogether from small affairs to turn all his energies toward large enterprises: by which he meant that he would leave to others the bringing of Germany to order and devote himself to driving the French from Italy and leading the world against Constantinople.

For the present, several small obstacles embarrassed his progress toward a triumphal entry into Constantinople. The Swiss, whose mercenary troops both Louis and Maximilian wanted to use and whose influential men both bribed as heavily as they could afford, finally voted not to allow their troops to be used against France, though they agreed that six thousand men might follow the imperial banner in an expedition to receive the crown at Rome. In the second place, Venice had refused to permit the Emperor to cross her territories on his way to Rome, unless he came without an army. It was difficult to see how he could get into Italy without the consent of the Swiss, the French who held Lombardy, or the Venetians. In the third place, the support promised by the Reichstag had not materialized. By February, 1508, less than one thousand men out of the fifteen thousand were with the colours, and only a quarter of the subsidy had been paid, while the contributions promised by some of the Italian cities were still on paper.

Maximilian could not get through the Alpine passes. It was very doubtful whether he could cross Italy to Rome. He determined therefore to take the title without the crown, and, after a ceremony in the cathedral of Trent, announced in proclamations that he was henceforth to be called "Elected Roman Emperor," instead of "King of the Romans." The Pope solemnly approved the act.

Under these circumstances, it is hard to imagine what motives worthy of a statesman's consideration, could have induced Maximilian to make war on Venice. Her trade increased the riches of German cities, and his own duchy of Tirol suffered especially from an interruption of commerce. It is difficult to find any reason but revenge and pride for leading his men down the Alpine valleys in an attack on Venice. He did not stay with them long but went back to Tirol to look after the finances. His generals met little but disaster. Fifteen hundred men were cut off and utterly destroyed near Pieve di Cadore. The Venetians took town after town around the northern shores of the Adriatic. The peasants and burghers were everywhere faithful to the Venetian masters who gave them better government and lower taxes than they had known under other rulers. The jealous imperial leaders, without any central control, scattered their strength. They could not save Trieste, which fell May, 1508. In vain did the Emperor call upon the German princes for further aid. Unable to properly defend his southeastern duchies against Venetian raids, he made a truce of three years with the Signory, on a basis which brought such loss of Austrian possessions, that Maximilian's faithful soldier, Eric of Brunswick, when he read the treaty, spat on it and trampled it under foot.

Maximilian's desire for revenge, increased by the humiliating treaty, was only deferred. To accomplish it he became the close ally of the monarch against whom he had repeatedly demanded from the Reichstag war to the knife. There is some reason to believe that Maximilian was more responsible than anyone else for the League of Cambray, which, in the end of December, 1508, united the Pope, France, Aragon and the Emperor against Venice. The war was to continue until she was stripped of all the conquests on the mainland she ruled so well. This booty was to be divided among the allies. England, Hungary and the Italian states were to be invited to join. The Pope was to release Maximilian from his oath to observe a truce with Venice for three years, and summon him as the protector of the Church to attack her.

Venice was the only state in Italy strong enough to make head against France. Whatever quarrels might arise with the Empire, self interest would in the long run make the Republic an ally of Maximilian if France tried to do what he said he feared she was planning. It is difficult to find an instance where a childish desire for revenge, for glory or for new lands and cities to call his own, has betrayed a ruler into a blunder in state craft more palpable than this activity of Maximilian in marshaling Europe for the destruction of Venice. His fancy led him into dreaming of the world as it had been, and he saw himself managing north Italy like another Frederick II. His imagination, always his master instead of his servant, was too weak to deal with facts, and his lack of knowledge of men made him constantly assume that allies as ambitious and crafty as himself, could be moved like pawns on a chess board wherever he wished them to go.

The Reichstag, when it met at Worms in the Spring of 1509, was not much interested in sending the men and money the Emperor asked to support this great scheme. They dissolved without any action. The Assemblies of Maximilian's personal duchies, the Austrian lands, also showed the greatest reluctance to attack Venice. It was only by granting new privileges that Maximilian could obtain a vote of half the supply he demanded. Nothing was left for him but to raise funds by mortgaging to the great Augsburg bankers, the Fuggers, almost everything as yet unmortgaged upon which they would lend. All this took time, and when the battle of Aquadello laid the Republic helpless before the allies, Maximilian was not on hand to get his share of the plunder. Aragon, France and the Pope seized the lands they wanted, but the banner of Maximilian was still on the other side of the Alps. When Verona Vicenza, Padua and the towns about the northern end of the Adriatic, bending before the storm, raised the imperial colours, no proper garrisons were at hand to man them. The Venetians were therefore able to surprise Padua, and make it a rallying point for their army broken at Aquadello.

It was the middle of August before Maximilian could invest the city so carelessly lost. His army, made up of four thousand French, a thousand Spaniards, a force of Burgundians, a small troop of Papal mercenaries and contingents from Italian princes, was about twenty thousand strong; a force which seemed to his contemporaries to insure success. While he waited for his siege guns, the Emperor took neighbouring towns, established his lines and collected provisions. His great cannon soon made a breach. But the troops which mounted to the assault were slaughtered by mines and the storm failed. A second attack ten days later met no better fate. Nevertheless, the chance to reduce the city was still good. The provisions and ammunition of the garrison were running low. The full strength of the besiegers had not been exerted. Then, if ever, was the time to set all on the hazard and play the game of glory to the end. Maximilian's reputation never recovered from the fact that, early in October, he abandoned the attempt to take the city and soon after returned to Tirol. The army, which was only held together by his presence, at once broke up, leaving the besieged astonished at their sudden release from mortal danger. As a result, the Venetians, with the favour of the inhabitants, recovered, before Winter, most of the fortresses they had lost.

Maximilian turned in every direction to find means to set on foot another army at whose head he could appear in Italy. The Reichstag would not give it to him. In vain he begged the King of France to lend him an army or the means to raise one, taking as security the conquests he was to make in Italy; and in the midst of his efforts the cumbrous league of Cambray suddenly began to go to pieces.

Pope Julius II was wiser than the Emperor. He had recovered from Venice the vassals the Signory had taken from the Church, and had no wish to lay Italy at the feet of the French King by the destruction of her strongest state. He suddenly announced himself an ally of the Signory to drive the French barbarians from Italy (May, 1510). He gained the support of Spain and the Swiss, and would have preferred to add Maximilian to his allies. He made, therefore, an effort to bring about peace between the Emperor and Venice; but Maximilian would make no concession that the Republic would accept. He acted as if he had so far won instead of lost in the war, demanding not only the towns Venice had taken, but also the chief cities of their possessions on the mainland. Venice was not disposed to lose the fruits of victory, and Maximilian stood by the alliance with Louis XII.

It is difficult to avoid the impression that this would have been an excellent opportunity to withdraw at any cost from what events had plainly shown must be a losing game. Maximilian was constantly changing his plans. An aptness to drop a half finished design and take up a new one, has been noted by all moderns who have written on any episode of his career. This lack of steadiness was, by this time, a commonplace among contemporary statesmen who knew him. Quirini thus describes this prominent trait to the Venetian Senate in 1507:[1] "He has a good intelligence, and one so alert that he is cleverer than any of his councilors in finding many expedients for every need. But he has one defect, that, however many expedients he may discover, he does not know how to carry out any of them, and so he is as lacking in power of execution as he is abundant in power of invention. And although, out of two or three remedies for an evil which may have suggested themselves to his mind, he has chosen one as the best, nevertheless he does not execute his design, because, suddenly, before he can execute it, some other design takes shape in his mind which he thinks better, and thus he is so eager to change from a better thing to a better thing that time and occasion pass for doing anything." But ready as Maximilian was to change his own plans, he was very unready to have them changed for him. Other contemporaries confirm Machiavelli's ob-

[1] Relazioni, etc. Serie I, Vol. VI, page 27.

servation that he never really consulted his councilors or acted on anybody's advice. Besides, like many men, usually good natured and slow to take offence, Maximilian had a temper exceedingly tenacious of a dislike once aroused. The offence the Venetians had given in 1507 by refusing passage for his army in a march to be crowned at Rome, overlaid in his mind the earlier hatred of Louis XII. He would not therefore change his attitude to the Republic.

It is easy of course to be unjust in judging Maximilian's attitude toward Italian affairs, and to blame him for not seeing what events made plain after his death. The forcible union of Italy and Germany in the Empire, was a curse to both peoples, and the full price they paid was the delay of national unity until 1870. But of all the rulers of Europe, only the Tudors, and they half unconsciously, had become aware that the strength of a dynasty lay in a national rather than in imperial policy. The wisdom not to join in the fight for the control of Italy, was, perhaps, too much to expect of any man in Maximilian's position. One of his titles was "at all times increaser of the Empire." In the oath of office he swore to defend its bounds. And as a knight it seemed impossible to him to refuse to resent an insult in arms. All his councilors, all his son's councilors and all the princes of the Empire, were, it is true, against his first descent into Italy. But he had reason to suspect the motives of many of these advisers, and the impulse to gratify his ambition and his love of action, might rather easily assume in his own consciousness the form of a sense of duty. The humanists, whose company delighted him, who were his great admirers, were constantly strengthening him in this delusion. Their utterances made it easier for Maximilian to live in a world of ideals long outworn, and to neglect the facts of the actual world. The critical methods of the New Learning of the Renascence, did not lead the early German humanists to a correct understanding of the genesis, or the nature, of the Holy Roman Empire of the German Nation. They clung to the delusion of the fifteenth century jurists, and thought it to be a direct successor of the Empire of Trajan. They transferred ideas from one to the other, in a way most misleading to any Emperor who read their writings or listened to their appeals. Worse political advisers than these men, who thought they had found in old books wisdom to direct a new world, could hardly be imagined. Their fundamentally wrong conceptions of the duty of an Emperor played into all Maximilian's weaknesses. The writings of Brant, Wimpheling, Celtes, Hutten, strengthened in him the erroneous ideas which carried him down into Lombardy in spite of all difficulties and against all protests, in order that he might display to an admiring world of which he was the rightful head, the combined virtues of his two namesakes, Fabius Maximus and Æmilius Paulus, and outdo the deeds of Julius Cæsar.[1]

But there was no reason why Maximilian should not have abandoned a position events had shown untenable, or given up a method of establishing his claims which common sense ought to have told him would lead to disaster. He had nothing to gain and much to lose by de-

[1] In one of his memorandum books is this entry (1501-1505): "In this affair his Majesty gave eight secretaries enough to write in order that his Majesty might outdo Julius Cæsar." Jahrbücher Kunsthistorischen Sammlungen, VI, page 9.

stroying Venice. No one paid any attention to the commands of an Emperor without an army. Germany would not give him an army. His attempts to raise one had completed the ruin of his finances, and cost him dangerous concessions in every contest to maintain his authority or claims within the Empire or on its borders. What reason was there to suppose that the King of France, whom he had repeatedly denounced as his deadly enemy and unscrupulous rival, would do anything for the German Empire in Italy? It was most fatuous for him to turn a deaf ear to the warnings of his clever, faithful daughter, Margaret, regent of the Netherlands for her young nephew, that Louis XII in advising him to continue the war with Venice was using him as a catspaw. The chief cause of his making such a mistake, was his instinctive disinclination to a policy of slow construction, and his longing for a course of adventurous action, preferably one which would make him the centre about which all events turned.

This seems to have been the reason for the most extraordinary of all his plans, the plan he attempted to put in execution in August, 1511. When Julius II was reported to be dying, Maximilian wrote letters, the face value of which is that he hoped to take vows of celibacy, lay down the imperial insignia and be crowned Pope. This is an idea so wild, that many of the more recent writers have insisted that it is possible to read all the phrases in an allegorical or jesting sense, which, they are inclined to believe, covered a plan to elect Cardinal Hadrian of Corneto, Vicar of Christ, while Maximilian received from him in return the temporal rule of the States of the Church. By ingenious argument, Maximilian's phrases can be made to fit the hypothesis; but the difficulty which suggested it, is not removed by its establishment. If it is difficult to believe that Maximilian cherished for a moment the idea that he could be elected Pope; it is scarcely less difficult to believe that he could have thought it possible for him to separate the spiritual and temporal power of the papacy. Nothing but the force of arms could have made such a revolution. How could an Emperor unable to defend against Venice the small towns at the head of the Adriatic, hope to take Rome and rule the Papal States?[1] Whatever the plan was, the unexpected recovery of Julius made it superfluous.

It was really a year later, before Maximilian permitted the Pope to arrange a ten months' truce with Venice which left him between France and the Holy League, sought by both and committed to neither. Within a week of the truce, the French army routed the army of the League in the slaughterous battle of Ravenna and seemed master of Italy. This spectacle was too much for Maximilian; he opened the passes of Tirol for the Swiss that they might march to the defense of the Pope, he ordered all the German mercenaries who had done so much to win the battle of Ravenna to leave the lilies. The result was the retreat of the French across the Alps. But in spite of this attack upon Louis XII, Maximilian still continued negotiations for the com-

[1] For this discussion references to literature Gebhardt Die Gravamina der deutschen nation gegen den Romischen Hof. Breslau, 1884, page 90.

Ulmann, Maximilian I, Vol. II, page 439.

Jäger Albrecht. Maximilian's verhältnisse zum Papsthum in Sitzungsberichte der Kais. Akad. d. Wissenschaften. Phil. Hist. Klasse, Vol. XII, 210.

pletion of the marriage between Louis's daughter and his own grandson Charles. The negotiations made the Pope uncertain of his support and anxious to persuade Venice to grant Maximilian's condition for a peace. Julius even went so far, as to threaten Venice with the interdict and an attack by papal troops under the command of Maximilian. Then Maximilian, having exacted the price of his adhesion, joined the Holy League. This was politics which seemed to promise the object he desired, the destruction of Venice. He forgot that the Venetians were not going to be idle while their destruction was carried out.

In March, 1513, they formed an alliance with their former deadly enemy, France. Maximilian's answer was a league with England, Spain and the new Pope, Leo X, to attack France and divide her territories, as the members of the League of Cambray had promised to divide the territories of Venice.

Once more the god of war, so long unfriendly, seemed to smile on him. The Swiss marched to defend the young Duke Maximilian Sforza, son of Ludovico, who had died a prisoner in France. At Novara, June 6th, 1513, they routed the French army, which retreated across the Alps. In northern France, the English army of invasion, which Maximilian joined without troops, to fight by the side of his ally, Henry VIII, won, largely by Maximilian's advice, the Battle of the Spurs (August 16th, 1513), a rout which temporarily demoralized the French army. In September the Swiss marched into Burgundy and invested Dijon, the capital, weakly garrisoned and unable to stand a strong attack. In October the imperial army made up of Spaniards and Germans totally defeated the Venetians near Vicenza, inflicting a loss of all their standards and artillery, together with five thousand men and the majority of their officers. But none of these victories were pushed home, and France gained time to prepare a strong defence.

The pieces were then moved on the board of diplomacy with bewildering rapidity. In order to make sure of the support of Henry of England for attacking France again in the spring of 1514, Maximilian promised to make Henry King of France and to appoint him Vicar and successor to the Empire. The alliance was to be sealed by the marriage of Henry's sister Mary, to Maximilian's grandson Charles.

The losses of the past campaign and the threat of continued attack, made the French King renew in the most flattering form the offer of a marriage between his daughter and Maximilian's grandson Ferdinand. He now promised the Duchy of Milan as a dowry. Tempted by the offer, Maximilian joined Ferdinand's maternal grandfather, Ferdinand of Spain, in a year's truce with France with this marriage in prospect. Thereupon the King of England, suspecting that he was deserted and betrayed by both his allies, broke the engagement of his sister Mary to Charles, married her to Louis XII, and made a close offensive and defensive league with France in October, 1514.

Louis, relieved from danger, broke the engagement of his daughter Renata to Ferdinand, and prepared to cross the Alps and reassert his mastery over north Italy. The country to which he took his journey was farther, for on the first of January, 1515, he died.

His successor, the youthful Francis I, enlarged and carried out his plan. In August he came down into Italy, and the next month, with the help of the Venetians, defeated the Swiss at Marignano in the greatest battle of the generation. Milan surrendered and the Duke, Maximilian Sforza, was sent to France a prisoner. Once more the pieces shifted on the diplomatic board where the armies for these brutal wars of treacherous and selfish princes were arrayed. Spain, England and Maximilian, fearing the overwhelming influence of France, joined another league against her. In the Spring of 1516, Maximilian appeared once more in Italy at the head of a force of Spaniards, Germans and Swiss paid for by English gold, and, towards the end of March, threatened an assault on Milan, whither the French army had retired. The English commissioners, the Swiss, German and Spanish captains, advised a fight, but suddenly, Maximilian, as at Padua seven years before, refused a decisive action and announced his intention of leaving the army. The Cardinal of Zion who had brought the Swiss into action, and Pace, the English agent, combatted this intention with all their power, and Maximilian's councilors told him that if he withdrew, "no man in Germany would esteem him the worth of a groat."[1] To the despair of all around him he persisted in abandoning the attack, although the Swiss sent word "desiring him, if he was afraid, to put himself in security in Brescia; and they, with his horsemen, would clear the French out of Italy."

[1] Letters and Papers of Henry VIII, Vol. II, number 1721.

The Emperor might have given some good reasons for his caution. The French army was strong and behind walls, the Swiss under his command were mutinous because their pay was delayed, and the Spaniards rivalled their insubordination. Such an army was, however, most easily controlled when it was fighting, and the plunder of Milan would have kept the soldiers with the standards. The Emperor afterwards said, he feared they would sack the city, and he wished to conquer Italy by kindness, not by fear. He had not shrunk from such violence before. He wasted Flanders with fire and sword to force the submission of Ghent. He sent word to the King of Spain that he intended to compel Florence to abandon the alliance of France, by devastating "all the villages, houses, gardens and vineyards outside of the city, and also all the country in the neighborhood belonging to the Florentines."[1] The truth probably was, that fear of betrayal by the Swiss—the idea that they would sell him to his enemies as other Swiss had sold Ludovico Sforza to France, sixteen years before—was the chief motive for his sudden preference for prudence over boldness. This fear was not very well based, for there was a marked difference between the two situations. In 1500, the Swiss were fighting against their cantonal standards. In 1516 they were with them. When the Swiss who fought with France sent messengers to Maximilian's Swiss captains a few days after the withdrawal, the imperial captains indignantly repudiated the invitation to betray their leader, reproached the French mercenaries and professed their

[1] Chmel Urkunden, page 128.

loyalty to Maximilian.[1] The Emperor's distrust of the Swiss was increased by two things. A letter proposing betrayal, intended to fall into his hands, was sent from the French camp, and the night after he read it, he saw in a dream his ancestors who had been defeated by the Swiss at Morgarten and Sempach. They warned him not to trust the hereditary foes of his house.[2]

Whether his reasons were good or bad, the world could see no good reasons why this man, usually so rash, should suddenly prefer caution to action. His friends were "greatly dispirited." In France it was thought that the King of the Romans had shamefully withdrawn.[3] The Venetian envoy wrote the Senate,— "The Emperor has gone back and to his great shame crossed the Adda." [4]

Spinelli wrote to Henry VIII,—"If the Emperor do not shortly return (to his army) his reputation is ruined."[5] Henry VIII exhorted him, "like a valiant captain, to resume his heart and put a stop to the dishonourable reports circulated about him." [6] And when Maximilian persisted in not trusting himself in the field at the head of his men, Pace finally wrote from Italy to Wolsey,— "The Emperor is so degraded it signifies not whether he is friend or enemy." [7] His own German landsknechts, mutinous for lack of pay, refused his orders to assault a Venetian castle on the Lago d'Idro and called him "Apple King and Straw King." The imperial army went

[1] Letters and Papers, Vol. II, number 1737.

[2] Historia und wahrhafftige beschreibung von Herr Georgen von Frundsberg, etc. Kriegsthaten, Frankfort, 1568, page 24. Confirmed also by Italian writers.

[3] Letters and Papers, Vol. II, 2017.

[4] Letters and Papers, Vol. II, 1841.

[5] Letters and Papers, Vol. II, 1763.

[6] Letters and Papers, Vol. II, 1753.

[7] Letters and Papers, Vol. II, 1877.

to pieces, and the French swept everything before them in north Italy.

From this time on, Maximilian hardly counted in Italian affairs. His grandson Charles, now King of Spain and Naples, advised him to save danger to his person by appointing a general captain of experience, and England leagued with the Swiss to re-take Milan, leaving out Maximilian altogether.

In August, Charles and Francis made the treaty of Noyon without Maximilian's advice and against his will. Nothing remained for the Emperor but to ratify it in December, 1516. It brought his nine years' war with Venice to a close which could have given him little pleasure. His effort to re-establish the power of the Empire south of the Alps, had added a small strip to his duchy of Tirol, and had left him a huge debt for which everything he owned was mortgaged.[1] The Venetians or the French were in possession of almost all he had claimed in north Italy. It is doubtful whether the Emperor, isolated and helpless as he was, would have agreed to such an arrangement if he had thought it permanent. He still trusted in the chances of the future and his own diplomacy.

In the Spring of 1517, another agreement was made between Francis, Charles and the Emperor. Secret articles promised the erecting of two new fiefs of the Empire. Maximilian was to create at once the kingdom of Lombardy for Francis, and the Kingdom of Italy, composed for Ferdinand, Maximilian's younger grandson, out of Venice, Tuscany and other middle Italian states. Per-

[1] Maximilian to the Estates of Tirol, January, 1518.
Archiv für Kunde Oesterreichischer Geschichte quellen. 1854, page 219.

haps neither Valois nor Hapsburg really expected to carry out this agreement. At all events, the influence of the Empire counted for nothing in Italy, until, five years later, Maximilian's grandson, under the title of Emperor, but using his resources as King of Spain, successfully renewed the struggle against the overmastering Valois.

The war against Venice thus ended in complete disaster. But in the east Maximilian had meantime met with a great success. A lasting agreement brought a final settlement to the question of the Hungarian and Bohemian crowns. In the spring of 1515, Maximilian met the King of Hungary and Bohemia and the King of Poland at Vienna. Maximilian was exceedingly proud of his ability at arranging banquets and masques, and has recorded it by pen and burin in the works which he designed to hand down his fame and posterity. He exerted his skill, and amid a magnificent series of entertainments which must have strained to the utmost his exhausted resources, these rulers reached an agreement very favourable to the house of Hapsburg. Louis, the Crown Prince of Hungary, was married by proxy to Maximilian's granddaughter Mary. His sister Anna was married to Maximilian himself, with the understanding that his younger grandson, Ferdinand, might, within a year, be substituted as titular husband. Maximilian adopted Louis, named him imperial Vicar, and issued a call to the Electors to choose him for the next Emperor. This was the same promise Maximilian had given to Henry VIII. Henry VIII apparently took it seriously; Louis may perhaps have done so, but it is certain that Maximilian never did. Six years later Ferdinand and Anna began their married life, and when King Louis, in 1526, lost his army and his life before the Turks at Mohacz, Ferdinand was able, after a civil war and much bribery, to secure the crowns of Bohemia and Hungary. Thus, east and west, the hopes of Maximilian for the power of his descendants, were successful. He could not reconquer Italy, but he did spread the lands of the Hapsburgs in almost unbroken line from the Carpathian mountains to the North Sea.

Far otherwise was it with his attempted reform of the Empire. When he called on various Reichstags to support him in maintaining the imperial influence south of the Alps against Venice and France, he had not entirely neglected the crying need of Germany for justice and peace. The reforms of Worms in 1495 proved entirely ineffective. Twelve years later, the condition of the Empire was no better than before. In 1507, Quirini, writing to the Venetian Senate, thus describes the conditions:[1] "There are in this nation four classes of people: princes of the Empire; gentlemen (knights); burghers of free cities; and peasants (populo minuto). The princes[1] generally have some quarrel among themselves or else with some free city, and, if they are poor, most of them permit their retainers to assault and rob on the roads. The gentlemen generally live in some castle outside of the cities or in the court of some prince or among the hills in solitary places. They are poor, enemies to the burghers, and so proud that, under no circumstances, will they intermarry with a mercantile family, or debase themselves to

[1] Relazioni. Serie I, Vol. VI, page 24.

practice trade with them. They make a living as captains of mercenaries, and when that fails, do nothing except hunt or rob on the roads. If this King (Maximilian) did not enforce a very strict justice, it would not be safe to ride through any part of Germany; in spite of it, in Franconia, where there are many of these gentlemen, and also around Nuremberg and in other places, the roads are most insecure."

This was just at the time when Maximilian, by war and political use of his influence, had really obtained power in the Empire; and he proposed to the Reichstag reforms to entirely suppress the habits of the robber barons. He had two objects in view. He wanted to provide an efficient court of justice, presided over by an imperial chief judge and composed of sixteen judges, two from the Hapsburg hereditary lands, six named by the Electors, six from each circle of the Empire, and two from the lesser nobility. To enforce its decisions, as well as to carry out the orders of the Imperial Council, he proposed an imperial police, to be commanded by four marshals, of the Lower Rhine, the Upper Rhine, the Elbe and the Danube. To each of these was assigned two councilors and twenty-four knights. For criminal matters, especially the repression of robbery, there was to be a Marshal for the Empire. He was to go from place to place, and enforce order, with the aid of the marshal of any circle whose roads were unsafe. For these propositions Maximilian found but little support in the Reichstag. They feared that such an arrangement would enable him to destroy all local power. The Reichstag refused to vote for the imperial police. For, in truth, the party Maximilian had rallied round him, was not the sort of a party from which he could have expected much help in any unification of the Empire. It was composed of princes, bishops and nobles, many of them selfish and ambitious, most of them promoted by his influence playing on personal desires. The opposition princes were many of them equally selfish. Those who complained bitterly of the disorders of the Empire, were not eager for any reform which threatened loss to their independence. The only possibility of forming an imperial party which would have backed him in meeting the crying needs of the Empire, lay in imitating the Tudors and seeking the aid of the burghers against the nobility. Around such a union of the middle classes and the crown, he might have rallied a support which would have enabled him to do his first duty. But this step Maximilian was, by his training, his tastes and his past experience, incapable of making. The classes whose privileges had survived from feudal times, always seemed to him superior to the classes who had won wealth and political influence in more recent generations, nor did the idea of turning for permanent support toward the burghers occur to him as a possibility.

To form such a party would have been very difficult, for the cities also were selfish and jealous. But the other support was shown by experience to be insufficient, and Maximilian, having refused the radical reform and accused its dead leader, Berthold of Mayence, of treachery and lack of wisdom, was bound to find some other plan to take its place. His great purposes in Italy required the support of Germany. He could not get it unless he gave Germany something beside a paper plan to subdue feuds and public disorder. This he did not do. In the Weiss Kunig, indeed, he wrote,—"He allowed in his realm no robbery, but it was perfectly safe to travel through his realm." The statement is false.[1] Successive Reichstags abounded in renewed complaints of feuds and robbery. The members of the Reichstag of 1517 informed the imperial commissioners that the imperial court was useless. Many of the judges were not fitted for their places—the calendar choked —the procedure intolerably slow. A decision in a suitor's favour did not help him, for it could not be enforced. Evil doers were not afraid even of the ban of the Empire. The lower courts were no better, and there was in Germany a frightful and general state of disorder. Travellers were not safe on land or river. The peasants who fed all, were going to destruction. Widows and orphans were not protected. No messenger, no merchant, no pilgrim, could traverse the roads to perform his pious work or give his message or attend to his affairs. These general complaints were accompanied by a large number of special instances, and they show that Maximilian's reforms had not worked. Perhaps they would have failed under all possible efforts. At all events it is certain that the greater part of Maximilian's energies were directed to his plans across the Alps. He did do something, but it lies on the face of the facts of his war against Venice and his eager engagement in the

[1] It is not true even of his own hereditary duchies. Representative committees from the Austrian duchies complained bitterly in 1518 of the prevalence of highway robbery.

Archiv für Kunde Oesterrichischer Geschichts Quellen. 1854, 239.

ten years of diplomacy spun like spider webs about its action, that he did not do all he could.

There were in Germany a lot of titled evil doers hardened in lawlessness. Kunz Schott, for example, caught a Nuremberg burgher and ordered him to lay his hand on a block. "At first he would not do it and then he said to him—'Lay it out or I'll thrust a sword through you.' The burgher said,—'Dear lord, I beg you have pity on my three children about this.' He answered,—'Lay it down at once.' Then he laid his left hand down, but he had to lay down the right hand. Schott said 'You won't write me any more letters,' and he drew his sword and struck. But the burgher jerked his hand and the blow fell on his fingers. But he had to put it down again. He struck again to cut off his hand at the joint. He jerked again and he struck him in the middle of the hand so that the thumb hung by the skin, and Schott thrust the cut off hand in his bosom, saying,—'Go carry that home to your masters' "[1] (the Nuremberg Councilors). Such scoundrels as are pictured in this rude miniature from a burgher's diary, were not uncommon in Germany, and if, instead of carrying the imperial banner over the Alps, Maximilian had spread it against selected examples of this class, and personally superintended their hanging on the towers of their own castles, it would have gained more for his own glory, for Germany, and ultimately for the house of Hapsburg, than the finest diplomatic arrangement by which he hoped to induce someone else to conquer north Italy and hand its best towns over to him.

But when peace with Venice and France left Maximil-

[1] Chroniken der deutschen Städte, Vol. XI, page 605.

ian's hands free in 1517, he did not propose to turn his energy toward the monotonous details of the administration of justice and finance. Two things occupied his attention and filled his speech. The first was the succession of his grandson Charles to the Empire. In spite of his promise to Louis of Hungary and Henry of England, Maximilian had thought for a long time about securing the succession to Charles. In 1517, signs of break down in his once extraordinary health began to appear. The doctors interfered with his habits and hampered his work, and his condition and their orders reminded him of the chances of mortality. There was only one effective argument to use with the Electors to induce them to elect Charles, King of the Romans, bribery. The Golden Bull expressly forbade both direct and indirect bribery, but the Emperor could grant dispensations, and offer the men he bribed exemptions from the law he asked them to break. This gave him a great advantage over the rival candidate, Francis I. Maximilian had no money and no means of raising any. Never did the ruler whom the Italians had long ago nicknamed "pochi danari," so well deserve his name. Progressive bankruptcy had brought him to the point where he literally lived on his debts. He could only secure one thousand gulden from his chief creditor the house of Fugger, after repeated attempts, and the plea that if he could not get the loan, "His Majesty would have nothing to eat." Charles had to raise the cash to bribe the Electors on his resources as the King of Spain. Prices were high, and the total of all the amounts promised was the enormous sum of between five and six hundred thousand gulden. Privileges and promises of good marriages were additional inducements. The result was, that on August 27th, 1518, four Electors and the ambassadors of a fifth, signed an agreement to elect Charles, King of the Romans.

But in spite of this triumph of influence, the four months Maximilian had to live, did not bring him the pleasure of being sure that the crown of Empire was to join the ducal crowns of the Netherlands, the royal crowns of Spain and Naples and many other diadems, on the head of his oldest grandson. Just what the hitch was does not appear with certainty. The Papal objection to the union of the crowns of Naples and the Empire, an objection surviving from the conflicts of the Papacy and the Empire in which the imperial family of Hohenstaufen had perished during the thirteenth century, played some part. But this formal objection, afterward overcome, could not have been the real obstacle. Probably Charles was unable to raise enough to pay cash on the completion of the bargain. The election therefore went over until after Maximilian's death, when the total price rose about sixty per cent.

The skillful conduct of this afterwards successful negotiation, was not the only matter which occupied Maximilian's attention when the close of the war with Venice and peace with France, gave him leisure. The reign of Mohammed II, who, in 1453, took Constantinople, marked a process of consolidation in the Turkish Empire and an extension of its power, which met its first serious disaster in arms at Lepanto in 1571. The victories of Selim I in Persia, Asia Minor and Egypt, between 1514 and 1517, as well as the boldness of his slave hunting fleets on the

Italian coasts,[1] pressed the standing menace of the Turkish power upon the attention of Pope Leo X. He wrote a letter to all Christian princes, exhorting them to lay aside their quarrels and unite under the standard of the cross against the common foe of Christendom. And in March, 1517, the Lateran Council voted to impose two taxes on Christendom. One resolution authorized the sale of indulgencies in order to restore St. Peters, so fallen into ruins that the relics of the Apostles were exposed to injury by the weather; the other ordered the payment of a tax on the clerical property of the world, and the sale of another indulgence to aid the Church in arming Europe for a crusade against the Turk. Many good churchmen did not believe that this money would be used for the purposes to which it was voted. A number of bishops of the council insisted that the Turkish tenth should not be raised or the Turkish indulgence sold, until the crusade had begun, and they were beaten on the vote by a very small majority. There is every reason to believe that their suspicions were justified by facts. There is absolute documentary proof of it in regard to parts of these monies. A receipt has been preserved, in which the Pope's nephew acknowledges one hundred thousand livres from the King of France, to be repaid out of the Turkish tenth. And it is perfectly plain that a large part of the income of the sale of the indulgence for the rebuilding of St. Peters, went to repay the banking firm of Fugger for advances to enable the Archbishop of Mayence to pay the papacy the

[1] One of these entered the Tiber and threatened to take the Pope himself prisoner. Letters and Papers, II, 2017.

customary enormous fees for the granting of the pallium, or badge of his office.

The way in which the indulgence traffic exploited the faith of the common people to line the pockets of greedy prelates or princes, and the reckless preaching which, to push the sale, often distorted to the injury of religion and the undermining of morality, the true doctrines of the Church concerning indulgences, had again and again been denounced by laymen and clergymen. An Augustinian monk who was one of the city pastors and University professors of Wittenberg, a small city in Saxony, became aware, through the confessions of his people, that great harm was being done to faith by the preaching of a vender of the St. Peter's indulgence. He issued in October, 1517, as a professor of theology sworn to defend the truth of God, a protest against these abuses and an appeal to the Pope to suppress them. Directed toward a professional audience, it called out a great popular response, and Martin Luther became a voice of Germany against the indulgence traffic, as an open and scandalous sign of manifest corruption in the ecclesiastical administration. For, as yet, he neither intended nor suggested attack upon the doctrine or constitution of the Church.

What Germany thought about the Turkish tenths, which, though levied on church property, must of course come finally out of the pockets of the people, found expression in various forms during the Reichstag which opened at Augsburg in the Spring of 1518.

The Emperor and the Papal Legate appeared before it in the attitude which corresponded to the mediæval ideal of the Empire as a double headed institution, where the sacred layman, chosen by God to bear the sword as a terror to evil doers, worked in perfect harmony with the Vicar of Christ, the head of the world in all spiritual things. The Legate, at high mass in the cathedral, bestowed a cardinal's hat on the Archbishop of Mayence, for the payment of whose debts the indulgence which roused Luther's protest had been sold, and gave a consecrated sword to the Emperor, exhorting him, in the name of the Vicar of Christ, to conquer Constantinople and Jerusalem and include the earth within the bounds of the Empire and the Church. How much the Emperor really expected the crusade to take the shape of an army, is hard to say. He had written, to the papal letter of the beginning of 1517, a most enthusiastic answer, in which the man who has studied Maximilian most profoundly, thinks he can detect the note of irony. He afterward worked out a military plan to occupy three years, which he sent to the various princes of the world. It was to begin with the conquest of north Africa by Hapsburg forces under the lead of the Emperor, while Francis and Henry remained at home to maintain European peace and keep down rebellion. It has been suggested that this plan may have concealed the desire to add north Africa to the Hapsburg domains, without any serious intention of assaulting Constantinople in the third year. This is possible. It is also possible, and more probable,[1] that Maximilian's errant fancy was again carrying him through the realms of glorious visions and his mind, drugged with egotism as

[1] Compare development of this plan in the successive sketches presented to the Auschüsse of the Austrian Duchies. See Archiv für Oest. Geschichts forschung, 1854, 207 ff. A reasonable motive for this plan is there shown in the desire to prevent the complete subjugation of the African prince by the Sultan and the consequent increase of his power to attack the Danubian lands.

with opium, was finding a pleasure in the world of dreams it had failed to find in the world of reality. At all events, Legate and Emperor exhorted the Reichstag to vote that every fifty householders should supply and arm a man against the Turks, and that a tax of a tenth should be paid by the German clergy, a tax of a twentieth by the German laity, for the support of the crusaders.

The feelings of the assembly, and indeed of all Germany, were shown with the least restraint in an anonymous pamphlet circulated at Augsburg. A few extracts will show its tone, which only expresses without reserve the meaning of a number of formal requests and exhortations sent to the Reichstag from many sides.

"To break the rule of the uncleanest foe who tries with all his strength to blot out the name of Christ, is a holy effort that can be blamed by no one who would rather serve Christ than the Turk. But under these pretences to plunder the ignorant people, to suck dry the milk of the nation, is a crime as bad as what the Turk does, not because of the money, but because it is unbearable that Satan should change himself into such an angel—should mingle in the cup of piety the poison of godlessness—that the people, giving for the glory of God, should really give to avarice, the mother of false religion." "If the money sent to Rome for fees for the induction of bishops were saved, it would be enough for the Turkish war." "The Pope is richer from his own lands than any other Christian prince, and still we buy palliums (Archbishops' cloaks) and send mule loads of gold to Rome, building gallows to hang Christ, promise presents, swap gold for lead" (the seals of papal bulls). "Where is there a college of priests that is not stained? Who has brought into Germany the wickedest imaginable habits and has taught things a decent man cannot even name? * * * This horrible flood has proved itself out of the Romish filth over the whole world, until there is no wilderness where before dwelt only wild beasts, which is free from it. * * * You wish to fight the Turk? * * * Seek him in Italy, not in Asia. Against the Asiatic Turk every Christian prince can defend himself, but the whole Christian world is not enough to restrain the other. You can only satisfy this hell-hound with streams of gold. It needs no weapon. Gold can do more than horse or foot."

Under the influence of such a spirit, the Reichstag prepared their Gravamina, or complaints of injuries and abuses inflicted by the Roman Curia on Germany. They repeated and sharpened similar charges which had been presented at Reichstags since the middle of the fifteenth century. These complaints did not come simply from laymen. The bishop of Lüttich sent, in the name of the clergy of his diocese, a complaint of abuses in the Church through corrupt use of patronage centering in the Roman Curia. It illustrated the counts of the indictments with instances. It denounced the hunting of benefices, the multiplication of chaplaincies and papal officials, pluralities, or the accumulation of many Church offices in one hand, the consequent terrible drain of money from churches and people, and the resultant degradation of religion and the service of God. "The offices are filled with false shepherds, who try to skin the sheep instead of feeding them." "Now, oh! Emperor and Reichstag, beg the Pope that out of fatherly love and the watchfulness of a shepherd, he may abolish these and other abuses, with the list of which a book could be filled."

These complaints must not be taken as the utterances of heretics. They came out of the consciousness that successive popes and large numbers of cardinals, cared more for the wealth and worldly power of their offices than for their spiritual duties. The court of Rome was so openly materialized—the money which flowed there from all parts of the world was so manifestly spent on worldly objects—many of the men in power there were so scandalously lacking in any vocation for the care of souls, that, all over the world, the zealous who knew the facts prayed, and those careless about religion, who saw their gold flowing over the Alps to enrich papal families, cursed. At the beginning of the sixteenth century, it was a commonplace among men of intelligence everywhere, that the Curia at Rome was desperately corrupt, and, in consequence, the Church terribly in need of reformation. Such a perception of obvious facts did not in the least imply heresy in the perceiver, and many of the noblest men who felt this situation keenly and helped to remedy it at the Council of Trent, hated and fought schism all their lives.

In no country of the world had the people suffered more from ecclesiastical abuses than in Germany, and, in the water-shed of the Rhine and the Elbe, the perception of the condition of the Church and the corrupt patronage, the greed, bribery and ambition which lay at the bottom of it, had passed from the classes to the masses.

Just as the Reichstag had prefaced every vote of supplies to Maximilian by a demand for a redress of grievances and a reformation of the Empire, so now they gave a negative or evasive answer to the demand for new ecclesiastical taxes, and pressed for redress of grievances. And in this instance, they backed their refusal by a strong statement that, in the present state of popular discontent with the administration of the Church, the attempt to levy a new ecclesiasical tax would not be borne by "the common man."

Maximilian had often entertained the idea of a reformation of the German Church, and even a violent reformation of the Universal Church in head and members. He considered joining the rebellion which Louis XII tried to create against Julius II. Had he done so, it would have been, historically considered, nothing extraordinary. It was only a hundred years since the largest assembly of the Church ever held, the council of Constance, had deposed the Pope and elected another. He had considered a more unprecedented intervention with the traditional government of the Church, in his plan, whatever it was, "to become Pope and Emperor." These schemes were to a large extent political moves, suggested to Maximilian's mind by the exigencies of the diplomatic entanglements resulting from the league of Cambray. A large motive for them in his mind, was to bring pressure to bear that should force the Pope into line with political or dynastic plans. But he was not without a real reformer's impulse. This double motive appears in his letter to his daughter Margaret, of June, 1510. "That cursed priest, the Pope, won't on any account let us go to Rome in arms for our imperial crown in company with the French, because he is afraid to be called before a council by us two for the great sins and abuses which he and his predecessors have committed and daily commit, and also some cardinals which fear reformation, etc." [1]

The touch of reforming zeal suggested in this letter, had moved him to ask (Sept. 1510) Jacob Wimpheling, formerly cathedral preacher at Spires, a zealous churchman and an orthodox theologian, most active in defense of the doctrine of the immaculate conception of the Virgin, to answer certain questions looking toward reform of the German Church. For years, Wimpheling, with his two intimates, the celebrated popular preacher, Geiler, cathedral preacher at Strassburg, and the pious satirist Brant, chancellor of Strassburg, had been denouncing the decay of religion and the corruptions and abuses of the Church which gave it opportunity to increase.

His reply pointed out ten distinct ecclesiastical abuses centering in the corrupt use of patronage at Rome, under which religion in Germany was suffering.

1. The way in which Popes violate by dispensations, revocations and suspensions, the agreements of their predecessors.

2—3. Interference with elections of German prelates and heads of cathedral chapters.

4—5. Granting of German church offices to members of the Roman court, even "expectations," conferring those offices on absentees before the incumbents are dead.

6. Annates, a heavy tax on new incumbents of higher offices.

7. Granting of pastorates "to unworthy candidates, fitter to pasture and guide mules than men."

[1] Le Glay, Vol. I, page 294.

8. The indulgence trade pushed to make money.

9. The Turkish tenths asked for war against the Turks—"and no expedition ever sails against them."

10. The summoning to Rome of ecclesiastical cases which ought to be tried in Germany.

"If these things go on and the drain of German gold to Rome continues, there is grave fear lest the common people, unable to bear that addition to their other burdens, should follow the example of the Bohemians in the last century, rise in arms and separate from Rome."

But to this clear and concise statement of abuses, repeating older documents of the same sort, he added no practicable plan to remove them. All he had to suggest was a request to the Holy Father to treat his German sons better. He even pointed out the danger of strenuous action. The three clerical electors might not stand by the Emperor, for fear of papal censures. The Pope might launch an interdict suspending all religious services in Germany, which the people would not bear. The begging friars might rouse the people against him. It was even possible that the Pope should do what popes had done to other emperors, deprive him of his crown and set up another.[1]

Such a counsel was not apt to strengthen the reforming, as against the political motive, in the Emperor's mind. And when a new combination made the Pope a factor

[1] See Un Réformateur Catholique . . . Jean Geiler de Kaysersberg. Par L'abbe L. Dacheux. Paris and Strassbourg, 1876.

Brieger's Zeitschrift für Kirchen geschichte, Vol. III, page 203 ff.

Gebhardt, Bruno; Die Gravamina der Deutschen Nation gegen den römischen Hof. zweite Auflage. Breslau, 1895.

Schmidt, Charles. Histoire Litteraire de L'Alsace a la fin du XVe at au commencement du XVIe siecle. Paris, 1879.

favourable to his political plans, Maximilian gave little attention to reform.

This neglect came, however, rather from preoccupation than from indifference. Maximilian was a genuinely religious man. He was regular and zealous in his devotions, and compiled a prayer book. In a crisis of his affairs, he wrote, with evident genuineness of feeling, to one of his faithful followers, that he was "become the scorn of the whole world," but he "lived always in hope, and comforted himself with the word of the Gospel that the Lord would not forsake the righteous and that he always chastised those whom He loved." [1] He showed his faith in conduct. He was free from the national disgrace of drunkenness, proverbial among the Germans of his day, and notorious among the princes. His singular decency of speech and his dislike of adultery, won him a high reputation for chastity [2] which, according to the moral standards of the age, was not impaired by the fact that he had, during the twenty years of his widowhood, eight illegitimate children.[3] In a chapter of his allegorical poem of Teuerdank he represents himself, in answer to the temptation of Satan, laying down three rules of life:—[4]

[1] MSS. in Dresden Archives, quoted by Ulmann, Vol. I, 164.

[2] Among others Cuspinian.

[3] See list of his children in Birk Fugger. Spiegel der Ehren des Ertz Hauses Oesterreich erweitert durch L. von Birken. The objections to relying on this work shown by Ranke would not apply to an item of general knowledge like this.

[4] The completed study of the MSS. has made evident to Laschitzer, editor of the final edition, that Maximilian is responsible for the entire poem. It is certain that "Without his consent no verse or illustration of the poem was sent to the printer." * * * "In short, not only the idea but also the general plan and order of the poem, not simply in the large but in all the details, is to be attributed to Maximilian." This does away with the old conclusion that the moralizing parts of the poem were to be attributed to the imperial secretary.

1. Bodily desires are to be ruled by God's commandments, and reason.

2. God's favour is worth more than honour among men.

3. A man who hopes in God must not break his oath.[1]

Religion influenced not only his feeling and his conduct but also his thought. His active mind turned towards problems of the spiritual realm. Abbot Trithemius of Boppard, published, together with his own answers, a series of questions the Emperor left with him after a journey in the imperial train along the Rhine, in 1508.

1. Why does God prefer being believed in by mortals, to being known by them?

2. Can heathen, ignorant of the Christian religion, and faithful to the religion they know, be saved?

3. Whence comes it that the prophets of false religions work miracles?

4. Why is the Holy Scripture neither complete nor perfectly clear, lacking much which is demanded for complete faith?

5. How is it that sorcerers are allowed power over evil spirits?

6. How is the doctrine of the righteousness of God reconcilable with the permission of so much evil, often injurious to pious men?

7. Can a special providence over the fortunes of men, more especially over everything that happens, be proved by Scripture and reason?

Not only was Maximilian a person of real religious

[1] Teuerdank Capitel, 10.

feeling, affected to some extent in all his activities by the doctrine of the church, but he had a strong feeling of his duty, to "the common man," who, as he was repeatedly told, suffered most in mind, morals and pocket from ecclesiastical abuses. He asked Geiler to form a collection of maxims upon the conduct which a prince, desirous of making his subjects prosperous and happy, ought to follow. He closes the little book of instructions on the beloved sport of hunting, which he wrote, towards the end of his life, for his grandsons and descendants, thus:—"Always rejoice in the great pleasure of hunting, for thy recreation and health, also for the comfort of thy subjects, because you can, through hunting, become known to them, the poor as well as the rich. The rich as well as the poor daily has access to you while you are hunting, so that they can complain of their necessities and present them to you, and you can hear their complaints with pleasure; because, during the enjoyment of the hunt, you can hear the petitions of the poor. To this end, you must always take your secretary and some councilors with you on your hunting trips, so that you are ready to give satisfaction to the common man when he comes to see you and comes near you; a thing you can do better on a hunting trip than in houses. In order to lose no time, you must never omit that except when the falcons fly or the hounds run." [1] A coloured picture he had made for his Fischerei buch, or list of fishing waters, interprets this word to his descendants of the house of Hapsburg, and shows us his

[1] Kaiser Maximilian I. geheimes Jagdbuch, etc. Ch. G. von Karajan zweite Auflage, Wien, 1881. The halting English of the translation is an attempt to reproduce the naïve style of the Emperor, who wrote the only MSS. of this little treatise entirely in his own hand and apparently without any criticism or help from his secretaries.

own habit. In one corner the Emperor has dismounted from his horse. On the ground lie his cloak and riding trousers. The climbing irons for following chamois on the cliffs, have just been buckled onto his feet, but he delays to receive a petition from a peasant who kneels before him.[1]

In spite of his sincere religious belief and the seriousness with which he took his office as the doer of justice to "the common man," these last appeals to lead in the reform of the Church, the most forcible of the many which had come to him during twenty years, seem to have made no impression upon him. To Luther's protest about indulgences he gave no heed. Maximilian never saw Luther, whose name was then on the lips of most Germans. But he was a poor judge of character and ability. And, in all probability, even if he had seen the Wittenberg professor, he would have failed to recognize that power, which, within a few years, even those who thought the power Satanic, admitted was in the man.

Signs of storms were common. In 1516 Aleander, afterward papal nuncio, wrote to the Pope,—"Germany is only waiting for some fellow to open his mouth against Rome." A thousand omens foretold the schism of Germany from the Holy See. By word and deed, a generation of discontented peasants, had giving warning of the terrible convulsion of the revolt of 1525. It does not appear that Maximilian read the signs of the times. It was afterwards said—"Germany is a magnificent horse which only needs a rider." Charles, whose ability was as much

[1] Das Fischereibuch Kaiser Maximilian I. Ludwig Frieherr von Lazarini und Dr. Michael Mayr. Innsbruck, 1901. Plate to page 1.

greater than that of his grandfather as his parts were less brilliant, tried for thirty-five years to make the horse go where he wanted, and then dismounted to put his son in the saddle. Perhaps no one could have ridden the horse. At all events, in 1518, Maximilian did not even try.

Probably the last reason why Maximilian never seriously undertook the reform of the Church which the humanists expected of him at his accession, was that he had added a personal article to the doctrine of the Church, and clung to it with the most passionate and intimate conviction. It was the belief that the house of Hapsburg was elected of God to play an enormous part in the destinies of the world. To his mind it was inconceivable that anything which injured their rights, could in the end help mankind. Inevitably, and as by natural law, out of any entanglement of motives and reasons, his mind drifted to the conclusion that his plans for the present power and future prospects of the Hapsburgs, had the right of way. Everything else must wait.

When the Emperor left the Reichstag of Augsburg the last week of September, 1518, he was in no mood for any action. In his youth, Maximilian had a fund of health and energy which seemed exhaustless. The secretary who wrote to his dictation, and under his supervision, the Latin autobiography, in one paragraph of it, tells how he saw Maximilian go out at dawn and bring in three stags —then exercise in arms, using up three horses, receiving a wound in the hand and giving a fall to his opponent that proved fatal. Then he changed to a magnificent court dress, danced and kept the ball going until the dawn of another day.[1] In 1518, Maximilian was not yet sixty, but he had drawn terribly on his reserve strength. The disastrous end of the long Venetian war, the decline of his reputation as a soldier, the arrangement with France forced on him by his own grandson, the refusal of the Reichstag to do anything he wanted, must have weighed heavily on his mind. With his usual courage he kept his disappointments to himself. During the Reichstag he was active in those great dances and banquets he liked to plan or share. He had always enjoyed the society of the wives and daughters of the city patricians. Once when he was ready to leave a Nuremberg dance, the ladies took off his boots and spurs, hid them and begged him to stay the dance out. Maximilian stayed and danced from noon until dark and, after supper, long into the night.[2] Of all the German cities, Augsburg had long been the pleasantest to him. He had a presentiment that he should never see Augsburg again, and he asked his old favourites to dance without the veils they were in the habit of wearing at public balls. But though he kept this smiling face as long as the Reichstag lasted, his heart was very heavy; and when it closed, he made for his beloved hunting grounds of Tirol.

At Innsbruck a new trouble met him. The government of Tirol was on the verge of bankruptcy, and the council had not been able to pay inn bills for twenty-four thousand gulden, he had contracted several years before. The inn keepers, therefore, refused to receive his court. This public shame, and the situation of the government, so

[1] Latin life. Jahrbucher der Kh. S., Vol. VI, page 432 (15).
[2] Chroniken der deutschen Städte, Vol. XI, page 723.

desperate that the council resigned and could be persuaded to keep merely the name of councilors for three months, deeply angered Maximilian. And two of his intimates think his excitement brought on the illness which attacked him. In spite of his weakness, he travelled in a litter and by boat some hundred and fifty miles, but at Wels, in Austria, in the end of November, it was plain that his life was in danger.

Doctors were sent for from Vienna. Maximilian had a high opinion of his own medical knowledge. He relates in the Weiss Kunig that, in his youth, a doctor who taught him medicine, told Frederick he could not teach his pupil anything more, and records how twice he saved his own life by acting against the mistaken orders of the physicians. This knowledge, or the Viennese doctors' advice, or the voice of nature, made him aware some time before death came that his end was near. In the end of December he made his will, and on the 12th of January he died.

All that we know of his last days is highly characteristic. He faced death with courage and self control, confessed and took the rites of the Church with a tranquil mind and the entirely good conscience that appears in all his references to his own life and deeds. His gentleness, kindness and patience to his attendants, were unchanged. His mind was active to the end, and he turned to the pleasures which had solaced his labours for many years. He had always been a patron of musicians and loved singing birds, which he kept near him in cages when he could. Tradition even assigns to him the Volkslied "Innsbruck Ich muss dich lassen." It is probable that music soothed the hours which must have been heavy for one so unused to confinement. We know that he clung to the pleasures of literature and art until the last.

Literature and art had to him a peculiar use and meaning. The bulk of his patronage had been expended in using the skill of masters of form, colour and words, to illustrate the glory of the house of Hapsburg and the deeds of its greatest descendant, Maximilian I. For this artists had drawn, cast bronze and painted; scholars had made geneological and historical researches; secretaries and writers had recorded his reminiscences and polished the style of his dictations. The scholars had reached results highly satisfactory to Maximilian. They had solemnly concluded that it was proved by authentic records,—"that the Archduchy of Austria was the first Kingdom privileged by Julius Cæsar and his successors when they had all the world in subjection." [1] They had, after long debates, established a genealogical line leading back through Hector to Noah.[2] They had discovered one hundred and twenty-three saints given to the Church by the house of Hapsburg, and Maximilian had ordered wood cuts made of all of them.[3] Dr. Mennel, one of the historiographers, was at Wels during Maximilian's last illness. He has told how the Emperor asked him, just before death came, if he had anything new and pleasant to read aloud to

[1] Chmel Urkunden, etc., zur Geschichte Maximilian I. Bibliothek des literarischen Vereins in Stuttgart, Vol. X. Instruction to the valet de chambre of the Archduke of Austria.

[2] See Laschitzer introduction to the Genealogy in Jahrbücher der Kh. S., etc., Vol. VII, and also the very amusing extract quoted from the Fugger MSS. in Deutsches Kunst Blatt, Vol. V.

[3] Jahrbücher, Kh. S., etc., Vol. IV.

shorten the sleepless nights. For several nights through, Mennel read him the legends of the saints of his race and stories of his ancestors. For the ruling passion of Maximilian was strong to the end of life.

His will, besides leaving full directions for the foundation of nine poor houses and for his burial in a coffin he had carried with him for five years, commended to his executors the publication of his books and chronicles. All of those which were left at all complete, were either accounts of the glories of his house, or illustrated catalogues of his own possessions, or records of his life and deeds for the instruction of his descendants, and, so far as we can judge, all those he ever planned were to be in some way related to the same topics.[1]

Maximilian also left in his will directions for the completion of his tomb. On the plan of this he had worked for many years. The general idea was his own, and he had constantly criticised and directed the sketches and castings for the details. His final design was a life-sized figure of himself kneeling on a bronze sarcophagus adorned with twenty-four reliefs showing his great deeds. The central mass was to be decorated and surounded by forty life-sized figures of Maximilian's heroic relatives, and one hundred smaller statues of saints of the lineage of the Hapsburgs.[2] The list of heroes included King Arthur, Theodoric, Charlemagne and Julius Cæsar. For

[1] The prayer book seems to be an exception. But the editor of the illustrations made for it holds that it was intended as a book of prayers for the Order of St. George, to which he invited all the princes and nobles of the world, in order that under his leadership they might drive the Turk from Constantinople, to the glory of God and the House of Austria, in the person of Maximilian. See Jahrbücher des Kh. S., etc., Vol. XX.

[2] Jahrbücher, Kh. S., etc., Vol. XI.

including Charlemagne and Julius Caesar in this family gathering he had the authority of his historiographers. But, so far as we know, King Arthur and Theodoric were added to the group as the result of his own historical studies. Only twelve of the large statues and a few of the smaller ones, were done. Two of them, Vischer's splendid figures of Arthur and Theodoric, made six years before, were still in pawn, and the debt for which they were held was not paid until 1532.

For Maximilian had been hampered in completing his tomb, as in all of his magnificent undertakings, by poverty. His large income was dwarfed by his larger designs. A statement could hardly be framed which would exaggerate the continuous influence of this lack of money upon his career. It was the immediate cause of almost all those delays in the execution of plans, which created the common opinion of his contemporaries, outside of the German humanists, that he was slow, inefficient or untrustworthy.

He recognized the fact that his finances were on an unsound basis, but he never really took it into account in his plans. He was fond of saying, in the peculiar Latin for which he was praised by the humanists, "Est enim una res miserabilis nostra paupertas," but he never learned to cut his coat according to his cloth. Extravagant habits, the outcome not only of taste and pride, but also of policy, grew upon him. He ordered in Augsburg a set of armor at one hundred thousand gulden, to appear before the Reichstag. And in 1515, when everything he owned was covered with mortgages, he spent two hundred thousand gulden in banquets to the visiting Kings at Vienna.[1]

The only part of Maximilian's estate which was in a sound condition at his death, was the treasure of the Hapsburgs. He had inherited a great amount of plate and jewels from his father. He kept adding to it, and his letters continually record orders for plate and the purchase of pearls, rubies or diamonds. To one of these, ordering the councilors at Innsbruck to pay one thousand gulden to the Fuggers for two jewels, they reply, that, if they settle this bill, they will have no money left to pay the personal expenses of the Archduchess. He occasionally pawned portions of his plate or jewels. His credit was so poor in the neighbourhood of his favourite city of Innsbruck, that he had to leave a ring in pledge with the hostesses of three inns for bills of six gulden.[2] But in spite of all obstacles, the treasure of the House of Hapsburg increased while Maximilian was its head. When his younger grandson, Ferdinand, opened the chests which contained it, he was astonished at its amount.

But though the treasure of his house had not suffered from Maximilian's poverty, his greatest artistic project had. When he tried, in 1517, to push the casting of the statues for his tomb, the council at Nuremberg refused to allow the artists of the city to accept commissions from the Emperor, lest the city should have to pay for the completed work. A compromise was arranged by which half

[1] Letters and Papers, Vol. II, part I, number 202.

[2] At least I can see no other explanation for entries in the accounts of the Council which record the redeeming of these rings from the hostesses of inns. Jahrbücher Kh. S., III, Nos. 2371-2391-2393. See the documents calendared here and in the back of other volumes for additions to the treasure of the Hapsburgs.

of the city tax was to be devoted towards extinguishing Maximilian's existing debt to the city. The other half was henceforth to be used to pay for the work on the monument. But the arrangement fell through, because the Elector of Saxony claimed the entire tax had already been pledged to him to cover a debt Maximilian owed.

Maximilian's death, therefore, left his tomb nothing but scattered fragments. It was not until the end of the century that descendants completed it on a smaller scale than the original design.

Though the greatest work he planned has probably gained by being freed from the forest and underbrush of statues big and little with which he proposed to surround it, Maximilian has won his most lasting fame as a patron of literature and art. The man whose features Holbein engraved in the Dance of Death, for whom Dürer drew the designs for the border of the Prayer-book, at whose orders Burgkmair handled the burin, whose suggestions Vischer cast in bronze, and whose tomb is ornamented by marble reliefs called by Thorwaldsen the most perfect works of their kind, cannot be forgotten in the history of art because of any criticisms of his taste or motives. His taste was not highly discriminating. Men who have followed with care and accuracy the details of his artistic commissions, suggest a lack of reason for believing that he could have seen any difference between the work of Sesselchreiber and the daring idealism of Vischer; and he seems to have been no better pleased with the illustrations Burgkmair or Dürer did for him than with those of inferior men. But what he may have lacked in critical power, he made up in zeal, and in a patron of art, readiness to recognize merit and find pleasure even in imperfect work, is better than keenness in detecting faults.

It is clear that his love for art centred around his dominant passions; thirst for distinction and family pride. But we must not be too quick to condemn it on that account. Few men have served the muses for naught. Many of the masters of literature, from the Greeks to Goethe, have shown in their works the love of fame mixed with the love of beauty. That combination of motives was very common in the age of Maximilian. General judgments comparing one epoch with another are apt to be false; but even a cursory comparison of mediæval and renascence art, suggests that the patrons of the former gave, and its servants worked, far less for their own glory and far more for the glory of God, than the patrons and artists of the latter. Maximilian may only have been more frank than his contemporaries, in so dispensing his patronage of art that it leaves upon one who reviews it all, an irresistible impression that the larger part of his interest in it, grew from the hope of presenting his figure to posterity as the greatest member of the glorious house of Hapsburg, and illustrating the lessons of his example to descendants who might raise the dynasty to the heights of power where his day dreams had placed it; with Italy, Spain, Portugal, England, part of a dismembered France, the Netherlands, Germany and the Danube Valley to the Black Sea, under the sway of its sceptre.

APPENDIX

REGINALD POLE AND THOMAS CROMWELL: AN EXAMINATION OF THE APOLOGIA AD CAROLUM QUINTUM

THOMAS CROMWELL, beginning life as a merchant's clerk without money or influence, finally rose to the highest authority ever wielded by a British subject. The portraits of this remarkable man presented by historians, have been most influenced by accounts of him left by two of his contemporaries. John Foxe put him into the Book of Martyrs as one who, having greatly served "the Gospel", died by the machinations of the enemies of truth. Reginald Pole, cardinal and Archbishop of Canterbury, denounced him as a false counselor who helped the descent of a once innocent and pious king into tyranny, crime, and irreligion by flattering evil passions for his own gain.

The first of these judgments upon Cromwell became prevalent in England during the lifetime of his grandson and continued dominant for many generations. But the image of the martyr, suggested by Foxe, has been to a great extent replaced by the picture of an unscrupulous adventurer, loving chiefly the profits of power, the English disciple of Machiavelli, flattering the ideals of his age while he sneered at them, cruel, treacherous, and, even when he sought great ends, pursuing them by means baser than those generally used by his contemporaries. The traits of which this latter image are composed, have been drawn from different sources, and the image, therefore, varies according to the emphasis which the writer may have chosen to lay upon this or that evil feature of the character of the earl of Essex. But about all these images of the unscrupulous adventurer type there is the same sinister atmosphere, and one who has read the account of Reginald Pole, easily recognizes that the presence of that sinister atmosphere, throwing Cromwell into relief as the "arch knave" of his time, is due to its influence. This is the first record of a critical examination of this often-quoted account of Cromwell, and it gives the writer's reasons for concluding that Pole's sketch of Cromwell's character and motives, is biased, improbable, and inaccurate.

Reginald Pole was of the blood royal, tracing descent from the Duke of Clarence and from Warwick the kingmaker. He was sent to Oxford by royal bounty, and, at twenty-one, went abroad to study, with a royal pension of 100*l.*, equal in modern value to some $5,000 or $6,000. In addition he enjoyed the income of three ecclesiastical benefices which had been presented to him. He stayed five years abroad as a student, and gained the friendship of some of the most distinguished scholars of the day. On his return to England, he was one of the very few English noblemen (he had entered Magdalen College as a nobleman) who might justly be called highly educated. When Henry VIII wanted to repudiate his wife, Pole, who had again gone abroad to study in Paris and still received his large pension as "king's scholar", was employed to collect opinions from the doctors of the university in favor of the invalidity of marriage to a brother's widow. Having successfully completed this task, which he so hated that he delegated its details to another, he returned to England by royal order in July, 1530, and shortly after was offered the archbishopric of York, rendered vacant by the death of Wolsey.

Knowing that if he accepted it he must approve the repudiation of Catherine, Pole manfully refused, had a stormy interview with the King, and in 1532 obtained permission to go abroad. His pension was continued and he received another ecclesiastical benefice.

Two years after Pole left England, a demand came to him from the King that he should write his opinion on two points: Is marriage with a brother's widow permissible? Is the supremacy of the pope instituted by God? Pole's answer to these questions grew into a treatise entitled *In Defense of the Unity of the Church (Pro Ecclesiasticæ Unitatis Defensione, etc.* It consists of four books, and expresses in places great affection for Henry and the grief Pole feels in being obliged to accuse him. The first book attacks the new royal title of Supreme Head of the Church in England, and threatens Henry with the divine vengeance for the death of More and Fisher. The second defends the supreme authority of the Pope, especially against the treatise of Sampson, which had been sent to him by the King. The third book exhorts Henry to prepare his mind to receive these arguments by laying aside his pride, and then proceeds, in an ever-rising storm of invective, to denounce his sins. Pole recites the facts in regard to Anne Boleyn and shows the injustice to Catherine, calls the King a robber and persecutor of the Church, charges him with having wasted in senseless extravagances more taxes than his predecessors had collected in five hundred years, calls him guilty of an infamous incest, applies the strongest possible epithets to Anne Boleyn, and asks Henry if he thinks her daughter will be accepted as queen by the aristocratic families of England. He denounces Henry for having slaughtered his nobles on slight pretenses and filled his court with wretched creatures. He calls up against him the blood of More, Fisher, and the Carthusian martyrs, saying that Nero and Domitian had not killed such men. He stigmatizes him as worse than the Tunisian pirates. In an apostrophe to Charles V, Pole begs him to defer the Turkish war in order to attack this new enemy worse than the Turk; for schism comes from the same source as paganism. Indeed, this English Turkish seed has produced worse results than are to be seen among the real Turks. The real Turks tolerate the true religion, but this king defends his false religion with the sword. Therefore let the orthodox head of the Christian republic draw the sword against him. And, pointing out that the English people have before driven kings from the throne, Pole calls upon England to renew her ancient spirit, looking to the Emperor for aid. Henry is a sacrilegious perjurer, who has broken his oaths and overthrown the foundations of his kingdom—justice, clemency, liberality. He has squandered England's treasures on unworthy favorites, and despoiled every condition of men. He has made sport of his nobility, plundered his clergy, never loved his people. He might be glad to have upon his tomb that epitaph of Sardanapalus which Aristotle said was fitter for a bull than for a man, that no room might be left for one not less true but more shameful; if, indeed, he might hope for any tomb, and not, in the words of Isaiah, be cast out from his sepulchre as a useless trunk, as a putrid corpse have no fellowship with his dead forefathers. His shame and ignominy are known to every one, and all powers sacred and secular are now leagued to cut off so pernicious a member from the body of Christendom. Whither can he flee for refuge? His riches stolen from the Church will not help him. No tyrant had perished from poverty. Neither will the many adherents who now support him save him; Richard III had been killed by his father in spite of a great army,

Henry had but one refuge from unexampled dangers—penitence. And in the fourth book, asking pardon for his harsh words, and "struggling with love and pity," Pole exhorts the King to penitence; that is, to repent of his sins, return to the Church, and ask for absolution, and "in the word of the prophet your iniquity will not be your ruin."[1]

Pole came to manhood at the crisis of a great conflict between two ideals for the European world. On the one hand, there was the mediæval ideal of Christendom as an organism with a visible head whose just sentence anticipated the sentence of the great day of judgment, made the rebel against divine commandment on whom it fell, an outlaw in this world, and sent him to hell after death. On the other hand, there was the forming ideal of Christendom as a series of distinct national institutions, each containing a divinely-constituted seat of authority that rightly rejected all outside interference in its own affairs, whose national church admitted no foreign authority to damn its apostate members, whose courts acknowledged no just power in any foreign tribunal to judge concerning the honor, the property, or the life of its citizens. These two ideals were to engage four generations in wars. The wars were complicated by theological opinions and religious beliefs, race hatred and class feeling, dynastic greed and personal ambition, but behind them all, from the battle of Mühlberg to the peace of Westphalia, there lay this central question, whether Christendom was or was not divinely constituted as an organic unity, possessing somewhere, either in pope or council, or in both, a common, visible, and ultimate au-

[1] Pole's description of his own book, in *Epistolarum Reginaldi Poli S. R. E. Cardinalis et aliorum ad ipsum Collectio*, Brescia, 1744-1757, 5 volumes, I. 74. Pole's characterization of the third book is expanded here by illustrative instances drawn from the book itself. Pole says it is written "acerbe et vehementer."

thority, appointed to define truth and judge righteousness for every nation and every man. The trumpet-call for that fight had come to Pole. Asked to say whether, in the last analysis, the supreme authority over England in questions involving a moral issue, was at Rome or in London, taste, reason, and conscience led him to stand by the old ideal. He threw down the glove to Henry as a tyrant who had betrayed England, because, in withdrawing from the papal obedience, he had broken the unity of Christendom, the God-given guarantee of saving truth and social order.

It is plain from Pole's letters at the time he was writing this treatise,[1] that he thought himself to be doing some great service to the cause of the Church. Just what service he hoped to do his cause by interpolating into his answer to Henry's questions a diatribe in a tone of such fierce invective that some of his intimate friends, ardent churchmen, advised the correction of the manuscript, does not appear to a modern reader at first sight. A search through his writings makes it plain that Pole hoped, now that the passion for Anne Boleyn which had driven Henry into his impiety was cooled, to frighten him back to the path of righteousness by the threat of insurrection backed by a crusade against England.[2] It seems strange that Pole could have thought it so easy to frighten a Tudor, or could have imagined that the insensate pride, backed by a morbid conscience, that ruled Henry's character, would submit to private contumely or bow to public disgrace without a furious struggle, but it is quite plain that he did cherish this hope, and sent his book to Henry in manuscript with this idea.[3] There was of course danger that the book might be used in pro-

[1] *Ibid.*, I, 427, 429, 438.

[2] *Ibid.*, I, 475; V, 155; also James Gairdner, *Letters and Papers, Foreign and Domestic, of the Reign of Henry VIII*, XII, part I, No. 429; part II, Nos. 107, 552.

[3] *Poli Epistolæ*, V, 61.

ducing the sort of civil war appealing to foreign aid which afterward desolated France and Germany. And Henry's effort to destroy the manuscript, strengthened Pole's resolve to keep it hanging over his head like a sword of Damocles. But in the year 1539, during his absence from Rome, it was printed, without his consent, by friends to whom he had confided it, and "not without the command of the pope."[1]

His writings show that at several different times in his life he contemplated publishing it. He wrote three prefaces, all printed for the first time two hundred years after his death. The first one is entitled by the editor *Apologia Reginaldi Poli ad Carolum V Cæsarem super quatuor Libris a se scriptis de Unitate Ecclesiæ.*[2] The second preface is entitled *Proemium alterum ejusdem libri a Reginaldo Polo transmissi ad Regem Scotiæ.* Internal evidence shows that it was written not long after the fall of Cromwell, who was arrested June 10, 1540. The third, which breaks off abruptly, is entitled *Espistola ad Edwardum VI. Angliæ Regem de opere adversus Henricum patrem,* etc. This must have been written 1547-1553. In it Pole says he had heard that the Protestants intended to publish his treatise in defense of the unity of the Church, and thought it better to do so himself. Shelhorn conjectures that he abandoned this intention on account of the death of Edward VI and the accession of Mary.

[1] *Epistola ad Edwardum VI,* Section xlviii, *ibid.,* IV.

[2] There are only four editions of the *Pro Ecclesiasticæ Unitatis Defensione:* (1) Rome, without date. (2) Strassburg, 1555. (3) Ingolstadt, 1587. (4) Bibliotheca Maxima Pontificia, Tome 18, 1698. Bibliographical manuals and catalogues assign the first to 1536 (*British Museum Catalogue,* 1535?; Brunel, *circa* 1536; Grässe, *vers* 1536; etc.). This assignment overlooks Pole's own account in the *Epistola ad Edwardum VI,* cited above, which fixes the date as 1539. This date also agrees with the preface of the Strassburg edition, which says (1555), "This book has been published as I suppose about fifteen years." Schelhorn pointed out in 1737 in his *Amoenitates Historiæ Ecclesiasticæ et Literariæ,* Leipzig and Frankfort, 2 vols., 1737-1738, I, some of the reasons for assuming this date.

In this third preface, Pole says that he had been very unwilling to have the book circulated, but some copies had been taken without his knowledge from the places where they were stored, and had come into the hands of many. The rarity of the first edition suggests the diligence of the author in preventing general circulation. The second edition was issued in 1555 by the Protestant apologist Vergerio, who said that Pole had concealed his book and given copies only to cardinals, popes, kings, bishops, princes. Pole's anxiety to prevent the general circulation of the book, appears in his answer to the letter of Damianus a Goes (October 12, 1540),[1] who had heard of a printed copy and asked for one. Pole replies, "Up to this time I have published nothing, and how my writings have come into those hands where you say they have come, I do not know. When I do publish, I will satisfy your desire." Now the *Apologia* shows, that, at the end of 1538, or the beginning of 1539, Pole did intend to publish this book and send it to the Emperor.[2] And in the *Proemium ad Regem Scotiæ,* he says, just about the time he refused to send Damianus a Goes a copy, that he intends to send one to the King of Scotland, and publish it under his auspices.[3] But, as copies of these prefaces do not seem to have been found in Spain or Scotland,[4] it is to be assumed that Pole changed his mind.

He changed his mind so completely, that in the last of these three prefaces, the letter to Edward VI, he asserted, that though he had tried to force himself to yield to the arguments of his friends, he had never been willing to publish his book. The reasons for this mental struggle, which we perceive when we thus compare the contemporary

[1] *Poli Epistolæ,* III, 37.

[2] *Apologia,* Section vi, "omnia tunc scripta quæ nunc edo," *ibid.,* I.

[3] *Ibid.,* I, 175, "In lucem exire volo."

[4] The *Apologia* was printed by Quirini from a manuscript found in Germany; *Præfatio ad Monumenta Præliminaria, ibid.,* I.

record of his feelings made by his own hand with his subsequent memories, are not far to seek. Any one who will read all Pole's writings and set them against the background of the age he lived in, can scarcely fail to see them.

The correspondence of Pole was printed in the middle of the eighteenth century, long after the close of the epoch of wars about religion. At that time a cardinal who fomented insurrection against a legitimate prince, or demanded war to drive him from his throne for religious causes, would have been regarded with disfavor by most orthodox churchmen and, under many popes, would have been reproved in Rome itself. The editor therefore shows in his notes a strong desire to clear Pole from the imputation of having been a rebel, even in the sense of those enemies of the Church who had condemned him for treason. The attempt is a vain one, as is admitted by Pole's best biographer, Father Zimmerman,[1] who points out that Pole believed the English people had the right to depose a king but not a bishop or a pope. But this anxiety of his editor, writing in a later age when all rebellion was apt to be regarded as sin, marks only the ultimate triumph of a sentiment which, even in Pole's day, exercised a strong influence on human action—the sentiment of patriotism, leading men to support, against every interference from men speaking other tongues, the action of the national government whose language they spoke. That sentiment, though not yet entirely prevalent anywhere, was stronger in England in the middle of the sixteenth century than in any other part of the European world, with the possible exception of Spain. Pole himself had formed his opinions and made his chief friendships among Italians, where the patriotic sentiment

[1] Athanasius Zimmerman, S. J., *Kardinal Pole, sein Leben und seine Schriften*, Regensburg, 1893.

was so extremely weak, that the destinies of Italy were swayed, down to our own generation, by foreign force. But there are plain indications that he had conquered it in his own mind only with pain, and we may well believe his assertion that he wrote, with bitter tears,[1] the book that made him an exile and a public enemy to England, in obedience to a conscience which bade him stand by the highest authority, established by God at Rome. But perhaps the struggle in his own mind, suggested to him the strength of the sentiment he was opposing. Therefore, while he hoped at times for insurrection backed by the sword of France, or of Spain, or of both,[2] he shrank from appearing before the world as a denouncer of war. That would be to draw down upon himself and the Church a renewal of the old reproach, most sharply expressed in Zwingli's epigram, that cardinals were appropriately clothed in red; their robes were stained with the blood they had caused to be shed. In saying this there is no intention of charging Pole with any extraordinary craftiness unexampled among his contemporaries. Pole, devoted to the institution he loved more than anything else in the world, was not superior to the temptation to which many men on either side of that great controversy whose issue was a war for life and death, yielded, the temptation to be—sometimes without being quite conscious of it—less than frank, if the cause might be helped by guile. Martin Luther, in the case of the bigamous marriage of the landgrave of Hesse, was willing to consent secretly to what he would not publicly approve, and Pole gave and shared secret counsels expressing hopes and intentions which he would not avow. This conclusion is derived from many instances in Pole's writings, even

[1] *Epistola ad Edwardum VI,* Section xl, *Poli Epistolæ,* IV.

[2] This is contrary to the opinion of several authoritative writers, but the references given below prove it beyond doubt.

stronger in the sum than in any instance. It comes perhaps to its most acute point in these particular passages.

On February 16, 1537, he wrote to the royal Council of England:[1] "You say the Pope is the King's enemy, to which I reply thus: I dare to affirm of this Pope, whose acts I see, whose talk I often hear, that I have never heard of a single act or word of his, either concerning the King or concerning those who are in his kingdom, which did not show the affection of a father, and that indeed the most indulgent father toward his son, or the affection of a most loving pastor toward his flock." This solemn asseveration was written on the eve[2] of Pole's departure on a Papal mission whose object, as the Pope told the Spanish ambassador, who repeated it to his master, was to aid the northern insurrection in England.[3] Pole must of course have known of this object to carry it out. That he did know of it, is shown positively by his letters to the Pope on starting from Rome and on returning.[4]

Now the motives that caused Pole to deny plans for promoting insurrection of which he was an instrument, would also be active in leading him, after hesitation, to suppress his book. For that book, as has already been said, he wrote three prefaces. The first, entitled the *Apologia*, contains the famous picture of Thomas Cromwell. In style and form it is not a preface, but an oration about two and a half times as long as this essay, arranged with art and most rhetorically written. Section viii shows that it was begun after the launching of the papal bull which commanded all faithful Christians to deprive Henry of his

[1] *Poli Epistolæ,* I, 185. Everything included in Pole's *Epistles* is either Latin or Italian. The passages are Englished by the writer.

[2] Although unwell, he was at Bologna on February 28, 1537.

[3] *Letters and Papers of Henry VIII,* XII, Part I, No. 123, confirmed by *Ibid.,* Nos. 463, 625, 1141.

[4] *Poli Epistolæ,* II, cclxxiv, 46.

crown, and either just before, or during, Pole's journey to Spain on a mission to Charles V, begun December 27, 1538. A passage about the middle of the *Apologia* shows, however, that it could not have been finished at that time; for the writer speaks of having seen, "per hos dies," the book which set forth the reasons the English Council gave for the attainder or execution of three members of Pole's family.[1]

That book was not ready for distribution on January 9, 1539,[2] and what must have been one of the first copies distributed, was sent to France by the French ambassador on January 16.[2] Pole could not therefore have seen the book before he passed through south France. (He was at Avingnon January 22.) It is not probable that he saw it then, for that supposition implies that he was writing during the rapid journey[3] to Toledo, which he reached on February 13. It is most probable, that after returning from Toledo, some time between the end of March and the end of September, 1539, he took up and finished the *Apologia*, which he certainly began when he was looking forward to seeing the Emperor as the representative of the Pope. It was written under great disappointment, for Pole had hoped that Henry would be forced back to the Church by the insurrection of the North and the invasion, which, as he had served notice in the manuscript of the *Pro Unitatis Defensione*, he would invoke, if the King did not yield to his prophetic denunciations of sin and exhortations to repentance.

He had now come to believe that his hopes of frighten-

[1] *An invective agenste the great and detestible vice of treason wherein the secret practices and traitorous workings of them that suffered of late are disclosed*, London, 1539.

[2] *Letters and Papers of Henry VIII*, XIV, Part I, Nos. 37, 72.

[3] *Ibid.*, No. 126.

ing and persuading Henry to repent and return to the Church, had been blocked first by the devil, and second, by an emissary of the devil, Thomas Cromwell. He might well have hated and attacked Cromwell bitterly on personal grounds, for Cromwell had been the chief agent in executing his brother, Lord Montague, and condemning his mother, the countess of Salisbury, for treason. But it is not to be assumed that the *Apologia* was written out of personal revenge. Its motive is a burning zeal to speak, as the exponent of God's justice, in denouncing the enemies of humanity and religion.[1] For Pole now saw plainly, what was the undoubted fact, that this man was the chief influence in frustrating the sacred hopes with which he had sailed on his mission (1537) to aid the English rebellion in defense of the Catholic Church, and on his other mission to induce the Emperor to force Henry back to obedience to the Vicar of Christ, which had just proved a failure. Pole, therefore, joins Cromwell to Henry as the object of invective in the name of God and the Church.

Let us now consider the historic value of this document, as a chief source for gaining a true impression of the work and character of Thomas Cromwell. In the first place, it must be noted that Cromwell was a man whose character and motives Pole could have appreciated, even under circumstances the most favorable to fair judgment, only imperfectly. Two more antipathetic personages could hardly be imagined. Pole was a man of the highest aristocratic lineage. Cromwell, as Pole is careful to point out, had risen from the common people. Cromwell's intelligence was a product of the Renascence training. Pole, though a correspondent of Erasmus and a friend of Bembo, was al-

[1] That the *Apologia* was not written merely as a private letter to the emperor is shown by its whole tone and by the end of Section viii: "Necessarium si cupimus multitudini prodesse hoc prius ostendere."

ways too much of a theologian of the old type to be really a man of the New Learning.[1] Cromwell expelled scholasticism from Oxford and made provision for the effective teaching of Greek.[2] When Pole became the first subject in England, he deplored the cessation of scholastic learning and changed the lectureship in Hebrew to one on the Master of the Sentences.[3] Pole was a believer in the old ideal liberties of a semi-feudal commonwealth defended by the two privileged classes of nobles and clergy.[4] Cromwell was a man of an era to come, who had been a chief instrument in the policy of ruthlessly smashing the remanent power of feudalism, breaking the political influence of the lay lords, destroying that of the ecclesiastical hierarchy, and making England a nation centered around an absolute throne resting on the consent of the middle classes.[5]

Pole belonged to an era that was past. Cromwell was destroying that ancient divine institution for which Pole had sacrificed everything in the world. To look for a judicious estimate of the character and aims of Abraham Lincoln in a letter of Jefferson Davis, written, in the midst of the Civil War, to gain the recognition of the Confederacy from some foreign government, would be far wiser than to approach without caution the *Apologia* which Pole addressed to Charles V. The expectation of finding in it a fair and final judgment on Thomas Cromwell is unreasonable.

[1] See his correspondence with Sadolet.

[2] *Letters and Papers of Henry VIII,* IX, Nos. 312, 350.

[3] *Poli Epistolæ,* V. 47, 84.

[4] Thomas Starkey, Dialogue between Pole and Lupset, in *England in the Reign of King Henry VIII,* edited by J. M. Cowper for The Early English Text Society, London, 1871. This is probably in accord with the general drift of Pole's views, and it agrees with the political allusions of his letters.

[5] The Tudors had no standing army. They destroyed the power of the nobility and clergy. By repeated legislation Henry VIII tried to make the people keep and practise arms. If his throne was not in the last analysis supported by the loyalty of the middle classes, what kept it from falling under the repeated attacks made upon it?

And this necessary caution is increased when we understand the purpose and feel the tone of the *Apologia*.

Pole's correspondence is not a common book, and the calendar of the *Apologia* to Charles V, printed in the *Letters and Papers of Henry VIII*, is so condensed that it gives no hint of the violent polemic tone of the writing. Nor does the description of Zimmerman enable the reader to form any idea of it. A few extracts from more characteristic[1] passages will suggest how little the historic, and how entirely the polemic, spirit ruled the mind of its author when it poured from his indignant soul against the enemies of God and His Church. The molder of the German tongue could never have forced his diction, virile to coarseness, into the artificial rhetoric of Pole's sixteenth-century Ciceronian, but not Martin Luther himself could write a polemic, which in effect, was more violent that the *Apologia*. The object of the treatise is to show that Henry is Antichrist, confirmed in his subjection to Satan by Cromwell, Satan's emissary, and its rhetorical climax is an appeal to the faithful for a holy war to free the world of his tyranny and impiety. Did Moses, Pole asks, have a juster reason for calling upon the Israelites to wipe out the crime of the worshipers of the golden calf even in the blood of brethren and friends, than the Vicar of Christ has to call to all the pious, in view of the worse crimes of Henry, Who is on the Lord's side let him gird his sword on his thigh? If it was said to the tribe of Levi, Blessed are ye of the Lord, ye who have consecrated your hands in the blood of your relatives, how much greater blessing will they deserve, who, at the call of the Vicar of

[1] The *Apologia* contains passages expressing the great sorrow it gives Pole to be compelled to denounce Henry. Such expressions are usual in the most comminatory writings of popes, cardinals, or bishops. But they are not characteristic of the *Apologia*. It is more denunciatory than that third book of the *Pro Unitatis Defensione,* which Pole himself said was written "acerbe et vehementer," "aspere." Regretful expressions are not applied to Cromwell at all.

God, consecrate their hands in the blood of those who have inflicted such slaughter joined with ignominy on the people of God? "Can it be, the chiefs of the tribes of the people of God, to whom I, one of those Levites, am sent to hold up that glorious and most pious example of the tribe of Levi," will fail to listen to me?

Henry is the vicar of the devil. Henry is worse than Nero, crueler than the Turk. "Unless Christian princes and peoples unite against him, God will give them no victory over the Turk." Strengthened by God's justice to the office of a prophet, Pole announces that, if they neglect this worst enemy of God, "He will not only not roll back the Turkish charge, but will make it prevail in the day of battle."

Henry has expressed the very form of the rule of Antichrist foretold in Scripture, as it has never been expressed before. Pole would gladly give his body to be burned to save him, but the king is so lost that his conversion would be a miracle never before heard of, "that one not four days dead, but long dead, should be restored to life, and, from that hell into which he descended, brought back living to the upper regions." An emissary of Satan had confirmed Henry in evil, and led him to set himself up in the place of God. His real name was that of the demon by whose impulse he worked. But if we begin with that human name he received from his family, before "he fell into the hands of devils and degenerated into their nature," we find it to be Cromwell. A man of no lineage, whose father, they say, earned his living in a little village by fulling cloth, he was like the man in the tombs possessed by a legion of devils—nay worse; "For if a legion of devils drove a herd of swine into the sea, how many legions, or rather how many armies of devils, must be in this Cromwell who has thrust such vast numbers of men down to hell?" No heretic, no schismatic has ever been so bad as Cromwell. They had cast crowds of men into the sea of death. But Cromwell had gone farther and destroyed the very foundation of righteousness, committing the sin for which Lucifer was cast into the abyss, the assertion that the norm of right and wrong is man's own will. Pole says that he is not talking mystically but in a common-sense way. He can prove what the commands of Satan brought by Cromwell to the King, were.

The greater part of his proof is as follows: He had had only one conversation with Cromwell,[1] and that was ten years before, soon after his own return from Italy (1528), when Cromwell was a "sycophant" of Wolsey's. Cromwell was trying, as the Duke of Norfolk tried, to persuade Pole (see Pole's letter to Edward VI) not to oppose the King. The keen man of the world doubtless told the young student of the cloisters things about kings' courts and the sort of arguments to use at them, which were true enough. And Pole did not know them, or else he would not have thought it possible to frighten Henry by the *Pro Unitatis Defensione* or raise a crusade against him by the *Apologia*. More, in the *Utopia,* made to Raphael some excellent remarks about not being a philosopher in the councils of princes, which might easily have been distorted by an enemy who repeated them after the lapse of ten years. And we may well believe that there was more cynical worldly wisdom than piety in Cromwell's talk, without turning his advice into that systematic attack upon the very foundations of morality which Pole says it was, as his judgment of Cromwell's devilish

[1] Pole says (*Apologia,* 132), "hoc fateor, me publice autem illum loquentum nunquam audivisse, privatim autem semel et iterum, nunquam amplius." This, as it stands, means twice. But a few lines farther down on the same page Pole contradicts it by saying "facile ex illo uno congressu et colloquio perspiciebam"; and in the next line, "Talem enim futuram ille uno sermone docuit." The only explanation I can suggest is to drop the editor's comma after *iterum* and take the phrase *iterum nunquam amplius* as loose Latin for "never again." The *Apologia* needs the file in many places, as its editor Quirini remarks.

work molded, across the lapse of years, his memories of a single talk. And we may easily believe that, in rejecting the temptation to justify the cruel injustice of Henry's divorce, Pole chose the better part, without seeing Cromwell as the diabolic personage Pole makes him appear in this trumpet-call to sacred war against him.

Pole says, that at the end of the conversation, Cromwell offered to lend him a book on statecraft if he would read it. It is expressly stated that Cromwell did not mention its name or send it. But Pole "took no less care to get it, by inquiring from those who knew the bent of his studies, than men take to intercept the despatches of a hostile general to know his plans." After these inquiries, Pole concluded that the book Cromwell had offered to lend him was the Prince of Machiavelli; and, as soon as he began to read it, he perceived that "though a man's name was on the title-page, the book was written by the finger of Satan even as the Holy Scriptures are said to be written by the finger of God." And this fact, that Cromwell once offered to lend him a book that had just appeared, and that he "afterward" found out that Cromwell read and approved Machiavelli's *Prince*, is Pole's proof that Cromwell, possessed of an army of devils, is an emissary of Satan to the King. Then he proceeds to tell also how Cromwell accomplished his mission from Satan.

Pole heard it from one who was present, that, on a certain occasion, the King, with a great sigh, said that, if he had known how difficult the divorce was, he would never have begun it. From this mood of hesitancy he was brought by Cromwell; and Pole gives a long speech of over 1,500 words made by Cromwell to the king. Pole says that he does not know that he has the order of this speech correct, for he was not present; but he can affirm that there is in it nothing which he has not heard, either from the speaker himself or from those who were the sharers of his counsel. Now when we remember that ten years had elapsed since the speech which Pole did not hear was supposed to be delivered, when we notice that he never referred to either conversation or speech in his writings during the interval, and perceive the unmistakable traces of Pole's reading of Machiavelli all through his version of Cromwell's supposed speech to the King, the conclusion seems inevitable, that it was largely constructed under the predominant influence of Pole's conviction that the diabolic activity of Henry's government, could best be accounted for by the belief that its chief councilor was the first man to introduce into English statecraft the principles of that Satan's Bible, *Il Principe.*

The reasons which Pole alleges for seeking some direct diabolic influence to account for Henry's conduct, should first be noticed. Pole was in no mood to recall the evils connected with the veneration of relics and pilgrimages, animadverted upon for more than a generation past by both schismatics and those who stood by the orthodox church. And to him, the wickedest things ever done by any tyrant in the history of the world, were the destruction of the shrine of Saint Thomas à Becket and the dishonoring of his bones, and the destruction of the tomb of Saint Augustine.[1] To one who shares this opinion, it may perhaps appear that the government of England under Cromwell's influence, was so uniquely and diabolically wicked that we must assume for it some peculiar relation to principles explicitly denying all the foundations of right and wrong. To one who does not share this view of the *unexampled* atrocity of the destruction of a saint's shrines and the brutal treatment of relics, the assumption that the government of England between

[1] These were deeds "quæ nullus unquam apostata tentavit unquam nullus hereticus est conatus," *ibid.*, 110.

1531 and 1538, so incomparably exceeded, in craft or cruelty or despotism, the reigns of Henry's contemporaries, men like Ferdinand of Spain, Charles V, Pope Clement VII, or Francis I, that it must of necessity have been guided by some uniquely immoral principles, is scarcely worthy of serious discussion.

Moreover, if Cromwell had owned a manuscript of the *Prince* in 1528—and, as we shall see, there is very strong reason for believing that he did not see the *Prince* until ten years later—there would have been nothing especially significant about that fact. The *Prince* was first printed in 1532, at Rome, by the same printer who printed Pole's book, and under the favor and sanction of the Pope,[1] who granted him a ten-years' copyright. It was then considered a perfectly proper book for a pious man to own. By 1554, some dozen editions had appeared, and the book was read by every one who read widely in politics at all. Sir Thomas Smith, a younger contemporary of Cromwell, and one of the fairest statesmen of his times, had it in his library of history and politics, of which a catalogue has survived. The possession of the *Prince,* between 1528 and 1540, would suggest no presumption whatever that its owner was a singularly sinister personage; "it is known that Charles V," for whom Pole wrote the *Apologia,* "carefully studied it, that his son and courtiers perused it."[2]

That Cromwell became, as Pole says, Henry's chief counselor in the process of breaking allegiance to Rome, destroying the political power of the clergy, and suppressing the monasteries, is true enough. In carrying out this plan,

[1] See G. Amico, *La Vita di N. Machiavelli,* Florence, 1875, 415.

[2] Pasquale Villari, *Niccolò Machiavelli,* Milan, 1895-1897, Volume II, Libro Secondo, Cap. v, 421, chapter on the critics of the *Prince.*

L. Alberti Ferrai makes a similar assertion in his essay on Francesco I e Carlo V in La Vita Italiana nel Ciuquecento. Milano, seconda edizione, 1897, page 7.

he used the ruthless and crafty methods common to the politics of the century; the condition of his power was willingness to serve the caprices of a despot whose morbid conscience gave to his evil deeds a singular stamp, which has thrown them into high relief among the many tyrannical acts of the age. But that Cromwell owed his policy or methods to the teachings of Machiavelli, is in itself highly improbable. Machiavelli did not create, he only interpreted the political methods of his age. Pole's direct proof that Cromwell was an emissary of the devil, is, to any one who knows that generation of the sixteenth century, entirely valueless. And it must be remembered that he himself, presumably with the advice of his friends, never gave the *Apologia* to the emperor, for whom he wrote it, nor to the world.

In addition to these considerations, there are the following detailed reasons to show that Pole's account of Cromwell as the messenger of Satan, drawing his policy from Satan's Bible, is untrustworthy: First we should observe that Pole, like most men, was capable of making mistakes in representing long afterward what he had felt at a certain time, and, in regard to small things, in relating what he had done. For example, the letter to Edward VI (1547-1553), denying the charge that he had undertaken his mission in 1539 to induce kings to take arms against Henry, asserts that he merely intended to persuade the Emperor and the French King to use the reasoning of love and friendship with Henry. He never wished that they should attack him by force of arms. He says he will not deny that he advised, in case love and kindness failed, that threats should be added, and that as a last extreme remedy they should declare a commercial blockade.[1] Now this does not necessarily

[1] *Epistola ad Edwardum VI,* xlv, *Poli Epistolæ,* IV.

involve any conscious misrepresentation of facts. But we may confidently affirm that it is, in effect, an entire misstatement. Pole was directed by the Pope to carry the bull of excommunication to Charles and ask his aid in its execution, so far at least as by recalling his ambassadors and forbidding all trade with England.[1] This of course was only an indirect way of using force, because we know from Pole's secretary that it was hoped by cutting England from all communication with Christendom, to cause such misery that the people would rise in rebellion against Henry.[2] But this consideration by no means measures the error of Pole's recollection. Section viii of the *Apologia* shows that the account Pole gave after 1547 of his motives and feelings in 1539, is explicitly contrary to fact. That section, written when he was about to undertake his mission, but not published until two hundred years afterward, plainly states that the motive of his mission, is to persuade the Emperor to postpone the Turkish war and turn his arms against England. Moreover we know that this is what Pole tried to persuade the Emperor to do; for the following despatch of Mocenigo, the Venetian ambassador, records the account the Emperor gave, soon after Pole left him, of his interview with Pole:—[3]

"On the one hand it seems that the Cardinal wishes me to forbid trade with this King of England as a sort of warning, on the other hand he appears to want me to make war on him: my answer is that I know full well what war means —that it is easy to begin and not so easy to end: * * * if His Holiness is counselling such enterprises, it is because

[1] Pope Paul III to Charles V, January 7, 1540, *Calendar of State Papers, Spanish*, VI, Part I, 97.

[2] Beccatelli's *Life of Pole*, 17, in *Poli Epistolæ*, I. Beccatelli was Pole's secretary and intimate companion.

[3] Quoted and summarized in *The Emperor Charles V*, by Edward Armstrong, M. A. (Macmillan, 1902), II. 21.

he is far distant from the said King; were he as near him as I am, his advice might be different."

Charles reminded Pole that at Nice the Pope had impressed upon him that the crusade was so important that all other enterprises must be postponed for this; he could not imagine why His Holiness had changed his mind. Pole urged that the English evil was intrinsic, the Turkish extrinsic,[1] and demanded that the intrinsic danger should receive the first attention. "But," replied the emperor, "if the Turk came to Italy and right up to Ancona, as come he undoubtedly would, would His Holiness regard that as an extrinsic evil?" Thus the Emperor's account of what Pole said on his mission, agrees entirely with Pole's own record in the *Apologia* of his feelings just before and after that mission, and shows that Pole's account of that mission written years afterward to Edward VI, was so incomplete as to be entirely misleading.

It may also be shown in the same connection, that Pole is capable, as most men are, not only of making mistakes as to the main meaning of what he felt and said in time past, but also capable of making mistakes in telling what he did long ago. He writes, in the *Epistola ad Edwardum VI,* that when his friends printed his *Pro Ecclesiasticæ Unitatis Defensione* without his consent, during his absence from Rome in 1539, they arranged it in several books, "which I never had done."[2] But in the first part of the *Apologia,* composed on the eve of that absence, as the eighth section shows beyond question, he writes, "I have divided the work into four books," and he then describes them one by one.

[1] The fatuousness of this argument, exposed by the humorous reply of the Emperor, is one of several indications that might be adduced to show how much Pole needed Cromwell's advice not to indulge in scholastic discussion at princes' councils.

[2] *Epistola ad Edwardum VI,* Section xlviii, *Poli Epistolæ,* IV.

Now, if Pole's memories about his feelings and acts were thus obscured and confused[1] in the interval between the writing of the *Apologia* (1539) and the *Epistola* (reign of Edward VI, 1547-1553), it is evident that his memories about his feelings and acts as regards Cromwell, might become confused in the interval between 1528 and 1539. That they did so become confused, is plainly shown by what he wrote in this interval. It is impossible to compare carefully the *Apologia* with the *Pro Unitatis Defensione* and Pole's letters between 1532 and 1539, without a suspicion, rising almost to certainty, that, in this elaborate rhetorical invective against Cromwell, he is telescoping, in a very misleading way, events long separated. In order to prove that Cromwell is a devil ("degeneravit in naturam dæmonum"), Pole tells the Emperor that long ago he had a talk with Cromwell about the duty of a prudent counselor with his prince. At the end of it Cromwell offered to lend him a book on the subject written by a certain acute modern of experience. The subject of the conversation and the offer to lend him the book, are facts that would be apt to remain in a man's mind. There is not the smallest reason to accuse Pole of inventing them.

There are, however, very strong reasons for doubting that the unnamed book which Cromwell offered to lend Pole, was Machiavelli's *Prince*. But does not Pole say that Cromwell offered to lend him Machiavelli's *Prince*? He says nothing of the kind. Cromwell offered to lend him a book which he did not name or send. But "afterward" Pole

[1] The suggestion which Pole's editor, Quirini, seems to imply (*Monumenta Præliminaria, ibid.*, I, lxxxvii) does not stand examination. If it did, it would free Pole from this mistake in memory only by involving him in another. Even taking Quirini's improbable suggestion, Pole's own writings show that he was mistaken either in the statement that he had never divided his treatise into four books or in the statement that he could never write a preface for the published work.

found out from Cromwell's friends that Cromwell admired Machiavelli's *Prince*, and he concluded that it was the book Cromwell had so much praised. How long "afterward"? There are the very strongest reasons for believing that it was not before 1537, conjectural reasons for believing that it was during 1538; or some ten years after the conversation took place.

Before examining these reasons, let us notice the very good ground for believing that the unnamed book which Cromwell offered to lend Pole in 1528 or 1529, was not the *Prince* of Machiavelli at all, but the *Courier* of Castiglione. (1) The *Prince* was not printed in 1529; the first edition was of May, 1532. This does not, as some writers have thought, render it impossible[1] for Cromwell to have had it, but it makes it improbable. Manuscripts of the *Prince* existed, but they were not very plentiful. (2) There is strong positive reason (to be afterward given) to believe that Cromwell did not see the *Prince* until long afterward, when a friend sent him a copy. (3) The *Courtier*, on the other hand, was printed in April, 1528, and was most widely read. In ten years it was published in seventeen editions and translated into Spanish and French. (4) We know that Cromwell had a copy, from the following letter written to him, in the summer of 1530, by Edward Bonner, afterward bishop of London:

Right worshipfull, in my veray hartiest maner I commende me to you. And wher ye willing to make me a good Ytalion promised unto me, longe agon, the Triumphes of Petrarche in the Ytalion tonge. I hartely pray you at this tyme by his beyrer, Mr. Augustine his seruant, to sende me the said Boke with some other at your deuotion; and

[1] It appears from the correspondence of Pietro Aretino that MSS. circulated in Italy in 1530 and copyists were still employed.

especially, if it please you, the boke called Cortigiano in Ytalion, etc.[1]

(5) The *Prince* has nothing whatever to say about the subject on which Cromwell was talking to Pole—the attitude of a prudent counselor toward his prince. Pole's recollections of this long-past conversation are not to be assumed as reliable in detail. He would not write it down, for in 1528 Cromwell was a man of no importance. But he would probably remember the subject and the general drift of the talk. This is his recollection:—

Pole said in opening, "In my judgment this belongs to the duty of a counselor, not to dissent from those honest and useful things which natural law and the writings of pious and learned men teach." Cromwell replied that scholastic discussion differs from a king's council; that much depends on when, where, to whom, and by whom a thing is said; and that it is the part of a prudent and experienced man to know this. In this matter the learned, who lack experience, often make mistakes, and, because of their abruptness, cause the hatred of princes, because they do not know how to accommodate themselves and their remarks to place, time, and person. Hence, those who come fresh from schools to princely councils, for lack of experience, often run on this rock; which he confirmed with some examples of those who, because they held too firmly to scholastic opinions, were hated by princes, and were, not only useless, but actually pernicious, as counselors. Hence he summed up his opinion about the duty of a prudent counselor that the first part of it is to study the will of his prince.[2]

(6) The *Courtier* is written about the character of princes' friends and the relation of counselors to their

[1] Sir Henry Ellis, *Original Letters,* Third Series, London, 1846, II, 178.
[2] *Poli Epistolæ,* I, 133.

sovereigns. It is all about the duty of a prudent counselor. And the following passages are curiously apposite to the advice which Pole says Cromwell gave him:—

Nor do I think that Aristotle and Plato would have scorned the name of perfect Courtier, for we clearly see that they performed the works of Courtiership, and wrought to this end,—the one with Alexander the Great, the other with the kings of Sicily. And since the office of a good Courtier is to know the prince's character and inclinations, and thus to enter tactfully into his favour according to need and opportunity, as we have said, by those ways that afford safe access, and then to lead him towards virtue,—Aristotle so well knew the character of Alexander, and tactfully fostered it so well, that he was loved and honoured more than a father by Alexander. * * * And of these achievements of Alexander the author was Aristotle, using the means of a good Courtier: which Callisthenes knew not how to do, although Aristotle showed him; for in his wish to be a pure philosopher and austere minister of naked truth, without mingling Courtiership therewith, he lost his life and brought not help but rather infamy to Alexander.[1]

This very close parallel strongly suggests that the unnamed book was the *Courtier* and not the *Prince*.

But, whether this book that Cromwell offered to lend was the *Courtier* or not, there is the strongest reason for believing that Pole did not think it was the *Prince* till a long time "afterward." He describes how he "sought out this book as carefully as one seeks out the despatches of an enemy to know his plans." He certainly did not do this immediately, for in 1528 (or 1529), when this talk took place, Cromwell was of no importance whatever in the English state. Pole himself describes him as a man of no family, a mere hanger-on of Wolsey. Nor did he rise at all, until, in the beginning of 1531, he became a member of

[1] Quoted after L. E. Opdycke's translation, New York, 1903, 284-285.

the royal Council. It is hard to understand why, previous to that time, Pole could possibly have been inclined to seek out, "as the despatches of an enemy's general," the book Cromwell had offered to lend. That he did so in 1531 is very improbable for the following reasons. Pole gives, as a proof of his accuracy in reporting this talk with Cromwell, that as soon as he saw Cromwell growing in authority with the King, he left England, fearing what would happen "when he held the helm of state." In regard to this one point of leaving England, there is very strong reason to believe Pole mistaken in his memories of his motives seven years before he wrote. He left England in January, 1532, and he had been trying to obtain permission to leave for some time.[1] In 1531, when he must have begun to ask license to go to Paris, it would have been very difficult for any one to foresee Cromwell's future great weight in the English councils of state. He was not important enough to be even mentioned in the despatches of the imperial ambassador until April 16, 1533, when he is spoken of briefly as "Cromwell, who is powerful with the King."[2] Norfolk and the other kindred of Anne Boleyn were in power at the time Pole left England. We have another account of the reason for Pole's leaving England besides that given here. It does not make any mention of Cromwell. Beccatelli, Pole's intimate friend, who wrote his life, says that he left England because of the fury of the King in an interview he had with him, when the King was so enraged at Pole that he gripped the hilt of his dagger as if to use it, "as Pole himself told me." "Moved by this offense of the King, Pole felt he ought to make every effort to leave England."[3]

[1] Despatch of imperial ambassador Chapuys to Charles V, *Letters and Papers of Henry VIII,* V, No. 737; *Epistola ad Edwardum VI,* Section xi, *Poli Epistolæ,* IV.

[2] *Letters and Papers of Henry VIII,* VI, No. 351.

[3] *Vita,* vi and vii, *Poli Epistolæ,* I.

This lacuna between 1528 and 1533 is filled up by Pole with the account of the long oration of Cromwell to the king alluded to on page 394. The implication that this hypothetical oration made Cromwell at a stroke chief councilor of the king, has been accepted without examination. But when tested by facts, by the *State Papers,* and by Pole's own writings, it appears very highly improbable. Pole was out of England from October, 1529, to July, 1530. On his return he lived in retirement. How did Pole find out that Cromwell was the real power behind the throne, when the Spanish ambassador, whose business it was to report the intrigues of the court, and who was in constant communication with the Queen and her friends, had no suspicion that Cromwell was of any determining importance until 1533? The straightforward account of Cromwell's rise to power given by Cavendish[1] agrees with all the facts and presents no mysteries. Cavendish, Wolsey's gentleman usher, saw Cromwell constantly, and talked with him just before he rode up to court to see the King on Wolsey's tangled affairs, and, as he said in his favorite phrase, "to make or mar." Cavendish did not approve of Cromwell's policy, and therefore could have had no prejudice in his favor. Moreover, as the account of Cromwell's rise comes as a side issue into Cavendish's account of Wolsey's life, there was no motive, conscious or unconscious, for distortion. Pole had spoken to Cromwell but once in his life. His account is in a highly rhetorical polemic. The hypothetical conversation of Cromwell with the King, is necessary to his argument that Henry is Antichrist inspired by the devil. Tried by every possible test for determining the value of historic evidence, the account of Cromwell's entry into the royal Council given by

[1] George Cavendish, *Life of Cardinal Wolsey,* first printed in London, 1641.

Cavendish, is far more trustworthy than the account of Pole. Cavendish says that Cromwell, in settling Wolsey's affairs, saw the King several times, and impressed him by "witty demeanour" and capacity for business. The King took him into his service and made him a royal councilor. The *State Papers* show that his influence in the Council was at first very small. He rose by capacity. In the summer of 1532 he was overwhelmed with business. In the fall he was the only commoner appointed to go with the King to France. In 1533 his power with the King was apparent to the Spanish ambassador.

Not only are there these reasons for doubting the accuracy of Pole's memory that he left England because of Cromwell's rise to power, but Pole's letters show unmistakably, that, nearly five years after he left England, he did not regard Cromwell as possessed by the devil. Therefore he had not yet "searched out" the book that Cromwell offered to loan him and found it to be the *Prince,* for he says, "I had hardly begun to read it, before I saw it was written by the hand of Satan." Four years after leaving England, Pole wrote to Cromwell as follows:—

"In my heartiest manner I commend me unto you." He says he is glad to hear through his brother of Cromwell's friendly words in assuring him of the continuance of the King's gracious favor, which "I cannot but accept for a great singular pleasure and acknowledge the same for such a benefit as few of my friends could a given beside." He desires Cromwell to do him "a yet greater pleasure": "That it may please you to ascertain His Highness of my serviceable and prompt mind to do him service at all times, wherein I can say no more but pray Almighty God to send me some good opportunity, who ever have you in his blessed keeping." He signs himself "Your assuredly bound Raynold Pole."[1]

Pole could not have written this letter to a man he thought was governing England by Satan's Bible. More than a year later (February, 1537) Pole still had not searched out this satanic book, for at that time Michael Throgmorton, a gentleman usher of the Cardinal, writes to his friend Richard Morison, "in the house of my Lord Privy Seal," (Cromwell) a long letter,[1] in which he "faithfully assures" Morison that Pole bears Cromwell "hearty affection, which, after long communication, by entire and hearty fashion of speaking, he manifestly declared, seeing that what chance soever should happen, he might be assuring of him to his power to shew him that friendly heart and pleasure that he, by his kindness and goodness showed toward him, hath deserved, with further words to the same tenor that at this time I will not rehearse. But briefly to conclude, I think, surely my Lord, your master, may assuredly rely of my master's heart to him as of any friend he hath in England"; so that, if the King's Highness will send any one into Flanders, (to confer with Pole) "I think my master would be most best content to speak with him than any other."

This suggestion Pole himself repeats in a letter to Cromwell written three days later. He says: "by writing meseemeth we do not understand one another, so that to reply more in this manner I see no point," suggests that learned persons from the King should meet him in Flanders, "and glad I would, if it might be that you might be one of them, for you pretending (the word had not yet acquired the sinister meaning of falsely putting forward) that affection to the King's honor that I no less (and with the greatest)

[1] *Nine Historical Letters,* etc., privately printed for J. P. C. (John Payne Collier), London, 1871; *Letters and Papers of Henry VIII,* IX, No. 701.

do bear to His Grace, if we spoke together, peradventure some better ways might be taken than can ever be brought to pass by writing; wherein there will never be that end that both would desire."[1] If Pole believed that Cromwell had degenerated into the nature of a devil and was the minister of Satan, preaching the overthrow of all foundations of right and wrong, out of a book written by the finger of Satan himself, in order to confirm Henry in the career of Antichrist, these are extraordinary messages for a cardinal of the Church to send and write to him.

Pole, unaware that Cromwell knew by advices from Rome and the French King, that the object of his mission to Flanders had been to aid the insurrection in England,[2] had steadily denied any rebellious intentions. In his letter to Cromwell of May 2, 1537,[3] he says the King's demand for his surrender as a rebel, was caused by "the sinister and false report of others that, by false conjectures of things they knew not, had ill informed the King of my purpose in coming to these parts." But the rebellion he had hoped to aid was extinguished. He thought himself in danger of assassination. He was in danger of being trapanned and taken to England, as in 1529 Charles V had seized and carried off from the very shadow of the Vatican a priest who had ap-

[1] This letter, printed in full in *Nine Historical Letters,* privately printed for J. P. C. (John Payne Collier), is not calendared. The following letter explains its omission:

PUBLIC RECORD OFFICE, 1st August 1902

Mr. Paul van Dyke
Dear Sir.
The letter from Pole to Cromwell 16 Feb. (1537), to which you refer is in this office but the abstract of it was accidentally omitted from the Calendar for the year 1537. The nine letters are all undoubtedly genuine.
I remain
Yours faithfully
R. H. BRODIE.

[2] See reference, page 387.

[3] *Nine Historical Letters,* etc.; *Letters and Papers of Henry VIII,* XII, Part I, No. 1123.

pealed from his authority to Rome.[1] What he wrote to the Pope was true enough. Ready as he might be to die if it could profit the Church, his death could now only be to her dishonor. Having permission to withdraw, he determined to leave Flanders secretly. Throgmorton wrote a letter[2] on August 20, insinuating that if Pole returned to Rome without obtaining some concession from the King about the papal authority, his book would be printed and the excommunication launched. The threat was repeated September 2 in the suggestion made to the English agent in Flanders,[3] that, if the King wished to stop such things as were likely to be put forth shortly in Rome, he should send at once to Pole.

This attempt to frighten Henry by the threat of publishing papal censures calling on all Christians to drive him from his throne, supported by a book denouncing civil war and appealing for foreign invasion, received as sharp an answer as one with real knowledge of human nature would expect. Two commissioners, one named by Pole himself, were appointed to go to Pole, with the demand that he lay aside his claim to represent the incarnate justice of God sitting in judgment on the sins of the King of England, or abide the issue which that claim made inevitable.[4] The time of threats was past. Cromwell, playing his game to destroy in England the political power of the clergy, who, in Pole's opinion, were able to appeal for support to a college of cardinals mainly composed of Italians, Frenchmen, and Spaniards who believed themselves appointed to speak the divine judgments to all peoples of the earth, forced

[1] *Journal d'un Bourgeois de Paris sous le Règne de François I,* publié par M. L. Lalanne, Société de l'Histoire de France, 1854, 403.

[2] *Letters and Papers of Henry VIII,* XII, Part II, No. 552.

[3] *Ibid.,* No. 635.

[4] *Ibid.,* Nos. 619, 620.

his adversary to show his hand—a hand which Pole thought contained infamy for Henry, serious danger of insurrection at home, and the imminent possibility of foreign invasion. But Pole, without waiting for the arrival of the commission he had asked for, was already on his way to Rome,[1] having started August 22. Throgmorton, as he afterward boasted, had tricked Cromwell;[2] and Cromwell answers this threat of publishing the book and loosing the anathemas of the Church to provoke rebellion and invasion, by a letter defying Pole and the Pope. "You have bleared my eye once," he writes to Throgmorton, "you shall not again." He threatens Pole with the most brutal agencies known to contemporary politics—assassination and proscription of his family.[3] Then Pole began to see in Cromwell what he had never seen before—the agent of Satan for hardening Henry in the career of Antichrist.

The words "had never seen before" are used advisedly. Not only are Pole's letters to Cromwell, up to the beginning of 1537, inconsistent with a belief on his part that Cromwell had become a devil and was the instrument of Satan hardening Henry in crime, but, in 1536, he wrote an altogether different account of the agent of Satan in that persuasion. When he had been asked to reply to the question,

[1] *Letters and Papers of Henry VIII,* Nos. 559, 598, 725.

[2] He had left England to return to Pole, telling Cromwell that if he could not persuade Pole to resign the cardinal's hat and resume allegiance to the King, he would desert Pole's service.

[3] In regard to these two letters from Cromwell, one sending commissioners, the other threats and defiance, Mr. Gairdner seems to have fallen into a slight error, a thing very unusual for that distinguished scholar. He says in the preface to *Letters and Papers of Henry VIII,* Volume XII, Part II, xxxvi, "In short the King . . . had entertained the idea of sending some one to confer with Pole . . . [but] had on second thoughts resolved to cast aside all decency and distinctly threaten," etc. No. 725, a letter from Hutton, shows that Cromwell's letter No. 619, promising to send the commissioners asked for by Pole, had been forwarded to Throgmorton, but that Pole and Throgmorton had already gone to Italy without waiting to receive it, the letter of Throgmorton not being delivered to Hutton

whether the supremacy of the pope had been established by God, a book by Richard Sampson[1] against the papal supremacy had been sent to him that he might consider its arguments. Pole's answer to the question, as already related, took the form of the book *Pro Ecclesiasticæ Unitatis Defensione.* He says,[2] addressing Henry: "God permitted Satan to come to you and persuade you that you would increase your glory by taking the name Supreme Head of the Church." "But how did Satan persuade you to this? Why should we ask how, when we have the book of Sampson, who was the instrument of Satan to persuade you to do it? Is anything hidden which Sampson and the other instruments of Satan said in thy ears, since they have been willing to commit it to writing?" Now if in 1536, when he wrote these words, Pole had been certain that Cromwell had come straight from Satan to Henry—he says in the *Apologia* (1539), "I knew who sent him and I knew the message he brought"—as the special emissary of the devil to persuade Henry to take the title Supreme Head of the Church, and that Cromwell had done it by arguments drawn from the book of Machiavelli, it is psychologically very hard to believe, that, while speaking of those implements of Satan, Sampson and Sampson's book, Pole should not have mentioned either Cromwell or Machiavelli's book. But neither Cromwell nor Machiavelli is mentioned, either here or any-

until twelve days after date (No. 635). It was after receiving this note from Hutton, telling him that Pole and Throgmorton had gone on without waiting and that there was no use in sending commissioners, that Cromwell wrote No. 795. In spite of this threat, there is nothing to show that any attempt was made to assassinate Pole. One instance where Pole was afraid of a certain man, which is cited in the preface of a volume of the *Letters and Papers of Henry VIII* as a proof of the attempt, is shown by documents in the volume to be a mistake. The supposed murderer was at the time trying to get pardon and employment from the King. An attempt was made to trapan Pole, bring him to England, and execute him, but Henry refused Wyatt's offer to have him assassinated.

[1] *Oratio quæ docet hortatur admonet omnes potissimum Anglos regiæ dignitati cum primis ut obediant,* etc., London, 1533.

[2] Ingolstadt edition, Book III, 401.

where else in the *Pro Ecclesiasticæ Unitatis Defensione.*

Having shown that up to February of 1537, Pole did not regard Cromwell as possessed of a legion of devils nor as preaching Satan's Bible, *Il Principe*, the next question would be, When did Pole first read Machiavelli, and so finding out, as he says, the principles of his action, discover Cromwell's devilish nature? For direct evidence on this question, I have searched in vain Pole's correspondence and that of his friends. In his extant writings to 1540, so far as printed, Pole does not mention Machiavelli except in the *Apologia*. This also is a strange thing, if he knew, for years before he wrote the *Apologia*, that Cromwell was responsible for the sins of Henry, that Machiavelli and the devil were responsible for Cromwell's advice. The omission is not however conclusive, for some of Pole's letters may be lost.

But it is a fact that, so far as we know, the only time Pole alluded to Machiavelli's evil influence, before he wrote the *Apologia*, was in March, 1538. This was not long after a trip to Florence (February or March, 1538),[1] where, as he tells us in the *Apologia*, he discussed Machiavelli's doctrines, and not long before he began the *Apologia*. A record of this conversation has been preserved in a curious way. John a Legh, a traveler to many lands, who had spent some years in Italy and had been conversant with Pole, returned to England in 1540. He was arrested and put in the Tower

[1] I have been able to date this visit to Florence by a process too long to be described in a note, but apparently certain in its result. Mr. L. A. Burd, in his admirable edition of *Il Principe* (Oxford, 1891), dates the passage of the *Apologia* that tells of discussing Machiavelli in Florence, 1534 (p. 37). He is doubtless misled by the idea that the *Apologia*, being a preface to the *Pro Unitatis Defensione*, was written when it was published, and he follows Grässe (*vers* 1536) and Brunel (*circa* 1536) for the publication of the *Pro Unitatis Defensione*. Professor Villari in his *Machiavelli* does the same thing. As already shown, page 388, the publication was in 1539. If, as seems probable, the *Apologia* was finished in the spring or summer of 1539, "superiore hyeme" would mean the winter of 1538 (Pole's usage often includes in "winter" the first month of spring and the last of autumn).

for examination. A deposition giving an account of his intercourse with Pole, has survived.[1] He writes that at a dinner given at the time when Pole, as head of the English Hospital at Rome, made a certain Hillyear master and a certain Goldwell custos, Pole talked about the sacrilege of the English King in "pulling Thomas of Canterbury from his shrine." He then asked "what stories I had read in the Italian tongue." I answered that as yet I had no leisure, but, on going home, I would get some and read them. He warned me against reading "the story of Nicolo Matchauello," which had already poisoned England and would poison all Christendom, and said he would do all he could to cause it "to be dystynkyd and put down howt off remberans." This conversation could not have taken place before March, 1538.[2]

Another strange chance has preserved to us a record of the fact that one of Cromwell's intimate friends, Lord Morley, a man who had frequently engaged with him in literary conversation, and more particularly in conversation about Florence (see passages in his letter), sent him, in the beginning of 1539,[3] a volume containing the *Florentine Histories* and the *Prince* of Machiavelli, as something which Cromwell had never seen before. Now if Pole explicitly asserted that Cromwell had Machiavelli before 1539, and

[1] *Letters and Papers of Henry VIII,* XV, No. 721.

[2] This is established by information kindly furnished by the head of the English College at Rome, which is the successor and literary heir of the English Hospital. All documents relating to these appointments were not found, and current statements about them are probably confused, but an index of documents which was found mentions a papal letter of March, 1538, appointing Cardinal Reginald Pole head of the Hospital.

[3] Sir Henry Ellis, who printed this letter in full (*Original Letters,* Third Series, III, 63), dated it 1537. It is dated only February 13. The editors of the *Letters and Papers of Henry VIII* (XIV, Part I, No. 285) have assigned it to 1539, for good reasons, which may be traced in Volume XIV. If it were written in 1537, it would make no great difference to the reasoning of this article.

Lord Morley, early in 1539, sent Cromwell the book as a novelty, the very strong probability would be that Pole was mistaken and Lord Morley right; for Pole had talked with Cromwell only once in his life, and Morley had often talked intimately with him on politics and literature. But the reader must again be reminded that Pole does not say that Cromwell had Machiavelli at any given time. He records an old conversation with Cromwell, and says that "afterward" he found out that he was a close student of Machiavelli. The conclusive reasons for believing that "afterward" must carry us on at least to March, 1537, have been given from Pole's own writings. What is more reasonable than to believe, that, in the spring of 1539, Pole had heard from his sympathizers in England that Cromwell was discussing with keen interest the book sent him by Lord Morley, and that in the *Apologia,* which Pole was finishing at the time, he should combine with an attack on Cromwell and Henry the fulfilment of the resolution expressed the preceding spring, which John a Legh naïvely reported as a plan to cause "Nicolo Matchauello" to be everywhere "dystynkyd and put down" out of all remembrance?

Besides this special line of investigation, many instances might be cited to show that the judgments of the *Apologia* are not those of a historian, but of a polemic, writing out of a mood the very honesty of whose intense zeal makes his work untrustworthy. Before doing so, it is well to recall that a partizan bias in forming moral judgments was common to the age. An intense partizan is apt, often unconsciously, to judge an opponent of his cause far more severely than a supporter of it; and the working of this natural tendency can be seen nowhere more plainly than among the judgments upon the morality of actions uttered by men of the sixteenth century. The delinquencies of the princes who embraced Lutheranism, bulk smaller in the pamphlets of Lutheran divines than those of Roman Catholic princes. Huguenot writings or speeches at the time of the civil wars, are apt to paint in vivid colors the atrocities of Roman Catholic soldiers. They seldom emphasize strongly the savage deeds of Huguenot partizan bands. And to Pole, as to most men of his time, circumstances, unconsciously to himself, altered cases.

According to the method pursued in this article, his tendency to suffer his moral judgments to be altered by circumstances, will first be illustrated by an instance taken from his writings outside the *Apologia*. Damianus a Goes, writing to Pole, spoke of the great ingratitude of Richard Morison, who, after being supported by Pole at Venice, had repaid his benefits by controversial attacks. Now this was precisely the charge his enemies made against Pole. He had been supported as a student on a royal pension for years, and had used his learning against the King. Pole answered, with unquestionable sincerity, that he had done so for conscience's sake. It never seemed to occur to him that there was any possibility of force in Morison's plea that he had stood by the King against his former benefactor, for conscience's sake. He answers Damianus a Goes: "Concerning what you write about Morison, you rightly detest his ungrateful soul. The vice of ingratitude is a very summary of evil. But if he has been so ungrateful to God, what wonder that he has been so ungrateful to me?" No one with any knowledge of human nature, would see in this a proof of insincerity. It only expresses a tendency common to all partizans, intensified in the death-struggle of opposing ideals in the sixteenth century. When Protestant Elizabeth ascended the throne, John Knox was not so positive as he had been under Roman Catholic Mary, in asserting that the rule of a woman was against the laws of God and nature. When the Huguenot, Henry of Navarre, came into sight as the legitimate heir of the throne of France, Huguenot controversialists began to feel the power of the divine right of kings, and Jesuit writers began to see new force in arguments for the supremacy of the people.

A very slight examination of the *Apologia* makes evident the fact that Pole's moral judgments are tremendously swayed by his partizan religious sympathies.[1] For instance, he denounces in the most unmeasured terms the lustfulness of Henry VIII. Most courts at that time were bad places, and Henry's was not one of the best. But it is hard to see that Henry was a more licentious man than James V of Scotland. James had illegitimate children by six different mothers, four of them being daughters of noblemen of his court. Pole could hardly have been unaware of this, for several of these children held important ecclesiastical benefices conferred at Rome. Yet, in his letters to James, Pole addresses him in terms of unbounded admiration: "You set yourself forth as the strenuous minister of Christ's piety, the noble offspring of pious kings, the constancy of whose piety you repeat in all things."

The conclusion is inevitable that the judgment expressed upon the *unique* and *unexampled* licentiousness of Henry in the denunciation of the *Apologia,* is, probably unconsciously, based upon the fact that Henry's passion for Anne Boleyn was the chief cause which led him to deny the papal supremacy. Pole would evidently have agreed with Sanders, who wrote in *The Rise and Growth of the Anglican Schism:*[2] "The royal household consisted of men utterly abandoned,

[1] The writer here intends no defense of Henry. He is only suggesting a method of testing the accuracy of Pole's judgment that Henry's deeds display a *unique* atrocity of lust and cruelty.

[2] Edition by David Lewis, London, Burns and Oates, 1877, 24.

gamblers, adulterers, panderers, swindlers, false swearers; blasphemers, extortioners and even heretics."

Pole's judgment upon the unexampled cruelty of Henry, is evidently inspired by the fact that its victims were largely supporters of the old relation of England to the Papacy. Henry shed more noble blood, but he did not put to death more people, than several other rulers of his age. In the year 1534, when Pole was writing the *Pro Unitatis Defensione,* which denounced Henry as guilty of inhumanity unmatched in history, Francis I, whose character Pole praises, burnt twenty-three Lutherans in Paris, presiding at the execution of six who were dipped in the *balançoire,* a machine which swung them up and down in the flame in order to prolong the death-struggle. Pole could scarcely have been ignorant of this.

Pole rebukes in the severest terms the cruelty of Henry's punishment of the northern rebellion which centered around the Pilgrimage of Grace. He has no word of blame for the comparatively greater severity of Mary in executing about one hundred for Wyatt's rebellion. He denounces the execution of More and Fisher as deeds worse than those of Nero and Domitian. It was a savage act; but when Pole was head of the English Church and chief councilor of the throne, to whom Philip had solemnly committed the care of his wife and kingdom, he expressly approved a deed, which, from the modern point of view, was, like the excution of More and Fisher, an act of savage and superfluous cruelty. In a letter to Philip he reports with full approval[1] the burning of Latimer and Ridley. And if, during those three years of Mary's rule whose record of executions cannot be matched during the entire reign of Henry, Pole used his authority as head of the English Church, or his influence as

[1] *Poli Epistolæ,* V, 84.

chief councilor of the throne, to save any one from death, no record of it has survived. He had, for Mary's conduct and character, nothing but the fullest praise. These observations do not imply the least doubt of the sincerity of Pole's denunciations of the crimes of Henry, nor question the entire honesty of his approval of the punishment of the two or three hundred heretics burnt by Mary. They simply illustrate the fact, that the controversial writers of the sixteenth century, used words like cruelty and wickedness from a standpoint of moral judgment which would be assumed by very few men of to-day, whether Roman Catholics or dissidents from the ancient church. And the *Apologia* of Pole, in purpose, tone, language, and judgment, is one of the most violently polemic writings of the century.

The writer ventures to suggest, in view of the foregoing examination, that there is far more reason for rejecting Pole's portrait of Cromwell in the *Apologia* than the portrait of Cromwell in Foxe's *Book of Martyrs,* now very properly set aside by modern writers as one-sided. The true portrait of Thomas Cromwell, is to be made out of the positive record of his acts. And he ought to be judged by his own ideals, not by ideals he rejected. Over seven thousand letters and papers relating to him, have been calendared. The inaccurate memories of his bitterest enemy should no longer distort their interpretation. Thomas Cromwell was no "Martyr of the Gospel." But the diabolically inspired disciple of Machiavelli, is a creation of the excited imagination of Pole. And the mysteriously sinister atmosphere which modern writers have borrowed from Pole to throw around their portraits of one of the most capable of English statesmen, is not the light of history.

LIST OF BOOKS CITED

AGRIPPA DE NETTESHEIM, HENRI CORNEILLE. Sur la *Noblesse* et *Excellence* du sexe feminin de sa *Preëminence* sur l'autre sexe et du Sacrament du Mariage. Leiden, 1716. 3 volumes.

ALBERI, EUGENIO. Relazioni degli Ambasciatori Veneti al Senato. Firenze, 1839. 14 volumes.

ALBERTI L., in La Vita Italiana nel cinquecento. Milano, 1897.

ALTMANN UND BERNHEIM. Ausgewählte Urkunden zur Erläuterung der Verfassungsgeschichte Deutschlands im Mittelatter. Berlin, 1895.

AMICO, G. La Vita di N. Macchiavelli. Firenze, 1875.

ARCHAEOLOGIA, or Miscellaneous Tracts relating to Antiquity published by the Society of Antiquaries of London. 1779, etc.

ARCHIV FÜR KUNDE OESTERREICHISCHE GESCHICHTSQUELLEN.

ARETINO, PIETRO. The works of Aretino, aside from his letters, exist in many old editions. The best collection of these is in the Bibliothèque Nationale at Paris, and a list of them may be found in the printed catalogue, of which the first volumes are already issued.

ARMSTRONG, EDWARD. The Emperor Charles V. London, Macmillan, 1902.

ASCHAM, ROGER. Works edited by the Rev. Dr. Giles. London, 1864. 4 volumes.

ASCHBACH, JOSEPH. Geschichte der Wiener Universität. Wein, 1865. 2 volumes.

BEMBO, PIETRO. Opere. Venezia, 1729.

BERTANI, CARLO. Pietro Aretino e le sue opere. Sondrio, 1901.

BRIEGERS ZEITSCHRIFT FÜR KIRCHENGESCHICHTE.

BURD. See Machiavelli.

CALENDAR OF STATE PAPERS. Spanish. London. Rolls Series.

CALENDAR OF STATE PAPERS. Venetian. Rolls Series. 8 volumes.

CAMDEN SOCIETY. Volume 37. A relation, etc., of the Island of England, etc., about the year 1500. London, 1847.

CAPELLI, A. Lettere d' Ariosto. Milano, 1887.

CASTIGLIONE, COUNT BALDESAR. The Book of the Courtier, translated from the Italian by Leonard Eckstein Opdycke. New York, Charles Scribner's Sons, 1903.

CAVALCASELLE AND CROWE. Tiziano. La Sua Vita e i suoi tempi. Firenze, 1877. 2 volumes.

CAVENDISH, GEORGE. The Life of Cardinal Wolsey, by George Cavendish, his gentleman usher. With notes and other illustrations by Samuel Weller Singer. Second edition. London, 1827.

CERVANTES. The ingenious gentleman Don Quixote of La Mancha. A translation with introduction and notes by John Ormsby. London, 1885. 4 volumes.

CHMEL, JOSEPH. Urkunden Briefe und Actenstücke zur Geschichte Maximilians I. Stuttgart, Bibliothek des lit. Vereins, 1845.

DIE CHRONIKEN DER DEUTSCHEN STÄDTE. Leipzig, 1862-1905.

CIAN, V. Un Decennio della Vita di M. Pietro Bembo. Torino, 1885.

DE MAULDE LA CLAVIÈRE, R. Procédures Politiques du Règne de Louis XII. Paris, 1886.

DE MAULDE LA CLAVIÈRE, R. La Diplomatie au temps de Machiavel. Paris, 1892. 3 volumes.

CONCILIUM DELECTORUM CARDINALIUM DE EMENDENDA ECCLESIA. British Museum.

CONTARINI, GASPARO. Opera. Parisiis, 1571.

CUSPINIANUS. Opera. 1601.

DACHEUX, L. Un Réformateur Catholique à la fin du XVe Siècle. Paris et Strasbourg, 1876.

DAGUET, ALEXANDRE. Histoire de la Conféderation Suisse. Septième edition. Paris, 1880. 2 volumes.

DEJOB, CARLO. De l'influence du Concile de Trent sur litterature et les beaux arts. Paris, 1884.

DONI, ANTON FRANCESCO. Il Terremoto, secondo la copia dell' anno 1556. Lucca, 1861. Edizione di 50 esemplari.

ELLIS, SIR HENRY. Original Letters illustrative of English History. 1824-1846. 11 volumes.

ERASMUS, DESIDERIUS. The Colloquies of D. E. Concerning Men, Manners and Things. Translated into English by N. Bailey. London, 1900.

GARDINER, SAMUEL RAWSON. Cromwell's Place in History. Founded on six lectures delivered in the University of Oxford. Third edition. London, 1897.

GASPARY, ADOLFO. Storia della Letteratura Italiana, volume secondo, tradotto dal tedesco da Vittorio Rossi, seconda edizione. Torino, 1901.

GASQUET, FRANCIS AIDAN. Henry VIII and the English Monasteries. London. John Hodges, 1889.

GEBHARDT, BRUNO. Die Gravamina der deutschen Nation gegen den römischen Hof. Zweite Auflage. Berlin, 1895.

GIORNALE STORICO DELLA LETTERATURA.

GÖTZ VON BERLICHINGEN. Lebensbeschreibung. Schönhuth. Heilbronn, 1859.

GRAF, ARTURO. Attraverso il Cinquecento. Torino, 1888.

GRÜNPECK. Die Geschichte Freidrichs III und Maximilian I. Geschichtschreiber der deutschen Vorzeit. Zweite Ausgabe. Band 3.

FISH, SIMON. Supplication of the Beggars. Early English Text Society, 1871.

FONTES RERUM AUSTRIACARUM. Wien.

FORSCHUNGEN ZUR DEUTSCHEN GESCHICHTE. Göttingen. 26 volumes.

FOXE, JOHN. Book of Martyrs. Edited by S. R. Catley. London, 1837. 8 volumes.

VON FRÜNDSBERG. Historia und Beschreibung Herrn Georgen von Fründsbergs Ritters Männlicher Kriegsssachen, etc. Franckfurt am Meyn, 1568.

FRIEDMANN, PAUL. Anne Boleyn. London, 1884. 2 volumes.

FUGGER. Spiegel der Ehren des Ertz-Hauses Oesterreich erweitert durch S. von Birken. Nürnberg, 1668.

HALL, EDWARD. Hall's Chronicle, etc. London, 1809.

HARPSFIELD, NICHOLAS. A treatise on the pretended divorce between Henry VIII and Catharine of Aragon. Printed for the Camden Society, 1878. New series, volume 21.

HERBERT, WILLIAM. The History of the Twelve Great Livery Companies of London. London, 1836. 2 volumes.

HUBER, A. Geschichte Oesterreichs. Gotha, 1885-1896. 5 volumes.

HUME, M. A. S. A Chronicle of Henry VIII of England translated by M. A. S. Hume. London, 1889.

JÄGER, ALBRECHT. Sitzungsberichte der Kaiserlichen Akademie der Wissenschaften. Philosophisch-Historischen Classe.

JÄGER, ALBRECHT. Archiv für Oesterreichische Geschichte LI.

JAHRBÜCHER DER KUNSTHISTORISCHEN SAMMLUNGEN DES ALLERHÖCHSTEN KAISERHAUSES, etc. Vienna.

JANSSEN, JOHANNES. Geschichte des deutschen Volkes zeitdem Ausgang des Mittelalters. Siebente verbesserte auflage, Freiburg im Breisgau, 1881.

JOURNAL D'UN BOURGEOIS DE PARIS SOUS LE RÈGNE DE FRANCOIS I. La Société de l'Histoire de France, 1854.

DEUTCHES KUNSTBLATT.

VON KRAUSS, VICTOR. See Maximilian.

KLAJE, HERMANN. Die Schlacht bei Guinegate. Greifs wald, 1890.

LAMPRECHT, KARL. Deutsche Geschichte. Berlin, 1894-1905. 7 volumes.

LAPSLEY GAILLARD T. The County Palatine of Durham. Harvard Historical Studies. Volume 8. New York and London, 1900.

LE GLAY. See Maximilian.

LETTERS AND PAPERS, FOREIGN AND DOMESTIC OF THE REIGN OF HENRY VIII. London, 1862-1905. 19 volumes.

LETTERE SCRITTE A PIETRO ARETINO EMENDATE PER CURA DI TEODORICO LANDONI. Bologna, 1873. 2 volumes in four parts. Edizione di Soli, 202 Esemplari.

LETTERE DI M. PIETRO ARETINO. Paris, 1609. 6 volumes. All quotations of letters are from this edition. It was apparently set, partly, by printers ignorant of Italian. It is called by an essayist on Aretino "Edizione scorrettissima." The first volume is accessible in the well edited volume of Daelli, Bibliotheca Rara, Vol. 51. Milano, 1864.

LORENZ, O. Reichskanzler und Reichskanzlei. Preuss. Jahrbücher, Vol. XXIX.

LUZIO, ALESSANDRO. Pietro Aretino nei primi suoi anni a Venezia e la Corte dei Gonzage. Torino, 1888.

LUZIO, ALESSANDRO. Un Pronostico Satirico di Pietro Aretino, Bergamo, 1900.

MACHIAVELLI NICCOLÒ. Il Principe. Edited by L. A. Burd. Oxford, 1891.

MAXIMILIAN I. A large number of his works and books he caused to be made, are magnificently printed in the Jahrbücher der Kunsthistorischen Sammlungen, etc., as follows:

Genealogie VII.

Heilige IV.

Weiss Kunig VI.

Latin Autobiography (fragment) VI.

Zeugbücher XIII and XV.

Teuerdank VIII.

His letters may be found in the following works:

Correspondance de l'Empereur Maximilien Ier et de Marguerite d'Autriche. Le Glay. Paris, 1839.

Maximilians I vertraulicher Briefwechsel mit Sigmünd Prüschenk. Victor von Krauss. Innsbruck, 1875.

Lettres inédites de Maximilien I sur les affaires des Pays Bas. Bruxelles, 1851. 2 volumes.

Lettres de Maximilien à l'Abbé de Saint Pierre à Gand. Messager Historique de la Belgique.

Other letters are scattered through a large number of journals.

Memorandum books. Printed in Hormayr's Taschenbuch für die Vaterländische Geschichte. Volumes IV, V, VIII.

Albrecht Dürers Randzeichnungen aus dem Gebetbuche des Kaisers Maximilian I mit eingedrucktem original-texte. München J. Roth.

Kaiser Maximilian's I Geheimes Jagdbuch. Herausgegeben von Th. G. von Karajan. Wien, 1881.

Das Jagdbuch Kaiser Maximilians I. Herausgegeben von Dr. Michael Mayr. Innsbruck, 1901.

Das Fischereibuch Kaiser Maximilians I. Herausgegeben von Dr. Michael Mayr. Innsbruck, 1901.

Freydal; des Kaiser Maximilian I Turniere und Mummereien Quirin von Leitner. Vienna, 1882.

The Triumphs of the Emperor Maximilian I, edited by Alfred Aspland for the Holbein Society. London, 1872.

MAZZUCHELLI, GIAMMARIA. La Vita di pietro Aretino. Edizione Seconda. Brescia, 1763.

MERRIMAN, ROGER BIGELOW. The Life and Letters of Thomas Cromwell. Oxford, Clarendon Press, 1902.

MOLMENTI. Storia di Venezia nella vita privata. Torino, 1885.

MORE, CRESSACRE. Life of Sir Thomas More. London, Pickering, 1828.

MORE, THOMAS. Workes. London, 1557.

MORISON, RICHARD. An Invective agenste the great and detestible vice of treason, wherein the secret practices, etc. London, 1539.

MORISON, RICHARD. Apomaxis Calumniarum. London, 1537.

MILTON, JOHN. The Prose Works of John Milton. Bohns Standard Library. London. 5 volumes.

NEUDECKER AND PRELLER. Freidrichs des weisen Leben und Zeitgeschichte nach Spalatins Handschrift herausgegeben.

NINE HISTORICAL LETTERS PRIVATELY PRINTED FOR J. P. C. London, 1871.

NUOVA ANTOLOGIA.

ORATIO QUAE DOCET ADMONET OMNES POTTISSIMUM ANGLOS REGIAE DIGNITATI, ETC. London, 1533.

PEARSON, CHARLES H. Historical Maps of England. London, 1883.

PHILIPS, THOMAS. History of the Life of Reignald Pole. Oxford, 1764.

PIRKHEIMER, WILLIBALD. Schweizerkrieg nach Pirckheimers Autographum im Britischen Museum, herausgegeben von Karl Rück. München, 1895.

POCOCK, NICHOLAS. Records of the Reformation. The Divorce. Oxford, 1870.

POLE, REGINALD. Epistolarum Reginaldi Poli S. R. E. Cardinalis et Aliorum ad ipsum. Brixiæ, 1744. 5 volumes.

POLE, REGINALD. Ad Henricum Octavum pro Ecclesiasticae Unitatis Defensione. Ingolstadt, 1587.

POLLARD, ALBERT F. Henry VIII. London, 1902.

POOLE, REGINALD LANE. Historical Atlas of Modern Europe. Oxford, Clarendon Press, 1902.

PRÜSCHENK, SEE VON KRAUSS.

ROSSI, VITTORIO. Pasquinate de Pietro Aretino. Palermo-Torino, 1891.

ST. PAUL'S. A Monthly Magazine. London.

SANDERS, NICHOLAS. Rise and Growth of the Anglican Schism, published A. D. 1585. Translated with introduction and notes by David Lewis. London, 1877.

SANUTO, MARINO. I Diarii di Marino Sanuto. Venezia, 1889-1903. 58 volumes.

SCHANZ, GEORG. Englische Handelspolitik gegen ende des Mittelalters, etc. Leipzig, 1881.

SCHELHORN, J. G. Amoenitates Historiae Ecclesiasticae et Literariae. Leipzig, 1737.

SCHMIDT, CHARLES. Histoire Littéraire de l'Alsace à la fin du XVe et au commencement du XVIe Siècle. Paris, 1879.

SCHULTHEISS, ALB. Pietro Aretino als Stammvater des modernen Litteratenthums. Sammlung gemeinverständlicher wissenchaftlicher Vorträge. Neue folge. Fünfte Serie, Heft 114. Hamburg, 1890.

DE SMET, J. J. Mémoire Historique sur la Guerre de Maximilien contre les Villes de Flandre. Mémoire de l'Académie de Bruxelles. Without date.

SOCIETY OF ANTIQUARIES. Catalogue of a Collection of Broadsides, etc. London, 1866.

SPEDDING, JAMES. The Works of Francis Bacon. Boston. 15 volumes.

STAFFETI, LUIGI. Il Cardinale Innocenzo Cybo. Firenze, 1894.

STARKEY, THOMAS. A Dialogue between Cardinal Pole and Thomas

Lupset, Lecturer in Rhetoric at Oxford. Edited by J. M. Cowper. Early English Text Society, 1871.

Statutes of the Realm. Record Commission 1810-1828. 10 volumes.

Stow, John. A Survey of the Cities of London and Westminster, etc. The sixth edition. London, 1754. 2 volumes.

Stow, John. The Annales or Generall Chronicle of England. London, 1615.

Stubbs, William, Bishop of Oxford. The Constitutional History of England. Oxford Clarendon Press, 1897.

Tunstall, Cuthbert. A Letter Sent unto Reginald Pole, etc. London, 1560.

Ulmann, Heinrich. Kaiser Maximilian I auf urkundlicher Grundlage dargestelt. Stuttgart, 1884. 2 volumes.

Valor Ecclesiasticus temp. Henr. VIII. 1810-1834. 6 volumes.

Vasari, Giorgio. Vite de' Pittori.

Villari, Pasquale. Niccolo Machiavelli. Milano, 1895.

Virgili, F. Berni. Firenze, 1881.

Wilkins, David. Concilia Magnae Britanniae, etc. Londini, 1737. 4 volumes.

Zimmerman, Athanasius. Kardinal Pole seine Leben und seine Schriften. Regensburg, 1893.

Zurich Letters, The. Parker Society. Cambridge, 1842.